Similar Languages, Varieties, and Dialects

Language resources and computational models are becoming increasingly important for the study of language variation. A main challenge of this interdisciplinary field is that linguistics researchers may not be familiar with these helpful computational tools and many natural language processing (NLP) researchers are often not familiar with language variation phenomena. This essential reference introduces researchers to the necessary computational models for processing similar languages, varieties, and dialects. In this book, leading experts tackle the inherent challenges of the field by balancing a thorough discussion of the theoretical background with a meaningful overview of state-of-the-art language technology. The book can be used in a graduate course or as a supplementary text for courses on language variation, dialectology, and sociolinguistics or on computational linguistics and NLP.

Part I covers the linguistic fundamentals of the field, such as the question of status and language variation. Part II discusses data collection and preprocessing methods. Finally, Part III presents NLP applications, such as speech processing, machine translation, and language-specific issues in Arabic and Chinese.

DR. MARCOS ZAMPIERI is an assistant professor at the Rochester Institute of Technology where he leads the Language Technology Group. He obtained his PhD from Saarland University in Germany with a thesis on computational approaches to language variation. He has previously held research and teaching positions in Germany and the UK. Dr. Zampieri published over 80 peer-reviewed papers on topics such as language acquisition and variation, offensive language identification, and machine translation. Since 2014, he is the main organizer of the workshop series on NLP for Similar Languages, Varieties and Dialects (VarDial). He is the lead organizer of the popular OffensEval shared tasks on offensive language identification at SemEval 2019 and 2020.

DR. PRESLAV NAKOV is Principal Scientist at Qatar Computing Research Institute at Hamad Bin Khalifa University. He leads the Tanbih megaproject, developed in collaboration with MIT. He coauthored a book on semantic relations between nominals, two books on computer algorithms, and many research papers in top-tier conferences and journals. He received the Young Researcher Award at RANLP 2011. He was also the first to receive the Bulgarian President's John Atanasoff Award, named after the inventor of the first automatic electronic digital computer. Dr. Nakov's research has been featured in more than 100 news outlets, including *Forbes*, the *Boston Globe*, and the *MIT Technology Review*.

Studies in Natural Language Processing

Series Editor:
Chu-Ren Huang, The Hong Kong Polytechnic University

Associate Series Editor:
Qi Su, Peking University

Editorial Board Members:
Nianwen Xue, Brandeis University
Maarten de Rijke, University of Amsterdam
Lori Levin, Carnegie Mellon University
Alessandro Lenci, Universita degli Studi, Pisa
Francis Bond, Nanyang Technological University

Volumes in the SNLP series provide comprehensive surveys of current research topics and applications in the field of natural language processing (NLP) that shed light on language technology, language cognition, language and society, and linguistics. The increased availability of language corpora and digital media, as well as advances in computer technology and data sciences, has led to important new findings in the field. Widespread applications include voice-activated interfaces, translation, search engine optimization, and affective computing. NLP also has applications in areas such as knowledge engineering, language learning, digital humanities, corpus linguistics, and textual analysis. These volumes will be of interest to researchers and graduate students working in NLP and other fields related to the processing of language and knowledge.

Also in the Series
Douglas E. Appelt, *Planning English Sentences*
Madeleine Bates and Ralph M Weischedel (eds.), *Challenges in Natural
    Language Processing*
Steven Bird, *Computational Phonology*
Peter Bosch and Rob van der Sandt, *Focus*
Pierette Bouillon and Federica Busa (eds.), *Inheritance, Defaults and
    the Lexicon*
Ronald Cole, Joseph Mariani, Hans Uszkoreit, Giovanni Varile, Annie
    Zaenen, Antonio Zampolli, and Victor Zue (eds.), *Survey of the State of the
    Art in Human Language Technology*
David R. Dowty, Lauri Karttunen, and Arnold M Zwicky (eds.),
    Natural Language Parsing
Ralph Grishman, *Computational Linguistics*

Graeme Hirst, *Semantic Interpretation and the Resolution of Ambiguity*
András Kornai, *Extended Finite State Models of Language*
Kathleen R. McKeown, *Text Generation*
Martha Stone Palmer, *Semantic Processing for Finite Domains*
Terry Patten, *Systemic Text Generation as Problem Solving*
Ehud Reiter and Robert Dale, *Building Natural Language Generation Systems*
Manny Rayner, David Carter, Pierette Bouillon, Vassilis Digalakis, and Matis
    Wiren (eds.), *The Spoken Language Translator*
Michael Rosner and Roderick Johnson (eds.), *Computational Lexical
    Semantics*
Richard Sproat, *A Computational Theory of Writing Systems*
George Anton Kiraz, *Computational Nonlinear Morphology*
Nicholas Asher and Alex Lascarides, *Logics of Conversation*
Margaret Masterman (edited by Yorick Wilks), *Language, Cohesion and Form*
Walter Daelemans and Antal van den Bosch, *Memory-Based Language
    Processing*
Chu-Ren Huang, Nicoletta Calzolari, Aldo Gangemi, Alessandro Lenci,
    Alessandro Oltramari, and Laurent Prévot (eds.), *Ontology and the Lexicon:
    A Natural Language Processing Perspective*
Thierry Poibeau and Aline Villavicencio (eds.), *Language, Cognition, and
    Computational Models*

Similar Languages, Varieties, and Dialects

A Computational Perspective

Edited by

Marcos Zampieri
Rochester Institute of Technology

Preslav Nakov
Qatar Computing Research Institute, HBKU

CAMBRIDGE
UNIVERSITY PRESS

CAMBRIDGE
UNIVERSITY PRESS

University Printing House, Cambridge CB2 8BS, United Kingdom

One Liberty Plaza, 20th Floor, New York, NY 10006, USA

477 Williamstown Road, Port Melbourne, VIC 3207, Australia

314–321, 3rd Floor, Plot 3, Splendor Forum, Jasola District Centre,
New Delhi – 110025, India

103 Penang Road, #05–06/07, Visioncrest Commercial, Singapore 238467

Cambridge University Press is part of the University of Cambridge.

It furthers the University's mission by disseminating knowledge in the pursuit of
education, learning, and research at the highest international levels of excellence.

www.cambridge.org
Information on this title: www.cambridge.org/9781108429351
DOI: 10.1017/9781108565080

© Cambridge University Press 2021

First published 2021

Printed in the United Kingdom by TJ Books Ltd, Padstow Cornwall

A catalogue record for this publication is available from the British Library.

Library of Congress Cataloging-in-Publication Data
Names: Zampieri, Marcos, editor. | Nakov, Preslav, editor.
Title: Similar languages, varieties, and dialects : a computational perspective /
    Marcos Zampieri, Preslav Nakov.
Description: 1. | New York : Cambridge University Press, 2021. |
    Series: Studies in natural language processing |
    Includes bibliographical references and index.
Identifiers: LCCN 2020014771 (print) | LCCN 2020014772 (ebook) |
    ISBN 9781108429351 (hardback) | ISBN 9781108565080 (epub)
Subjects: LCSH: Language and languages–Variation. | Dialectology. |
    Sociolinguistics. | Computational linguistics.
Classification: LCC P120.V37 S556 2020 (print) | LCC P120.V37 (ebook) |
    DDC 417–dc23
LC record available at https://lccn.loc.gov/2020014771
LC ebook record available at https://lccn.loc.gov/2020014772

ISBN 978-1-108-42935-1 Hardback

Contents

Contributors

ŽELJKO AGIĆ Unity Technologies

BENGT J. BORGSTRÖM MIT Lincoln Laboratory

CHARLOTTE GOOSKENS University of Groningen

NIZAR HABASH New York University Abu Dhabi

WILBERT HEERINGA Fryske Akademy

CHU-REN HUANG The Hong Kong Polytechnic University

MENGHAN JIANG Peking University/The Hong Kong Polytechnic University

STEFFEN KLAERE University of Auckland

JINGXIA LIN Nanyang Technological University Singapore

NIKOLA LJUBEŠIĆ Josef Stefan Institute

MIRIAM MEYERHOFF Victoria University of Wellington

PRESLAV NAKOV Qatar Computing Research Institute, HBKU

JOHN NERBONNE University of Freiburg

DONG NGUYEN Alan Turing Institute

JELENA PROKIĆ Leiden University

TANJA SAMARDŽIĆ University of Zurich

YVES SCHERRER University of Helsinki

DINGXU SHI Guangdong University of Foreign Studies

RACHAEL TATMAN Rasa Technologies

JÖRG TIEDEMANN University of Helsinki

PEDRO A. TORRES-CARRASQUILLO MIT Lincoln Laboratory

VINCENT J. VAN HEUVEN   University of Pannonia, Leiden University

JAMES A. WALKER   La Trobe University

MARTIJN WIELING   University of Groningen

HONGZHI XU   Shanghai International Studies University

MARCOS ZAMPIERI   Rochester Institute of Technology

Foreword

Over the past decade, we have witnessed a revolution in Natural Language Processing (NLP) driven by advances in machine learning, growing amounts of natural language data, and increased computing power. As a result, computational linguists have made major advances across a range of tasks with diverse technological applications. Crucially, these advances are changing the lives of people around the world, who are increasingly interacting with NLP as part of their daily routine. These innovations are also starting to revolutionise the field of linguistics, where very large corpora and NLP methodologies are being used to expand our scientific understanding of language, allowing linguists to study language at scale for the first time, as demanded by the inherent complexity of this most basic of human behaviours. However, although these technological advances are improving our world in many ways, they are also creating new problems.

Perhaps most obvious of these problems is that NLP technologies tend to work best for speakers of the dominant languages of the world – thereby inadvertently increasing the power of speakers of these languages. Modern NLP workflows generally rely on large collections of training data, often carefully annotated by hand, which are usually only available for major languages. As a result, the benefits of the AI revolution in NLP have largely been reserved for speakers of a small number of high-resourced languages, especially English. To address this issue, there have been calls for NLP researchers to clearly acknowledge the languages upon which they work – especially if that language is simply English, as is often the case – and by extension to accept that NLP applications that are trained and evaluated on high-resourced languages will not necessarily perform as well on languages of the world more generally. This is popularly known as the 'Bender Rule', named after Emily Bender, the computational linguist who has championed this perspective over the past decade. The rule has even been evoked in linguistics, primarily to encourage linguists who work on the English language to acknowledge how this naturally limits the generalisability of their research.

But speakers of low-resourced languages are not the only ones who are being left behind by the current NLP revolution. In addition to zooming out to acknowledge the typological diversity of human language, computational linguists must zoom in and acknowledge the sociolinguistic diversity of human languages. Even English is not simply English – it is a complex system of mutually and sometimes not-so-mutually intelligible dialects, characterised by systematic patterns of variation, changing over time in ways and for reasons that linguists are only beginning to understand. Treating this variation as noise or assuming that speakers of non-standard dialects will be adequately served by tools trained on standard dialect data amounts to contributing to the entrenchment of social inequities.

Speakers of non-standard dialects are being technologically disenfranchised by NLP. For speakers standard American English or Standard British English, NLP tools for English work well and will inevitably continue to improve over time, but performance necessarily falls for speakers of non-standard dialects, especially those associated with the most marginalised communities. As NLP tools increasingly become embedded into our daily lives, it is crucial that these technologies work for regular people regardless of their social background. Computational linguists have a responsibility to make sure this is the case – to fight against the inequalities they have helped create. The challenge is to build robust NLP technologies that model linguistic variation directly, probably at the expense of maximising economic value.

This situation presents a clear intellectual challenge for computational linguists. It is arguably as complex as any problem currently faced in NLP. It is certainly a far greater technical problem than the divide between high- and low-resourced languages, where the solution at least is clear – the compilation and annotation of large corpora for low-resourced languages. Alternatively, there is no clear approach to building NLP tools that can handle language internal variation, not least because linguists do not have anywhere near a complete understanding of how language internal variation is patterned. For example, building corpora that represent languages, regardless of their size, is often fairly straightforward, as languages are often delimited by relatively hard borders – be they defined politically or based on mutual intelligibility – but dialects generally blend into each other, making even compiling representative dialect corpora a difficult task, and at least part of the solution.

This volume represents an important first step to address the challenge of language-internal variation in NLP. By bringing together linguists who specialise in language variation and change and computational linguists who develop NLP tools capable of working with language-internal variation, this collection provides an indispensable introduction for any researcher in NLP who takes this challenge seriously. This volume also meets the Bender Rule by considering language-internal variation cross-linguistically, highlighting the fact that all language, be they low- or high-resourced, contain internal variation.

Crucially, this volume also opens up a dialogue between NLP researchers and linguists interested in variation. It is sometimes remarked that linguists do not have much to offer NLP these days, at least for high-resourced languages like English, given that the grammars of these languages are fairly well understood. Such an attitude reflects a narrow view of language and linguistics that artificially simplifies the endeavour of NLP, in much the same way that generative linguists once artificially simplified the endeavour of linguistics. When the NLP community takes variation seriously, sociolinguists, dialectologists, historical linguists, and corpus linguists should be the first port of call. Similarly, given the complexity of linguistic variation, these are probably the same linguists that have the most to gain from engaging with computational linguistics, as demonstrated by the emerging interdisciplinary field of computational sociolinguistics, with which a number of the contributors to this volume are affiliated. Ideally linguists and computational linguists will work together to better understand and process language variation, with research in one area informing the other, accelerating progress in both.

Jack Grieve
University of Birmingham
February 18, 2020

Introduction

Variation is intrinsic to human language. Language differs from speaker to speaker, from community to community, as well as across time, genre, media, etc. Natural language processing (NLP) systems are typically trained on standard contemporary language varieties such as the language found in books and newspapers. Such systems work very well on the kind of language they are trained on, but their performance degrades when faced with variation.

One of the most relevant dimensions of variation from a computational perspective is diatopic language variation, or the variation of language spoken (and written) in different places and/or regions of a linguistic area, e.g., language varieties and dialects. Dialects are per se nonstandard, thus posing challenges to most off-the-shelf NLP tools. On the other hand, the similarity between closely related languages such as Dutch–Flemish, Bulgarian–Macedonian, and Turkish–Kazakh can provide opportunities for researchers and developers.

With these challenges and opportunities in mind, we introduce you to the present book, *Similar Languages, Varieties, and Dialects: A Computational Perspective*. The book consists of fourteen chapters written by well-known researchers in dialectology, language variation, sociolinguistics, computational linguistics, and natural language processing.

The idea for this book came from the success of the series of workshops – Natural Language Processing for Similar Languages, Varieties and Dialects (VarDial) – that have been organized yearly since 2014 and have been co-located with international NLP conferences such as COLING, EACL, NAACL, and RANLP. VarDial has become an important forum for scholars working on topics related to the study of diatopic language variation from a computational perspective and the application of NLP methods to dialects and similar languages. Since the workshop's first edition, there has been an uphill trend in the number of submissions as well as in the number of research papers published on related topics in specialized journals and conferences.

Even though the interest of the research community has seen steady growth, to the best of our knowledge, so far there have been no books approaching diatopic language variation from a computational perspective. While there have been several well-known handbooks and edited volumes published on topics such as dialectology (Chambers and Trudgill, 1998); language variation, and change (Chambers et al., 2002); and sociolinguistics (Meyerhoff, 2015), the computational aspect has remained largely underexplored.

We believe that this book fills an important gap in the existing literature. It is interdisciplinary by nature, and it can be useful for both experienced researchers and (graduate) students in computer science, linguistics, natural language processing, and related areas. The book provides a concise introduction to core topics in language variation and an overview of the computational methods applied to similar languages, varieties, and dialects.

The book is divided into three parts. Part I covers the fundamentals of language variation and the study of dialects and similar languages. Chapter 1 discusses different dimensions of language variation and how they are manifested. Chapter 2 focuses on the phonetic variation in dialects. The question of status, i.e., dialect versus language, is discussed in Chapter 3. Mutual intelligibility between similar languages and dialects is discussed in detail in Chapter 4, with several examples from languages such as Danish, Spanish, and Portuguese. Closing the first part of the book, Chapter 5 presents a concise yet comprehensive overview of dialectology for computational linguists.

Part II covers methods and resources for data collection, preprocessing, and annotation for similar languages, varieties, and dialects. Chapter 6 deals with data collection and representation, covering social media and speech transcripts. Chapter 7 discusses preprocessing and adaptation of taggers used to annotate similar languages. Finally, Chapter 8 deals with methods to learn dependency parse trees from one language and to project them to a related language.

The last part of the book, Part III, covers applications and language-specific issues when processing similar languages, varieties, and dialects. Chapter 9 presents an overview of computational methods for similar languages and dialect identification. Chapter 10 presents an account of computational methods applied to diatopic language variation in social media. Chapter 11 deals with machine translation between similar languages, varieties, and dialects. Chapter 12 discusses speech processing applications. The last two chapters deal with language-specific issues when processing dialects and varieties of two major languages: Arabic (Chapter 13) and Chinese (Chapter 14).

We would like to take this opportunity to thank all chapter authors for their valuable contribution and the colleagues who kindly helped us by giving the authors feedback and suggestions. We are grateful to Željko Agić, Patricia Cukor-Avila, Charlotte Gooskens, Wilbert Heeringa, Vincent J. van Heuven, Chu-Ren Huang, Menghan Jiang, Steffen Klaere, Jingxia Lin, Nikola Ljubešić, Miriam Meyerhoff, John Nerbonne, Dong Nguyen, Jelena Prokić, Tanja Samardžic, Dingxu Shi, Rachael Tatman, Jörg Tiedemann, Pedro Torres-Carrasquillo, James A. Walker, Martijn Wieling, and Hongzhi Xu.

Finally, we would like to thank the series editor, Chu-Ren Huang for the interest in our volume and for the continuous support, and Kaitlin Leach and Amy He at Cambridge University Press for their support throughout the editorial process.

References

Chambers, J. K. and Trudgill, P. (1998). *Dialectology*. Cambridge: Cambridge University Press.

Chambers, J. K., Trudgill, and P. Schilling-Estes, N. eds. (2002). *The Handbook of Language Variation and Change*. Oxford: Blackwell.

Meyerhoff, M. (2015). *Introducing Sociolinguistics*. New York: Routledge.

Part I

Fundamentals

1   Language Variation

James A. Walker

1.1   Introduction: Defining Language Variation

Language variation can be defined as "different ways of saying the same thing," where "different ways" refers to differences in the **form** of language (sounds, words, sentences, ways of speaking) and "the same thing" refers to the intended **meaning** conveyed by those forms: talking about things or events in the world, marking distinctions required by the language's grammar, conveying the speaker's intention, or indicating something about the speaker's social position or relationship to the listener. Let us start by distinguishing variation *between* languages (**interlinguistic** variation) from variation *within* languages (**intralinguistic** variation).

1.1.1   Interlinguistic Variation

Different languages say the same thing in different ways. The words *jī* (Chinese), *frango* (Portuguese), and *kuku* (Swahili) are different sequences of sounds that all refer to the same animal as the English word *chicken*. Since the relationship between form and meaning differs arbitrarily from language to language, and there is no way to figure out the meaning of a word based *only* on its sounds, learning a language involves making the connection between forms and the meanings conveyed by those forms.

Interlinguistic variation goes beyond the words that each language uses to refer to things. The human vocal apparatus is capable of producing many different sounds, but each language uses only a subset of these sounds for the purposes of speech and uses them in ways that differ from the way that other languages use them (**phonology**). The English sounds represented by the spelling *th* (as in *thin* or *the*) are not used in other languages, while sounds such as German *ch* (as in *Bach*) or the "click" sounds in languages such as Xhosa are not used in English. These differences make it difficult for some learners of English to pronounce *th* or for speakers of English to pronounce German *ch* or Xhosa clicks.

Languages differ from each other in the way that they put words together (**morphology**). English uses a number of word-formation strategies to indicate grammatical distinctions and to create new words. Plural can be indicated by adding a suffix to the noun (*cat* ~ *cat-s*) or by changing its stem vowel (*goose* ~ *geese*). New words can be formed by adding a prefix to another word (*read* ~ *re-read*) or by compounding two words into one (*black* + *board* > *blackboard*). Word-formation strategies vary quite a bit across languages: languages like Turkish and Finnish use many prefixes and suffixes to indicate grammatical distinctions, while languages like Thai and Chinese do not use word-formation strategies to indicate grammatical distinctions but use compounding extensively to form new words.

Languages differ in how they group words to form clauses and sentences (**syntax**). In English, subjects tend to come before verbs, which come before their objects (subject–verb–object). In Japanese, the verb comes after everything else (subject–object–verb), while in Gaelic the verb comes first (verb–subject–object). Morphology and syntax are interrelated: some languages indicate the roles of nouns in the sentence through their position, while others mark these roles on the nouns, which allows more freedom in the syntax.

Finally, languages differ from each other in the strategies used to indicate the speaker's belief in, source of, or attitude toward what they are saying or to indicate elements of their relationship to the hearer (**discourse** and **pragmatics**). Japanese indicates levels of politeness through the choice of pronouns and marking on the verb, and some languages indicate how the speaker came to hear about what they are stating. In English these functions are usually not conveyed grammatically but through discourse strategies, such as indirectness (*"Could you open the door?"*) and across verbs in multiple clauses (*"I heard that ..."*).

1.1.2   *Intralinguistic Variation*

Variation within languages is less apparent, largely because we learn to filter out a lot of that variation when we learn to speak a language. Speakers sometimes refer to differences between the way people speak their language as a matter of "dialect," but from a linguistic perspective the distinction between dialect and language is not straightforward. Some languages are similar enough to each other to be mutually understandable, but cultural, social, or political attitudes can influence the extent to which their speakers think of them as different. Norwegian, Swedish, and Danish are so similar to each other that their speakers can understand each other, but they are considered to be languages rather than dialects because they are spoken in different countries. In contrast, the many types of "Chinese" spoken in China are very different from each other and not mutually understandable, but they are considered dialects of the same language because of their speakers' shared history, culture, and political unity. Dialects differ from each other on a number of levels, just as languages do.

Focusing on a single dialect (or even a single speaker), we still find variation in form. The English plural suffix -*s* has different realizations: a voiceless sound [s] (*cats*), a voiced sound [z] (*dogs*), or a full syllable [ɪz] (*bushes*). The object of a verb with a particle sometimes occurs after the particle (*he picked up the* **children**) and sometimes before it (*he picked* **them** *up*). However, we do not normally think of these differences in form as variation because they can be predicted on the basis of the linguistic context: the plural alternation is triggered by the type of consonant that comes before the suffix, and the object's position depends on whether it is a pronoun or a noun phrase. The goal of linguistic analysis is to correlate differences in form with differences in meaning or with elements of the linguistic context.

Nevertheless, in linguistic analysis there always remains a certain amount of variation that we are unable to predict, traditionally referred to as "free variation." The use of the word *free* implies that the realization of form is completely random, due to forces outside of language and therefore not of interest to linguistics.

In the 1960s, William Labov and his associates and students began to develop an approach to linguistic analysis that saw variation as an inherent feature of language rather than something to be eliminated or ignored (Labov 1963, 1966). The goal of the **variationist** approach is to conduct linguistic analysis through correlating quantitative patterns of variation with elements of the linguistic and social context.

Central to the variationist approach is the **linguistic variable**, which embodies our definition of linguistic variation as "different ways of saying the same thing": the "different ways" are the **variant** forms and "the same thing" is their common meaning or function. English speakers exhibit variation in the pronunciation of the consonant in the suffix -ing, alternating between a velar form [ɪŋ] and an apical form [ɪn] (*singing ~ singin'*). These forms are in "free variation," as the same speaker can produce either variant under the same circumstances. Determining the circumstances under which a speaker is free to vary between forms is a crucial component of the variationist analysis, known as defining the **variable context** (or the envelope of variation). In the case of (ING), we must restrict the variable context to word-final unstressed -*ing*, as the variation is not observed outside of this context (that is, the word *ring* is never pronounced *rin'*). Defining the variable context determines how we go about looking for examples of the variable (occurrences, or tokens) to count.

1.2   Types of Linguistic Variables

Since variation occurs at all levels of the linguistic system, variables can exist at each of these levels. At the lexical level, different words can refer to the same thing (synonyms). The English words *running shoes*, *runners*, and *sneakers* may all be used to refer to the same type of athletic footwear. Phonetic variables reflect different pronunciations of the same underlying sound. Consonants can be deleted or inserted or can change in their place or manner of articulation or their voicing, or they may vary in secondary articulation. A couple of well-studied consonantal phonetic variables in English are (t/d)-deletion, which involves the variable pronunciation of /t/ and /d/ at the end of words (*west* ~ *wes'*, *sand* ~ *san'*), and (ING), which involves the variable realization of word-final *-ing* with a velar [ŋ] or coronal [ɪn] nasal. Phonetic variables define their variable context in terms of structural positions – (t/d)-deletion occurs word-finally in consonant clusters, and (ING) occurs only in unstressed word-final syllables. Variation in vowels involves alternations in height, frontness/backness, and rounding; realization as a monophthong or a diphthong; and devoicing. In Canadian English, the vowels /ɪ/, /ɛ/ and /æ/ are variably lowered and retracted. The variable context for vowels may be defined on the basis of their underlying sounds, as above, or may be defined through classes of words that act similarly and are identified by keywords (the KIT, DRESS, and TRAP vowel classes). Consonant variables are normally considered to be categorical – each variant can be classified into a different category (deleted or not deleted, velar or coronal). Since vowel variants form a continuum, they may be classified impressionistically (lowered or not lowered) or the properties of their soundwave may be measured for identifying formant frequencies. Suprasegmental variables involve considerations of pitch (tone, intonation) or rhythm (prosody, stress). In some varieties of English a declaration may be uttered with a rising intonation, making it sound more like a question. As with vowels, classification of variants may be made impressionistically or acoustically.

Morphological variables concern the variable occurrence of forms that function to indicate grammatical differences. Normally these functions reflect inflectional properties such as number, gender, or case for nouns or tense, mood, aspect, or person–number agreement for verbs. For morphological variables the definition of the variable context is usually made on the basis of grammatical function – since the function itself may alternate between overt and unmarked forms, the grammatical function sometimes must be inferred from the wider discourse context. If a speaker alternates between saying "three cats" and "three cat" or "Yesterday she walked a mile" and "Yesterday she walk a mile," we can infer that there is variation in the formal marking of plural or tense, respectively. Syntactic variables concern alternation in the position of constituents in the sentence or the presence or absence of grammatical words. The given example of verbs with particles demonstrates predictable variation with pronoun objects, but if the object is a noun phrase, the particle placement is variable: *he picked up **the children*** ~ *he picked **the children** up*. English shows alternation in the occurrence of the complementizer *that*: *she knew that he was lying* ~ *she knew* *he was lying*. Note that there is often no neat division between morphological and syntactic variation, and in fact some variables may cut across this division. In French, reference to future time alternates between inflection on the verb (*j'acheterai*, "I will buy") and a multiword construction (*je **vais** acheter*, "I'm going to buy").

Extending the study of linguistic variation into the realm of morphology and syntax brings us into considerations of meaning, which creates problems for defining the variable context. If linguistic variation is "different ways of saying the same thing," can we interpret differences in morphology and syntax as referring to the same thing or are all such differences indicative of changes in meaning?

This question occupied the variationist approach in its early years (Lavandera 1977; D. Sankoff 1988), but recent research has relaxed the requirement of strict equivalence of meaning as a criterion for defining variables. Instead, variables are defined on the basis of their shared function. The different forms of the French future are often said to indicate subtle distinctions of meaning (such as "near future" vs. "far future"), but in practice these distinctions are not always evident. If we define the different forms as fulfilling the same (grammatical) function – referring to states or events after the time of speaking – we sidestep the need to determine whether in fact there are subtle differences of meaning.

The question of equivalence of meaning becomes even more controversial when we move into variation at the level of discourse or pragmatics, both because differences in form are here themselves normally taken to indicate differences in meaning and because the meaning of forms is not always clear or may be multilayered. People often comment on the prevalence of the word *like* as a discourse marker in English, but it is not clear exactly what its meaning is (or meanings are), where it can (and cannot) occur, and what (if anything) it varies with (D'Arcy 2017). Nevertheless, there are variables for which a discourse function can be isolated. One use of *like* that has accelerated in recent years in English is in reporting speech (*she was like, "How are you?"*), where it alternates with verbs of saying as well as the verb *go* (*she went, "How are you?"*). All of these forms have in common the discourse function of introducing speech made outside of the current speech event, which can then serve as the variable context (Buchstaller 2014).

1.3 Dimensions of Variation

The variationist approach is concerned not only with the simple fact of linguistic variation or with how frequently each of the variants occurs but also, and more importantly, how variants are distributed across contexts. Some contexts are language internal – for example, we might ask how frequently the deletion of a consonant occurs when the following sound is a consonant or when it is a vowel.

Examining the distribution of variants according to elements of the linguistic context (which simply represents a quantitative extension of linguistic analysis) can provide us with further evidence of how the language works.

Contexts that are external to language are just as important to the variationist approach. Some of these distributions may reflect underlying linguistic differences – groups of speakers may show differences because they speak different dialects or languages – but more often they demonstrate that the choice of variant has social meaning. Speakers of a language use linguistic variation to construct and express how they view themselves and their social world.

1.3.1   Region (Dialect)

Long before the beginning of the variationist approach, variants were noted to be distributed differently according to geographical region. Regional differences arise because people tend to talk like the people that they talk to: people who live near each other are more likely to interact, meaning that their speech will resemble each other's more closely.

The systematic study of regional variation in language (**dialectology**) began in the middle of the nineteenth century, when researchers in France and Germany who were concerned about the loss of traditional dialects under pressure from language standardization began to carry out **dialect surveys**. Traveling to different parts of the country, they would ask inhabitants for the local words and pronunciations of common items, or they would send these questions by post to be answered by local literate officials such as schoolteachers. Recent dialect surveys have relied on advances in technology to ask questions over the telephone or by internet or social media, but the tool of the **dialect questionnaire** remains the same (Chambers and Trudgill 1989).

The goal of a dialect survey is to map the distribution of variants according to their geographical location. Dialect maps allow for graphic interpretation of regional distribution, revealing geographic concentrations of speakers who agree in their choice of variant. Where groups of speakers differ, a line (**isogloss**) can be drawn between geographical areas. The isoglosses for a number of variables often coincide, revealing dialect areas that are characterized by differences across a set of features (Kretzschmar 2017). For example, the traditional distinction between Low German and High German is made on the basis of a number of lexical and phonological variables whose isoglosses coincide.

Traditional dialect surveys are limited by providing a single response to each question. Proportions represent the number of speakers or locations within a region who agree on the choice of variant. As we have seen, individual speakers may vary in their pronunciation, in which case a single response would not capture that variation. A larger number of responses from each speaker or locale would more accurately reflect linguistic behavior. Recent work in the study of regional variation has incorporated larger datasets that use extended recordings of speech rather than responses to questionnaires, as well as employing more sophisticated statistical and mapping techniques (**dialectometry**) (Szmrecsanyi 2013). The goal remains the same: to understand the geographic distribution of linguistic variation.

1.3.2   Style

As noted, individual speakers do not behave the same under all circumstances. Instead, they alter their way of speaking according to the social situation in which they find themselves (**style**). On a broad level, we can distinguish formal and informal contexts. In certain situations or topics, speech is expected to be more formal or informal. Discussions in a church or about religious topics call for more formal variants than do discussions in a pub or about what you did on the weekend. In addition to the setting or topic, the type of relationship that exists between speakers and their audience calls for different levels of formality. Speaking to a family member involves less formal variants than speaking to an outsider – although even within the family, speaking to a relative of an older generation may call for more formal speech than speaking to a relative of the same generation. Levels of formality may be asymmetric, with lower-status speakers required to use more formal variants with higher-status interlocutors. It is normal for employees to address their employer more formally than vice versa.

In some languages, these distinctions of style related to situation, topic, and status are conveyed grammatically. In Japanese, the choice of pronoun and verb marker reflects these considerations. In other languages, the choice of word depends on situation and status. In Javanese, which word you use for "eat" is determined by who you are talking to and what situation you are in. Even in English, the choice of word that we use or how indirect we are in making a request or command depends on the situation, the topic, or the audience. This type of variation, in which there is a clear-cut and qualitative relationship between the variants and elements of the social situation, we can refer to as differences of **register**. In other words, given our knowledge of the social context, we can make a pretty firm prediction about which variant will occur.

However, other types of variation may show differences of a quantitative nature. I note that my use of *-in'* is higher when I am talking to my friends than when I am making a presentation at work. Over the years, studies of variables that are sensitive to style show that speakers exhibit different rates of variants depending on the context (**style shifting**).

The observed effects of style shifting have been attributed to a number of different explanations. In his work in New York City in the 1960s, Labov (1966) argued that speakers shift according to how much attention they pay to *how* they are speaking (rather than what they are saying). Under this view, asking the speaker to engage in tasks that focus more and more attention on language (such as reciting a list of words or pairs of words that differ minimally) rather than content should elicit increasingly formal speech. Conversely, more informal or casual speech is elicited by focusing the speaker's attention on content. In relating narratives of personal experience (such as "danger of death" narratives, in which speakers are asked to relate a time when they thought that they were about to die), speakers tend to get so caught up in reliving the experience that they focus less on their speech. Most research since then has either followed or challenged Labov's techniques or explanation.

The effects noted in Labov's study were acknowledged by Allan Bell (1984), but he identified a common theme to the different contexts in which speaker behavior changed: the characteristics of the person or people being spoken to. His audience design model argues that variants that are perceived as being formal or informal derived that interpretation from their association with the social characteristics of the people who use them. In other words, speakers change the way they speak to adapt to the perceived characteristics of their audience. Bell provided an overview of different studies showing how differences in the composition of the audience could be related to greater or lesser degrees of style shifting.

These views of style characterize speakers as reacting or responding to elements of the social context (situation, topic, audience). In contrast, more recent work led by Penelope Eckert (2000) and others has offered an alternative view in which speakers take an active role in defining the sociolinguistic situation. In contrast to responsive or reactive theories of style shifting, agentive approaches view speakers as acting together to define the sociolinguistic situation through their use of linguistic variants. Under this view, linguistic variants have potential rather than fixed meaning, and the interpretation of their meaning depends on the context in which they are used in conversational interaction. Rather than passively relating social meaning to variants, speakers and their interlocutors co-construct the meaning of variants.

1.3.3   Social Group (*Sociolect*)

Since speakers make use of the fact of linguistic variation to construct, express, and interpret social meaning through language, an important task of the variationist approach is to determine which divisions are socially meaningful, whether and how those divisions are expressed linguistically. While the most straightforward approach would be to ask people directly, language speakers are not always consciously aware of their own behavior. Paradoxically, people can exhibit quite complex sociolinguistic behavior without being able to discuss this behavior! For this reason, the variationist approach relies primarily on observations of linguistic behavior in natural contexts.

Within the variationist approach, there is often a tension between "macro-level" and "micro-level" (or local) definitions of groups. Macro-level definitions involve grouping speakers in ways that are measurable and objective and can be replicated and compared across studies (**etic**). Categories such as occupation, amount of income, level of education, biological sex, and racial-physical characteristics are relatively easy to determine and measure and can be compared across studies. However, these categories, while objectively useful, may not be meaningful to the community or the individuals being studied and may not be conveyed linguistically. An alternative approach, more commonly adopted in recent years, is to seek explanations for sociolinguistic divisions in micro-level or local categories (**emic**). Local categories, being more subjective, are less easy to code and may require supplementing observations of linguistic behavior with long-term ethnographic analysis or social-psychological questionnaires or experiments, but they often provide more socially motivated explanations for the observed patterns of variation than do the macro-level categories (Eckert 2000; Hoffman & Walker 2010).

1.3.3.1   Social Class – Social Network – Community of Practice   In New York in the 1960s, Labov noticed a correlation between style shifting and the speaker's socioeconomic status: speakers with lower status tend to use more informal variants and speakers of higher status use more formal variants (Labov 1966). This finding reflects a common observation across different communities that a person's social status is correlated with his or her linguistic behavior.

Distinctions in socioeconomic status were operationalized by Labov as **social class**, defined on the basis of three (etic) measurements: occupation, income, and education. Together these measurements placed people on a scale which could then be divided into sectors such as "middle class" and "upper working class." The correlation between socioeconomic status and linguistic behavior has been established across a number of studies conducted in English-speaking communities, but the relative effect of each of the components of the socioeconomic scale differs across communities. Labov traced the differences in social-class behavior to two competing pressures: pressure from above (we try to sound like those of higher social classes when considerations of power or prestige are invoked) and pressure from below (we try to sound like those of lower social classes when we want to display solidarity).

Social class has not figured as prominently in subsequent variationist research, which has taken a couple of different directions in accounting for sociolinguistic divisions on the basis of power and status. In a study of Montreal

French, David Sankoff Suzanne and Laberge (1978) adapted Pierre Bourdieu's idea of language as a form of **social capital** to reimagine social class as access to the "linguistic market." In their analysis of different variables in Montreal French, they found correlations between the formal variants associated with standard French and the degree of access that speakers had to this form of capital.

Another direction of research in sociolinguistic stratification has looked at the relationships that exist among speakers. As I noted, geographical variation forms dialect regions because people tend to talk like the people they talk to. In a study of English in Belfast, Northern Ireland, James and Lesley Milroy made use of the notion of **social networks** (Milroy 1987). Under this approach, individuals form social ties with others in order to carry out the different functions of life. Social networks can be characterized by a couple of dimensions: density (the extent to which people you know know each other) and multiplexity (the number of types of relationships). Urban working-class speakers tend to have dense and multiplex networks, which leads to reinforcement and preservation of informal and nonstandard variants, whereas middle-class speakers tend to have looser and more simplex networks, leading to pressure to use more standard and formal variants. The Milroys found a high degree of correlation between the type of social network and the use of local Belfast variants. Because social classes are characterized by different kinds of social network, this approach can be seen as complementary to, rather than in competition with, the socioeconomic approach. Later work has looked in more detail at the types of social networks speakers engage in. Penelope Eckert and Sally McConnell-Ginet (1992) introduced the notion of the "**community of practice**" (CoP) from education theory. The social networks studied by the Milroys were formed on the basis of voluntary (friendship) and involuntary (family, neighborhood, work) bases. In contrast, the CoP is formed by groups of speakers who come together purposefully to achieve certain ends. Their work and subsequent studies have shown that the volitional component of networks can have a strong correlation with patterns of linguistic behavior.

1.3.3.2 Sex/Gender   As sex is a basic biological distinction that figures prominently in most social systems, it should not be surprising that it also serves to distinguish speaker behavior in many communities. We should be careful to note that although there are physiological differences between men and women that produce differences in the speech signal – men tend to have longer vocal cords than women, which lowers overall pitch– not all sex-based differences in linguistic behavior can be traced to physiology. In many languages the sex of the speaker is conveyed through their choice of pronouns or the use of particular discourse markers. English does not convey sex distinctions grammatically, but certain discourse strategies and lexical choices are popularly believed to be more common among men or women.

Speaker sex has been a social factor since the earliest days of variationist studies. Most studies have agreed in finding that women tend to use more formal variants than men do. Early studies suggested that, because women traditionally lack power and capital, they compensate for this lack through their manipulation of the "symbolic capital" of formal or standard language. These studies were later criticized for framing women's behavior as deviant from men's, and therefore in need of explanation. More recent studies view any sex-based differences as arising from different processes of socialization during childhood, which (stereotypically) orients girls and boys to different behavioral norms (Eckert 1989; Labov 1990). In their study in Belfast, the Milroys (Milroy 1987) found that men and women in urban working-class communities tend to have different types of social networks: men's networks are denser and more multiplex, while women's are looser and more simplex. These differences can be seen to result from patterns of employment, in which men worked locally, whereas women had to travel outside of the neighborhood to find work, coming into contact with a greater variety of people.

1.3.3.3 Ethnicity   Ethnicity is a fundamental social division that also entails differences in linguistic behavior, but defining ethnicity as a general concept is made difficult because it arises from different sources. Ethnicity is sometimes defined on the basis of physical characteristics, such as skin and hair color and eye and nose shape (race). In the United States, the major ethnic division is between black people (most of whom trace their origins to Africa) and white people (most of whom trace their origins to Europe). Ethnicity may be defined on the basis of adherence to a particular religious tradition. In many societies around the world, people are divided according to whether they are Muslim, Christian, Jewish, Buddhist, etc. Ethnicity may be defined on the basis of place of origin, even if that origin lies in the distant past. In an immigrant society such as Australia, people are divided ethnically according to where their ancestors originally migrated from. Ethnicity may be defined on the basis of a heritage or community language, even if that language is no longer spoken. In the United States there is a sizable Hispanic population whose ethnicity is based on Spanish as their heritage or community language, although many people categorized as Hispanic do not speak Spanish.

Ethnicity serves as the basis for a number of qualitative and quantitative differences in linguistic behavior (ethnolects). A common assumption is that ethnolects stem from a process of language acquisition from the heritage or community language to the majority language, but tracing ethnolectal features to the original language is not straightforward after the first generation. Much of the variationist work on ethnicity in the United States has been concerned with the black–white division. In the way they speak English, many African Americans differ on all linguistic levels from Americans of other origins

(Labov 1972). Some researchers have suggested that these differences arose from an earlier African American creole (a mixture of English and African languages with some second-language features) (Rickford 1998), while others have suggested that the long period of social segregation led to linguistic divergence (Poplack 2000). For other groups, variationist research has shown that ethnic boundaries, whatever their source, can serve to maintain different linguistic systems over time and impede participation in ongoing change. The variants that make up ethnolects may also serve as a way of constructing and expressing a particular ethnic identity, particularly when the original heritage or community language is no longer spoken and cannot serve this function (Hoffman & Walker 2010).

1.3.3.4 Age and Time   As with sex, age is a biological reality that divides people into groups, whether expressed as generations (cohorts of people born at the same time) or life stages (periods of life characterized by different social roles and responsibilities). Age groups may correlate with different patterns of linguistic behavior, but these patterns may result from different sources: changes going on in the community or social expectations of membership in each age group.

Quantitative differences in linguistic behavior may be inferred to reflect ongoing change in the language (**apparent time**) if we assume that individual speakers do not change the way they speak once they acquire their language. People born in 1966 should speak the same whether they are studied in 1986 or 2016, and their speech should reflect the state of their language as spoken in the community in the late 1960s. On the other hand, age-based differences may reflect patterns of linguistic behavior associated with each life stage, repeated by each generation as they go through each stage (**age grading**). A person born in 1966 studied in 1986 and a person born in 1996 studied in 2016 should behave the same.

The only way to definitively decide whether age-based differences reflect ongoing change or age grading is to conduct a longitudinal study of the same community over an extended period of **real time**, either by resampling the same community similarly each time (**trend study**) or by rerecording the same individuals over time (**panel study**). Until recently, real-time studies were difficult to conduct. A real-time study of spoken data is obviously limited by the lack of recorded speech before the twentieth century. Written data can serve as a proxy for spoken data, but we are limited to using whatever documents have happened to survive, and since the rate of literacy in previous centuries was very low, the documents are unlikely to represent the range of variation that existed in the community.

Nevertheless, there is now enough spoken-language data recorded for the purposes of variationist research from the 1960s to the present that real-time studies have become more feasible. Real-time studies suggest that the assumptions of apparent time are largely valid: most speakers do not substantially change their rate of use of incoming variants across the course of their life. The few cases where change has been observed across the life span are correlated with changes in the individual's life situation, and speakers tend to change in the same direction as the community (G. Sankoff & Blondeau 2007). These studies suggest that we can continue to conduct apparent-time studies, so long as we understand the social characteristics of ongoing change.

When mapped across time or across age groups, changes in progress show an S-shaped curve, starting out slowly, accelerating in the middle, and slowing at the end. Changes in progress are also characterized by particular types of distribution across social categories. Although I noted that women tend to be more conservative in greater use of standard forms, they are at the same time more innovative in ongoing changes. Women, especially young women, are likely to adopt or lead in changes ahead of men. Ethnic groups exhibit different rates of participation in ongoing changes. African Americans have been shown not to participate in changes going on in the wider English-speaking community. Changes will show different patterns of distribution according to the origins of the change. As seen in the case of Belfast, changes involving the introduction of standard variants into the community are usually initiated through the type of social network that characterizes middle-class speakers. Such **changes from above** begin with higher social classes and filter down the social-class hierarchy. In contrast, **changes from below** are initiated by lower social classes and percolate to higher levels of the socioeconomic scale.

1.4   Conclusion

Variation is a fact of language, from differences between languages and dialects to differences between speakers and even within an individual speaker. The variationist approach to the study of language allows us to use the fact of linguistic variation to understand the workings of linguistic systems and the way that speakers make use of variation to construct and express aspects of their social life.

References

Bell, A. 1984. Language style as audience design. *Language in Society* 13, 145–204.
Buchstaller, I. 2014. *Quotatives: New Trends and Sociolinguistic Implications*. Oxford: Wiley-Blackwell.
Chambers, J. K., and Trudgill, P. 1998. *Dialectology*. 2nd edn. Cambridge: Cambridge University Press.
D'Arcy, A. 2017. *Discourse-Pragmatic Variation in Context: Eight Hundred Years of Like*. Amsterdam: John Benjamins.

Eckert, P. 1989. The whole woman: Sex and gender differences in variation. *Language Variation and Change* 1: 245–267.

Eckert, P. 2000. *Linguistic Variation as Social Practice*. Oxford: Blackwell.

Eckert, P., and McConnell-Ginet, S. 1992. Think practically and look locally: Language and gender as community-based practice. *Annual Review of Anthropology* 21, 461–490.

Hoffman, M. F., and Walker, J. A. 2010. Ethnolects and the city: Ethnic orientation and linguistic variation in Toronto English. *Language Variation and Change*, 22, 37–67.

Kretzschmar, W. A. 2017. Linguistic atlases. Pages 57–72 of: C. Boberg, J. Nerbonne, and D. Watt (eds.), *The Handbook of Dialectology*. Oxford: Wiley-Blackwell.

Labov, W. 1963. The social motivation of a sound change. *Word*, 19, 273–309.

Labov, W. 1966. *The Social Stratification of English in New York City*. Washington, DC: Center for Applied Linguistics.

Labov, W. 1972. *Language in the Inner City: Studies in the Black English Vernacular*. Philadelphia: University of Pennsylvania Press.

Labov, W. 1990. The intersection of sex and social class in the course of linguistic change. *Language Variation and Change* 2: 205–254.

Lavandera, B. 1977. Where does the sociolinguistic variable stop? *Working Papers in Sociolinguistics*, 40, 6–19.

Milroy, L. 1987. *Language and Social Networks*. 2nd edn. Oxford: Blackwell.

Poplack, S. (ed.). 2000. *The English History of African American English*. Oxford: Blackwell.

Rickford, J. R. 1998. The Creole origins of African-American vernacular English: Evidence from copula absence. Pages 154–200 of: S. Mufwene, J. R. Rickford, G. Bailey, and J. Baugh (eds.), *African-American English: Structure, History and Use*. London: Routledge.

Sankoff, D. 1988. Sociolinguistics and syntactic variation. Pages 140–161 of: F. J. Newmeyer (ed.), *Linguistics: The Cambridge Survey. Vol. IV: Language: The Socio-Cultural Context*. Cambridge: Cambridge University Press.

Sankoff, D., and Laberge, S. 1978. The linguistic market and the statistical explanation of variability. Pages 239–250 of: D. Sankodff (ed.), *Linguistic Variation: Models and Methods*. New York: Academic Press.

Sankoff, G., and Blondeau, H. 2007. Language change across the lifespan: /r/ in Montreal French. *Language*, 83, 560–588.

Szmrecsanyi, B. 2013. *Grammatical Variation in British English Dialects: A Study in Corpus-Based Dialectometry*. Cambridge: Cambridge University Press.

2   Phonetic Variation in Dialects

Rachael Tatman

2.1   Introduction

Even if you've never studied linguistics, you already know that a lot of social information is reflected in the ways that we use language. You've almost certainly met someone for the first time and been able to immediately figure out something about their social background based on the way they speak or sign. Linguistic features associated with social or regional identity occur at every level of the grammar, from speech sounds to syntactic constructions to the cues that people use to show that their conversational turn is over. Such features can also encode a wide variety of social information, from social class to gender to how formal a speaker is being. Investigating the relationships between linguistics features and social identity is the focus of the field of sociolinguistics.

In this chapter, we will focus on a very small part of sociolinguistics: how variation in the sounds of speech[1] reflect the regional origin of the speaker.

The study of the production and perception of speech sounds is called *phonetics*, and the differences in speech sounds between language varieties is commonly called *phonetic variation*. Rather than focusing on the specific differences between a small handful of dialects we will discuss the ways speech sounds can vary across dialects and what causes these differences, illustrated with a handful of examples. This will give you the general framework and vocabulary you will need to begin reading the sociophonetic literature for the specific dialect(s) of interest to you and your work.

Before we began investigating specific reasons for differences between dialects, we will need to cover some introductory phonetic principles and vocabulary: phonemes, vowels, consonants, and suprasegmentals. Then we will briefly discuss why differences between dialects arise. After this introduction, the rest of the chapter will consist of a discussion of processes that affect

---

[1] While sign languages are beyond the scope of this chapter, they also show sociolinguistic variation. See Lucas (2001) for an overview.

different classes of phonemes, along with examples of dialect differences arising from each kind of process.

2.1.1   What Are Phonemes?

Phonemes are the smallest unit of sound in a language (Trubetzkoy, 1969). A change in a single phoneme can change an existing word into a different word or make it a non-word. For example, if you change the first sound of the word *shrimp* (*sh* as in *ship*) into *s* (as in *sip*) you are left with the non-word *srimp*. This is good evidence that *sh* and *s* are different phonemes in English. However, if you replaced the *r* sound in the Japanese ア ロ エ (said *ah-row-ey*) with the American English *l* sound (so that it would sound more like *ah-low-ey*), a native Japanese listener would probably still accept is as ア ロ エ. This is because the American English sounds *l* and *r* are not separate phonemes in Japanese. While not all linguists agree about the existence or nature of phonemes, phonemes are a useful shorthand for discussing clusters of similar sounds and most texts, including this one, will use them.

Phonemes can generally be divided into two large classes: vowels and consonants. They are distinguished by the shape of the vocal tract. The *vocal tract* is the term that linguists use to refer to the throat, mouth, and nasal cavity. In order to make speech sounds, we use our lungs to push air through our vocal chords, up through the throat and then out through either the mouth and/or the nasal cavity. By manipulating different parts of the vocal tract, we can change the quality of the sound produced.

Phoneme-level transcriptions of speech are almost always done using the specialized international phonetic alphabet, or IPA. However, as learning to read and write IPA is very time-consuming, it will not be used in this chapter. I would point interested learners to *A Course in Phonetics*, by Ladefoged and Johnson (2014), and the associated website.[2]

2.1.1.1   Vowels   Vowels are the class of sound produced without a constriction or closing of the vocal tract. They are louder, longer, and easier to hear than consonants. In the vast majority of languages, each syllable (and thus each word) must contain at least one vowel. All languages have at least three distinct vowels and some have many more. Dutch, for instance, may have as many as thirteen (Mees and Collins, 1983). If a language does have only three vowels, it will generally be the vowels in the American English[3] words *beet*, *bot*, and *boot*.

Vowels are conventionally graphically represented in a two-dimensional space. The *x*-axis represents whether the tongue is more forward or more

---

[2] See www.phonetics.ucla.edu/course/contents.html.
[3] The author is a native speaker of American English.

backward in the mouth, with the left of the diagram representing the front of the mouth. The *y*-axis represents the tongue height or degree of opening of the jaw, with a *high* vowel having the jaw more closed and thus the tongue closer to the roof of the mouth. The vowel in *beet*, for example, is a high front vowel, while the vowel in *bat* is a low front vowel. If you place your hand under your chin and alternate between saying *beet* and *bat*, you will find that your jaw is more open while producing the *bat* vowel than the *beet* vowel. You can observe the difference in backness by gently holding a spoon in your mouth with the end resting on your tongue and repeating the vowel in *beet* and *boot*. The spoon will move toward the front of your mouth while producing the *beet* vowel and toward the back of your throat while producing the *boot* vowel.

The position of individual vowel is usually measured by the location of formants. Formants, or distinct bands of high acoustic energy in the time/frequency domain, are important cues to human vowel perception and fairly easy to annotate. The frontness of the tongue body is captured by the inverse of the first formant and the height is captured by the inverse of the second formant. (The inverses are used so that high vowels are at the top of the graph and back vowels are at the right.) The first formant is abbreviated *F1* and the second, *F2*. Some vowels may be produced with movement of the tongue body during articulation, such as the vowel in American English *buy*. These are called diphthongs and are generally show as vectors, rather than static points, in the F1 by F2 space.

Vowels may also be distinguished by other qualities, such as whether air escapes through the nose during articulation, how long the vowel production is held, and whether the lips are rounded. These differences cannot be easily seen in an F1 by F2 space.

2.1.1.2 Consonants

Consonants are sounds that have at least one point of construction or closure of the vocal tract. Consonants are generally distinguished by the place and degree of restriction. The constriction can range from a complete closure (in which case the consonant is called a *stop*) to a slight movement of the tongue toward the side of the mouth (which is called a *lateral*). Consonants can be produced anywhere in the vocal tract from the vocal folds themselves (*glottal*) to the lips (*bilabial*).

In addition to the place and manner of articulation, many consonants can be produced either with or without sound being produced by forcing air through taut vocal folds. If sound is produced in this way while articulating the consonant, the resulting consonant is called *voiced*. If no sound is produced, the consonant is *voiceless*. You can feel the differences in voice quality by placing your hand on your throat. For voiced sounds, like the *z* in *zip*, you should feel a buzzing sensation in your throat. For voiceless sounds, like the *s* in *sip* this sensation will be absent.

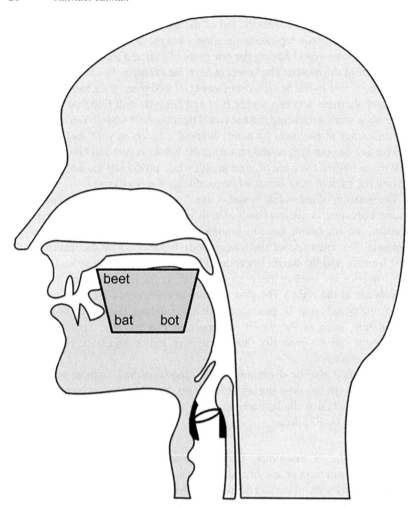

Figure 2.1 A vowel quadrilateral superimposed over a midsagittal diagram of
the vocal tract. The position of each word corresponds to the position of the
center of the tongue body while producing the vowel in that word.

We can combine these qualities: place and manner of articulation and whether
the sound is voiced or voiceless, to precisely describe different consonants.

The sound *t* as in *tee*, for example, is a voiceless alveolar (produced at the
alveolar ridge) stop. The sound *m* in *me*, on the other hand, is a voiced bilabial
nasal (produced by forcing air through the nasal cavity). I will not discuss all
the possible places and manners of articulation here, but interested readers are
encouraged to refer to "The Sounds of the World's Languages" (Ladefoged and
Maddieson, 1998) as an authoritative guide.

Languages tend to have more constants than vowels, often around twenty-two or so. However the number of consonants in a language can range from six, like the Rotokas language spoken in Papua New Guinea, to over a hundred, like the !X language spoken in Botswana (Haspelmath et al., 2005).

2.1.2   What Are Suprasegmentals?

So far we have discussed only vowels and consonants. However, there is a third category of sound that is used to indicate differences between words: suprasegmentals. Suprasegmentals are the acoustic aspects of speech associated with words or syllables rather than individual speech sounds. Examples include lexical tone, stress, and intonation.

Perhaps the simplest example of a suprasegmental is lexical tone. Lexical tone is the use of pitch (whether the fundamental frequency of the voice has a high or low frequency) to distinguish between words. In Mandarin Chinese, for example, the words for "horse," "mother," "hemp," and "to scold" are all pronounced *ma*. It is the pattern of the pitch used while producing the word that determines the meaning.

Pitch, particularly when looking at prosody or intonation, is sometimes annotated using the ToBI system, developed by Silverman et al. (1992). However, there are many different standards for annotating pitch and tone and they often depend on the language being annotated.

2.1.3   Why Does Dialectal Variation Exist?

Language in use constantly varies. Even a single speaker producing the same word in the same environment will never produce it in exactly the same way twice. Two instances of the same speaker saying the same word will, however, probably be more alike than two different people saying the same word. And two individuals who share many social characteristics (gender, socioeconomic status, level of education, profession, friend network etc.) will probably produce language more similar to each other than two individuals who share none of those characteristics. These systems of variation that pattern with social identity tend to be systematic to the point that they can be summarized by systems of rules. They also occur for groups smaller than "all speakers of a particular language."

It is common to refer to a language as a single monolithic entity: French or Thai or Twi. However, this hides the complexity of language in use. It's more accurate to say that there are many versions of a language. For English, for example, we might refer to American English or British English. Or we might make even finer grain distinctions within American English and talk about Nevada English or Boston English. At an even finer grain, we might talk about the patterns of language use that occur in from a particular social network or even an individual speaker's idiolect. For this chapter, however, we will focus mainly on differences in language use between geographical regions. This has long been a focus of sociolinguistic research, and many large-scale research projects, such as the *Dictionary of American Regional English* (Cassidy et al., 1985) or *The Atlas of North American English* (Labov et al., 2005), focus on finding and describing language differences between regions.

These different versions, or *dialects*, of a language come from a single historical language. For example, at one time French, Italian, and Spanish would all have once been considered dialects of Latin. However, all living languages are constantly changing at every level of the grammar. (We will discuss some of the specifics of phonetics change later in this chapter.) Since the French, Spanish, and Italian language communities were not in daily contact with each other, as they changed, they slowly diverged from each other to the point where they were no long mutually intelligible. When say that two language varieties are *mutually intelligible* when a speaker of variety A can understand a speaker of variety B and vice versa.

Other than historical changes, the other major source of differences between language varieties is migration. When speakers of a language variety move to a new area and either establish a new language community or integrate with the existing community, features of their language variety will often be incorporated into the dialect of that region. For example, the migration of Hindi-speaking indentured laborers to Fiji resulted in the emergence of new dialect of Hindi known as Fijian Hindi, which incorporates English and Fijian words (Kerswill, 2006).

2.2   Vowels

Dialectal variation in vowels has been extensively studied. There are two main ways that the vowel systems of two varieties may differ from one another: each variety may have a different number of vowels or they may have the same number of vowels but produce them in different ways.

Because dialects share a historical root with each other, it is common to compare an existing dialects to an earlier one. Thus, when we talk about something like a vowel *split*, we mean that where there was historically a single vowel in the vowel space there is now more than one. Similarly, a *merger* refers to a single vowel in the area of the vowel space that was previously occupied by more than one vowel. Finally, a vowel *shift* refers to the movement of vowels in the vowel space from some historical starting point, but without changing the total number of vowels.

2.2.1   Splits

Vowel splits generally start as *conditioned* splits that appear only in certain environments. For example, in the Haroi language spoken in Vietnam, the vowel *u* (as in American English *boot*) is pronounced as *o* (as in Canadian English *boat*) when it comes before a syllable that starts with a vioceless fricative, affricate, or stop (Lee, 1977). If this conditioning environment is lost over time, the result is words that are distinguished only by differences in vowels. This is the case in Swiss German, where the vowel *ai* as in *bait*, split into the *bait* vowel in some words and the *e* as in *bet* vowel in others (Moulton, 1961).

2.2.2   Mergers

Like splits, mergers may be either conditioned or unconditioned. The *pin/pen* merger, for example, found in the Southern United States, means that the vowels in *pin* and *pen* are pronounced in the same way before nasals (Labov et al., 2005). This results in pairs of words like *Wendy* and *windy* or *djinn* and *Jenn* being pronounced the same. Some mergers occur in all contexts, however. The *cot-caught* merger, which is ubiquitous in the United States west of the Rocky Mountains, occurs in all contexts and results in words like *body* and *bawdy* or *hall* and *haul* being pronounced in the same way (Wolfram and Schilling, 2015).

2.2.3   Shifts

In vowel shifts, all or part of the vowel system moves within the F1 by F2 space. Generally, this will be started by a single vowel moving. If it does not merge, it will either crowd another vowel or leave an empty space in the vowel space. This will cause a second vowel to move, either to scoot out of the way or to fill the vacuum, which in turn will push or pull a third, and so on. This process is known as a *chain shift*.

English's vowel system is particularly active. Perhaps the most notable vowel shift in English was the great vowel shift, which took place between the fourteenth and seventeenth centuries and affected all long vowels (Baugh and Cable, 1993). There are also many currently on-going vowel shifts in English, including the New Zealand vowel shift (Hay et al., 2008), the Canadian vowel shift (Clarke et al., 1995), the northern cities vowel shift, and the southern vowel shift (Labov et al., 2005).

2.3   Consonants

Historically, sociolinguistic variation in consonants has been the focus of less research than variation in vowels. This is due in part to the fact that consonants, which are generally shorter and quieter than vowels, are harder to measure.

Like vowels, consonantal sounds can undergo both splits and mergers between dialects of the same language. This may result in two related varieties that have a different number of consonants. In Spanish, for example, a historical distinction between the *s* and *th* sounds has been maintained in Spain, while in American Spanish both sounds are now produced as *s* (Penny, 2002). These differences can also be conditioned: while most varieties of Mandarin have dropped all consonants at the ends of words, the Yue dialects (including Cantonese) have preserved most of them (Norman, 1988).

It is also common for the same underlying sound to be produced in different ways in different dialects. One example is the French *r* sound. In Parisian French, it is produced with the back of the tongue near the uvula (the pink "punching bag" visible at the back of the throat when yawning). In other varieties, such as that produced by older speakers of Midi French, the *r* sound is produced with the tip of the tongue against the alveolar ridge (behind the front teeth) (Klingler and Lyche, 2012).

2.4   Suprasegmentals

Dialectal variation in suprasegmentals is less well studied than variation in vowels or consonants. As with vowels and consonants, suprasegmentals may vary in the number used by differing dialects or in the way in which they are realized. As an example of the former, Mandarin spoken in Yantai has three lexical tones, rather than the four found in varieties such as Beijing Mandarin (Bao, 1999). As an example of the latter, while many dialects of Japanese make use of a pitch accent system where the pitch accent used is determined by the word, Japanese spoken in Miyakonoj assigns pitch accent based the position of the word in a sentence instead (Haraguchi, 1988).

2.5   Conclusion

Vowels, consonants, and suprasegmentals can all vary between dialects. These differences arise due to historical changes that start in and speech sounds. However, sociophonetic variation is reflected in text as well. Differences in how speech sounds are produced and perceived are often reflected in spelling, particularly in informal user-generated text, such as social media posts. Spelling variation sometimes reflects the user's own linguistic perception, such as a Twitter user from Kentucky tweeting "going to eat at windys." Since the *pin/pen* merger is common in Kentucky, it seems reasonable and *windy's* and *Wendy's* (an American fast-food restaurant) are homophones for this speaker, and this is reflected in their spelling.

The use of spelling to reflect regional phonetic variation is sometimes called *eye dialect* (Bowdre, 1964). In general, users are more likely to use an eye dialect to reflect their spoken variety if they have a strong regional identity (Shoemark, 2017). They are also more likely to write out phonetic markers that are stereotypically associated with the dialect they're attempting to show (Tatman, 2016).

The fact that these variant spellings appear only in user-generated text can lead to poor performance on user-generated text data for models trained on corpora of more formal text. One example of this is the fact that many identification algorithms have been shown to be unable to correctly identify African American English as English (Blodgett et al., 2016). This may be due in part to spellings such as *dis* for *this* or *wit* for *with*, which reflect the merger of interdental fricatives (the *th* sound in English) with alveolar stops (the *d* and *t* sounds) (Mufwene et al., 1998).

In short, different dialects have systemic phonetic differences, and these differences are sometimes reflected in text. Natural language processing researchers who are aware of these differences and how and why they occur won't be surprised when they encounter them in data and are better prepared to build models to handle such variation.

Vowels, consonants, and suprasegmentals can all vary between dialects. These differences arise due to historical changes that occur in one dialect but for some reason do not spread to others. As a result, different dialects may have more, fewer, or different speech sounds in the same words or phonetic contexts.

References

Bao, Zhiming. 1999. *The structure of tone*. Oxford University Press on Demand.

Baugh, Albert C., and Cable, Thomas. 1993. *A history of the English language*. Routledge.

Blodgett, Su Lin, Green, Lisa, and O'Connor, Brendan. 2016. Demographic dialectal variation in social media: A case study of African-American English. Pages 1119–1130 of: *Proceedings of the 2016 conference on empirical methods in natural language processing*.

Bowdre, Paul Hull. 1964. *A study of eye dialect*. Ph.D. thesis, University of Florida.

Cassidy, Frederic Gomes, et al. 1985. *Dictionary of American regional English*. Belknap Press of Harvard University Press.

Clarke, Sandra, Elms, Ford, and Youssef, Amani. 1995. The third dialect of English: Some Canadian evidence. *Language variation and change*, **7**(2), 209–228.

Haraguchi, Shoshuke. 1988. Pitch accent and intonation in Japanese. *van der Hulst & Smith*, 123–150.

Haspelmath, Martin, Dryer, Matthew S., Gil, David, and Comrie, Bernard. 2005. *The world atlas of linguistic structures*.

Hay, J., Maclagan, M., and Gordon, E. 2008. *New Zealand English*. Dialects of English. Edinburgh University Press.

Kerswill, Paul. 2006. Migration and language. *Sociolinguistics/Soziolinguistik. An international handbook of the science of language and society*, **3**, 1–27.

Klingler, Tom, and Lyche, Chantal. 2012. Cajun French in a non-Acadian community: A phonological study of the French of Ville Platte, Louisiana. *Phonological variation in French: Illustrations from three continents*, 274–312.

Labov, William, Ash, Sharon, and Boberg, Charles. 2005. *The atlas of North American English: Phonetics, phonology and sound change*. Walter de Gruyter.

Ladefoged, Peter, and Johnson, Keith. 2014. *A course in phonetics*. Nelson Education.

Ladefoged, Peter, and Maddieson, Ian. 1998. The sounds of the world's languages. *Language*, **74**(2), 374–376.

Lee, Ernest W. 1977. Devoicing, aspiration, and vowel split in Haroi: Evidence for register (contrastive tongue-root position). *Pacific linguistics. Series A. Occasional papers*, 87.

Lucas, Ceil. 2001. *The sociolinguistics of sign languages*. Cambridge University Press.

Mees, Inger, and Collins, Beverley. 1983. A phonetic description of the vowel system of standard Dutch (ABN). *Journal of the international phonetic association*, **13**(2), 64–75.

Moulton, William G. 1961. The dialect geography of hast, hat in Swiss German. *Language*, **37**(4), 497–508.

Mufwene, Salikoko S., Rickford, John R., Baugh, John, and Bailey, Guy. 1998. *African-American English: Structure, history, and use*. Psychology Press.

Norman, Jerry. 1988. *Chinese*. Cambridge University Press.

Penny, Ralph John. 2002. *A history of the Spanish language*. Cambridge University Press.

Shoemark, Philippa. 2017. Debnil Sur, Luke Shrimpton, Iain Murray, and Sharon Goldwater. 2017. Aye or naw, whit dae ye hink? Scottish independence and linguistic identity on social media. Pages 1239–1248 of: *Proceedings of the 15th conference of the European chapter of the Association for Computational Linguistics*. Vol. 1.

Silverman, Kim, Beckman, Mary, Pitrelli, John, Ostendorf, Mori, Wightman, Colin, Price, Patti, Pierrehumbert, Janet, and Hirschberg, Julia. 1992. ToBI: A standard for labeling English prosody. In: *Second international conference on spoken language processing*.

Tatman, Rachael. 2016. Ima spawts guay: Comparing the use of sociophonetic variables in speech and Twitter. *University of Pennsylvania Working Papers in Linguistics*, **22**(2), 18.

Trubetzkoy, Nikolai Sergeevich. 1969. Principles of phonology.

Wolfram, Walt, and Schilling, Natalie. 2015. *American English: Dialects and variation*. Vol. 25. John Wiley & Sons.

3   Similar Languages, Varieties, and Dialects: Status and Variation

Miriam Meyerhoff and Steffen Klaere

3.1   Introduction

This chapter builds on the introduction to the nature of sociolinguistic approaches to language variation presented in Chapter 1. It focuses in more detail on the problems associated with assessing the similarity and difference between closely related varieties. In particular, it discusses methods for extracting meaningful patterns of variation from different speakers from the same place. We use a data set collected in three villages on a small island in the Caribbean to illustrate how sociolinguists approach questions such as how similar, abstract patterns of variation can serve to cluster speakers; how some aspects of variation seem to index subgroups; and what the relationship is between the group and the individual. We show how different computational perspectives can be brought to bear on these problems in order to visualise and analyse the significance of interindividual and intergroup difference.

The purpose of this chapter is to address three problems: The status of discrete varieties – What do labels like *language, dialect, creole,* and *variety* mean? How can we investigate these labels? What is the role of variation in doing so? Can the variation inherent in natural languages be a means for differentiating or unifying varieties under these labels?

The first half of the chapter consists of a brief review of some of the issues associated with the often contested terms *language, dialect, creole,* and *variety* and indicate how linguists have approached the task of making systematic and principled distinctions between them. The distinction between *language* and *dialect* is an important one in language policy and planning, and the question of whether creoles are a unified class of natural languages has generated a lively literature since the 1990s. We will review some of the key points in this literature, while attempting to keep a focus on practical implications of the debates and how they have impacted the implementation of linguistic practice.

The second half of the chapter takes a closer look at some of the ways in which different analytic practices might explore these difficult spaces using data from an English-based creole. We document our efforts to use the systematic patterns inherent to language variation as a means of building a bottom-up case that validates speakers' strong beliefs that linguistically differentiated groups can emerge even on a relatively small island and in a relatively short time period.

3.2   Language: More Than Communication

As we will shortly see, linguists have sometimes been reluctant to engage with the distinction between *language* and *dialect*. However, they have been more than ready to engage with the task of identifying the properties that characterise human language and what makes it distinct from other (animal) forms of communication. We will sidestep some lively, and at times intemperate, contemporary debate about (1) how and when human language evolved and (2) whether it is distinguished from other forms of communication because of a single, game-changing evolutionary innovation or whether the emergence of human language is simply another step on a gradual continuum of changes in natural communication systems, differentiating humans from animals in a less dramatic way (Corballis, 2017, is a useful introduction).

One of the problems with the debate over the origins of human language is a lack of clarity about what the object of enquiry is. In some instances, it seems that researchers are interested in dating the emergence of and mechanisms by which very rudimentary oral communication systems emerged in early humans, and in other cases it seems that researchers are more interested in when and how more sophisticated social aspects of human communication emerged.

Hockett (1960) presented a checklist of features which he argued evolved from the building blocks of animal communication but which – taken altogether – uniquely define human language. A crucial criterion was what he referred to as 'duality of patterning'. This is an opaque way of expressing the fact that basic, meaningless sounds can be combined in numerous permutations to create words that do have distinct meaning. Thus, *cat*, *tack*, *act* all share the same basic sound units (/t/, /k/, /æ/) but depending on how they are ordered, the results have different meanings for speakers of English. Hockett suggests that this feature is unique to human language (while many of the other twelve design features would have been shared by protohominoids and are clearly a feature of some animal communication systems).

So, descriptively, there has long been agreement among linguists about what is a useful and appropriate means of differentiating *language* from *communication*. However, the differentiation between *language* and *dialect* is much more fraught.

3.3   Language and Dialect

Delimiting the terms *language* and *dialect* is perhaps one of the most painful tasks a linguist can be set. Is mutual intelligibility what differentiates dialects from languages? Is historical relatedness (and time depth for separation) what differentiates them? Is the distinction sociopolitical and therefore something that exists outside of the scope of linguistics? Faced with such difficulties, many English-speaking linguists have thrown up their hands, disavowed the distinction, and sought refuge in even fuzzier and indeterminate terms such as *variety*. Meyerhoff (2019), along with a number of other sociolinguists, chooses to refer to language *varieties* precisely in order to avoid the complex structural and sociological issues raised when trying to distinguish between language and dialect. Maxwell (2018) points out, this is rather disingenuous of (socio)linguists. For professional linguists to avoid the political freight associated with distinguishing *language/dialect* and to suggest that the distinction between them is simply an artefact of inexpert views about language neither erases the use of the two terms in everyday speech nor (more importantly) engages with the substantial sociopolitical disadvantage that is often vested on speakers of speech varieties labelled dialects.[1] As Lo Bianco, an authority on the formation of national language policies observes, 'language is a problematic object for planning because of the much greater quotient of identity, ideology and interests which languages carry' (Lo Bianco, 2008, 162).

For virtually every measure that can be forwarded, problems and counterexample exist. We find cases of mutually unintelligible varieties that are nevertheless referred to as *dialects*, as is the case in China where the various indigenous Sinitic languages are recognised officially as dialects even though linguists can point to numerous and very profound structural differences between them. We find cases of mutually intelligible varieties that are nevertheless referred to as *languages* (as is the case in much of Scandinavia), and even varieties that are asymmetrically intelligible (Speaker A claims not to be able to understand Speaker B's language, but Speaker B has no trouble understanding Speaker A). (See Chapter 4 and Chapter 9, for more on this).

If structural factors and relatedness are used as the criteria, similar problems arise and may even be amplified. We might find that in respect to some parts of the grammar, two varieties seem to be closely related – hence they appear to be dialects of a single language. Meanwhile, in other aspects of the grammar, they appear to be only distantly connected. Should sound changes be given more weight than grammatical changes or less? Many sound changes can occur on a continuum, allowing for (say) more or less fronting of a vowel, while many

---

[1] Not all sociolinguists of English are so pusillanimous. Since 1998, Kirk Hazen's West Virginia Dialect Project has embraced the term *dialect* and foregrounded regional dialects as an object of valorisation and study. Their work focuses on providing practical tools for exploring the systematicity of nonstandard varieties (dialects) of American English and for raising awareness of the social politics underlying attitudes to standard and nonstandard varieties of a language (Hazen, 2018).

grammatical changes are binary, e.g., negative particles occur before or after the main verb. It's true that there may be periods of variability when negatives can occur both before and after the main verb or periods when some verbs are more likely to occur with a negative before and others are more likely to occur with the negative after them, but the fundamentally binary nature of this feature is qualitatively different to the gradient nature of a feature like the degree of fronting (and lowering) of a vowel such as /u/.

This ultimately creates challenges for modelling similarity and difference[2] – if the measures of sameness and difference can have only two possible settings and if it is possible for languages to switch back and forth between the two settings over time, then a comparison of two languages may appear to be unchanged with respect to a grammatical feature, when in fact there might have been multiple opportunities for the grammatical feature to have switched that are now occluded by a poor historical record. For instance, if we find two languages both place the negative article before the verb at a given point in time, this could be because neither has ever changed and they both retain a shared, earlier setting for negation. However, if there are only two possible places for negation, one language might have moved negation from before the verb, to after the verb and back again to before the verb (a process known to linguists as Jespersen's Cycle), and this would not necessarily be apparent without careful consideration of an entire language family reconstructed on the basis of multiple, independent features. Furthermore, as Greenhill et al. (2017) point out, where a feature has only a binary setting, this restricts a priori the degrees of difference that are possible between varieties. Such problems and restrictions are not associated with continuous variables, such as vowels, which have continuous values associated with at least two major formant frequencies. Hence, the models used for testing hypotheses about how closely languages are related (i.e., whether they are languages or dialects) should ideally be sensitive to these qualitative differences between measures of similarity/difference or control for them.

We might also ask whether every sound change should be given the same weight when differentiating between language and dialect? Should changes that are phonetically predictable, such as the palatalisation of consonants immediately adjacent to a high/tense vowel, be conceptualised differently from less predictable changes, such as the loss of a segment in a consonant cluster?

---

[2] From a computational linguists' point of view, these problems may be otiose. Whether parsing or identifying unknown varieties, it would appear the question of status (dialect versus language, for instance) doesn't usually play a role in which natural language processing (NLP) methods to choose and how they perform (Zampieri et al., 2017).

All these sorts of considerations complicate the business of differentiating language and dialect – something that one might think was absolutely fundamental to the business of linguistics.

Added to this are the attendant social attitudes that the labels language and dialect stir up. In many contexts, dialect functions as a means of downgrading or minimising the status and rule-governed systematicity of a linguistic system. The oft-quoted (and oft-misquoted, Maxwell, 2018) saying that 'A language is a dialect with an army and a navy' points to the widely held perception that the only reliable differences between the two terms are sociopolitical and prestige or power based. Maxwell's insightful analysis of this phrase in Weinreich's work observes that it is frequently misattributed as an aphorism Weinreich himself subscribed to. Maxwell shows that this is not accurate and furthermore points out that attributing this belief to Weinreich stands at odds with Weinreich's advocacy for recognition of Yiddish as a bona fide language, rather than some broken form of Germanic or Slavic languages.

Nevertheless, in some subfields of linguistics, the business of distinguishing languages and dialects has been of central concern for centuries and in these fields, various methods have been developed for making the study of languages and dialects more transparent and accountable. Historical linguistics uses the comparative method to infer relatedness (degrees of similarity and difference) between languages and to infer how long varieties might have separated from each other. This essentially involves comparing how different languages realise (express) similar concepts and working out whether there have been systematic sound changes over the centuries and millennia that have resulted in the different shapes of words that are observed today. Where such changes can be reconstructed (inferred), linguists can specify the changes that have resulted in related languages diverging over time. Where such changes cannot be reconstructed, linguists can infer different lineages (see Chapter 1). New computational methods have allowed linguists to boost the scope of some of this work, but the empirical and theoretical underpinnings are little changed from the principles laid down by nineteenth-century dialectologists (as discussed in Chapter 5).

The side of historical linguistics that is concerned with reconstructing the dates of divergence between different languages gave rise to a methodology known as lexicostatistics. Here, there is an indirect implication that mutual intelligibility is an important distinction between languages. This method involves using versions of Morris Swadesh's list of core vocabulary (a set of 100 or 200 lexical items deemed to be universal to all human languages, such as *louse, hand, sun, ashes*; Swadesh, 1971) as the starting point for reconstructing the past relatedness of languages. Generally, at least 80 per cent shared cognate vocabulary on the Swadesh list is taken as indicating a very close relationship, such as would warrant being considered *dialects* of a single *language*, while shared cognate rates of between 36 and 80 per cent indicate different *languages* within the same *family* (Crowley, 1992, pages 168–183).

However, this definition knowingly abstracts away from the behaviours of speakers, who – as we have already noted – may invoke nonstructural criteria when making commonsense or lay differentiations between language and dialect (Lo Bianco's 'identit[ies], ideolog[ies] and interests', mentioned earlier).

3.4   Creoles as a Class of Natural Languages

Similar tensions over the role of linguistic structure and the social, political, and historical contexts of a language characterise debates over whether or not creoles constitute a distinct class of natural languages. This discussion is interesting for linguists because it differs from the debates over the identification of language versus dialect. It is manifestly not the case that all languages known as creoles were at some point related to each other (early theories of creole genesis that posited a single source for all creoles have been conclusively refuted; Velupillai, 2015, section 5.1). Hence, what is at question is not Have these varieties diverged sufficiently from a common ancestor to warrant separate status? but rather Are there enough features shared by these independent varieties to warrant considering them a separate class or family of languages? That is, a family of languages such as Romance or Algonquian can be classified as such because they share systematic sound and grammatical correspondences due to their descent from a common ancestor. If many or all creoles share key grammatical and phonological features, can we likewise categorise them as a distinct language family?

The principal exponents of what is (currently) known as 'creole exceptionalism' argue that creoles are more likely to share a common set of structural features (e.g., lack of productive inflectional and derivational morphology, small phoneme inventory, higher levels of polysemy), than other natural languages do. Since we know that this is not because of a common ancestor, the proposal is that the intense language contact giving rise to creoles is what triggers the appearance of these particular traits (Bakker et al., 2011). Alternatively, it has been argued that when cross-linguistic comparisons are based on well-constructed data sets that do not overrepresent some language families or linguistic features and underrepresent others, there is no statistically significant difference between the languages known as creoles and all other natural languages (Velupillai, 2015). Hence, what we might call the nonexceptional perspective suggests that what unifies creoles and sets them apart from other languages (to the extent that they are) are sociohistorical and sociopolitical facts. The details of this debate and the methods being used to underpin arguments for and against exceptionalism have changed as technology and resources have changed, but the debate itself is a rather old one; we can find its antecedents in the structural view of creolistics expounded by formal and cognitive linguists such as Bickerton (1980) and the more socially situated analysis of creolisation among ethnographic linguistics such as Jourdan (1985).

Both sides of this debate seem to agree on one thing – namely that creoles are rather new or young languages, many having only stabilised as the regular medium of communication in a community within the last two hundred years (Velupillai, 2015); an eyeblink in the context of hundreds of thousands of years of human language (Pinker and Bloom, 1990). They also seem to agree that this social fact, i.e., the comparative newness of these languages, has implications for their structural makeup. Their fundamental difference lies in whether the social facts alone are seen as sufficient for defining any class of languages or whether the structural facts alone are sufficient. We will not weigh in on one side or another on this debate; interested readers can explore a widening pool of primary research in this area and articles that contrast different modes of quantitative analysis (e.g., Fon Sing, 2017). Nonetheless, the quantitative approaches we will outline could in principle be adapted to the question of creole exceptionalism, should a researcher be so inclined. We will conclude by observing that another lesson one might take away from the ongoing debates over creole exceptionalism is the tremendous importance of thoughtfully constructed and linguistically rich data sets when attempting to make any claims about structural similarity or difference (see Chapter 6).

In the remainder of this chapter, we introduce one such linguistically rich data set and use it to exemplify a number of different quantitative techniques and modes of visualisation that can be used to explore diversity and unity within a single speech community. Any analysis of human behaviour experiences a tension between top-down, external (etic) and bottom-up, internal (emic) perspectives on variation. Sociolinguistics is committed to the primacy of the grammar that underlies spontaneous and unscripted speech, and these are the kind of data that we will present in the next section. Having stated this commitment to what might be construed as an emic approach to the identification and analysis of variation, we must recognise that it is impossible for any analysis to be entirely theory neutral. As we will see, the linguist has to decide which features (from the many features that vary in natural languages) will be the object of enquiry. We present these forays into different methods of exploring and visualising the relationships between speakers and between linguistic variables as an indication of the wide range of options that are available to linguists who might be concerned with questions of uniformity and divergence between and among languages, dialects, or creole and non-creole varieties of English.

3.5   Introducing the Corpus of Spoken Bequia Creole English

The Corpus of Spoken Bequia English (henceforth, Bequia Corpus) was collected by Jack Sidnell, James A. Walker, and Miriam Meyerhoff between 2004 and 2006. It consists of recordings with older residents of the island of Bequia (St Vincent and the Grenadines), the northernmost of the Vincentian Grenadine islands. The history of Bequia (pronounced *bek'way*) and what has been able to be reconstructed of the sociolinguistic history of the island are summarised in Meyerhoff and Walker (2013a). We surmise that some form of creole English was brought to the island in the late eighteenth century – historical data suggest close ties between Bequia and not only neighbouring St Vincent but also probably Barbados. Today, what is known locally as Dialect is spoken in one form or another by all native-born residents on the island; increased mobility among Bequians and increased inbound tourism means that there is ongoing change in the way younger residents speak (Daleszynska, 2013). Our study focused on older speakers (more than forty years at the time of recording) to control for this. Our speakers were all people who had grown up in a single village on Bequia before tourism on ferries, cruise ships, and planes became an important part of the island's economy. All speakers had at least one parent who was also born in their home village, many had two parents who grew up there, and sometimes two to four grandparents, too. Our speakers therefore are people with very dense networks in their home village.

Remarkably, given the small size of the island, the comparatively shallow time depth for settlement, and a total population of only about 5,000 people today, Bequians claim to be able to tell which village someone comes from simply by hearing them speak. We were initially not sure how to evaluate these claims – perhaps because there are so few people on the island, residents can place individuals in different villages based on social knowledge, not purely linguistic facts. However, despite the close network ties within villages (which make it unlikely that a speaker would not be related to or somehow know everyone else in their village), it became evident that there might be some substance to the claim across villages. Accordingly, we decided to investigate this folk linguistic (Niedzielski and Preston, 2000) ideology of difference, using a corpus of conversational speech collected over three seasons of fieldwork.

Since most people on Bequia switch to a supralocal version of Caribbean English that they use when talking to tourists or other outsiders (such as visiting linguists), our study used local interviewers. In most cases, the interviews were done by local teenagers who were recording members of their extended family or their neighbours. While they had been trained to be able to draw on a range of topics known to be successful in eliciting the kind of animated conversation that we were interested in recording, any given interview might cover very different topics from the others (e.g., politics and construction projects in one;

a miscarriage and family dynamics in another). The conversations vary in length, but on average run for between one and two hours. The recordings were transcribed exactly (but not phonetically), and these transcriptions were subsequently the basis for detailed analysis of a range of linguistic features.

As we noted, the choice of these features is not entirely theory neutral. We know, from previous research, that the verb phrase is a very rich source of structural diversity among varieties of English (Holm and Patrick, 2007; Kortmann and Luckenheimer, 2013). Consequently, our analysis focused heavily on features of the verb phrase (e.g., Walker and Meyerhoff, 2006; Meyerhoff and Walker, 2013b). What sets our method of analysis apart from the methods used by other researchers struggling with the distinction between *dialect*, *language*, and *creole* is the fine level of granularity that we adopted.

As variationist sociolinguists, we are interested in not just the categorical features that vary from one variety to another (the typical input for quantitative and qualitative assessments of linguistic sameness and difference) but with features that are probabilistic components of the grammar. This requires full accountability to the data (Labov, 1972), i.e., all and only the possible sites of variation must be examined. For instance, using examples from Walker and Meyerhoff (2006), we might observe that Bequians sometimes use a full or contracted form of the copula verb BE in sentences like (1) and (2), and that they sometimes do not use a copula at all (zero form), as in sentence (3).

(1) The boy and them is forward and fresh.
(2) Now he's twenty-one.
(3) When your head Ø bad, your foot Ø bad.

In order to describe accurately the likelihood of seeing a full, reduced or zero form of the copula, we must consider every possible place where a copula could occur in every utterance of every speaker, and we must document exactly which variant was used in each possible occurrence. Previous research on the copula has shown that documenting mere frequencies of the zero variant is rather uninformative; Labov (1969) famously demonstrated that by considering where speakers are more or less likely to use a zero variant, we can see a logic to the distribution of this variant which exactly parallels the logic that underlies the use of a contracted form in Standard English. Hence, careful coding of the variants as they occur is not enough for a solid analysis of variation; we also need to code the context in which the variant occurs – in this case, details about the phonology and syntax of the immediately surrounding words.

The methods of variationist sociolinguistics also mean we can ask similarly detailed questions about the social context for any variant: What are the social characteristics associated with the speaker who uttered it (their age, sex, history of mobility)? Who were they talking to when they uttered this and who else was around?

The resulting data sets can be very large and are quite time-consuming to construct, as (to date) much of the annotation cannot be automated, however, as advances are made with automated part-of-speech tagging and forced alignment of sound with transcripts, we can hope to see significant time savings over the next decade or two for researchers undertaking this kind of detailed coding. The Bequia Corpus was manually coded for its numerous variables. In the next section, we explain how the Bequia Corpus was manipulated to enable us to undertake an analysis of multiple variables that would enable us to determine whether a subset of highly salient features of creole grammar might serve as reliable diagnostics of what village a speaker comes from.

3.6   Transforming Spoken Word into Categorical Data

The recording of each speaker was encoded for twenty grammatical features. This necessitated narrowing the scope of the enquiry to nineteen speakers (out of more than sixty recorded as part of the study). They came from three villages that we knew, from our fieldwork, to be strongly identified on the islands with a distinct identity and an identifiable speaking style. From the twenty linguistic variables, we selected six for their potential to discriminate among the communities (based on our fieldwork observations) and for their linguistic coherence. The six features are subject type (STY), form of copula (FCO), tense aspect marker (TAM), auxiliary modal (AMO), form of negation (FNE), and negative copula (NCO). The overall number of encoded lines of interview are 10,621, at an average of 559 lines per speaker. The nineteen speakers have quite a diverse range, from 300 to 823 lines recorded. To assess the interrelationships between these variables and the communities, the number of states of each feature needs to be reasonable. Table 3.1 shows the number of states for each of the six features.

In a purely combinatorial sense, this means we have $11 \times 15 \times 9 \times 13 \times 6 \times 5 = 579,150$ possible grammatical feature combinations. The observed

Table 3.1 *Number of possible states every feature can attain.*

Feature	Number of States
STY	11
FCO	15
TAM	9
AMO	13
FNE	6
NCO	5

Table 3.2 *Marginalisation of states for each feature Here the variation is reduced to a four-way contrast between typically creole, typically Standard English, ambiguous variants, and coding where the feature is not applicable. The table shows the number of states marginalised to the smaller set and the number of lines of code that contributed towards the state.*

Feature	Ambiguous		Creole		English		Not Applicable	
STY	2	2,106	3	1,582	6	6,933	0	NA
FCO	2	279	4	1,528	8	2,978	1	5,836
TAM	2	237	4	120	1	244	1	10,020
AMO	2	1,865	0	NA	11	5,115	1	3,641
FNE	1	561	3	1,192	1	1,642	1	7,226
NCO	0	NA	3	1,185	0	NA	2	9,436

number of joint states is 907. The discrepancy between possible and actual is not least because we assume that the features have some form of correlation. For instance, a negative copula cannot exist in a line where no negation is observed. Statistical models usually operate on the full space of grammatical features, especially if one wishes to model interactions between the features. Thus, fitting a model to this sparse data set without any modifications leads to overfitting and potentially will result in the wrong conclusions being drawn from the models.

One way to accommodate this is to marginalise the states, i.e., group states of a feature into a smaller number of groups. Since we want to identify features that discriminate by community, it seemed sensible to marginalise by whether a realisation is of creole or English style or is ambiguous between the two (i.e., occurs in both creoles and Standard English). Table 3.2 shows the assignments we made within the data. We see that subject type is present in every line (no 'not applicable' state), while the auxiliary modal has no pure creole form and that negative copula is a pure creole form, although it can also be used with other forms of negation.

With this marginalisation, the number of potential groupings drops to $3 \times 4 \times 4 \times 3 \times 4 \times 2 = 1,152$, of which we observe 213. This is still quite a discrepancy, but with 10,621 lines of primary data, we have a much better coverage of the observed marginalised states.

Some questions are better asked with the original feature set rather than the marginalised feature set. For instance, when exploring the interrelationship of feature states, we would want to use the detailed basic coding, while investigating the use of Creole by any speaker is more sensibly explored using the marginalised feature set.

3.7   Feature Interrelationship

In this section, we discuss methods of visualising and quantifying feature interrelations. Feature interrelations explore the way in which features co-occur, e.g., if a speaker uses subject type 'i' (pronounced *it*) will we observe primarily the copula form 'H' (pronounced *ah*)?

We first investigate the utility of co-occurrence networks. A co-occurrence network visualises common patterns within a population or data set. For instance, if STY 'i' and CFO 'H' co-occurred 25 out of 10,621 times we would expect to see a hairline connecting the two variables. Such a network would explore the strength of connections between different features. It therefore would give us an indication of important features in the spoken language of Bequia.

Using the package `igraph` (Csardi and Nepusz, 2006), we created a circular network to visualise co-occurrences of pairs of feature realisations. Since for six features there are $\binom{6}{2} = 15$ pairings, we will have up to fifteen edges per line added to the network. Note that from now on, *line* will refer to a transcribed line from the interviews, while *edge* will refer to the co-occurrence of a pair of feature states within the interviews.

Pairs in which at least one feature had state 'not applicable' were not included. Since there are 2,820 lines in which only STY has an applicable state, the overall number of edges is reduced. After the edges have been extracted and thinned out, the count for each edge is extracted. This process leads to a network that contains 55 vertices and 635 edges. The combination of STY 's' (subject forms of a pronoun, e.g., *she, I*) and FNE 'n' (suffix - *n't*) occurred 1,226 times and is the thickest edge in the network. The state TAM 'i' (*iz* with a following bare verb) occurred exactly once in the data and is connected by only a single edge. Other, low-occurrence states affect repulsion algorithms (e.g., Fruchterman and Reingold, 1991) such that all other vertices are clumped together, and their connections are hardly visible. Due to this, we decided to rely on circular graphs for graph visualisation. To highlight abundance within the graph, edge width corresponds to the abundance of each edge.

Figure 3.1a shows the described visualisation for the full data set, while panels b through d show the breakdown by community. We can see that there are a few features which seem to dominate the Bequia corpus, such as the aforementioned STY 's' and FNE 'n' connection. The strong combinations are identified by the thick lines showing a few dominant patterns.

The main task throughout this work is to harness the discriminative power of the grammatical features. We will use this approach to look at the differences between the communities. Figures 3.1b–3.1d show the community-specific graphs. We see Mt Pleasant (panel c) and Paget Farm (panel d) appear

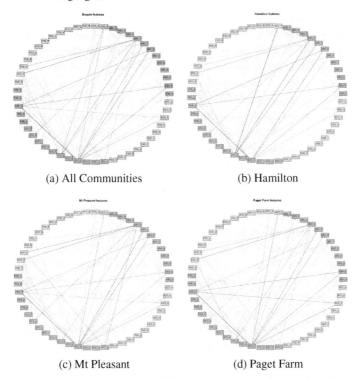

(a) All Communities   (b) Hamilton

(c) Mt Pleasant   (d) Paget Farm

Figure 3.1 Circle graphs visualising the pairwise relationships of feature states. Shades indicate feature group.

reasonably similar while Hamilton (panel b) shows a different pattern. This form of discrimination has before been discussed using multidimensional scaling (Meyerhoff and Klaere, 2017). Of the 635 edges in the full data set, Hamilton shows 515, Mt Pleasant shows 412, and Paget Farm shows 434, suggesting more evidence for a difference between the communities. To further investigate this difference, we created a Venn diagram showing the number of unique and shared edges within the data. Figure 3.2 indicates that Hamilton has about twice as many unique edges compared to the other two communities. This further indicates a difference in Hamilton. Note that there were 870 potential edges that have not been observed in the data set.

Comparing the abundance vectors we find that the abundances between Mt Pleasant and Paget Farm are highly correlated ($\varrho = 0.88$), while Hamilton's correlation coefficients with Mt Pleasant and Paget Farm are 0.73 and 0.74, respectively.

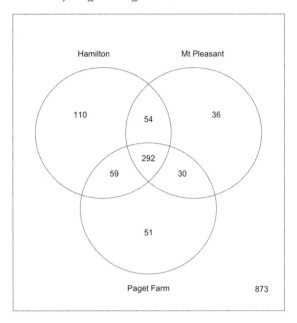

Figure 3.2 Venn diagram of edge distribution across communities. Numbers refer to number of edges present in the combination of communities. For example, 291 edges were present in all three communities, while 30 edges were present in Mt Pleasant and Paget Farm but not in Hamilton.

3.8   Graphical Models to Visualise Interactions

A widely used modern tool in data analysis is the Bayesian network; these graphs are linked to a stochastic process operating on the network and quantifying the links between variables. The states are now realisations at the nodes of the network rather than the nodes themselves. Two features are connected in the network if the co-occurrences in the data suggest an actual dependency between the features.

Using the R-package `bnlearn` (Scutari, 2010), we generated a graph connecting the six grammatical features accordingly. The bnlearn package provides a large number of training algorithms to infer a Bayesian network. These algorithms are classified as *score-based, constraint-based structure learning, local discovery*, or *hybrid* algorithms. Score-based algorithms use simple heuristics to infer networks from data. They are fast but cannot guarantee optimality. Local discovery algorithms restrict themselves to pairwise mutual information to infer a graphical structure. They are also quite fast but rely on very reduced data. Constraint-based learning attempts to include as much information as possible to infer an as accurate as possible structure. It is the slowest family but is also the most conservative, awarding relationships only under quite strong restrictions. Finally, hybrid algorithms combine features of the other classes. Such hybrids utilise certain structures in the data to speed up the inference without losing too much information. The bnlearn package provides multiple instances for each family. Throughout our inference we are using the pairwise method ARACNE (algorithm for the reconstruction of accurate cellular networks; Margolin et al., 2006), the heuristic method tabu (Tabu greedy search; Daly and Shen, 2007), the learning method pc (practically constraint; Colombo and Maathuis, 2014) and the hybrid method mmhc (max–min parents and children; Tsamardinos et al., 2006). Note that undirected edges in a Bayesian network indicate that the algorithm was unable to identify a causal direction of the relationship of the connected nodes.

To test model adequacy of our inferred networks, we created 500 boot-strapped samples of 10,621 joint feature states each and recorded the frequency with which each edge occurred in the sample. Edge width in the graphs corresponds to bootstrap support of the edge.

The two simplest methods, pairwise and score-based, provide quite intricate networks where everyone is connected (Figure 3.3a). However, when using hybrid and learning methods, this observation collapses to a single edge connecting AMO with FCO, whereas all other variables appear independent, (Figure 3.3b). Note, that about 4 per cent of the bootstrap samples for the hybrid learning algorithm included an edge between FNE and NCO. The score-based approaches are quite liberal in their acceptance of relationships leading to an overestimate of relationships. Hybrid and learning methods are more reliant on the general information coming from the data and are thus more trustworthy. From this we would conclude that the states are not particularly strongly related.

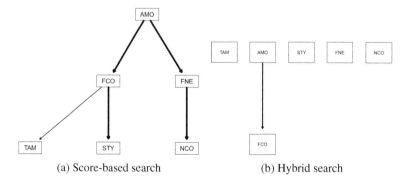

(a) Score-based search   (b) Hybrid search

Figure 3.3 Networks for the interaction of features obtained from the score-based and the hybrid methods. Edges indicate connections between features. Edge width corresponds to bootstrap support.

From here, we can drive the analysis in two additional directions: (1) Will the features relate on a marginalised level? and (2) Is the lack of relationship between features due to an underlying confounder?

3.9   Feature Relations at a Marginalised Level

Recall that we have combined realisations to four consistent groups within each feature: ambiguous, creole, English, not applicable. Investigating the interrelationship of these marginalised groups may reveal consistency in usage. Figure 3.4 shows the results using a learning algorithm and a score-based algorithm. Both networks show the same connectivity, although the learning network shows some undirected edges connecting AMO and FNE, AMO and TAM, and FNE and NCO. We had expected the connection between FNE and NCO before since one cannot show a negative concord without negating. For both networks in Figure 3.4 the edge connecting TAM and FNE is thin, indicating weak evidence for this relationship. Overall, this indicates that at a marginalised level there is a stronger connection between these variables. While a connection between the auxiliary/modal (AMO) and tense and aspect marking (TAM) is hardly surprising (a great deal of tense and aspect information is carried in English by modals), a connection between auxiliary/modal and form of negation (FNE) is less expected. This suggests promising lines for future enquiry into the grammar of Bequia Creole, perhaps integrating negative modality with other modals.

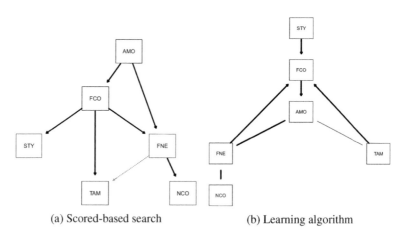

(a) Scored-based search   (b) Learning algorithm

Figure 3.4 Networks for marginalised data using score-based (a) and learning algorithm (b) approaches.

3.10   Feature Interrelationship within Communities

To paraphrase question (2) from the previous section: What if some features strongly interact within each community but are different enough that they appear unrelated within the generalised framework? To answer this question, we re-create the networks from the detailed coding just within each community and assess whether there are differences between the networks. For each subset we will generate the network using the learning approach. The graphical structure recovered is the same for all three communities (see Figure 3.5 for the graph).

Considering the obvious difference to the graph we initially obtained from the full data, we have to assume that there are notable differences in the underlying graphical models. We can do this by looking at the transition kernels available. The model depicted earlier has only two transition kernels: The transition from AMO to FCO and the conditional array of AMO and NCO to FNE. For the purpose of visualisation, we will visualise and discuss only the two-dimensional matrix of AMO to FCO. Figure 3.6 shows a heat map of the three kernels. There are some differences visible, especially due to the fact that Hamilton has no instance of the use of the AMO state 'h'. But we can see more obvious differences in the use of some combinations. Using the Manhattan distance, we see that the kernels for Mt Pleasant and Paget Farm are 2.8 units apart, while the kernels for Hamilton to Mt Pleasant and Paget Farm are 4.9 and 4.5 units apart, respectively.

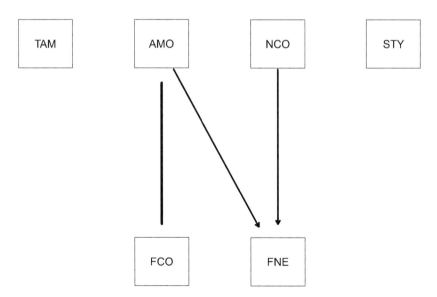

Figure 3.5 Graph depicting feature relations as obtained for each community. Note that the structure was the same for all communities.

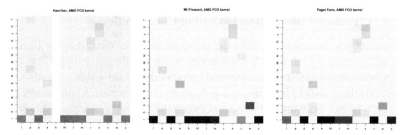

Figure 3.6 Visualisation of transition kernels. Light grey cells indicate entries close to zero; dark grey cells indicate entries closer to one. The white column in the Hamilton matrix indicates no entries in the column since AMO 'h' has not been observed.

To add some form of statistical significance one could invoke Fisher's exact test to compare the columns of the transition matrices. Essentially, this tests the hypothesis that the transitions in all three models are identical and any differences observed are due to random variation. We multiplied the transition vectors for each model with the frequency of observations for the respective column label, i.e., how often each state of AMO was observed in each data set. The p-values of the thirteen resulting tests were corrected using false discovery rate. We found that six columns showed p-values below 0.005 while the remaining seven showed p-values above 0.05. Thus, we can conclude that the transition kernels were significantly different, suggesting that there is indeed a difference in the way AMO and FCO are employed within the communities, pointing to a linguistic difference in the dialect grammars.

The application of Fisher's exact test might be sensible but should be invoked only if an omnibus assessment of the employed models has shown evidence of difference. Unfortunately, such an omnibus test has not been implemented for Bayesian network models as of yet.

3.11   Community Distinction

So far, the influence of community on language was explored by conditioning the whole of the graph on features from the community. A different approach that explores the dependency more directly includes community as an extra node in the networks. Edges connecting community with a grammatical feature would then indicate (significant) differences in use of a feature. Figure 3.7 shows the network obtained by learning methods using (1) the original states and (2) the marginalised realisations. We see that for the full set of states no real significant relationship was found, while the marginalised states show some relationships and community is seen to interact with NCO and STY.

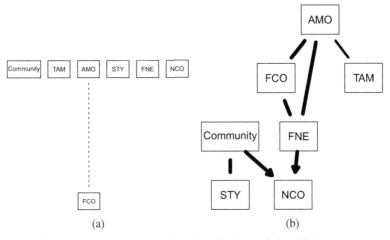

Figure 3.7 Bayesian networks depicting interrelationship between community and grammatical features, using detailed states (a) and marginal states (b).

The relationship of community to STY and NCO has been posited before (Walker and Sidnell, 2011) with the network providing further evidence for the validity of this approach. Figure 3.7a on the other hand appears to not provide evidence in support of the observed differences in Figures 3.1b–3.1d, which seemed to suggest that there are differences between the communities. Conversely, the noise visible in Figures 3.1b–3.1d could also suggest that the lack of structure in Figure 3.7a is due to noise washing out the signal instrumental for a visualisation. Appropriately identifying the features that provide signal within a large amount of noise is a standard challenge in data science.

Another approach to assessing the dependencies between vertices is the underlying stochastic process, which could provide us with insights how the community affects STY or NCO. However, the structure of Figure 3.7b contains an undirected edge between community and STY, which means the algorithm was unable to predict the causal link between those vertices from the data. In such cases, the algorithm will also not provide a prediction of the outcome (Scutari, 2010), and we cannot comfortably conclude more than the existence of a relationship.

3.12   Speaker-Specific Creole Frequency

Another interesting question raised was visualising language usage throughout the interview, i.e., utilising the line order (as a measure of temporal progression through the conversation) for another look at the interview. For each line, the frequency of the four marginalised states across the six features is taken into

Speaker 1 , Community: H , Window size: 1

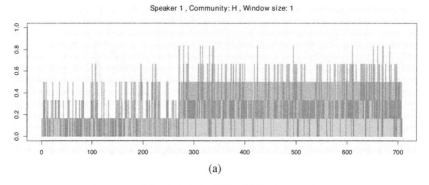

(a)

Speaker 1 , Community: H , Window size: 10

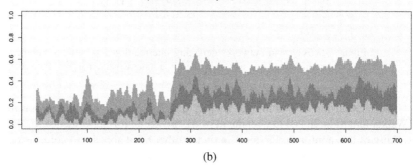

(b)

Speaker 1 , Community: H , Window size: 25

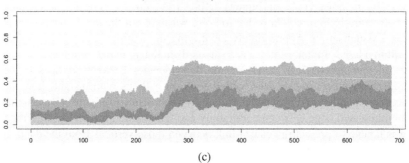

(c)

Figure 3.8 Stacked bar charts to visualise temporal changes in feature usage at different levels of smoothing.

account. The four states are differentiated in grey scale. Using a stacked bar chart, the height of dark grey at each line indicates the proportion of the six features that are of creole-type. Figure 3.8a shows the chart for a speaker from Hamilton. We see that the plot is quite choppy, and not much can be said about it. To reduce this type of variability, we use a moving window approach where the lines following the indexed line are included in the frequency calculations. The effect of the moving window is seen in Figures 3.8b and 3.8c, where the following 9 and 24 lines are included in the calculation, respectively.

Interestingly, the frequency of not applicable states seems to drop drastically after the first 250 lines, resulting in a perceived increase in creole-type realisations (the other two types are increasing at about the same proportion). This feature has been observed consistently among all speakers. The first interpretation could be that the speakers used longer sentences later in the interview, thus producing more of the features. Unfortunately, what it actually highlighted was a change in the mode of data extraction and coding. For the first 250 lines every sentence had been transcribed, and afterward only those sentences incorporating a copula were recorded.

While the ultimate reason for this apparent change in the quality of co-occurring features over time is somewhat disheartening, one has to also see the positive feature of discovering this in the first place. Knowing this, means we can adapt the questions we ask. Instead of taking all of the data into account, we can split the data into one set of the first 250 lines and look at these data, while the second attempt involves looking only at copula across the lines.

Figure 3.9 shows the distribution of copula forms across the speakers. There do not seem to be noticeable differences here. A quasi-Poisson model fitted with the counts as response and copula level and community as

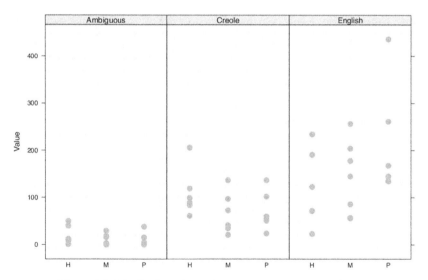

Figure 3.9 Distribution of copula counts per community by copula state. English is the most used in all three communities, with ambiguous states the lowest counts.

independent variables found community was not significantly affecting the counts ($p > 0.15$). Significance was assessed using analysis of variance with a χ^2 test for signficance.

3.13   Conclusions: Principled Methods for Exploring Systematic Dialects within Languages

The purpose of this chapter was twofold: in the first part of the chapter, we introduced epistemological problems surrounding common terms used by linguists and laypeople alike – *language, dialect, variety, creole*. In drawing attention to these problems, we hoped not to suggest that distinguishing between languages, dialects, and creoles is impossible but rather to highlight the structural and social dimensions of the terms. Quantitative measures have always played a role in how confident linguists are in applying these terms and have been used to bolster, refute, or complement qualitative means for using them as denotational measures.

In the second part of the chapter, we demonstrated a number of quantitative methods that can be profitably used to help find the coherence of subgroups within a population of speakers. As far as we know, none of these has been widely deployed in tackling fundamental problems, such as the distinction between language and dialect or the debate over creole exceptionalism. Yet we would suggest that they all have potential as statistically informed visualisation techniques for not only grouping speakers but also for exploring how different linguistic features cluster (a matter of interest to historical linguists and typologists as well as sociolinguists) and how much of the differentiation between groups can be accounted for by different specific states of, e.g., the copula.

Using a wide array of approaches (as in this chapter) provides us with new ways of conceptualising dialect subgroups. In principle, the methods lend themselves well to questions about the similarities and differences of different languages in different geographic locations and might provide additional tools for addressing phylogenetic questions about language subgroupings and the validity of creoles as a natural class of human languages. But most importantly and most concretely, by highlighting facts such as the connection between community type and negative concord and subject type in Bequia Creole or the affinity between negation and auxiliaries, these approaches generate new questions and hypotheses specific to this speech community.

References

Bakker, Peter, Daval-Markussen, Aymeric, Parkvall, Mikael, and Plag, Ingo. 2011. Creoles are typologically distinct from non-creoles. *Journal of Pidgin and Creole Languages*, **26**, 5–42.
Bickerton, Derek. 1980. *The Roots of Language*. Ann Arbor, MI: Karoma.

Colombo, Diego, and Maathuis, Marloes H. 2014. Order-independent constraint-based causal structure learning. *Journal of Machine Learning Research*, **15**, 3921–3962.

Corballis, Michael C. 2017. *The Truth about Language*. Chicago and Auckland: University of Chicago Press and Auckland University Press.

Crowley, Terry. 1992. *An Introduction to Historical Language*. Oxford: Oxford University Press.

Csardi, Gabor, and Nepusz, Tamas. 2006. The igraph software package for complex network research. *InterJournal, Complex Systems*, 1695.

Daleszynska, Agata. 2013. The local, the global, and the authentic: Language change and authenticity in Bequia. *Zeitschrift für Anglistik und Amerikanistik: A quarterly of Language, Literature and Culture*, **60**, 275–294.

Daly, Rónán, and Shen, Qiang. 2007. Methods to accelerate the learning of Bayesian network structures. In: *Proceedings of the 2007 UK Workshop on Computational Intelligence*. London: Imperial College.

Fon Sing, Guillaume. 2017. Creoles are not typologically distinct from non-Creoles. *Language Ecology*, **1**, 44–74.

Fruchterman, Thomas M. J., and Reingold, Edward M. 1991. Graph drawing by force-directed placement. *Software – Practice & Experience*, **21**(11), 1129–1164.

Greenhill, Simon, Wu, Chieh-Hsi, Dunn, Michael, Levinson, Stephen C., and Gray, Russell D. 2017. Evolutionary dynamics of language systems. *Proceedings of the National Academy of Sciences USA*, **114**(42), E8822–E8829.

Hazen, Kirk. 2018. *West Virginia Dialect Project*. West Virginia University.

Hockett, Charles F. 1960. The origin of speech. *Scientific American*, **203**, 88–111.

Holm, John, and Patrick, Peter L. (eds.). 2007. *Comparative Creole Syntax: Parallel Outlines of 18 Creole Grammars*. Westminster, UK: Battlebridge Publications.

Jourdan, Christine. 1985. *Sapos Iumi Mitim Iumi: The Social Context of Creolization in the Solomon Islands*. Ph.D. thesis, The Australian National University, Canberra.

Kortmann, Bernd, and Luckenheimer, Kerstin. 2013. *The Electronic World Atlas of Varieties of English*. Leipzig, Germany: Max Planck Institute for Evolutionary Anthropology.

Labov, William. 1969. The logic of non-standard English. In: Alatis, James E. (ed.), *Report of the Twentieth Annual Round Table Meeting on Linguistics and Language Studies*. Washington, DC: Georgetown University Press.

Labov, William. 1972. *Sociolinguistic Patterns*. Philadelphia, PA: University of Pennsylvania Press.

Lo Bianco, Joseph. 2008. Tense times and language planning. *Current Issues in Language Planning*, **9**(2), 155–178.

Margolin, Adam A., Nemenmann, Ilya, Basso, Katja, Wiggins, Chris, Stolovitzky, Gustavo, Dalla Favera, Riccardo, and Califano, Andrea. 2006. ARACNE: An algorithm for the reconstruction of gene regulatory networks in a mammalian cellular context. *BMC Bioinformatics*, **7**(Supplement 1), S7.

Maxwell, Alexander. 2018. When theory is a joke: The Weinreich witticism in linguistics. *Beiträge zur Geschichte der Sprachwissenschaft*, **28**, 263–292.

Meyerhoff, Miriam. 2019. *Introducing Sociolinguistics*. 3rd ed. London: Taylor & Francis.

Meyerhoff, Miriam, and Klaere, Steffen. 2017. A case for clustering speakers and linguistic variables: Big issues with smaller samples in language variation. Pages

23–46 of: Buchstaller, Isabelle, and Siebenhaar, Beat (eds.), *Language Variation – European Perspectives IV: Selected Papers for the Eighth International Conference on Language Variation in Europe (ICLaVE 8)*, Leipzig, May 2015, vol. 19. Leipzig, Germany: John Benjamins.

Meyerhoff, Miriam, and Walker, James A. 2013a. *Bequia Talk: St Vincent and the Grenadines*. Westminster, UK: Battlebridge Publications.

Meyerhoff, Miriam, and Walker, James A. 2013b. An existential problem: The sociolinguistic monitor and variation in existential constructions on Bequia (St Vincent and the Grenadines). *Language and Society*, **42**(4), 407–428.

Niedzielski, Nancy A., and Preston, Dennis R. 2000. *Folk Linguistics*. Berlin/New York: Mouton de Gruyter.

Pinker, Steven, and Bloom, Paul. 1990. Natural language and natural selection. *Behavioral and Brain Sciences*, **13**, 707–726.

Scutari, Marco. 2010. Learning Bayesian Networks with the bnlearn R package. *Journal of Statistical Software*, **35**(3), 1–22.

Swadesh, Morris. 1971. *The Origin and Diversification of Language*. Chicago: Aldine Transaction.

Tsamardinos, Ioannis, Brown, Laura E., and Aliferis, Constantin F. 2006. The max-min hill-climbing Bayesian network structure learning algorithm. *Machine Learning*, **65**(1), 31–78.

Velupillai, Viveka. 2015. *Pidgin and Creole Languages: An Introduction*. Amsterdam: John Benjamins.

Walker, James A., and Meyerhoff, Miriam. 2006. Zero copula in the Caribbean: Evidence from Bequia. *American Speech*, **81**(2), 146–163.

Walker, James A., and Sidnell, Jack. 2011. Negation in Bequia. Pages 39–56 of: Hinrichs, Lars, and Farquharson, Joseph (eds.), *Variation in the Caribbean*. Amsterdam: John Benjamins.

Zampieri, Marcos, Malmasi, Shervin, Ljubesic, Nikola, Nakov, Preslav, Ali, Ahmed, Tiedemann, Jörg, Scherrer, Yves, and Aepli, Noëmi. 2017. Finding of the VarDial evaluation campaign. Pages 1–15 of: *Proceedings of the Fourth Workshop on NLP for Similar Languages, Varieties and Dialects*.

4   Mutual Intelligibility

Charlotte Gooskens and Vincent J. van Heuven

4.1   Introduction

4.1.1   Intelligibility in Speech Communication

When two persons communicate through spoken language, thoughts that enter into the mind of the speaker first have to be expressed in terms of the vocabulary and grammatical structures of the speaker's language. The mental linguistic structures are then used to make the speaker's vocal organs move so that they produce audible sound. The sounds travel through the air (or some other medium – e.g., a telecommunication channel) and then impinge on the ear of the listener. The result is that the listener hears a stream of sounds. If the listener is familiar with the language, he or she will recognize (the same) linguistic units (e.g., words) in the same order in which they left the speaker's mouth. This part of the communication process is what we call *speech recognition*. If a sufficient number of units have been correctly recognized in the correct sequential order, the listener will be able to reconstruct the original thoughts and intentions of the speaker. This last part of the process is what we call *speech understanding* or *comprehension*. The sequence of events sketched here is known as the *speech chain* (Denes and Pinson 1963), and it has been the blueprint of Levelt's (1989) model of speech production and Cutler's (2012) model of native listening.

The intelligibility of a speaker, or of a speech utterance, is the degree to which a listener is able to recognize the linguistic units in the stream of sounds and to establish the order in which they were spoken. If the listener does not know the language the speaker uses, the speaker's intelligibility is (close to) zero – even if the utterance(s) would be perfectly intelligible to native listeners of the language. The comprehensibility of a speaker (or a spoken text) is the degree to which a listener is able to understand the speaker's meaning and intentions. Intelligibility, then, is the correlate of speech recognition and the comprehensibility of speech understanding. In this view speech understanding is a higher-order process than speech recognition. Different methods are required to assess a speaker's intelligibility than to assess that individual's comprehensibility. For instance, a strict intelligibility test would be ask a listener to take down by way of dictation, a series of nonsense utterances produced by the speaker. This is what the semantically unpredictable sentences (SUS) test (Benoît et al. 1996) does with utterances like *The state sang through the whole week*. A speech comprehension test would, for example, ask a listener to determine whether a spoken sentence embodies a truth or a falsehood. If a listener would think that *Most human babies are heavier than a full-grown elephant* is true, he or she obviously has not understood the sentence. Section 4.2 reviews a range of experimental methods that have been used to establish the intelligibility of speakers and spoken utterances. It is important here to point out that intelligibility, in our view, is the joint product of the combination of a particular speaker and a particular listener. Speakers may differ from one another not only in their command of the language but they may also differ in the quality of their speech production due to personal habits, such as weak versus loud voice, fast versus slow tempo, and sloppy versus clear articulation. By the same token, listeners may differ in their familiarity with the language being spoken, hearing acuity or even motivation to understand what the speaker is trying to convey.

We spell this out in some detail because other disciplines and other researchers have used the terms differently from the way we do. For instance, applied linguists (Munro and Derwing 1995; Munro et al. 2006) use the term *intelligibility* as the degree to which a speaker can be understood using functional tests and the term *comprehensibility* for the listener's opinion as to how well a speaker (or utterance) can be understood. Our position is that intelligibility and comprehensibility address two different stages in the speech chain and that each can be measured both by functional tests (see earlier) and by opinion tests.

Some researchers also make a further distinction between *comprehensibility* and *interpretability*, where the former concept refers to the ease with which the listener may extract the propositional content of the sentence(s) produced by the speaker and the latter to the ease with which the speaker's intentions can be understood by the listener even if there is a cultural gap between the two interactants (Kachru and Smith 2008, chapter 4). In our own research we tend to ignore this subdivision because the languages and cultures we study tend to be closely related and do not regularly require large cross-cultural gaps to be bridged.

4.1.2   Mutual Intelligibility

Until the 1950s it was assumed that the mutual intelligibility between two languages would be *symmetrical* (also called *reciprocal*). It was also assumed that the structural difference (or *distance*) between two languages A and B would be symmetrical. This, at first sight, is a reasonable proposition, since generally the distance between any two locations on the map is symmetrical: the distance from London to New York is the same as the distance from New York to London. In Section 4.4, however, we will see that linguistic distance is not necessarily symmetrical.

Given symmetrical differences between two related languages A and B, language A should be as intelligible to native listeners of language B as the other way around. Casad (1974: 73) points out that reciprocity was part of the definition of mutual intelligibility in the work by the American structuralists in the early 1950s. Any deviation from perfect reciprocity would then be the result of either measurement error or of differences in extra-linguistic factors such as previous exposure to the other language. Pierce (1952), in fact, used *mutual intelligibility* for linguistically determined (and necessarily reciprocal) intelligibility versus *neighbor intelligibility* for nonreciprocal intelligibility, where the asymmetry could be due only to extra-linguistic differences (mainly contact). Small deviations from perfect symmetry in intelligibility were averaged out by computing the mean of the intelligibility scores for the two directions, AB and BA, as an index of mutual intelligibility. Such an index, however, will fail to predict the success of communicating if there is a large discrepancy between the AB and BA scores. An intelligibility index of 70 percent, for instance, would suggest reasonably successful communication between speakers A and B. However, if listener A understands speaker B at 90 percent, but listener B gets only 50 percent of speaker A's utterances (yielding an average of 70 percent), communication may well break down, and one-way communication would be the best possible result. Adopting Weinreich's (1957) term *cross-language communication* we prefer to use the term *cross-language intelligibility* when talking about the separate directions AB and BA (see also Ladefoged 1968). We will use *mutual intelligibility* as the mean of the two directions, with the caveat that the measure will fail when the cross-language intelligibility strongly deviates from reciprocity.

4.1.3   *Inherent versus Acquired Intelligibility*

Listener A may be able to understand a speaker of a related language B for two (sets of) reasons, which are unrelated in principle. When the related languages (or language varieties) A and B are spoken in neighboring countries, or more generally on opposite sides of a shared geographic boundary, there will usually be contact between the speakers of the two languages, caused by, e.g., trade, tourism, personal relationships, and mass media. The speakers may also have become familiar with the other language as the result of formal teaching in a school setting. These reasons can be subsumed under the heading of extralinguistic or social factors. These will be discussed in detail in Section 4.3. Several terms have been proposed to capture the notion of intelligibility as determined by extralinguistic factors, such as *acquired intelligibility*, *social intelligibility*, and *contact-based intelligibility* (Simons 1979). These terms can be used interchangeably.

When we are dealing with written language (rather than spoken language) a special extralinguistic factor influencing cross-language intelligibility may be the use of a shared ideographic writing system, as in China. Intelligibility between Sinitic languages across the Mandarin–Southern divide may be close to zero (Tang and Van Heuven 2007, 2009, 2015) for the spoken modality. However, since the same characters tend to be used to represent the same concepts across all Sinitic languages, no matter how the words are pronounced, printed text will still be understood. The opposite has also been found. Some closely related languages are spelled with such divergent orthographic conventions (but still using the Roman alphabet) that printed texts cannot be understood even though the spoken forms are mutually intelligible. For instance, Dutch readers generally fail to understand written Frisian (with spelling conventions that depart grossly from those of Dutch – and from any other language), but they will understand spoken Frisian rather well (Van Bezooijen and Gooskens 2005, 2006; Van Bezooijen and Van den Berg 2000).

Even if the interactants have never been exposed to the other language, we may still find considerable cross-language intelligibility, depending on how much the two languages are alike. This part of the cross-language intelligibility would then be based entirely on the degree of linguistic similarity between the two languages. Linguistic similarity is multidimensional and subsumes differences in any of the linguistic subdomains, such as lexicon (shared cognates with shared meanings), phonology (same or similar sound systems, transparent correspondences between the sound systems), morphology (same or similar word structure), and syntax (same or similar word order). The dimensions of linguistic similarity will be dealt with in Section 4.4. The terms *inherent intelligibility* and *similarity-based intelligibility* (Simons 1979) were introduced to represent the theoretical degree of understanding between two language varieties whose speakers have never had any contact.

It has been suggested that communication might be possible between two languages A and B that are not mutually intelligible if the interactants A and B both know a non-native language (variety) C that may bridge the gap between A and B. Language C should then be genealogically "in between" language A and B in terms of shared vocabulary and phonological distance. Shared familiarity with an in-between language helps extend the range of language varieties within a language family (or dialect group) within which speakers may use receptive multilingualism as a means of communication. This is a form of communication in which each interactant speaks his or her own language but is able to understand the language of the other enough to sustain a meaningful exchange of information. The mediating language C (also referred to as a *bridge language*) is not necessarily genealogically in between the related languages A and B. It may also be the case that interactants are familiar with the mediating language C because it was taught in school. For instance, in eastern Europe Russian used to be a compulsory subject taught at secondary schools. Although Russian is not structurally and lexically halfway between Estonian (a Finno-Ugric language) and Ukrainian (Slavic), Estonian listeners will understand a Ukrainian speaker, simply because Ukrainian and Russian are mutually intelligible, and Estonians have learned Russian at school (Branets et al. 2020). In this example, of course, the Ukrainian listener will not understand the Estonian speaker, so this would end as a case of one-way intelligibility.

4.1.4   Symmetry versus Asymmetry in Intelligibility

As explained in the foregoing, it was assumed in the 1950s that cross-language intelligibility should be reciprocal and that any deviations from perfect reciprocity (or symmetry) would be due to nonlinguistic factors such as exposure. Since then, however, many pairs of languages have been identified in which the cross-language intelligibility was far from symmetrical, and could not be attributed to differences in exposure or some other social variable. For instance, Jensen (1989) showed that Latin American Spanish speakers were better understood by Brazilian-Portuguese listeners (58 percent correct), than Brazilians were understood by the Spanish listeners (50 percent). The discrepancy was even stronger in recent experiments done with European Spanish and Portuguese speakers and materials (Gooskens and Van Heuven 2017). Similarly, Danish speakers are rather poorly understood by other Scandinavian listeners (Norwegians, Swedes), whereas Danes have less difficulty understanding spoken Norwegian or Swedish (see Gooskens et al. 2010; Schüppert 2011, and references therein).[1] Although partial explanations of these asymmetries based on sociological factors (differences in attitude, contact) cannot be ruled out entirely, it is generally agreed that another cause of the asymmetries is in the different linguistic structures of the languages involved. Typically, phonological lenition processes (such as consonant deletion and vowel apocope) have corrupted Danish and Portuguese words beyond recognition by listeners of the neighboring Scandinavian and Romance languages. Danish and Portuguese listeners, however, easily recognize the non-lenited forms in

---

[1] Kluge (2007: 11) lists the following examples of asymmetrical intelligibility: Gurage speech varieties of central Ethiopia (Gutt 1980; Ahland 2003); the Kaansé, Kpatogoso, Dogosé, and Khisa varieties of southwestern Burkina Faso (Showalter 1994); the Mazatec and Trique speech varieties of southwestern Mexico (Casad 1974: 76 ff.), as well as a number of speech varieties of southern Nigeria (Wolff 1959). The original publications should be consulted to determine the direction of the asymmetries for each language group.

the neighbor languages, especially if the orthography abstracts away from the lenition processes (Schüppert 2011; Schüppert et al. 2016, for the Scandinavian languages; Voigt and Schüppert 2013, for the Iberian languages).[2] If this is indeed the case, then symmetric distance measures quantifying the difference in linguistic structure between Spanish and Portuguese or between Danish and Swedish will be inadequate as explanations of the asymmetries found. In Section 4.4 we discuss a number of attempts to establish structural asymmetries between related languages, which may account for nonreciprocal intelligibility.

4.1.5   Why Study Mutual Intelligibility?

Languages change over time. Changes are driven by internal linguistic forces as well as by social pressures. Sounds that are difficult to articulate or are difficult to hear as different from some other sound may be replaced by, or merged with, easier sounds. The way we speak and pronounce sounds may also be used as an identity marker by which we show that we belong to one particular group of speakers, and not to any other. Every time a group of speakers adopt a new way of speaking (called an *innovation*) and become different from some other group in what up to that moment was one homogenous linguistic community, a new language variety has come about. Over the centuries the language of a single linguistic community may have diversified into a great many varieties, differing from one another in the type and number of innovations that were implemented over the years. It is customary in (historical) linguistics to represent this process of diversification by means of family trees (or cladistic trees). A parent language (or ancestor language) splits up into younger varieties every time an innovation takes place. It is generally held that two languages are related to one another if they can be shown to have descended from the same parent language. Language varieties that differ from one another in only a few (recent) innovations are referred to as dialects of a language (see, e.g., Chapter 5 in this volume). If the number of innovations is large and such innovations were introduced many generations ago, we usually consider the varieties different languages.

---

[2] These explanation of the asymmetries were proposed in the literature several decades earlier. For instance, Chambers and Trudgill (1980: 4) write:

> Mutual intelligibility may also not be equal in both directions. It is often said, for instance, that Danes understand Norwegians better than Norwegians understand Danes. (If this is true it may be because, as Scandinavians sometimes say, 'Norwegian is pronounced like Danish is spelt', while Danish pronunciation bears a rather more complex relationship to its own orthography. It may be due, alternatively or additionally, to more specifically linguistic factors).

Casad (1974: 73) writes "since Portuguese has undergone a consonant deletion rule that Spanish has not, the surface phonological forms of Spanish correspond more closely to underlying proto-forms than the surface forms of Portuguese do. One might therefore predict that Portuguese speakers can understand Spanish better than Spanish speakers can understand Portuguese."

There is, however, no consistent way to quantify the number, type, and recency of innovations that differentiate two language varieties such that a clear-cut boundary can be drawn between what are different dialects of one language and what are different languages. Inherent mutual intelligibility was introduced by the American structuralists as a practical solution to this problem. If there is mutual intelligibility between the members of two different language varieties, these are considered dialects of one language; if there is no mutual intelligibility, the varieties belong to different languages. Mutual intelligibility as a criterion to distinguish dialects from languages generally works well, but it is known to fail when varieties are arranged along a dialect continuum. In a dialect continuum the geographically adjacent varieties differ only in a few innovations and are mutually intelligible. However, varieties at one extreme of the continuum will not be mutually intelligible with varieties at the other end, possibly hundreds of kilometers away. In the case of a dialect continuum the criterion of mutual intelligibility should then be applied as if it were a transitive relationship: if A understands B, and B understands C, then A also understands C.

It should be noted that neither the innovation-based nor the intelligibility-based language versus dialect dichotomy necessarily corresponds with the status currently attributed to many language varieties. Danish, Norwegian, and Swedish are mutually intelligible (e.g., in general Danes, Norwegians, and Swedes communicate with their own L1s rather than using a lingua franca such as English) and yet are considered different languages. Conversely, there are many pairs of geographically adjacent Chinese varieties that are not mutually intelligible (e.g., Tang and Van Heuven 2009) and yet are called dialects of Chinese. This means that the choice of whether two language varieties are dialects of the same language is basically a practical, political matter and not a question with any scientific import or theoretical status.

Mostly, the study of cross-language intelligibility has no theoretical import but is exclusively motivated by practical questions. It has been suggested, for instance, that spoken language varieties that are mutually intelligible – i.e., are dialects of one language – may well be served by a single orthography, which should then abstract away from superficial differences in pronunciation and realization of lexical tones. A single orthography, of course, would save time, effort, and development of teaching resources.

Testing of cross-language intelligibility is a prerequisite to building a theory that predicts how well speakers of two different but related languages will be able to communicate with each other through receptive multilingualism. Generally, establishing the degree of cross-language intelligibility is a time-consuming process involving large numbers of experimental participants. One of the goals of our work is to build a model that predicts the degree of cross-language intelligibility between two languages from a detailed comparison of the lexicon, phonology, morphology, and syntax of the languages concerned and, if the written modality is included, also the orthographies. Once such a predictive model is available, it may help policy makers decide whether, for instance, television programs in a neighboring language should be dubbed or subtitled, whether receptive multilingualism would be a viable option for cross-linguistic communication or whether the use of (English as) a lingua franca should be promoted. If cross-language intelligibility is predicted to be insufficient, the model should be able to pinpoint the source of the difficulties that block intelligibility. Dedicated teaching programs can then be devised to help overcome the difficulties and permit receptive multilingualism (e.g., Golubovic 2016, chapter 5). In various parts of Europe, educational programs have been developed to teach receptive multilingualism, mostly in the written modality (e.g., the GalaNet and GalaPro,[3] EuroCom,[4] Linee,[5] and Dylan[6] projects). However, only little research has been conducted to investigate the effects of these programs.

4.2   How to Measure Intelligibility

A large number of methods have been devised to determine the degree of intelligibility of a speaker or of a speech utterance. Speech intelligibility testing has seen a wide range of applications, such as quality assessment of talking computers, determining the severity of a patient's speech or hearing defects, foreign language proficiency testing, and mutual intelligibility testing. A typology of test techniques can be given, using a limited number of parameters. Here we will concentrate on test techniques developed for spoken language. It is not difficult to see how the techniques should be adapted for the testing of written language.

4.2.1   Typology of Intelligibility Tests

A first division of techniques is that between *opinion testing* (also called *judgment testing*) and *functional testing*. In an opinion test, listeners are asked how well they think they would understand a speaker or a spoken text. This is what the American structuralists called "ask the informant" (Voegelin and Harris 1951). Opinion testing can be done without using a physical stimulus. Assuming that the informants have had ample experience with another language, they can be asked to indicate on some scale (e.g., between 0 and 100) how well they would understand speech in the target language, where 0 would mean nothing and 100 would stand for perfect intelligibility. However, since it is

---

[3] http://e-gala.eu/.   [4] EuroComprehension, www.eurocomprehension.eu.
[5] https://cordis.europa.eu/docs/results/28/28388/124376831-6_en.pdf.
[6] Dylan, www.dylan-project.org.

unclear what conception the participants have of the typical speaker of the target language, opinion testing is usually based on a selection of speech materials produced by one or several representative speakers of the target language. Opinion tests are relatively simple to carry out and take little time. Moreover, the same materials can be presented to the listeners repeatedly, either spoken by the same talker or by different talkers, without affecting the judgments. In functional testing, listeners have to actually show they have recognized linguistic units in a particular order and/or understood the meaning of what they just heard. This is what the American structuralists called "test the informant." Obviously, functional testing cannot be done without a physical stimulus being presented. A drawback of functional tests is that listeners can be presented with the same word or sentence only once. Once a listener has recognized a word, the same word – even when spoken by a different speaker or in a degraded condition – will be recognized much faster and more effectively. The problem can be circumvented by blocking multiple versions of the same stimulus over different groups of listeners, but this is time-consuming and presupposes the availability of large numbers of listeners. We usually find strong correlations between test scores obtained from judgment tasks and functional tasks. Moreover, the opinion scores are realistic in the sense that respondents do not overestimate or underestimate how well they would do in a functional test using the same materials (Gooskens and Swarte 2017).

The second parameter concerns the *linguistic level* that is tested. A test may address low-level intelligibility, requiring the listener to judge or show how well he or she recognized the words and the order in which they occurred. Alternatively, higher-order speech understanding may be targeted by asking the listener to judge or show how much of the content of what was said he or she understood. Since there may be substantial interaction between lower-order recognition and higher-order understanding processes, it is often necessary to construct the stimulus material in such a way that higher-order processes cannot be employed. Access to the mental lexicon can be blocked by presenting non-words only, as in 'Jabberwocky' (Carroll 1871). Speech understanding based partly on contextual cues can be blocked by using semantically unpredictable sentences (Benoît et al. 1996). The relative importance of semantic context can be assessed by systematically comparing the listener's word recognition scores obtained from constraining and nonconstraining sentences (Kalikow et al. 1977; Wang 2007, chapter 9).

Addressing different linguistic levels overlaps to some extent with another parameter in the typology of intelligibility tests, viz. *black box* versus *glass box* test testing.[7] If the researcher is interested in only the overall interlingual

---

[7] Also called "white box" testing, "clear box" testing, or "open box" testing. The concept was developed in the software testing industry (see e.g., Ehmer Khan 2011).

intelligibility between interactants, the process by which the communication takes place is considered a black box, the inner workings of which need not be known. However, if the researcher wants to pinpoint the causes of imperfect interlingual intelligibility, some form of diagnostic testing is required. Diagnostic intelligibility testing presupposes a modular view of the communication process, and specific tests that address each of the modules separately. The ultimate black box test would consider only the success rate of some interactive task performed by two participants who use receptive multilingualism – i.e., the interlingual communication type in which each interactant speaks only his or her native language and tries to understand the nonnative language as much as possible, relying on the lexical and structural similarity between the languages. The successful task completion rate in a (simulated) information service game would be an example of such a black box test. One interactant would be the information giver, the other the information requester. Together they must complete a communicative task – e.g., finding out how to travel from A to B, ordering a meal from a menu of choices, booking a seat on a plane, or obtaining the telephone number of a particular person. The first step on the way to glass box testing would be to test the success of the information exchange separately for the A-to-B and B-to-A directions. On a more fine-grained level, the separate contributions of vowels, consonants, prosody, non-cognates, morphological structure, and word order can be experimentally controlled and tested.

The third parameter, which applies only to functional intelligibility tests, is whether the test is online or offline. *Online* test techniques aim to tap into the listener's mind while the recognition and comprehension processes are being carried out. The results of online tests inform the researcher about the speed, sequential ordering, and interaction of modules involved in the processing of the spoken input. Reaction time measurements are claimed to provide an indirect indication of relative difficulty experienced during the processing of the input. More immediate access to the information processing can be obtained from eye tracking techniques (matching pictures on screen with words or sentences) or from neurological techniques such as evoked response potential (ERP) and or functional magnetic resonance imaging (fMRI), which tell the researcher exactly when and where in the brain decisions are being made by the listener, although we are not familiar with such neurolinguistic approaches in the area of mutual intelligibility testing.

Most of the intelligibility tests, however, are *offline*. Here the listener is allowed time to consider a response, and only the result of the response, rather than the time course, is considered. These results are typically the percentage of correctly recognized or translated linguistic units. Offline tests are used much more often than online techniques because they require no special and/or expensive equipment. It is not unusual to run online techniques in an offline mode. For instance, lexical decision tasks (decide whether a string of sounds or letters exists as a word in the lexicon) or category monitoring tasks (decide whether a word is a member of some semantic category, e.g., denotes a concrete object) are online if the decision time can be measured (with millisecond precision). Such reaction time measurements can be done only by computers that are disconnected from a network. This precludes administering reaction time tests long distance over the internet. In such cases the correctness of the decision is the only measure of intelligibility.

4.2.2   Considerations

In our view, measuring mutual intelligibility between two languages breaks down into separately assessing the cross-language intelligibility of language A for receivers of language B (AB) and of language B for receivers of A (BA). Moreover, measuring cross-language intelligibility is not principally different from measuring the intelligibility of a sender (speaker, writer) to a receiver (listener, reader) who both communicate in the same language. In our own work, we are mainly interested in establishing inherent (similarity-based) cross-language intelligibility. We are not interested in interactive strategies, and therefore assess the speaker's intelligibility in strictly one-way tests in a laboratory setting. How intelligible a sender is, can be determined only by studying the responses of the receiver to the signals (stimuli) produced by the sender.

Even healthy adult speakers of a language differ substantially in the quality of their speech production, depending on their habitual rate of delivery, fluency and pausing strategy, clarity of articulation, liveliness of melody, loudness, and overall voice quality (as determined by the efficiency of the vocal fold vibration). Intelligibility tests (Markham and Hazan 2004: 733) have shown that the scores obtained for a random selection of 33 speakers of British English (18 men) producing simple CVC words (and legal non-words) in a fixed carrier ranged between 82 and 97 percent correct as determined from the responses of 45 adult native listeners. Sentence intelligibility (100 Harvard Sentences; IEEE 1969) scores ranged between 81 and 93 percent correct for 20 American speakers (10 men) (Karl and Pisoni 1994; Bradlow et al. 1996; Bent et al. 2007).[8] If we want to compare the cross-language intelligibility in both directions, the speakers should be matched for intelligibility within their own speech community. This can be ensured either by using a large random sample of speakers (which is unpractical) or by selecting a small number of optimally representative speakers, or even a single one, from the

---

[8] In both the British and the American data, there is a small but significant effect of gender: women are slightly more intelligible than men, with a difference of 2 percentage points in the British word data and of 3 points in the American sentence data. No gender effects could be found in similar Dutch data (Tielen 1992).

larger group. The representative speaker(s) should be in the middle of the range of intelligibility scores found for the larger peer group. A clever way of circumventing the speaker variable is using one perfectly bilingual speaker. This would be a speaker who has learned both languages under comparison from childhood onward, and who cannot be identified as being different from monolingual native speakers of either language (using a voice line-up procedure as used in forensic phonetics, see, e.g., Broeders et al. 2002).

Listeners, like speakers, differ in how well they recognize and understand speech. Healthy adult native listeners in the British research cited obtained scores ranging between 88 and 96 percent correct across all talkers; no indication of between-listener variation is given in the American publications. When running cross-language intelligibility tests, researchers would therefore do well to recruit a fairly large number of listeners and at some later stage exclude those listeners who find themselves at the extremes of the score distribution.

It is often assumed that communication between native speakers and listeners of the same language is flawless. However, since even normal speakers differ in intelligibility, and listeners vary in their listening skills, we recommend measuring between-native intelligibility of the test materials used in the experiment as a baseline condition.

4.2.3   Survey of Intelligibility Testing Methods

We will now present a nonexhaustive survey of techniques that have been employed in the field of cross-language intelligibility testing, concentrating on functional tests only. For more complete surveys of intelligibility tests, including opinion tests, we refer to chapters in handbooks such as Lawson and Peterson (2011) and McArdle and Hnath-Chisolm (2015) for speech audiometry, Gooskens (2013) for measuring interlingual intelligibility, Van Bezooijen and Van Heuven (1997) on the assessment of intelligibility of text-to-speech systems, and Kang et al. (2018) for intelligibility testing in the foreign language curriculum.

The first set of tests can be, and have been, used to test the intelligibility of single words presented out of context. The tests necessarily involve low-level, signal-driven word recognition and can be used to determine how difficult it is to recognize a (cognate) word in spite of a (strongly) deviant sound shape.

- *Word translation.* Listener hears isolated words in the non-native language, and writes down, types, or pronounces a word in the native language that captures the same meaning. Alternatively, the listener selects the correct translation from a closed list of alternatives.
- *Word-to-picture matching.* As word translation, but used when the listener is not required to respond using language. Listener hears a word and identifies

its meaning with one of (usually) four pictures presented on screen. This is an online technique using either a touch screen or eye tracking.

- *Lexical decision.* Listener hears a word-like sequence of sounds in the non-native language and has to decide as fast as possible, without making any errors, if the sequence exists as a word in the language or not. This is primarily an online word recognition technique. Decision time can be measured as an indication of processing difficulty. The assumption is that the sequence can be identified as a word only if the listener recognizes it. The paradigm can be complicated by presenting a prime word that is or is not (semantically) related to the test word. When related, the response time will be shorter. Impe (2010) used this technique to find very small differences in cross-lingual intelligibility between regional varieties of Standard Dutch as spoken in the Netherlands and Belgium.
- *Word category monitoring.* Listener hears a word and has to decide, as fast as possible while avoiding errors, which of a range of pregiven categories the word belongs to. The choice can be binary (e.g., tangible or intangible; animate or inanimate) or multivalued. Tang and Van Heuven (2009) used ten semantic categories such as body parts, family members, animals, and plants. Assigning category membership presupposes word recognition. Online decision time can be used as an additional indication of processing difficulty.

The next group of test techniques measures the intelligibility of words at the sentence level. Sentence context makes the target words predictable to a greater or lesser extent (if the context part is understood).

- *Full sentence translation.* Listener hears a (recorded) spoken sentence, possibly repeated at regular intervals to reduce memory load, and produces a translation in the native language, typically by writing or typing. This is an off-line task. The scoring of the response may be a problem. The technique was first used by the American structuralists (test the informant) to assess the interlingual intelligibility of Native American languages (e.g., Voegelin and Harris 1951; Hickerton et al. 1952; Pierce 1952; Biggs 1957).
- *Partial sentence translation.* Listener hears a sentence in a non-native language. The task is to write down the translation of the last word heard. The target word may or may not be highly predictable from the earlier part of the spoken sentence. Comparing the difference between the two conditions provides an indication how much of the semantic context was used by the listener to recognize the target. This is a interlingual adaptation of the Speech in Noise test (Kalikow et al. 1977), and was used by Tang and Van Heuven (2009) to measure the interlingual intelligibility of fifteen Chinese languages, and by Wang (2007) and Wang and Van Heuven (2013) for non-native Englishes.

- *Cloze test with written gaps*. Listener hears a spoken (sequence of) sentence(s) and sees a printed translation of the speech utterance in the native language. One or more words in the translation are replaced by blanks. The task is to write down (or choose from a list of alternatives) the blanked-out word(s). The task is easier (faster completion times, fewer errors) as the blanked-out words are contextually more constrained. Cloze testing was used by, e.g., Smith and Rafiqzad (1979) to assess the cross-lingual intelligibility of Asian World Englishes. It was also used to test the intelligibility of Frisian for Dutch listeners (Van Bezooijen and Van den Berg 2000).
- *Cloze test with spoken gaps*. Listener hears a spoken sentence in the non-native language in which one word is replaced by a beep. The task is to select one word from a printed list of alternatives (in the listener's L1) such that it optimally expresses the meaning of the missing word. This technique was used to assess the cross-lingual intelligibility in seventy pairs of European languages by Gooskens and Van Heuven (2017), and Gooskens et al. (2018).
- *Translation of semantically unpredictable sentences*. SUS sentences are quasi-random but syntactically grammatical sequences of short (monosyllabic, high-frequency) words. Five basic syntactic frames are used to generate sentences up to eight words long, as, e.g., *The state sang by the long week* or *Why does the range watch the fine rest?* There are SUS generators for most European languages (Benoît et al. 1996). The score is the percentage of correctly translated (content) words. Word recognition potentially benefits from top-down information on lexical category and sentence prosody. Responses are not constrained by semantic dependencies. SUS sentences were used by Gooskens et al. (2010) to assess the (asymmetrical) cross-lingual intelligibility of Danish and Swedish.
- *Sentence verification*. Listener hears a sentence that contains a logical proposition that is either true or false, e.g., *Horses are known to climb up trees*. The listener's task is to decide, as quickly as possible and without making any errors, whether the proposition is true or false. The technique can be used either as an offline task or as an online measure of sentence processing. In the latter case, the decision times have to be lined up with the earliest moment in the acoustic stimulus where sufficient information is available to correctly decide on the truth value of the sentence. Responses given before the temporal alignment point should be discarded as guessing. Since the response is binary (true/false), the number of test items should be large so as to reduce the influence of guessing. In an alternative application of the test, the listener is asked not to judge the truth of the proposition but its plausibility (e.g., Hilton et al. 2013 on the interlingual intelligibility of Scandinavian languages).
- *Carry out spoken instructions*. A straightforward method of measuring sentence understanding of a non-native language is having the listener carry

out instructions. Dependent variables are (1) the success rate with which the instructions are carried out, (2) the time it takes the respondent to start carrying out the description, and (3) the time it takes to successfully carry out the instruction. The instructions usually ask the listener to move or arrange objects in a virtual world on a computer screen. Van Heuven and De Vries (1981) used this technique to measure the intelligibility of Dutch spoken by Turkish immigrants (see also Van Heuven 1986).

Speech understanding is generally measured at the text level, using short texts composed of several sentences making up a coherent story or reasoning. Comprehension is then tested either by asking questions or by having the listener retell (i.e., translate or interpret) the text in his or her own language.

- *Text comprehension.* The participant reads or listens to a text of some length and answers questions about the contents. Usually the questions are asked after the presentation of the printed or spoken text, but some researchers maintain that it more realistic to present the questions beforehand so the participant knows what aspect of the contents to focus on. The questions are typically presented in multiple-choice format (three or four alternatives, only one of which is correct), which facilitates the scoring of the responses. Questions should be about the general ideas developed in the text and should not hinge on one specific word. As a precaution the questions should be tried out on a separate group of participants without any text presented to make sure that correct responses cannot be chosen on the basis of world knowledge or on logical grounds. The questions and the alternatives should be presented in the participant's L1, so that only the comprehension of the text (and not that of the questions) is measured. The recorded text testing (RTT) technique (Casad 1974) is an example of this type of test. In the RTT-Q version the questions are in open format. Interlingual comprehension testing based on this method was done in Scandinavia. Delsing and Lundin Åkesson (2005), for example, asked participants to answer just five open questions about short passages of continuous text.
- *Text translation.* This is the same technique, with the same advantages and drawbacks as sentence translation. Typically the text is presented sentence by sentence, while the participant responds by either reading out or typing the translation. Again, the scoring of the translations is a problem. In the RTT-retelling technique (Kluge 2007) the participant is asked to listen to a story in the non-native language and then to retell the story in the L1, keeping in as much detail of the original as possible. The result of the retelling is scored in terms of number of propositions in the original that are reflected in the retelling. This places a burden on the fieldworker, who has to analyze the original text and the retold versions in terms of propositions and then assess how well each of the propositions is maintained in the retelling. Retelling a

spoken story is basically the same task as *consecutive interpreting* (also called *conference interpreting*).

- *Story to picture matching*. A text is shown or played to the participant in its entirety after which the participant has to select one of four pictures shown on screen such that the picture chosen optimally matches the contents of the passage presented. In Gooskens et al. (2018) the four pictures were constructed such that they embodied the correct or wrong representation of two key propositions in the passage. For instance, if the passage was about driving a car in winter, one picture showed a car driving in a wintery landscape, another picture showed a car driving in summer (with a sunny landscape and trees and flowers in full bloom), a third picture would show a plane flying over a wintery landscape and a last picture contained a plane in a summer setting. When both content features were correctly identified the participant got full marks, when both aspects were wrongly identified no mark was given, when one feature was correct, the participant was given half marks. The technique is very fast and scoring is done automatically. In Gooskens et al. (2018), however, the test insufficiently discriminated among languages with high interlingual intelligibility, due to ceiling effects.[9]

We end this survey with a few examples of recent attempts to determine interlingual intelligibility at the discourse level. These tests involve live interaction between two participants, each using his or her own language, who have to solve a problem together.

- *Map task*. One interactant is the instruction giver and the other, the instruction follower. Both interactants have a map with roads and landmarks. The giver's task is to tell the follower how to trace a route between two landmarks that are known to the giver but unknown to the follower. To complicate the task, the two maps may differ in subtle ways. After completion of one task, new maps are provided and giver and follower switch roles. Dependent variables are success rate and time to completion (Anderson et al. 1991).
- *Spot the differences task*. Each of two interactants (who cannot see one another) has a copy of a picture that displays a large number of objects (e.g., toiletry articles) arranged in arbitrary order. There are differences between the two pictures in shapes, sizes, colors, and presence/absence of the objects. The participants' task is to identify as many of these differences as possible within

---

[9] There are many ways to systematically reduce the intelligibility of a spoken text to avoid ceiling effects, such as artificially speeding up the spoken text (Janse et al. 2003; Syrdal et al. 2012), adding (babble) noise (Gooskens et al. 2010), applying filtering (Wang et al. 2011), or using signal compression as used, for instance, in GSM telephony (Nooteboom and Doodeman 1984) or by varying the number of electrodes in simulated cochlear implants (Friesen et al. 2001).

a certain time frame. Dependent variables are the number of differences correctly identified and the number of spoken words used in the interaction (Van Mulken and Hendriks 2015).

4.3   Extra-linguistic and Para-linguistic Factors Influencing Intelligibility

The methods for establishing the level of intelligibility discussed in the previous section were developed for various purposes and capture the extent to which speakers of language A understand language B. Of course, linguistic overlap between the language of the listener and that of the speaker plays an important role in explaining how well listener A will understand speaker B. However, since intelligibility measurements are based on experiments with living persons, the results of the measurements depend on a large number of extra-linguistic and para-linguistic factors. An overview of such factors is provided in Gooskens (2019). Extra-linguistic factors include personality traits that have been identified within psychology to influence language learning, such as the ability to adapt to new situations, knowledge of the world, and access to sociocultural and cognitive resources.

Also age of the listener has been shown to affect the intelligibility of a related language. Vanhove and Berthele (2015) showed that in the written modality, cognate guessing skills, i.e., the ability to recognize words that are related to the historically related word in the L1, improve throughout adulthood while in the spoken modality, cognate guessing skills remain fairly stable between ages twenty and fifty but then start to decline. The speech-specific decline in cognate-guessing ability was tentatively attributed to different reliance on fluid intelligence (reasoning and problem-solving skills) and crystallized resources (in particular L1 vocabulary knowledge). Fluid intelligence tends to increase sharply into young adulthood and then declines, while crystallized resources stay stable or even increase throughout adulthood. Possibly, this interaction with modality is due to the fact that sounds differ between languages but letters do not. Older people are used to recognizing letters even though type fonts and personal hand-writing styles differ widely. But they no longer have the cognitive flexibility to accept atypical exemplars as tokens of their native sound categories. Alternatively, the authors suggest that it may be the time pressure associated with auditory stimulus presentation that caused the difference between the modalities. Spoken items were presented only once and thus required the quick application of cognitive flexibility, whereas speed was a lesser issue in the written mode because the words remained on the screen until the participants had entered their translations.

Attitudes toward the language and country of the speakers may affect the listener's willingness and motivation to understand an L2 speaker. Negative attitudes or social stigmas attached to languages are often seen as a potential obstacle for successful communication between speakers of different languages. If people do not have the will to try to understand each other, linguistic similarity between languages is of little help. However, experimental support for the relationship between attitude and intelligibility has been rather weak (e.g., Gooskens and Van Bezooijen 2006; Impe 2010; Schüppert et al. 2015) probably due to the fact that it is difficult to elicit (subconscious) attitudes in experimental settings.

An important factor in explaining the level of intelligibility is the nature and amount of previous exposure to the language of the speaker. The more exposure listeners have had to a language, the more likely they are to understand it. Listeners who have learned the language in a formal setting will generally understand the language better than listeners who have not, but also exposure outside the class room (e.g., via television, music, social media, and personal contact) may improve intelligibility, because the listeners will learn some of the vocabulary and become conscious about sound correspondences between the L1 and the L2 (Gooskens and Swarte 2017).

Most listeners have at least some knowledge of other languages or dialects than their own L1. Often, this knowledge can be used to understand a closely related language. Listeners may understand some non-cognate words in the language of the speaker because they are loanwords from a language that they are familiar with. In addition, multilingual listeners tend to have a higher level of metalinguistic awareness and are better able to use cross-linguistic similarity to understand a language. Listeners with experience in listening to other languages are also likely to develop strategies to guess the meaning of cognates in a related language (inferencing strategies; Berthele 2011). Examples of competences for good guessing capacities are the ability to make a flexible and selective comparison of features and patterns, focusing on consonants and neglecting or systematically varying the vowels, and the ability to use contextual information to make decisions. Listeners should know when to stop searching for correspondences between the L1 and the L2 in order not to waste time. They can also make clear when they do not understand the speaker and provide feedback to show whether they have understood or not (back-channeling). The speakers on the other side can also use various strategies to improve intelligibility, such as speaking slowly, reformulating sentences, and avoiding words they know to be difficult in their own language and using words known to be cognates in the two languages.

Orthographic knowledge may play a role in the intelligibility of a closely related language, even when the interaction takes place in the spoken modality. For instance, divergence between orthographic and spoken similarity between the two languages has been suggested as the explanation for the asymmetric mutual intelligibility between Danish and Swedish (Chambers and Trudgill 1980; Schüppert 2011). Danes understand spoken Swedish better than Swedes understand Danish, as has been borne out by an abundance of studies (see Gooskens et al. 2010) for a summary). How orthography helps can be illustrated by the following example. Literate Danes confronted with the spoken Swedish word *land* /land/ "country" can probably use their orthographic knowledge to match this word to their native correspondent *land* /lan$^?$/. On the other hand, this is not the case for Swedes listening to the Danish word because of the absence of the phoneme /d/, which is present in Swedish pronunciation as well as orthography. Gooskens and Doetjes (2009) showed that there are more Swedish words that Danes can understand by means of the orthography in the corresponding Danish cognates than Danish words that Swedes can use their orthography to recognise. This difference can be explained by the fact that spoken Swedish is close to both written Swedish and written Danish, whereas spoken Danish has changed rapidly during the last century and has undergone a number of reduction processes that are not reflected in the orthographic system. This means that Danes can often understand spoken Swedish due to its close similarity to written Danish, while Swedes get less help from written Swedish when understanding spoken Danish. Schüppert (2011) used event-related brain potentials (ERPs) to collect evidence that online activation of L1 orthography enhances word recognition among literate speakers of Danish who are exposed to samples of spoken Swedish. On the basis of these investigations, it can be concluded that Danish listeners indeed seem to make more use of the additional information that the L1 orthography can provide when listening to Swedish than Swedes when listening to Danish.

Paralinguistic factors include speech phenomena such as pitch, volume, speech rate, modulation, and fluency and nonvocal phenomena such as facial expressions, eye movements, and hand gestures are often included in the list of paralinguistic factors (Lyons 1977). Many linguists stress the importance of such factors for successful communication (Crystal 1975), but little research has been carried out to experimentally test the role of paralinguistic factors for the intelligibility of a closely related language.

The short overview of extra linguistic and para-linguistic factors provided in this section makes clear that predicting the level of intelligibility between languages is a complicated matter involving a large number of factors that may influence intelligibility to varying degrees. Simons (1979) notes that such factors may often explain asymmetric intelligibility between language pairs and he suggests that "discrepancies larger than 10% are due to social factors rather than linguistic factors" (quoted in Grimes 1992: 26). Grimes therefore suggests this threshold as a way to recognize such factors. However, he continues by noting that for some language combinations specific areas of phonology may play a role in explaining asymmetry. In Section 4.1.4 we provided examples of languages that are known to show asymmetric intelligibility. We will discuss possible linguistic explanations for asymmetric intelligibility in Section 4.4.4.

4.4   Linguistic Determinants of Intelligibility

The multilingualism factor discussed in Section 4.3 places many situations of intelligibility somewhere on the scale between inherent and acquired intelligibility. However, often the main interest of the researcher is to establish inherent intelligibility, i.e., the level of intelligibility that is linked to linguistic factors only, without any influence from previous exposure to the language of the speaker (acquired intelligibility) or another related language (mediated intelligibility). However, in practice inherent intelligibility is almost a theoretical construct since most listeners have had at least some exposure to the language of the speaker or some related language. In addition, some researchers note that functional testing is often very labor intensive and that the wide varieties of tests, test situations, and personal backgrounds of listeners involved in intelligibility research make it hard to compare levels of intelligibility between different language pairs. A way to circumvent these problems may be to measure objective linguistic distances by means of methods that have been developed for dialectometric research. By means of such measures, the degree of linguistic overlap at various linguistic levels can be expressed. Various investigations have shown that linguistic distance measures correlate with measures of inherent intelligibility. In this section, a number of computational approaches to measuring linguistic overlap between closely related languages are presented and discussed, and in particular it is shown how the measurements have been used to model intelligibility.

4.4.1   Lexical

Many researchers have argued that the degree of lexical overlap between two languages is likely to be very fundamental for predicting the level of intelligibility. If two languages share no vocabulary, the languages are in principle not mutually intelligible, and the larger the lexical overlap, the larger the mutual intelligibility will be. A simple way of measuring lexical distance between two languages is to calculate the percentage of non-cognates. Cognates are historically related words in the vocabularies of the two languages. Cognates share form and meaning even though both may have changed so much across time that they are difficult to recognize as cognates. For example, the cognate word pair English *fish* and Danish *fisk* obviously has the same origin, but the word pair Eng. *year* and Da. *år* may be difficult to recognize since the forms have changed more. Note that lexical distance from language A to language B maybe be different from that from B to A. This can be part of the explanation for asymmetric mutual intelligibility. For example, A might have two synonyms for a concept that has only one equivalent in B. An example is *rom* ("room") in Swedish, and *rum* or *værelse* in Danish. On first confrontation, a Swede will probably understand the Danish cognate word *rum* but not the non-cognate *værelse*. On the other hand, a Dane will easily understand Swedish *rom*.

To measure lexical distance between two languages the percentage of non-cognates needs to be established. This is not always a straightforward task and a number of decisions need to be taken.

First, in the strict definition, cognates are such word pairs that have developed from the same word in a common ancestor language, but for the purpose of predicting intelligibility it makes sense to also count borrowings that have the same origin as cognates, since they are often easily recognizable for a listener. They are generally more similar to the corresponding word in the L1 because they have had less time to change than inherited words that have been part of the lexicon for a much longer time than loanwords. For example, many Low German words were borrowed into Danish during the Middle Ages while more recently French and English were sources of borrowing into the languages. Examples are Da. *køkken* and Ge. *Küche* ("kitchen"), Da. *kusine* and Fr. *cousine* ("cousin"), and Da. *teenager* ("teenager"). In addition, many loanwords have specific segmental and/or prosodic properties that make them resistant to linguistic changes that affected inherited words (Gooskens et al. 2012). For example, French loans are stressed on the final syllable, cf. Sw. *mil'jö* and Da. *mil'ieu* ("environment"), whereas Germanic languages stress the stem-initial syllable. While in Germanic languages vowels in unstressed final syllables are often reduced, final syllables mostly maintain the full vowel in French loans.

Second, when measuring the lexical distance between two languages it is important to consider carefully what data set will be used for the measurements. It should contain enough words for a stable measurement. Furthermore, the selection of words used for the calculations depends on the purpose of the measurements. In traditional research on glottochronology and lexicostatistics the Swadesh list has often been used to calculate the genealogic relationship between languages (Swadesh 1971). However, to model intelligibility it is important to base the measurements on lists of words that represent the modern languages well. In recent years many corpora have been compiled for larger languages. Some researchers base their measurements on the most frequent words in such corpora, assuming that this is a good representation of the language as a whole. The 1000 most frequent words in a large corpus generally cover more than 70 percent of the word tokens in running English text (Nation and Waring 1997). Other researchers use running texts as a basis for measurements. Gooskens and Van Heuven (2020) established the degree of mutual intelligibility of sixteen closely related spoken languages within the Germanic, Romance, and Slavic language families in Europe using the same uniform methodology (cloze tests based on translations of the same four texts of in total 800 words). They measured the lexical distances between all language pairs within the same language family on the basis of the test material and found high correlations with intelligibility scores of listeners with little or no previous exposure to the test language ($r = -.69$ for the Romance languages, $r = -.80$ for the Slavic languages, and $r = -.95$ for the Germanic languages).

To establish whether the results could be generalized, i.e., whether the results would be the same if the intelligibility scores were predicted by means of linguistic distance measurements based on another data set they repeated the analysis with distance measures based on translations of a list of the 100 most frequently used nouns in the British National Corpus.[10] The correlations with intelligibility were just as high as the correlations with the distances based on text data. This shows that inherent intelligibility can be predicted quite well by lexical distances and that a short word list provides sufficient input for computing the distance measures needed.

Third, the researcher needs to consider what kinds of words to include in lexical distance calculations. Some non-cognate words in a text can easily be interpreted from the context or have little negative influence on intelligibility. The meaning of other words may be more difficult to predict or be more important for understanding the text. It is often assumed that content words (nouns, adjectives, numerals, main verbs) are more important for intelligibility than are function words (articles, conjunctions, prepositions, pronouns, auxiliaries, modals, particles, adverbs) because they express the content of the message (Van Bezooijen and Gooskens 2007). The importance of content words becomes clear when looking at the vocabulary in telegrams and newspaper headlines. To express a message as shortly as possible, most function words are left out; yet it is possible to understand the message. And even within the group of content words, some words are more important than others in certain contexts. Salehi and Neysani (2017) found that Turkish listeners had more difficulties guessing the meaning of Iranian-Azerbaijani verbs and nouns than the meaning of adjectives and adverbs. They explain this by the higher semantic load of nouns and verbs. This means that it may be possible to improve lexical distance measurements as predictors of intelligibility by weighing differences in verbs and nouns more heavily than differences in function words, adjectives, and adverbs. On the other hand, the results by Gooskens and Van Heuven (2020) summarized earlier show that measurements based on whole texts including all word classes are equally good predictors as measurements based on frequent nouns.

Fourth, it is not a straightforward task to decide what words are cognates. They can be coded qualitatively by the researcher on the basis of etymological knowledge. The information can be found in etymological dictionaries for the largest languages of the world. Ciobanu and Dinu (2014) describe a method that can do this manual work automatically by means of electronic dictionaries. However, when such etymological information is not available or if the researcher wishes to measure distances on the basis of large numbers of words, the researcher may use a quantitative method where string

---

[10] See British National Corpus at www.natcorp.ox.ac.uk.

distances are automatically computed (McMahon and McMahon 2005; Holman et al. 2008). Schepens et al. (2013) compared how well qualitatively (cognates in the Swadesh-200 word lists) and quantitatively established percentages of cognates predict speaking proficiency scores among 30,066 immigrants with thirty-five different mother tongues and found that the qualitative expert scores were better predictors ($r = -.77$) than quantitative measures ($r = -.66$). The intercorrelation between the qualitative and quantitative distance measures was $r = .90$. Partial semantic overlap can be taken into account when coding words lists for cognacy. For example, the English word *queen* is historically related to Danish *kvinde* ("woman") but shares only part of the meaning. Also compounds may cause coding problems. For example, in Danish *barnevogn* only the second part of the word is cognate of Dutch *kinderwagen* ("baby pram"). A pragmatic solution to such coding problems is to count such words as half cognates and assign them half a point for cognacy.

Finally, when calculating lexical distances with the aim of modeling intelligibility, the researcher also needs to decide how to deal with so-called false friends – i.e., words that sound similar but are not historically related and mostly have different meanings. An example of a false friend is German *Dach* /daχ/ ("roof") Dutch *dag* /dɑχ/ ("day") by the German subjects. The German word is more similar to the Dutch word than the German cognate *Tag* /tak/. A false friend cannot be recognized by a listener with no previous knowledge of the language of the speaker. While regular non-cognates will in principle hinder intelligibility, false friends may cause even larger problems because they may actually mislead the listener. In addition, listeners are less likely to use contextual cues to guess the meaning of false friends than in the case of other unknown words because they do not realize that they are non-cognates. For this reason, it may be sensible to give such words an extra (negative) weight when coding for cognacy.

Neighborhood density is another lexical property that may influence intelligibility. Neighbors are defined as word forms that are similar to the stimulus word but differ from it in the presence, absence, or substitution of just one sound (or letter). A large number of neighbors broadens the pool of recognition candidates, causing delay or even failure of successful word recognition (see Luce and Pisoni 1998). Kürschner et al. (2008) found neighborhood density to be a significant predictor of intelligibility of Swedish words for Danish listeners. For instance, the Swedish word *säng* ("bed") was less often correctly translated (as *seng*, which has four Danish neighbors: *syng* ["sing"], *senge* ["beds"], *hæng* ["hang"], and *stæng* ["close"]), than the Swedish word *adress* ("address"), which has no neighbors. A measure of lexical distance might be refined by taking neighborhood density into consideration.

Lexical distance measurements are generally good predictors of experimental measurements of intelligibility, as was shown in early publications by, for example, Bender and Cooper (1971), who found an *r* of .67 between morpheme cognateship (established on a variant of the Swadesh-100 word list) and interlingual intelligibility for all twenty-five combinations of five Cushitic languages.[11] Results of more recent investigations showing the relationship between lexical distances and intelligibility measures are summarized in Sections 4.4.2 and 4.4.5.

4.4.2   *Phonetic*

The research discussed in the previous section shows that there is a strong relationship between lexical similarity and intelligibility but that lexical distances are not perfect predictors of intelligibility. As discussed, the lexical distance scores themselves could be improved, but also other linguistic levels might play a role in predicting intelligibility. The fact that a word is a cognate does not mean that the listener will always be able to match it with the counterpart in his or her own language. Two cognate words may have changed beyond recognition (see Tatman, Chapter 2 this volume, on phonetic variation in dialects). Various methods have been developed within dialectometry to measure dialect distances and draw dialect maps. These distance measurements can also be used to predict the intelligibility of cognates.

An early investigation was carried out on Chinese dialects on the basis of phonetic transcriptions of over 2,700 cognate words in seventeen dialects (Cheng 1997). The complexity of the correspondence patterns needed to convert the word strings from one dialect to their counterparts in the other was computed (systemic mutual intelligibility). Arbitrary reward and penalty points were assigned to sound correspondences in onset consonants, post-onset glides, nuclear vowels, coda consonants, and tones. Frequent sound correspondences (above the mean frequency for a particular sound) were assigned positive values, while relatively rare correspondences were negatively weighted. Cheng reasoned that the larger the complexity of the rule system needed to convert cognate strings between dialects, the lower the cross-dialect intelligibility would be, but he never tested the prediction against experimental results. Moreover, Cheng's phonetic distance measure is asymmetrical when fewer and simpler correspondences are needed in one direction than in the other. Tang and Van Heuven (2015) correlated Cheng's phonetic distance measure

---

[11] In Biggs (1957) lexical distance and interlingual intelligibility (averaged over AB and BA pairs and excluding AA pairs) for six Yuman languages (spoken in Arizona, USA) are even correlated at $r = .990$ (computed by us). This correlation is inflated, however, due to the bimodal distribution of the intelligibility scores. When computed separately for language pairs above 70 percent mutual intelligibility and those below 20 percent (there are no scores between 20 and 70 percent; see Figure 4.1a), we find $r = .882$ and $r = .533$, respectively.

with functional sentence intelligibility scores for 210 Chinese dialect pairs, and confirmed this prediction ($r = .772$).

The complexity of Cheng's computations makes it difficult to apply them to other language situations. However, other dialectometric distance measurements have been used successfully to model intelligibility. The Levenshtein distance measure has become the most widely used algorithm for predicting intelligibility. Phonetic distance between two language varieties is computed for aligned cognate word pairs as the smallest number of string edit operations needed to convert the string of phonetic symbols in language A to the cognate string in B. Possible string operations are deletions, insertions, and substitutions of symbols. Each string edit operation needed incurs a penalty of one point. The total number penalty points is then divided by the length of the alignment (number of alignment slots) to yield a length-normalized Levenshtein distance. The overall phonetic distance from language A to language B is the arithmetic mean of the normalized distances for all cognate word pairs in the research corpus (Nerbonne and Heeringa 2010). The Levenshtein algorithm was used to explain mutual intelligibility between various Germanic language varieties – e.g., Gooskens et al. (2008) for eighteen Scandinavian languages and dialects among standard Danish speakers, Gooskens and Swarte (2017) for twenty Germanic language combinations, Vanhove and Berthele (2017) for intelligibility of Swedish among German participants – and recently the algorithm has been used for intelligibility research in a large number of language combinations in other language areas – see, e.g., Golubovic (2016) for Slavic, Kaivapalu and Martin (2017) for Finnish-Estonian, Tang and Van Heuven (2015) for Chinese dialects, Salehi and Neysani (2017) for Turkish-Azeri, Čéplö et al. (2016) for Arabic dialects, Gooskens and Schneider (2019) for Pacific dialects, and Feleke et al. (2020) for Amharic and two Tigrigna varieties spoken in Ethiopia. All of these investigations found high correlations between intelligibility measurements and Levenshtein distances, typically at $.7 < r < .9$. Many of the investigations combine the Levenshtein measurements with measurements of lexical overlap, as described in Section 4.4.1 in regression analyses. For example, in an investigation by Beijering et al. (2008) and Gooskens et al. (2008) a regression analysis including lexical and Levenshtein distances resulted in a proportion explained variance of $R^2 = .81$ for the intelligibility of seventeen Scandinavian language varieties and standard Danish as assessed among young Danes from Copenhagen.

The simplest version of the Levenshtein algorithm uses binary differences between alignments; more advanced versions use graded weights that express acoustic segment distances. For example, the pair [i, o] is seen as being more different than the pair [i, ɪ]. However, for the purpose of modeling intelligibility, it is not clear how the differences should be weighted. Gooskens et al. (2015) found that minor phonetic details that could hardly be captured by Levenshtein distances may sometimes have a major impact on the interlingual intelligibility of isolated words. The optimal weighing is likely to differ for different language combinations and depends on predictability and generalizablity of sound correspondences. Improvements of the algorithm should take into account the human decoding processes. For example, Gooskens et al. (2008) tested the intelligibility of eighteen Scandinavian language varieties among Danish listeners and correlated this with Levenshtein distances split up into consonant and vowel distances. Their results showed higher correlations with consonant distances than with vowel distances, suggesting that consonants convey more lexical information than vowels and therefore play a more important role in predicting intelligibility. However, the relative contribution of consonants and vowels to intelligibility may be different across languages since the size of consonant and vowel inventories can vary considerably and so can the number of vowels and consonants used in running speech. Čéplö et al. (2016) tested mutual intelligibility between three Arabic varieties and found vowel differences to affect mutual comprehension more than consonants. They explain this finding with the large interdialectal and allomorphic variation in consonants that listeners seem to be well able to deal with.

Gooskens et al. (2008) also found that insertions are better predictors of intelligibility than deletions. This is confirmed by Kaivapalu and Martin (2017) who found that Finns perceive more similarity between Finnish and Estonian than Estonians do. They explain this by the fact that Finnish word forms often contain material that is not present in the corresponding Estonian form, both within the inflectional formative and within the stem. They therefore conclude that the fact that something is missing compared to the L1 results in a larger perceived similarity than when something is added. We will come back to this point in Section 4.4.4.

Kürschner et al. (2008) correlated the intelligibility of 384 frequent Swedish words among Danes with eleven linguistic factors and carried out logistic regression analyses. Phonetic distances explained most of the variance. However, they also found that individual characteristics of words influence intelligibility. Word length, different numbers of syllables in L1–L2 words pairs, Swedish sounds not used in Danish, neighborhood density (see Section 4.4.1), and word frequency also correlated with intelligibility. Berthele (2011) and Möller (2011) note that listeners rely more on word beginnings than on later parts of words, and similarities of word onsets have been found to be more important than similarities in the rest of the word. Van Heuven (2008) showed that correct recognition of words synthesized from low-quality diphones was severely reduced if stress was shifted to an incorrect position in Dutch words. He therefore assumes that unexpected stress positions play a negative role in understanding speech in a closely related variety. Wang et al. (2011) monotonized Chinese sentences and presented these (and the original sentences as well) to listeners in versions with high, medium, and low segmental quality. The results showed that lexical tone information is important, especially when the segmental quality is poor. Tone is therefore a potentially important factor in the interlingual intelligibility of tone languages. Yang and Castro (2008) computed tonal distance between dialects of tone languages spoken in the south of China in several different ways and found substantial correlations with functional intelligibility scores around $r = .7$. Tang and Van Heuven (2015), however, correlated similar tonal distance measures with functional and judged intelligibility measures for fifteen Mandarin and non-Mandarin Chinese dialects but found no significant correlations.

4.4.3   Morpho-syntactic

Most investigations on linguistic determinants of intelligibility have focused on lexical and phonetic distances. It is generally assumed that these two linguistic levels are most important for intelligibility and in addition, most dialectometric measures for other levels have only recently been developed. However, there is evidence that morpho-syntax plays a role in predicting intelligibility and should therefore not be ignored. For example, by means of reaction time and correctness evaluation experiments, Hilton et al. (2013) investigated whether certain Norwegian grammatical constructions that are not used in Danish may impede Danes' comprehension of Norwegian sentences. Their results showed that when Danish listeners were presented with sentences with Norwegian word orders and morphology not used in Danish, they needed longer decision times and made more errors in a sentence verification task.

Recently various methods for measuring morphological and syntactic distances have been developed and applied in intelligibility research. Nerbonne and Wiersma (2006) introduced the "trigram measure," a measure of aggregate syntactic distance. Trigrams (different sequences of three lexical category labels) are inventoried and counted. Syntactic distance is then defined as 1 minus the Pearson correlation coefficient between the trigram frequencies. Heeringa et al. (2017) developed two additional measures, the "movement measure," which measures the average number of words that has moved in sentences of one language compared to the corresponding sentences in another language, and the "indel measure," which measures the average number of words being inserted or deleted in sentences of one language compared to the corresponding sentences in another language. Swarte (2016) measured mutual intelligibility between five Germanic languages by means of a spoken cloze test. She correlated the intelligibility scores with the three syntactic distance measures. The trigram measure showed the highest correlation with intelligibility ($r = .26$). Gooskens and Van Heuven (2020) found significant correlations between syntactic trigram distances and inherent intelligibility

($r = .72$ for fourteen Germanic language combinations, $r = .77$ for fifteen Romance language combinations, and $r = .53$ for twenty-nine Slavic language combinations).[12]

Heeringa et al. (2014) measured orthographic Levenshtein distances between five Germanic languages separately for stems and affixes. They found that orthographic stem variation among languages does not correlate with orthographic variation in inflectional affixes. This suggests that a distinction needs to be made between stem and affix distances. Gooskens and Van Heuven (2020) found significant correlations between affix distances and intelligibility for fifteen Romance ($r = .54$) and twenty-nine Slavic ($r = .81$) language combinations. The correlation for fourteen Germanic language combinations was insignificant.

4.4.4   Asymmetric Intelligibility

As discussed in Section 4.1, mutual intelligibility may sometimes be asymmetric. This asymmetry is often caused by social factors. However, as we will demonstrate, the linguistic relationship between two languages may be asymmetrical and can therefore be part of the explanation for asymmetric mutual intelligibility.

The following example of the lexical correspondences between Dutch and German shows that lexical relationships can be asymmetric. A word in language A may have a cognate in language B, but a word in language B need not have a cognate synonym in language A. For instance, the Dutch word *plek* ("place, spot, location") has no cognate in German. The equivalent for *plek* in German would be *Ort*, which is cognate to Dutch *oord*. A German person may be able to understand the Dutch cognate *oord* but not the non-cognate *plek*. On the other hand, a Dutch person will probably understand *Ort*. Gooskens et al. (in preparation) modeled this asymmetry in an investigation of the mutual intelligibility of seventy closely related languages in Europe. The texts used for the functional intelligibility experiments (Gooskens and Swarte 2017) were all translated from the same original English text into each of the test languages. However, when calculating the lexical distances, they translated the words in the texts of each of the test languages to the corresponding cognates in the languages of the listeners if such cognates existed. The lexical distances were expressed as the percentages of non-cognates for each combination of stimulus text and the corresponding translations. This sometimes resulted in different distances from language A to language B and from language B to language A.

---

[12] The correlations are lower in Swarte (2016) because the participants had often had exposure to the test language. In the study by Gooskens and Van Heuven (2020) only the results of participants with very limited or no exposure were included.

For example, the distance from French to Romanian is 49 percent while it is 58 percent from Romanian to French. This would predict that Romanian is more difficult to understand for French speakers than the other way around and this is also what Gooskens and Van Heuven (2017) found.

Grimes (1992: 26) noted that asymmetric intelligibility between Spanish and Portuguese and between Chinese dialects can be traced to specific areas of phonology, and also for other language pairs it has been suggested that characteristics of the pronunciation may cause one language to be more difficult to understand for speakers of a closely related language than the other way around. For example, Bleses et al. (2008) have shown that the early language development of Danish children is somewhat slower than that of children with other mother tongues, such as English and Swedish. Bleses et al. attribute this result to the poor segmentability of Danish, which is caused by prosodic phenomena such as lack of specific juncture cues, compulsory sentence accents, and local signals to utterance function. At the segmental level, lenition of consonants and other reduction phenomena, in particular schwa assimilation and schwa deletion, would result in poor segmentability. These characteristics of Danish may be part of the explanation for the Swedish–Danish asymmetric intelligibility and ideally phonetic distance measurements should be able to capture such asymmetries.

The Levenshtein algorithm does not capture asymmetric phonetic relations between language varieties; the distance from language A to language B is equal to the distance from language B to language A. However, as discussed, it may be possible to improve the Levenshtein algorithm in such a way that it takes into account the human decoding process by assigning different weights to different operations. If insertions are given higher values than deletions, the distances measured may be asymmetric.

Other algorithms have been developed that are able to express phonetic asymmetries. The complexity scores developed by Cheng (1997) for Chinese dialects (see Section 4.4.2) result in different scores between AB/BA pairs of dialects. Somewhat misleadingly, Cheng calls the computed mean of the phonetic complexity scores "mutual intelligibility." It should be kept in mind that this computed mean is a prediction of mutual intelligibility at best, but that the actual mutual intelligibility can only be obtained from experimental results with live listeners and speakers. Tang and Van Heuven (2007) renamed Cheng's computational phonological distance measure the Phonetic Correspondence Index (PCI). Tang and Van Heuven (2009) established cross-lingual intelligibility scores at the word and sentence level for fifteen Chinese languages. Six of these languages were members of the Mandarin group. Standard Chinese, which is based on Beijing Mandarin, is a compulsory subject in primary education throughout China, so that Mandarin languages are not a good testing ground for exploring the potential of the PCI as predictor of asymmetrical cross-lingual intelligibility. The cross-lingual intelligibility within any language pair involving Beijing (acquired intelligibility) or any other Mandarin language (using the Standard Mandarin as a bridge language) will be substantially better than can be predicted from linguistic distance measures. However, if we limit the comparison to only the nine non-Mandarin languages in the sample, the PCI asymmetry (the AB score minus the BA score) correlates significantly with the asymmetry found in the functional word and sentence scores for the thirty-six language pairs, where the correlation is predictably better at the word level ($r = .454, p = .003$, one-tailed) than at the sentence level ($r = .331, p = .024$, one-tailed).[13]

Moberg et al. (2007) used conditional entropy for accounting for asymmetric phonetic relations. This algorithm measures the complexity of a mapping, and is sensitive to the frequency and regularity of sound correspondences between two languages. Moberg et al. used conditional entropy measures in an attempt to explain the asymmetrical intelligibility between Danish, Swedish, and Norwegian by measuring the amount of entropy in both directions for each language combination. Conditional entropies do not measure how similar two languages are, but how predictable the correspondence is in a certain language pair. Given a certain sound in language A, how predictable is the corresponding sound in language B? The more predictable this sound is, the lower the entropy. Higher predictability aids intelligibility; therefore, the hypothesis is that a low entropy measure corresponds well with a high intelligibility score. The results suggest that conditional entropies correspond well with the asymmetric results of intelligibility tests that have been carried out between the three languages. Other researchers found similar results. Kyjanek and Haviger (2018) measured entropies between Czech, Slovak, and Polish that correspond with most of the results found in previous intelligibility research. Stenger et al. (2017) calculated entropy scores for written Czech–Polish and Bulgarian–Russian and refined these scores with the information-theoretic concept of surprisal. On the basis of the measurements they predict that no asymmetry can be expected for Russian–Bulgarian and, like Kyjanek and Haviger (2018), they predict that Czech readers may have more difficulties reading Polish than a Polish reader reading Czech.

No entropy-based asymmetry measures have been tested on experimental intelligibility data. To be more certain about the relationship, intelligibility experiments should be carried out that test the hypothesis that the most regular

---

[13] Tang and Van Heuven (2015) limited the prediction of word and sentence intelligibility from objective linguistic distance measures only after eliminating asymmetries from the data by taking the mean scores of the AB and BA pairs. The analysis of the asymmetry given here is new.

and frequent correspondence rules are more transparent for listeners. If this is indeed the case, then we would also expect the results of listeners who have had exposure to the test language to show higher correlation with high entropy measures since the listeners will have had the chance to discover correspondence rules. Listeners with no previous exposure can recognize words in the test language only on the basis of similarities with their native language and on their intuitions of possible sound correspondences. In this context the distinction between item similarity (similarity of individual forms such as sounds, morphemes, words or phrases) and system similarity (a set of principles for organizing forms paradigmatically and syntagmatically) introduced by Ringbom and Jarvis (2009) is relevant.

Another point to consider when applying the asymmetry measures discussed here is the fact that a large corpus is needed for stable results. According to Moberg et al. (2007) at least 800 words are needed for entropy measures, while measures with the Levenstein algorithm have given stable results with only 100 words.

Also morpho-syntactic asymmetries may play a role in explaining asymmetric intelligibility. For example, Gooskens and Van Bezooijen (2006) found that Dutch speakers tend to understand Afrikaans better than vice versa. They showed that one of the reasons for this is the simplified grammar of Afrikaans resulting in a higher degree of morphological and syntactic transparency for speakers of Dutch than for speakers of Afrikaans. Heeringa et al. (2017) measured mutual intelligibility between five Germanic languages on the basis of four texts of in total 800 words. The distances were measured from the source texts in the five languages to the five languages of the listeners, resulting in a total twenty distance measurements involving two distances per language combination, from language A to language B and from Language B to language A. They used the three different methods described in Section 4.4.3. Because of the nature of the database used for measuring the distances, they were able to detect asymmetric relationships between the languages. For example, all three measures suggest that asymmetric syntactical distances could be part of the explanation why native speakers of Dutch more easily understand German texts than native speakers of German understand Dutch texts (Swarte 2016).

4.4.5   Modeling Mutual Intelligibility

Languages do not differ along just one dimension but may differ at all linguistic levels (lexical, phonetic/orthographic, morpho-syntactic, prosodic), and at each of the linguistic levels, languages may furthermore vary on many different parameters. Ideally, we would like to express the linguistic distance between language varieties using a single number on a one-dimensional scale. However, there is no a priori way of weighing the different linguistic dimensions. Intelligibility is mostly expressed in one number (for example, the percentages of correct answers in an intelligibility test) and intelligibility measurements are an adequate way of determining the relative importance of the various linguistic dimensions. On the other hand, correlations between intelligibility measurements and linguistic distance measurements reveal which linguistic dimensions are most important for the intelligibility of a closely related language.

The investigations presented show that all linguistic levels can play a role in predicting how well speakers of closely related languages can understand each other's languages. Often there is a strong relationship between the various levels, but this does not always have to be the case. In their investigation of seventy European language combinations Gooskens and Van Heuven (2020) found that especially lexical distances show overlap with other linguistic distances. However, the correlations differ between different linguistic levels and languages. For example, Gooskens and Swarte (2017) found a small lexical distance between Danish and Swedish (5 percent) but a relatively large phonetic distance (46 percent), while for Dutch and German, the lexical distance was larger (20 percent) and the phonetic distance smaller (37 percent). They found a correlation of $r = .95$ between intelligibility scores and lexical distances, while the correlation with phonetic distance was nonsignificant ($r = .28$). Salehi and Neysani (2017) also found lexical distance to be more important than phonetic distance for explaining the intelligibility of Turkish among Iranian-Azerbaijani speakers. They explain this finding by the fact that the phonetic distances between Turkish and Azerbaijani are small and highly rule governed. Gooskens et al. (2008), on the other hand, correlated lexical and phonetic distances with the intelligibility of seventeen Scandinavian language varieties among Danes and found phonetic distance to be a better predictor of intelligibility ($r = .86$) than lexical distance ($r = .64$) for this particular set of closely related language varieties.

Differences at the morphological and syntactic levels are generally assumed to be less important for intelligibility than lexical and phonetic differences. Hilton et al. (2013; details in Sections 4.2.3 and 4.4.3) found that the non-native phonology impeded comprehension to a larger degree than morpho-syntactic differences, confirming the important role of phonetic similarities besides lexical similarities for comprehension. Gooskens and Van Heuven (2020) included lexical, phonetic, orthographic, and syntactic distances in a regression analysis in order to explain mutual intelligibility among closely related Germanic, Slavic, and Romance languages. Lexical distance was the best predictor of intelligibility in the case of Germanic and Slavic. However, for Romance languages, syntactic distance was the only predictor included in the model, and it was also included in the model for Slavic languages.

4.5   Relationship between Intelligibility and Language Trees

Generally, the greater the historical depth (also called *glottochronology*: how long ago did language A undergo an innovation that language B was not part of?), the less the two languages resemble one another, and the more difficult it will be for speakers of language A to be understood by listeners of language B and vice versa. Computational linguists have developed algorithms to assemble phylogenetic trees that represent hypotheses about the evolutionary ancestry of languages (see Dunn 2015; Bowern 2018). In this section we review some attempts at testing how well present-day intelligibility patterns of (inherent) cross-language intelligibility reflect genealogic taxonomies established by comparative linguists.

In terms of data processing, cross-lingual intelligibility scores are best presented in a matrix with speaker language in the rows against listener language in the columns. The scores in the cells can be seen as a distance measure between the two languages. Within-language intelligibility scores, which should be near perfect, are in the cells along the main diagonal of the matrix. The full square matrix can be simplified to a triangle by computing the mean of the contra-diagonal cell contents, which abstracts away from any asymmetries (see above). The matrix data can be converted to either hierarchical tree structures or to maps. The maps are generally two-dimensional and can be compared with geographic maps, which tend to congrue with intelligibility-based maps. Three-dimensional maps may be drawn, which are a combination of the geographic maps, with hierarchical tree structures superposed as contours or colors (delineating islands of equal interlingual intelligibility). Matrices, trees, and maps can be constructed with any kind of distance measures, including the various objective linguistic distance measures discussed in Section 4.3. In the present section we will only compare the congruence between interlingual intelligibility and diachronic distance using hierarchical tree structures.

The comparison, however, is not without problems. Linguists often disagree on the exact family relationships among languages. Cladistic trees they suggest may be based on synchronic counts of lexical correspondences rather than on glottochronology, which is indeed difficult to establish. Also, the fact that two languages split away from another a long time ago need not by itself compromise mutual intelligibility. If the innovation involved only a small detail of the phonology, for instance the change of all stem-initial voiceless plosives to affricates, and is not followed by many other changes in later years, intelligibility will hardly be affected. Moreover, there is no agreement among linguists that glottochronology is the only or even the preferred criterion for establishing the genealogy of languages. An alternative approach is based on counting the number of differences among (related) languages and so defining isogloss bundles that set apart groups of language varieties from one another. But then again, there will be disagreement on which isoglosses should be considered important and which ones are insignificant (Chambers and Trudgill 1980: 112).

In the following we give the family tree structure suggested for the Yuman languages by Kroeber (1943) and for the Iroquoian languages by Julian (2010: 10). The trees we present have been pruned so as to contain only the languages that were tested (in italics) for mutual intelligibility.

Yuman	Northern Iroquoian
North-West Arizona	*Onondaga*
Walapai	*Seneca*
Havasapai	*Cayuga*
Yavapai	Mohawk-Oneida
Colorado River	*Mohawk*
Yuma	*Oneida*
Mohave	Tuscarora-Nottoway
Gila River	*Tuscarora*
Maricopa	

Figure 4.1 shows the distance matrices that can be filled with the cross-lingual intelligibility data reported by Biggs (1957) for six Yuman language varieties (with filling in of two missing cell contents by imputation) and for six Iroquoian languages by Hickerton et al. (1952, detailed tests only). Hierarchical trees were drawn below the matrices using average linking between groups.

The intelligibility-based tree conforms closely to Kroeber's (1943) linguistic tree, with the exception of Maricopa, which Kroeber placed in a separate (Gila River) group. Kroeber's family structure, however, was mainly based on

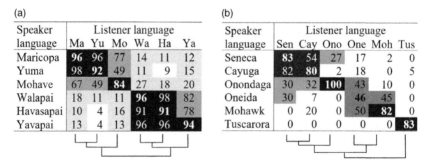

(a)

Speaker language	Listener language					
	Ma	Yu	Mo	Wa	Ha	Ya
Maricopa	96	96	77	14	11	12
Yuma	98	92	49	11	9	15
Mohave	67	49	84	27	18	20
Walapai	18	11	11	96	98	82
Havasapai	10	4	16	91	91	78
Yavapai	13	4	13	96	96	94

(b)

Speaker language	Listener language					
	Sen	Cay	Ono	One	Moh	Tus
Seneca	83	54	27	17	2	0
Cayuga	82	80	2	18	0	5
Onondaga	30	32	100	43	10	0
Oneida	30	7	0	46	45	0
Mohawk	0	20	0	50	82	0
Tuscarora	0	0	0	0	0	83

Figure 4.1 Cross-lingual intelligibility scores for all combinations of six Yuman languages (a) and six Iroquoian languages (b). The better the intelligibility, the darker the shading of the cell. Affinity trees are given below the matrices.

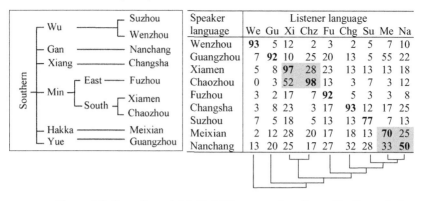

Figure 4.2 Cross-lingual intelligibility scores for all combinations of nine southern Chinese languages, based on functional sentence intelligibility test. Affinity tree (average linking between groups) is drawn below the matrix. The diachronic classification (left panel) is based on Li (1987a; 1987b: A1–2).

counting synchronic sameness in the lexicon and phonology, without much attention for historical depth, which strictly speaking renders this an invalid test. Similarly, the Iroquoian family tree predicts the intelligibility data reasonably well, although Mohawk and Oneida should have shown better cross-lingual intelligibility. Also, Cayuga has clearly better cross-lingual intelligibility with Seneca than with Onondaga, which is not predicted by the family tree.

Tang and Van Heuven (2007, 2009) established cross-lingual intelligibility (using opinion tests and functional tests) for $15 \times 15 = 225$ pairs of Chinese languages. Leaving out the six Mandarin languages (which pollute the results due to acquired intelligibility; see Section 4.4.4), Figure 4.2 shows the cross-lingual scores for the remaining $9 \times 9 = 81$ pairs of non-Mandarin languages based on functional sentence intelligibility.

Congruence with the diachronic taxonomy (Figure 4.2, left) is found only for the pair Xiamen–Chaozhou, which both belong to the South Min branch in the family tree. The close-knit pair Meixian–Nanchang, however, cannot be predicted from the genealogical tree.[14]

Gooskens et al. (2018) compared the congruence between cross-lingual intelligibility scores obtained from experiments with genealogies of Germanic (five), Romance (five) and Slavic (six) languages (seventy language pairs in total). In Figure 4.3 we show the genealogies, intelligibility data, and the affinity trees based on the experimental data. The intelligibility scores are based on a

---

[14] The affinity tree in Tang and Van Heuven (2009: 722) contains one incorrectly drawn branch, by which Wenzhou forms an early cluster with Suzhou. The tree presented here (and also in Tang 2009: 81) is correct.

Speaker language	Listener language				
	Da	Sw	Du	Ge	En
Da		56.0	9.9	12.5	7.9
Sw	43.8		10.4	10.0	8.7
Du	13.3	13.0		25.5	9.6
Ge	-	13.1	-		9.5
En	-	-	-	-	

Speaker language	Listener language				
	Sp	It	Pt	Ro	Fr
Sp		56.0	62.0	46.6	11.0
It	38.2		44.1	47.2	22.9
Pt	35.7	23.4		20.7	18.0
Ro	13.7	8.7	14.7		10.5
Fr	-	18.6	-	-	

Speaker language	Listener language					
	Cz	Sk	Pl	Cr	Sl	Bu
Cz		-	24.0	18.1	18.1	10.8
Sk	87.5		40.6	23.0	18.8	16.0
Pl	34.3	48.7		9.5	12.6	7.1
Cr	19.9	24.5	14.6		71.8	29.2
Sn	16.7	16.0	13.4	41.3		20.2
Bu	13.4	10.1	13.7	19.7	18.6	

Figure 4.3 Cross-lingual intelligibility scores (cloze test) for all combinations of five Germanic, five Romance, and six Slavic languages. Affinity trees are given below the matrices.

cloze test, done by listeners who indicated to have had minimal prior exposure to the test language. For some language pairs, no such listeners could be found. For instance, since English is a compulsory school language in Scandinavia, Germany, and the Netherlands from age ten or earlier, the cells for English as a test language remain empty for listeners with some other Germanic L1. In order to compute the affinity trees, such empty cells were given the value of the contra-diagonal cell, assuming reciprocity for cross-lingual intelligibility.

The family trees for the languages are given in the following list. They are excerpted from Harbert (2007), Hall (1974), and Sussex and Cubberley (2006), for Germanic, Romance and Slavic, respectively.

Germanic	Romance	Slavic
West	Italo-Western	West
North Sea	West	Northern
English	Ibero	*Polish*
Continental	*Portuguese*	Southern
Dutch	*Spanish*	*Czech*
German	Gallo	*Slovak*
North	*French*	South
East	Italo	Western
Danish	*Italian*	*Slovene*
Swedish	Eastern	*Croatian*
	North	Eastern
	Romanian	*Bulgarian*

For the Germanic and Slavic groups the intelligibility-based trees are isomorphic with the linguistic taxonomy. The Romance tree, however, is a rather poor predictor of the Romance intelligibility results. The Ibero cluster (Spanish–Portuguese) is not reproduced, and French, which should be in a cluster with the other Italo-Western languages, is more remote even than Romanian. We computed correlation coefficients for the distances within language pairs based on the intelligibility data and on the linguistic taxonomies, using the cophenetic (tree distance) measure as the criterion. Correlations were $r = .75$ for the Germanic group, $r = .41$ for the Romance group, and $r = .86$ for the Slavic group.

We conclude from the data presented here that the correlation between intelligibility-based distances and linguistic tree distance (based on the ordering of innovations in the history of the languages), is substantial but clearly imperfect – as was only to be expected given the disparity between the historical innovation-based approach, the synchronic shared vocabulary approach, and the rather noisy effects of these factors on contemporary intrinsic cross-lingual intelligibility. Nevertheless, if decisions about genealogic taxonomies are hard to make, present-day intelligibility results may well be given the casting vote.

4.6   Conclusions, Discussion, and Desiderata for Future Research

In this chapter we provided an overview of research on mutual intelligibility between closely related languages. We defined intelligibility as the degree to which a listener is able to recognize the linguistic units in the stream of sounds and to establish the order in which they are spoken. Mutual intelligibility is the mean of the two directions, i.e., the degree to which listener A understands speaker B and vice versa. It should be noted that the two directions can be asymmetric, i.e., can yield different scores. We gave an overview of methods for measuring intelligibility and considerations that have to be made when choosing a method.

One thing that strikes us is that it is very difficult to find cross-lingual intelligibility studies across widely differing language families that use the same methodology. Even the recorded text retelling technique used worldwide by the SIL researchers does not use standardized materials. The stories that are recorded and have to be retold differ from language group to another, thereby precluding cross-family comparisons. Methods used to study cross-lingual intelligibility among European languages (as in Gooskens et al. 2018) use rather different experimental methods than, e.g., Tang and Van Heuven (2009) for Chinese languages. If the same experimental method and the same materials (translations of some language and culture neutral text) were used, we could begin to say with some authority that the differences in cross-lingual intelligibility between certain European languages are larger than those between some Chinese "dialects." This would be a step on the way toward an internationally respected linguistic criterion to distinguish between languages and dialects.

For practical and theoretical reasons it is interesting to be able to explain and predict the results of intelligibility measurements and to understand why mutual intelligibility can be asymmetric. Extra-linguistic factors such as previous exposure to the language of the listener play an important role in predicting acquired intelligibility. However, often the main interest of the researcher is inherent intelligibility and the relationship with linguistic factors. We showed how linguistic distances can be measured at different levels. The methods have been developed for dialectometric purposes, but the results of the investigations discussed in this chapter show that we are able to a large extent to predict mutual intelligibility of closely related languages by computational distance measurements.

However, since correlations between intelligibility measurements and linguistic distances are not perfect there are more linguistic and extra-linguistic factors that should be taken into consideration. We gave some suggestions for improvements of the computational algorithms for measuring linguistic distances, but future research should target more detailed knowledge of the mechanisms behind the intelligibility of language varieties. Methods that have been developed by experimental linguists and psycholinguists should be exploited when setting up controlled experiments that will give us more detailed insight into the relative importance of various linguistic and extra-linguistic factors that impact the intelligibility of language varieties.

References

Ahland, Colleen. 2003. Asymmetry in the interlectal intelligibility of Gurage lects: Can implicational patterns explain and predict this phenomenon? Paper presented as coursework for a historical linguistics course at the University of Texas-Arlington.

Anderson, Anne H., Miles Bader, Ellen G. Bard, Elizabeth Boyle, Gwyneth Doherty, Simon Garrod, Stephen Isard, Jacqueline Kowtko, Jan McAllister, Jim Miller, Catherine Sotillo, Henry S. Thompson, & Regina Weinert. 1991. The Hcrc map task corpus. *Language and Speech* 34(4). 351–366.

Beijering, Karin, Charlotte Gooskens, & Wilbert Heeringa. 2008. Predicting intelligibility and perceived linguistic distance by means of the Levenshtein algorithm. *Linguistics in the Netherlands* 25(1). 13–24.

Bender, Marvin L. & Robert L. Cooper. 1971. Mutual intelligibility within Sidamo. *Lingua* 27. 32–52.

Benoît, Christian, Martine Grice, & Valérie Hazan. 1996. The SUS test: A method for the assessment of text-to-speech synthesis intelligibility using semantically unpredictable sentences. *Speech Communication* 18(4). 381–392.

Bent, Tessa, Adam Buchwald, & Wesley Alford. 2007. Inter-talker differences in intelligibility for two types of degraded speech. *Research of Spoken Language Processing, Indiana University, Progress Report* 28. 316–330.

Berthele, Raphael. 2011. On abduction in receptive multilingualism. Evidence from cognate guessing tasks. *Applied Linguistics Review* 2. 191–220.

Biggs, Bruce. 1957. Testing intelligibility among Yuman languages. *International Journal of American Linguistics* 23. 57–67.

Bleses, Dorthe, Werner Vach, Marlene Slott, Sonja Wehberg, Pia Thomsen, Thomas O. Madsen, & Hans Basbøll. 2008. Early vocabulary development in Danish and other languages: A CDI based comparison. *Journal of Child Language* 35. 619–650.

Bowern, Claire. 2018. Computational phylogenetics. *Annual Review of Linguistics* 4. 281–296.

Bradlow, Ann R., Gina M. Torretta, & David B. Pisoni. 1996. Intelligibility of normal speech I: Global and fine-grained acoustic-phonetic talker characteristics. *Speech Communication* 20(3). 255–272.

Branets, Anna, Daria Bahtina, & Anna Verschik. 2020. Mediated receptive multilingualism: Estonian-Russian-Ukrainian case study. *Linguistic Approaches to Bilingualism* 10(3). 380—411.

Broeders, Ton P. A., Tina Cambier-Langeveld, & Jos Vermeulen. 2002. Case report: Arranging a voice lineup in a foreign language. *The International Journal of Speech, Language and the Law* 9(1). 1350–1771.

Carroll, Lewis. 1871. *Through the Looking-Glass, and What Alice Found There.* London: Macmillan.

Casad, Eugene H. 1974. *Dialect Intelligibility Testing.* Norman, OK: Summer Institute of Linguistics of the University of Oklahoma.

Čéplö, Slavomír, Ján Bátora, Adam Benkato, Jiří Milička, Christophe Pereira, & Petr Zemánek. 2016. Mutual intelligibility of spoken Maltese, Libyan Arabic, and Tunisian Arabic functionally tested: A pilot study. *Folia Linguistica* 50(2). 583–628.

Chambers, Jack K. & Peter Trudgill. 1980. *Dialectology.* Cambridge: Cambridge University Press.

Cheng, Chin-Chuan. 1997. Measuring relationship among dialects: DOC and related resources. *Computational Linguistics and Chinese Language Processing* 2(1). 41–72.

Ciobanu, Alina M. & Liviu P. Dinu. 2014. On the Romance languages mutual intelligibility. In Nicoletta Calzolari, Khalid Choukri, Thierry Declerck, et al. (eds.). *Proceedings of the 9th International Conference on Language Resources and Evaluation, LREC,* 3313–3318. Reykjavik: European Language Resources Association (ELRA).

Crystal, David. 1975. Paralinguistics. In Jonathan Benthall & Ted Polhemus (eds.). *The Body as a Medium of Expression,* 162–174. London: Institute of Contemporary Arts.

Cutler, Anne. 2012. *Native Listening: Language Experience and the Recognition of Spoken Words.* Cambridge, MA: MIT Press.

Delsing, Lars-Olof & Katarina Lundin Åkesson. 2005. *Håller språket ihop Norden? En forskningsrapport om ungdomars förståelse av danska, svenska och norska* Copenhagen: Nordic Council of Ministers.

Denes, Peter B. & Elliot N. Pinson. 1963. *The speech chain. The physics and biology of spoken language.* Murray Hill, NJ: Bell Telephone Laboratories.

Dunn, Michael. 2015. Language phylogenies. In Claire Bowern & Bethwyn Evans (eds.). *The Routledge Handbook of Historical Linguistics,* 190–211. London: Routledge.

Ehmer Khan, Mohammed. 2011. Different approaches to white box testing technique for finding errors. *International Journal of Software Engineering and Its Applications* 5(3). 1–13.

Feleke, Tekabe L., Charlotte Gooskens, & Stefan Rabanus. 2020. Mapping the dimensions of linguistic distance: A study on South Ethiosemitic languages. *Lingua* 243, 1–31. DOI: 10.1016/j.lingua.2020.102893.

Friesen, Lendra M., Robert V. Shannon, Deniz Baskent, & Xiaosong Wang. 2001. Speech recognition in noise as a function of the number of spectral channels: Comparison of acoustic hearing and cochlear implants. *Journal of the Acoustical Society of America* 110. 1150–1163.

Golubovic, Jelena. 2016. *Mutual Intelligibility in the Slavic Language Area.* Groningen: University of Groningen.

Gooskens, Charlotte. 2013. Experimental methods for measuring intelligibility of closely related language varieties. In Robert Bayley, Richard Cameron, & Ceil Lucas (eds.). *The Oxford Handbook of Sociolinguistics*, 195–213. Oxford: Oxford University Press.

Gooskens, Charlotte. 2019. Receptive multilingualism. In Simona Montanari & Suzanne Quay (eds.). *Multidisciplinary Perspectives on Multilingualism*, 149–174. The Hague: De Gruyter.

Gooskens, Charlotte & Gerard Doetjes. 2009. Skriftsprogets rolle i den dansk-svenske talesprogsforståelse. *Språk och stil* 19. 105–123.

Gooskens, Charlotte, Wilbert Heeringa, & Karin Beijering. 2008. Phonetic and lexical predictors of intelligibility. *International Journal of Humanities and Arts Computing* 2(1–2). 63–81.

Gooskens, Charlotte, Wilbert Heeringa, & Vincent J. van Heuven. In preparation. Comparing Germanic, Romance and Slavic: Relationships among linguistic distances. *Quantitative Linguistics.*

Gooskens, Charlotte, Sebastian Kürschner, & Renée van Bezooijen. 2012. Intelligibility of Swedish for Danes: Loan words compared with inherited words. In Henk van der Liet & Muriel Norde (eds.). *Language for Its Own Sake*, 435–455. Amsterdam: Amsterdam Contributions to Scandinavian Studies.

Gooskens, Charlotte & Cindy Schneider. 2019. Linguistic and non-linguistic factors affecting intelligibility across closely related varieties in Pentecost Island, Vanuatu. *Dialectologia* 23. 61—85.

Gooskens, Charlotte & Femke Swarte. 2017. Linguistic and extra-linguistic predictors of mutual intelligibility between Germanic languages. *Nordic Journal of Linguistics* 40(2). 123–147.

Gooskens, Charlotte & Renée van Bezooijen. 2006. Mutual comprehensibility of written Afrikaans and Dutch: Symmetrical or asymmetrical? *Literary and Linguistic Computing* 23. 543–557.

Gooskens, Charlotte, Renée van Bezooijen, & Vincent J. van Heuven. 2015. Mutual intelligibility of Dutch-German cognates by children: The devil is in the detail. *Linguistics* 53(2). 255–283.

Gooskens, Charlotte & Vincent J. van Heuven. 2017. Measuring cross-linguistic intelligibility in the Germanic, Romance and Slavic language groups. *Speech Communication* 89. 25–36.

Gooskens, Charlotte & Vincent J. van Heuven. 2020. How well can intelligibility of closely related languages in Europe be predicted by linguistic and non-linguistic variables? *Linguistic Approaches to Bilingualism* 10(3). 351–379.

Gooskens, Charlotte, Vincent J. van Heuven, Jelena Golubovic, Anja Schuppert, Femke Swarte, & Stefanie Voigt. 2018. Mutual intelligibility between closely related languages in Europe. *International Journal of Multilingualism* 15(2). 169–193.

Gooskens, Charlotte, Vincent J. van Heuven, Renée van Bezooijen, & Jos J. A. Pacilly. 2010. Is spoken Danish less intelligible than Swedish? *Speech Communication* 52(11–12). 1022–1037.

Grimes, Joseph E. 1992. Correlations between vocabulary similarity and intelligibility. In Eugene H. Casad (ed.). *Windows on Bilingualism*, 17–32. Dallas, TX: Summer Institute of Linguistics and the University of Texas at Arlington.

Gutt, Ernst-August. 1980. Intelligibility and interlingual comprehension among selected Gurage speech varieties. *Journal of Ethiopian Studies* 14. 57–85.

Hall, Robert A. 1974. *External History of the Romance Languages.* New York: Elsevier.

Harbert, Wayne. 2007. *The Germanic Languages.* Cambridge: Cambridge University Press.

Heeringa, Wilbert, Femke Swarte, Anja Schüppert, & Charlotte Gooskens. 2014. Modeling intelligibility of written Germanic languages: Do we need to distinguish between orthographic stem and affix variation? *Journal of Germanic Linguistics* 26(4). 361–394.

Heeringa, Wilbert, Femke Swarte, Anja Schüppert, & Charlotte Gooskens. 2017. Measuring syntactical variation in Germanic texts. *Digital Scholarship in the Humanities* 33(2). 279–296.

Hickerton, Harold, Glen D. Turner, & Nancy P. Hickerton. 1952. Testing procedures for estimating transfer of information among Iroquois dialects and languages. *International Journal of American Linguistics* 18. 1–8.

Hilton, Nanna H., Charlotte Gooskens, & Anja Schüppert. 2013. The influence of non-native morphosyntax on the intelligibility of a closely related language. *Lingua* 137(4). 1–18.

Holman, Eric W., Søren Wichmann, Cecil H. Brown, Viveka Velupillai, André Müller, & Dik Bakker. 2008. Explorations in automated language classification. *Folia Linguistica* 42(3–4) 331–354..

IEEE. 1969. IEEE recommended practices for speech quality measurements. *IEEE Transactions on Audio and Electroacoustics* 17. 227–246.

Impe, Leen. 2010. *Mutual Intelligibility of National and Regional Varieties of Dutch in the Low Countries.* Leuven: Catholic University of Leuven.

Janse, Esther, Sieb Nooteboom, & Hugo Quene. 2003. Word-level intelligibility of time-compressed speech: Prosodic and segmental factors. *Speech Communication* 41. 287–301.

Jensen, John B. 1989. On the mutual intelligibility of Spanish and Portuguese. *Hispania* 72(4). 848–852.

Julian, Charles. 2010. *A History of the Iroquoian Languages.* Winnipeg: Department of Linguistics University of Manitoba.

Kachru, Yamuna & Larry E. Smith. 2008. *Cultures, Contexts and World Englishes.* New York/London: Routledge.

Kaivapalu, Annekatrin & Maisa Martin. 2017. Perceived similarity between written Estonian and Finnish: Strings of letters or morphological units? *Nordic Journal of Linguistics* 40(2). 149–174.

Kalikow, D. N., K. N. Stevens, & L. L. Elliott. 1977. Development of a test of speech intelligibility in noise using sentence materials with controlled word predictability. *Journal of the Acoustical Society of America* 61. 1337–1351.

Kang, Okim, Ron I. Thomson, & Meghan Moran. 2018. Empirical approaches to measuring the intelligibility of different varieties of English in predicting listener comprehension. *Language Learning* 68(1). 115–146.

Karl, John R. & David B. Pisoni. 1994. The role of talker-specific information in memory for spoken sentence. *Journal of the Acoustical Society of America* 95. 2873.

Kluge, Angela. 2007. *"Sorry, Could You Repeat That, Please?!" – Where Does One Language End and the Next Begin?* Jakarta: SIL International-Indonesia.

Kroeber, Alfred L. 1943. *Classification of the Yuman Languages.* Berkeley/Los Angeles: University of California Press.

Kürschner, Sebastian, Charlotte Gooskens, & Renée van Bezooijen. 2008. Linguistic determinants of the intelligibility of Swedish words among Danes. *International Journal of Humanities and Arts Computing* 2(1–2). 83–100.

Kyjánek, Lukáš & Jiří Haviger. 2018. The measurement of mutual intelligibility between West-Slavic languages. *Journal of Quantitative Linguistics* 26(3). 205–230.

Ladefoged, Peter N. 1968. *The measurement of Cross-Language Communication.* Washington, DC: Office of Health, Education, and Welfare.

Lawson, Gary & Mary Peterson. 2011. *Speech Audiometry.* San Diego CA: Plural Publishers.

Levelt, Willem J. M. 1989. *Speaking: From Intention to Articulation* (ACL-MIT Press Series in Natural-Language Processing). Cambridge, MA: MIT Press.

Li, Rong. 1987a. Chinese dialects in China. In Stephen A. Wurm, Benjamin T'sou, David Bradley, et al. (eds.). *Language Atlas of China*, map A-2. Hong Kong: Longman.

Li, Rong. 1987b. Languages in China. In Stephen A. Wurm, Benjamin T'sou, David Bradley, et al. (eds.). *Atlas of China*, map A-1. Hong Kong: Longman.

Luce, Paul A. & David B. Pisoni. 1998. Recognizing spoken words: The neighborhood activation model. *Ear and Hearing* 19. 1–36.

Lyons, John. 1977. *Semantics,* vol. 2. Cambridge: Cambridge University Press.

Markham, Duncan & Valérie Hazan. 2004. The effect of talker- and listener-related factors on intelligibility for a real-word, open-set perception test. *Journal of Speech, Language, and Hearing Research* 47(4). 725–737.

McArdle, Rachel & Theresa Hnath-Chisolm. 2015. Speech audiometry. In Jack Katz, Marshall Chasin, Kristina English, Linda J. Hood, & Kim L. Tillery (eds.). *The Handbook of Clinical Audiometry*, 61–75. Philadelphia: Wolters Kluwer.

McMahon, April M. S. & Robert McMahon. 2005. *Language Classification by Numbers* (Oxford Linguistics). Oxford: Oxford University Press.

Moberg, Jens, Charlotte Gooskens, John Nerbonne, & Nathan Vaillette. 2007. Conditional entropy measures intelligibility among related languages. In Peter Dirix, Ineke Schuurman, Vincent Vandeghinste, & Frank Van Eynde (eds.). *Computational Linguistics in the Netherlands 2006: Selected Papers from the 17th CLIN Meeting*, 51–66. Utrecht: LOT.

Möller, Robert. 2011. Wann sind Kognaten erkennbar? Ähnlichkeit und synchrone Transparenz von Kognatenbeziehungen in der germanischen Interkomprehension. *Linguistik Online* 46(2). 79–101.

Munro, Murray J. & Tracey M. Derwing. 1995. Foreign accent, comprehensibility and intelligibility in the speech of second language learners. *Language Learning* 45. 73–97.

Munro, Murray J., Tracey M. Derwing, & Susan L. Morton. 2006. The mutual intelligibility of L2 speech. *Studies in Second Language Acquisition* 28(1). 111–131.

Nation, Paul & Rob Waring. 1997. Vocabulary size, text coverage, and word lists. In Norbert Schmitt & Michael McCarthy (eds.). *Vocabulary: Description, Acquisition and Pedagogy*, 6–19. Cambridge: Cambridge University Press.

Nerbonne, John & Wilbert Heeringa. 2010. Measuring dialect differences. In Jürgen E. Schmidt & Peter Auer (eds.). *Language and Space: Theories and Methods*, 550–567. Berlin: Mouton De Gruyter.

Nerbonne, John & Wybo Wiersma. 2006. A measure of aggregate syntactic distance. In John Nerbonne & Erhard Hinrichs (eds.). *Linguistic Distances Workshop at the Joint Conference of International Committee on Computational Linguistics and the Association for Computational Linguistics, Sydney, July 2006*, 82–90.

Nooteboom, Sieb G. & Gert J. N. Doodeman. 1984. Speech quality and the gating paradigm. In M. P. R. Van den Broecke & A. Cohen (eds.). *Proceedings of the Tenth International Congress of Phonetic Sciences, Utrecht, August*, 481–485. Dordrecht: Foris.

Pierce, Joe E. 1952. Dialect distance testing in Algonquian. *International Journal of American Linguistics* 18. 208–218.

Ringbom, Håkan & Scott Jarvis. 2009. The importance of cross-linguistic similarity in foreign language learning. In Michael H. Long & Catherine J. Doughty (eds.). *Handbook of Language Learning*, 106–118. Oxford: Blackwell.

Salehi, Mohammad & Aydin Neysani. 2017. Receptive intelligibility of Turkish to Iranian-Azerbaijani speakers. *Cogent Education* 4(1). 1–15.

Schepens, Job, Frans Van der Slik, & Roeland van Hout. 2013. The effect of linguistic distance across Indo-European mother tongues on learning Dutch as a second language. In Lars Borin & Anju Saxena (eds.). *Approaches to Measuring Linguistic Differences*, 199–230. Berlin: De Gruyter Mouton.

Schüppert, Anja. 2011. *Origin of Asymmetry: Mutual Intelligibility of Spoken Danish and Swedish*. Groningen: University of Groningen.

Schüppert, Anja, Nanna H. Hilton, & Charlotte Gooskens. 2015. Swedish is beautiful, Danish is ugly? Investigating the link between language attitudes and intelligibility. *Linguistics* 53(2). 275–304.

Schüppert, Anja, Nanna H. Hilton, & Charlotte Gooskens. 2016. Why is Danish so difficult to understand for fellow Scandinavians? *Speech Communication* 79. 47–60.

Showalter, Stuart D. 1994. How attitude, use, and bilingualism data help define language shift and dialect choice in a rural cluster. *Notes on Sociolinguistics* 40. 3–26.

Simons, Gary F. 1979. *Language Variation and Limits to Communication*. Ithaca, NY: Department of Modern Languages and Linguistics, Cornell University.

Smith, L. E. & K. Rafiqzad. 1979. English for cross-cultural communication: The question of intelligibility. *TESOL Quarterly* 13. 371–380.

Stenger, Irina, Klára Jagrova, Andrea Fischer, Tania Avgustinova, Dietrich Klakow, & Roland Marti. 2017. Modeling the impact of orthographic coding on Czech–Polish and Bulgarian–Russian reading intercomprehension. *Nordic Journal of Linguistics* 40(2). 175–199.

Sussex, Roland & Paul Cubberley. 2006. *The Slavic Languages.* Cambridge: Cambridge University Press.

Swadesh, Morris. 1971. *The Origin and Diversification of Language: Edited Post Mortem by Joel Sherzer.* Chicago, IL: Aldine.

Swarte, Femke. 2016. *Predicting the Mutual Intelligibility of Germanic Languages from Linguistic and Extra-Linguistic Factors.* Groningen: University of Groningen.

Syrdal, Ann K., H. Timothy Bunnell, Susan R. Hertz, Taniya Mishra, Murray Spiegel, Corine Bickley, Deborah Rekart, & Matthew J. Makashay. 2012. Text-to-speech intelligibility across speech rates. In *Proceedings of Interspeech–2012*, 623–626.

Tang, Chaoju. 2009. *Mutual Intelligibility of Chinese Dialects: An Experimental Approach.* Utrecht: Netherlands Graduate School of Linguistics (LOT).

Tang, Chaoju & Vincent J. van Heuven. 2007. Predicting mutual intelligibility in Chinese dialects. In William J. Barry & Jürgen Trouvain (eds.). *Proceedings of the 16th International Congress of Phonetic Sciences, Saarbrücken,* 1457–1460. Saarbrücken: Universität des Saarlandes.

Tang, Chaoju & Vincent J. van Heuven. 2009. Mutual intelligibility of Chinese dialects experimentally tested. *Lingua, an International Review of General Linguistics* 119(5). 709–732.

Tang, Chaoju & Vincent J. van Heuven. 2015. Predicting mutual intelligibility of Chinese dialects from multiple objective linguistic distance measures. *Linguistics* 53(2). 285–312.

Tielen, Mirjam. 1992. *Male and Female Speech: An Experimental Study of Sex-Related Voice and Pronunciation Characteristics.* Amsterdam: Universiteit van Amsterdam.

Van Bezooijen, Renée & Charlotte Gooskens. 2005. Intertalig tekstbegrip. De begrijpelijkheid van Friese en Afrikaanse teksten voor Nederlandse lezers. *Nederlandse Taalkunde.* 10(2). 129–152.

Van Bezooijen, Renée & Charlotte Gooskens. 2006. Waarom is geschreven Afrikaans makkelijker voor Nederlandstaligen dan andersom? In Tom Koole, Jacomine Nortier & Bert Tahitu (eds.). *Artikelen van de Vijfde Sociolinguïstische Conferentie in Lunteren,* 68–76. Delft: Eburon.

Van Bezooijen, Renée & Charlotte Gooskens. 2007. Interlingual text comprehension: linguistic and extralinguistic determinants In Jan D. ten Thije & Ludger Zeevaert (eds.). *Receptive Multilingualism and Intercultural Communication: Linguistic Analyses, Language Policies and Didactic Concepts,* 249–264. Amsterdam: John Benjamins.

Van Bezooijen, Renée & Rob J. H. van den Berg. 2000. Hoe verstaanbaar is het Fries voor niet-Friestaligen? In Piter Boersma, Pieter Breuker & Lammert G. Jansma (eds.). *Philologia Frisica Anno 1999,* 9–26. Leeuwarden: Fryske Akademy.

Van Bezooijen, Renée & Vincent J. van Heuven. 1997. Assessment of speech synthesis. In Dafydd Gibbon, Roger Moore, & Richard Winksi (eds.). *Handbook of Standards and Resources for Spoken Language Systems,* 481–653. Berlin/New York: Mouton de Gruyter.

Van Heuven, Vincent J. 1986. Some acoustic characteristics and perceptual consequences of foreign accent in Dutch spoken by Turkish immigrant workers. In Jeanne Van Oosten & Johan P. Snapper (eds.). *Dutch Linguistics at Berkeley, Papers Presented at the Dutch Linguistics Colloquium Held at the University of California,*

Berkeley on November 9th, 1985, 67-84. Berkeley, CA: Dutch Studies Program, University California, Berkeley.

Van Heuven, Vincent J. 2008. Making sense of strange sounds: (Mutual) intelligibility of related language varieties. A review. *International Journal of Humanities and Arts Computing* 2(1–2). 39–62.

Van Heuven, Vincent J. & Jan W. de Vries. 1981. Begrijpelijkheid van buitenlanders: de rol van fonische versus niet-fonische factoren. *Forum der letteren* 22. 309–320.

Van Mulken, Margo & Berna Hendriks. 2015. Your language or mine? or English as a lingua franca? Comparing effectiveness in English as a lingua franca and L1–L2 interactions: Implications for corporate language policies. *Journal of Multilingual and Multicultural Development* 36(4). 404–422.

Vanhove, Jan & Raphael Berthele. 2015. The lifespan development of cognate guessing skills in an unknown related language. *International Review of Applied Linguistics in Language Teaching* 53(1). 1–38.

Vanhove, Jan & Raphael Berthele. 2017. Interactions between formal distance and participant-related variables in receptive multilingualism. *International Review of Applied Linguistics in Language Teaching* 55(1). 23–40.

Voegelin, Charles F. & Zellig S. Harris. 1951. Methods for determining intelligibility among dialects of natural languages. *Proceedings of the American Philosophical Society* 45. 322–329.

Voigt, Stefanie & Anja Schüppert. 2013. Articulation rate and syllable reduction in Spanish and Portuguese. In Charlotte Gooskens & Renée van Bezooijen (eds.). *Phonetics in Europe: Perception and Production*, 317–332. Frankfurt a.M: Peter Lang.

Wang, Hongyan. 2007. *English as a Lingua Franca: Mutual Intelligibility of Chinese, Dutch and American Speakers of English.* Utrecht: Netherlands Graduate School of Linguistics (LOT).

Wang, Hongyan & Vincent J. van Heuven. 2013. Mutual intelligibility of American, Chinese and Dutch-accented speakers of English tested by SUS and SPIN sentences. In *Proceedings of Interspeech 2013, 2 July 2013, Lyon, France*, 431–435.

Wang, Hongyan, Ligang Zhu, Xiaotong Li, & Vincent J. van Heuven. 2011. Relative importance of tone and segments for the intelligibility of Mandarin and Cantonese. In Wai S. Lee & Eric Zee (eds.). *Proceedings of the 17th International Congress of Phonetic Sciences*, 2090–2093. Hong Kong: City University of Hong Kong.

Weinreich, Uriel. 1957. Functional aspects of Indian bilingualism. *Word* 13. 203–233.

Wolff, Hans. 1959. Intelligibility and inter-ethnic attitudes. *Anthropological Linguistics* 1. 34–41.

Yang, Cathryn & Andy Castro. 2008. Representing tone in Levenshtein distance. *International Journal of Humanities and Arts Computing* 2(1–2). 205–219.

5   Dialectology for Computational Linguists

John Nerbonne, Wilbert Heeringa, Jelena Prokić and Martijn Wieling

5.1   Introduction

This chapter provides an overview of computational work in dialectology. We have published similar surveys in the not-too-distant past (Wieling and Nerbonne, 2015; Heeringa and Prokić, 2018), but these were aimed at dialectologists and general linguists, respectively. This chapter is written for computational linguists, so that we will focus less on the technical details of exploiting the computer in research on dialects (which is documented in the articles we cite) but rather more on background assumptions and emerging issues and opportunities.

5.2   Dialectology

James Walker's and Miriam Meyerhoff and Steffen Klaere's introductory chapters clarify that one normally reserves the term *dialect* for what they also call *diatopic variation*, in particular, a geographically restricted language variety, and we focus our attention here on the study of this sort of variety, ignoring the other dimensions of variation, including social, situational, and temporal. We hasten to add both that these are interesting (see other chapters) and also that many of the same issues arise in the (computational) analysis of nongeographical variation.

5.2.1   *Research Questions and Research Perspectives*

Many researchers and laypeople alike are fascinated by dialects, what makes them up, and where they are spoken. This means that there is a substantial intrinsic motivation for the study. The two questions – what is special about a given dialect and where is it spoken – are the two main research questions that are asked in dialectology, the scientific study of dialects.

Lay interest seldom extends to explanations of dialectal facts – why certain language elements are different and why the geographical distribution takes the form it does, but dialectologists are passionately interested in these questions, too, and we will include attempts at explanation arising from computational work as well. Naturally we strive as scientists to provide not only accurate answers to these questions but also insightful ones, i.e., compact characterizations with defensible assumptions.

Computational linguists interested in developing classifiers for dialectal material, i.e., procedures to assign dialectal material to one of a given set of varieties, may note that this is indeed a natural way to construe the first research question. It will be sufficient if the classifiers to be developed are discriminative rather than generative in the sense of Ng and Jordan (2002). See also Chapter 9 in this volume.

5.2.2 Comparative, Nongenerative Perspective

Implicit in the way we have sketched the research questions is that we are seldom interested in a complete description of a dialect in the sense of generative grammar, i.e., a description that would allow one to decide for any putative utterance, whether it belongs to the dialect or not. This goal has been abandoned in Chomskyan generative linguistics in any case (Nerbonne, 2018). Instead we are primarily interested in what is different in the dialect under study with respect to other dialects, and we largely ignore what is common. In any case, there have been few attempts at developing comprehensive grammars of a range of dialects.[1] The focus on comparison means that computational techniques that proceed by processing comparable material from a range of dialects will be most useful, as we shall see in this chapter.

This does not mean, however, that there has been no interest in dialectology on the part of generative grammar; on the contrary, many generativists have been interested. Barbiers (2009) explores *syntactic microvariation*, i.e., the sort of detailed variation that one finds across a range of dialects, in an attempt to characterize that range in generative terms. See Hinskens (2018) and references therein for a recent survey of generative work in phonology. But their interest is also primarily comparative, e.g., in exploring how a syntactic phenomenon such as inflected complementizers or a phonological phenomenon such as final devoicing varies from one dialect to another. They add to this an interest in what's common with respect to a particular phenomenon under study, but their perspective is likewise discriminative.

5.2.3 Data Collection

Dialectologists have experimented with myriad data collection techniques, attending carefully to sampling (Macauley, 2018), which must go beyond random sampling of the usual sort in order to ensure coverage of the entire

---

[1] Wagner and O'Baoill's *Linguistic Atlas and Survey of Irish Dialects* (1958) is perhaps a counterexample, but well outside the generative tradition (see discussion in text).

area where a variety is spoken. Dialectologists have experimented not only with questionnaires (Llamas, 2018) and other written surveys (Chambers, 2018), which better guarantee that responses are comparable, but also with personal interviews (Bailey, 2018), which, in the hands of a good interviewer, provide a better chance at obtaining natural speech. Increasingly, dialectologists are turning to the World Wide Web as a means of conducting surveys, e.g., the *Atlas zur deutschen Alltagssprache* at www.atlas-alltagssprache.de (Möller and Elspaß, 2008), as well as to smart phone apps and crowdsourcing (Scherrer et al., 2012; Goldman et al., 2014).

Dialectology has always been a discipline that has cherished data, collecting notably it in the form of *dialect atlases* (Kretzschmar et al., 1993), which in modern times, are normally accompanied by a database of dialect speech material (Van den Berg, 2003; Elspaß and König, 2008). Computational linguists interested in pursuing research in dialectology should definitely consider collaboration with one of the many dialect atlases across the world.

5.3   Dialectometry

As the opening chapters of this handbook note, one of the primary data analysis steps in traditional dialectology involved decorating a map with codes corresponding to the different ways of expressing the same thing in the language area under study. This might be [ɑr] vs. [a] (the latter represents the "r-less" "ah" in the pronunciation of *car* in eastern New England and in most of Great Britain). In a following step the researcher attempted to draw an *isogloss* separating the area with the one code ([ɑr]) from the area with the other ([a]). In fact this would run north–south in New England (see Labov et al. (2006a, Map 11.12) for a larger geographical view). If several linguistic features share their geographical distributions, one might speak of *isogloss bundles*, groups of isoglosses with roughly the same geographical course. But the problems with this rough procedure have long been appreciated. Even in simple cases it might be impossible to draw a single line, and since one can draw tens of thousands of isoglosses, the choice of which to regard as definitive was vexing (Nerbonne, 2009). Areas were normally drawn with sharp borders, even while dialectologists conceded that they often witnessed gradual, unsharp boundaries.

Traditional dialectology often relied on extremely knowledgeable practitioners – both field workers and project managers. They drew dialect maps without resorting to counting the number of differing features or to recording the reactions of dialect speakers. As Bill Kretzschmar (2009) once said of Kurath, the dean of American dialectology in his time "Kurath knew that he wanted to subdivide the survey region, and he only needed to find diagnostic isoglosses to match his perceptions, guided by his long experience."

In the absence of more replicable methods, the authority of researchers such as Kurath were accepted.

Jean Séguy (1971, 1973) initiated the work in *dialectometry*, i.e., the "measure of dialect." He worked on the dialect atlas of Gascony in southwest France, and sought a way to avoid choosing the basis for his dialect characterizations and his dialect maps in an arbitrary way. His solution was simple: he examined the differences per item between the data collection sites, counting different items as contributing one to a difference and identical ones as contributing zero. He derived from this an aggregate difference, which in fact is a distance: zero for identical sites, symmetrical, and conforming to the triangle inequality. Séguy published only the two papers cited on his ideas before he met an unexpected death in an automobile accident.

Hans Goebl (1982) was in correspondence with Séguy and adopted his ideas enthusiastically even while elaborating a great deal on them. Goebl examined each point (data collection site) and the distribution of distances (actually, Goebl always preferred to analyze similarities, i.e., inverse distances) to all the other sites, e.g., in an effort to characterize transitional zones.

Although Goebl emphasizes the care that he has always taken in collecting and codifying data (a step he refers to as "taxation"), a clear disadvantage in his work from a computational point of view is that care *must* be taken. Only categorical data are analyzed by the later step in Goebl's procedures. This is perhaps okay as the basis to analyze lexical differences, since lexemes are either the same at two sites or different.[2] Pronunciation (a sound shift) or even syntax might have been part of the data collection in early dialectometry, but then manual procedures were used to extract the categorical differences that are then subject to further analysis. There are enormous opportunities for computational linguistic work in extracting the interesting differences automatically.

Perhaps Goebl's most lasting contribution to dialectometry was the introduction of *clustering* as a means of detecting dialect areas. The number of features that two varieties share may be regarded as the inverse of a distance, as we just noted, and that distance gives rise to a half matrix of distances when the entire set of data collection sites is analyzed. Goebl noted further that dialect areas are often hierarchically organized – e.g., Badisch, Swabian and Bavarian are all southern German dialects, meaning that they share features that distinguish them from the northern varieties. This made *hierarchical clustering* the method of choice (as opposed to *k-means*, for example, which simply partitions the input without attention to potential further internal structure), and Goebl was the first to champion this. When a half matrix of aggregate differences (or, conversely,

---

[2] But this identity can be difficult to ascertain. See Heeringa and Nerbonne (2006) for an example of a set of five word forms that is difficult to partition into lexeme subsets.

similarities, which Goebl always preferred to work with) were clustered – with no reference to their locations, the results normally projected nicely to convex geographical regions. This was in itself a confirmation of the approach. Goebl's work on clustering pushed the discussion concerning the determination of dialect boundaries to a new, more replicable level.

Clustering algorithms are, however, notoriously unstable: small differences in the input can be magnified to quite large differences in results. For this reason further work has been conducted to develop more stable versions. One technique, the *bootstrap* (and note that the term we took from biological work is used differently from computational linguistics), re-clusters several times (typically 100 or 1000) using random subsets of the original data, e.g., the distances among a subset of the entire set of words. Alternatively, one may recluster using variable small amounts of noise. These procedures indeed solve the stability problem when parameters are chosen judiciously (Nerbonne et al., 2008). A further problem arises in the choice of algorithm. Further computational linguistic work has examined several of the various hierarchical algorithms, concluding that those where distances between non-atomic clusters were determined using nearest neighbor regimens or schemes using the (weighted) means of distances between cluster elements (WPGMA amd UPGMA) yield acceptable results, while centroid-based elements and complete-link (aka "farthest neighbor") did not. Evaluation using standard measures of cluster quality, such as the modified Rand index, cophenetic correlation coefficient, entropy, and purity (Prokić and Nerbonne, 2008) as well as a comparison to the more stable multi-dimensional scaling procedure (MDS, see later).

As computational linguists are well aware, the interest in clustering and in developing novel algorithms and techniques is large and is not likely to diminish, given the impossibility of designing perfect clustering algorithms (Kleinberg, 2004).

5.4   Edit Distance on Phonetic Transcriptions

In the past three decades, the computational analysis of dialects has been performed at various linguistic levels, including phonetics, morphology, lexicology and syntax, with pronunciation differences being the most studied. In this section we discuss *edit distance* – a very simple, yet efficient way commonly used in dialectometry to infer pronunciation differences between language varieties. It has successfully been applied to many languages in aggregate analysis of dialect varieties: Dutch (Nerbonne et al., 1996; Heeringa, 2004; Wieling et al., 2007), Sardinian (Bolognesi and Heeringa, 2002), Norwegian (Gooskens and Heeringa, 2004), German (Nerbonne and Siedle, 2005), American English (Nerbonne, 2015b), and Bulgarian (Osenova et al., 2009).

Edit distance, also known as *Levenshtein distance* (Levenshtein, 1965), is a measure of how distant (or dissimilar) two strings are by computing the minimal number of substitutions, insertions, and deletions needed to transform one string into the other. At the same time, it can be used to align two strings. For example, given two pronunciations of the Dutch word *hart* – [hɑrt] and [ærtə] – the algorithm produces the following alignment:

$$
\begin{array}{cccc}
\text{h} & \text{ɑ} & \text{r} & \text{t} \\
& \text{æ} & \text{r} & \text{t} & \text{ə} \\
\hline
1 & 1 & & & 1
\end{array}
$$

In order to transform [hɑrt] into [ærtə] 3 edit operations are needed: the [h] has to be deleted, the [ɑ] replaced by [æ], and [ə] has to be inserted. If all operations are assigned cost 1, the total distance between these two strings is 3.

Kessler (1995) introduced the use of edit distance in dialectometry by successfully utilizing it to compare phonetic transcriptions of Gaelic Irish and compute linguistic distance between each pair of sites under investigation. In his approach, the strings are compared by simply counting the number of mismatching segments in phonetic transcriptions, i.e., assigning all operations the cost of 1 as in the example. This simple technique is called *phone string comparison*, and two segments are always counted either as the same or as different, never as partially similar or similar to a certain degree. For example, in this simple approach [e] is considered equally different from [ɛ] and [s]. In a following step, Kessler applied clustering to the calculated distances and automatically obtained dialect boundaries that corresponded fairly well to those in traditional scholarship.

The most comprehensive study of the application of edit distance in dialectometry can be found in Heeringa (2004). In order to take into account the varying dissimilarity between different segments, Heeringa examines feature representations of segments, where each segment is represented as a bundle of phonetic features, but also acoustic segment representations, using canonical spectograms. The results showed that the more discriminating feature and acoustic representations, although linguistically more intuitive, do not lead to better results in the task of dialect classification. When compared to perceptual studies of dialects, the use of binary costs (0/1) (in the phone string comparison) actually outperforms distances obtained using gradual costs of segments.

In his work on automatic sequence alignment and cognate detection, List (2012a) groups sounds into predefined classes in order to reduce the number of phonetic segments and achieve more efficient and accurate string comparison. The concept of sound classes was introduced to historical linguistics by A. B. Dolgopolsky (1986), who grouped sounds into different classes based on observations of sound frequency correspondences. The main idea is that sounds within one sound class correspond more often with each other than with sounds from other sound classes. In List's approach transition probabilities between sound classes are automatically computed from the data and then employed by the alignment algorithm. Sound classes have been successfully applied in a couple of approaches, including phonetic alignment (List, 2012b), and automatic cognate detection (List, 2012a). The method is implemented as a part of the LingPy library, an open-source software package for quantitative historical linguistics (List et al., 2017).

5.4.1   Automatically Induced Segment Distances

Wieling et al. (2009) proposed a data-driven solution to segment comparison in edit distance algorithm. They collect the frequencies of the segments aligned by the phone string comparison in a large contingency table. They then weighted the edit operation costs using (an inverse of) *pointwise mutual information* (PMI) with edit distance algorithm in order to let operation costs reflect the likelihood of two segments being involved in a substitution. PMI is an information-theoretic association measure that estimates the amount of information one event tells us about the other. Applied to the phonetic transcriptions of words, PMI can gauge how similar or distant two phones are; the more often they are aligned, the bigger the similarity between them and vice versa. The procedure of calculating the association strength between the phones and improving the alignments at the same time is iterative: (a) all word transcriptions are initially aligned using the binary (0/1) Levenshtein algorithm; (b) from the obtained alignments, for all pairs of phone segments PMI association values are calculated; (c) all word transcriptions are aligned once more using Levenshstein algorithm, but based on the phone distances generated in the previous step; and (d) steps b and c are repeated until there are no further changes in phone distances and alignments.

Wieling et al. (2009) showed that Levenshtein PMI produces more correct alignments when compared to the simple Levenshtein algorithm and to two slightly modified versions of this algorithm. Wieling et al. (2012) found that PMI induced segment distances correlate well with acoustic distances in formant space ($0.61 < r < 0.76$) measured on six dialect data sets.

A similar procedure has been used in computational historical linguistics by Gerhard Jäger (2013, 2015) to infer language phylogenies from word lists using PMI-weighted alignments. Naturally, the concept of string similarity in historical linguistics is to be understood as relative to the sound changes that related languages have undergone. This need not be the same as the global similarity that one sometimes perceives among dialects. By discounting the substitution of sounds related by regular sound change, PMI alignments reflect the results of those changes. Jäger (2013) has shown that applied to

5644 word lists taken from the Automated Similarity Judgment Project database (Wichmann et al., 2012), the PMI-weighted alignment improves the accuracy of phylogenetic inference in comparison to plain Levenshtein-based alignments by 1 to 3 percent, depending on the evaluation method used. Applied to a collection of approximately 1000 Eurasian languages and dialects, PMI-weighted alignments, combined with phylogenetic inference, produced a classification in excellent agreement with established findings of historical linguistics as well as strong statistical support for several putative macrofamilies (Jäger, 2015).

5.4.2   Some Criticisms

Although successful in detecting dialect groups at the aggregate level, edit distance has often been criticized as linguistically naive and too simple. The criticism arises because linguists are interested not only in determining main dialect areas, but also in discovering linguistic details behind those divisions (see Section 5.5). An aggregate approach based on simple edit distance fails to provide such details and thus fails to shed light on the linguistic processes that lead to the observed dialect divisions. In order to overcome the simplicity of the edit distance approach, several advances in dialectometry have been put forward in the past decade. These include a technique to automatically induce a more sensitive measure between individual sound segments in phonetic transcriptions (see Section 5.4.1), and a method that enables researchers to identify characteristic features of dialect areas.

   Another point of criticism of edit distance as applied in dialectometry is that it is based on manually prepared phonetic transcriptions, often extracted from traditional dialect atlases. These manually prepared data are on the one hand expensive to acquire and on the other hand do not represent natural speech but data already selected and transcribed by linguists. Further research in acoustic phonetics but also in articulography promises to overcome the problem of relying too heavily on phonetic transcriptions (see Section 5.6.3).

5.4.3   Distinctive Elements

In order to identify distinctive characteristics of dialect areas, Prokić et al. (2012) suggested a method inspired by Fisher's linear discriminant that seeks features that differ little within the group in question and a great deal outside that group. The method starts from a number of sites already grouped into two or more dialects and examines one candidate group at a time, seeking features that characterize it best in distinction to elements outside the group. It does not assume that the groups were obtained via clustering, only that candidate groups have somehow been identified. This method, in comparison to others proposed earlier (see remarks in Section 5.5 on multidimensional scaling), is general and it can be used with any type of dialect charateristic – word, segment, or syntactic construction – as long as one can define a numerical difference metric between the features. Prokić et al. (2012) tested the method on German and Dutch dialect sets that were first analyzed by means of the Levenshtein algorithm to calculate distances between each pair of sites and Ward's clustering algorithm to detect main dialect areas. The results show that the words identified successfully distinguish the group of dialects in focus from the rest.

Even if we are able to detect which individual variables are most characteristic for a given variety, the scientific challenge of characterizing these remains. We do not suppose that dialect speakers monitor all the thousands of potential variables individually. In keeping with the quantitative spirit of computational dialectology, we focus here on dimension reduction techniques that are used in the attempt to detect commonalities among these variables. We refrain from an explanation of alternative dimension reduction techniques, referring the reader to Tabachnick and Fidell (2012) for detailed information at a practical level.

Shackleton (2010) applies principal component analysis (PCA) to the a site × variable matrix, where his matrix contained not aggregates of differences but rather, variable values.[3] This allowed him to show, e.g., that certain vowel shifts patterned similarly across English dialects and, in particular, that vowel shifts involved several vowels. This is, of course, scientifically more satisfying than simply noting where patters seem to overlap. The commonalities (the PCs) may be regarded as latent variables that are shared across varieties.

Nerbonne (2006) applied factor analysis, a technique similar to PCA, to site × vowel matrices, where the vowels were characterized by vectors of feature values. The results were similar to Shackleton's, but Nerbonne's analysis really succeeded only in showing that some vowel tokens (for example, the reduced vowel in the the English plural morpheme {əz}) behaved in a common fashion, suggesting that a single sound (phoneme) varied from one set of varieties to the next. This might be seen as an indication that the phoneme was playing a role in variation, which is encouraging, but less insightful than linguists would like.

The search for compact and insightful characterizations of dialect differences is essential for the scientific study of dialect and worthy of much more attention.

5.5   Geography of Distributions

Let's return to the research question on the location of dialects, which, as we noted, was answered wisely in traditional dialectology, but in a way that left the justification for the answer often unclear. Séguy's step to examine

---

[3] Labov et al. (2006b) had used PCA on the acoustic values of twenty-one vowels in American English.

large aggregates of dialectal material brought clarity into the basis of dialectal division, which Goebl's clustering elaborated on algorithmically to extract relatively similar groups of collection sites. Subsequent work examined alternative clustering algorithms and various means of making results more reliable (see Section 5.3 above).

From there it was a small step to project those collections of sites onto maps, with the gratifying result that they often projected to (nearly) coherent dialect regions, which, moreover, normally differed little from those that experts had outlined earlier. There was a difference, naturally, in the explicitness of the methods, and in the efficiency with which analyses could be conducted.

An alternative to clustering arose when Embleton (1993) suggested the use of *multi-dimensional scaling* (MDS) as a means of analyzing the site × site matrix of dialect distances (in fact, since distances are symmetric, half matrices suffice). MDS (Kruskal and Wish, 1978) was originally developed for psychometric applications, and it inputs a half matrix of distances and outputs coordinates of the sites in a low-dimensional space from which the original distances can be derived (approximately). The number of dimensions need not be specified in advance, and existing software normally produces solutions in one, two, and more dimensions. The quality of the solution is specified via a loss function known as *strain*, or alternatively, as the correlation coefficient of the scaled distances with those in the input. As might be expected, strain falls as the correlation rises.

Nerbonne et al. (1999) took advantage of the fact that three-dimensional solutions accounted for 80–90 percent of the variance in the dialect material they studied, in order to take the the further step of interpreting coordinates chromatically, mapping the three coordinates to red, green and blue (RGB). Each site was then colored using each color to the degree of its coordinate in the three-dimensional MDS solution. Figure 5.1 shows the results of applying MDS to the results of an analysis of Dutch pronunciations (see Heeringa (2004) for details on the data set).

With respect to our second research question, how are varieties geographically distributed, the MDS analysis is noteworthy for two reasons. First, unlike cluster analysis, MDS does not assume that varieties are aligned with discrete sets of data collection sites that then project to convex (and exhaustive) dialect areas. Instead, *dialect continua* can likewise be detected. Leinonen (2010) analyzes Swedish varieties as a continuum, where areas play no role. Second, when we examine the MDS coordinates of data collection sites, these are distributed continuously, not categorically, so that "borders" between areas of relative concentration are typically gradual. MDS analyses thus do away with dialect maps showing areas, which often unfortunately suggest that a traveller might move from one dialect area to another in a single step. In general this is found congenial among dialectologists.

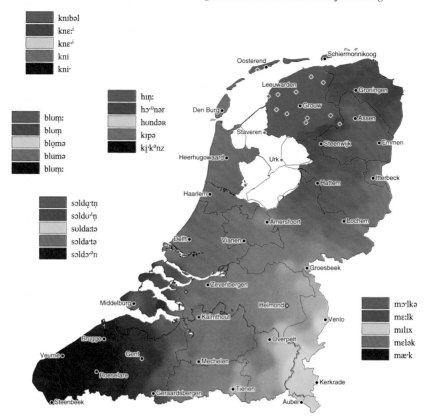

knıbəl
knɛːⁱ
knɛˑⁱ
kni
kniˑ

blʊm̩ː
blʊm̩
blǫmə
blumə
blʊm̩ː

hɪm̩ː
hɔˑⁿnər
hʊndəʀ
kɪpə
kįˑkᵊnz

sɔldɑˑtn̩
sɔldʊˑⁱn̩
sʊldaːtə
sɔldaˑtə
sɔldɔˑᵊn

mɔˑlkə
mɛːlk
mɪlɪx
mɛlək
mæˑk

Figure 5.1 Heeringa (2004) first compared the pronunciations of 125 words at each pair of 360 sites, aggregated the site × site differences, and analyzed those results via MDS. The first three MDS dimensions were then interpreted chromatically (see text). The legends (added later) indicate the pronunciations of some indicative words at sites with the given color.

It is important to attempt to interpret the MDS dimensions. Naturally, the maps described constitute one dimension of interpretation, the geographic one, but linguists are likewise passionately interested in the linguistic basis of the differences. The legends in Figure 5.1 were obtained by examining which words correlate most strongly with each MDS dimension, yielding indications of the linguistic basis. But words – taken as sequences of sounds (phonemes) – are rougher indications than most linguists want. In the analysis behind Figure 5.1 entire word pronunciations served as the input to the (edit distance) analysis, so finer indications are not possible.

Pickl (2013) suggests using *factor analysis* (FA) rather than MDS (see Tabachnick and Fidell (2012) for detailed information at a practical level on the different dimension-reducing techniques), and distinguishes twenty factors, whose geographic projections he also examines. Most of these are nearly negligible ($\leq$ 1 percent) in explained variance, but the attempt to go beyond the usual aggregate analysis in dialectometry should not be the last. See Nerbonne (2015a) for more discussion of Pickl's work.

5.5.1   Geostatistics and Topography

Jack Grieve has pioneered the effort to include a geostatistical perspective on dialect distributions (Grieve et al., 2011; Grieve, 2018). *Geostatistics* is a well-developed field motivated not only by geography proper, but also by the many other fields where geography plays an important role, e.g. epidemiology, geology, ecology and environmental protection. It has studied various sorts of geographic sampling regimes as well as interpolations, and it is perhaps surprising that dialectology was pursued for so long without attending to this major potential source of further insight. Grieve's work is therefore important for bridging the gap.

Burridge (2017) is intrigued by the parallelism between dialect distributions on the one hand and borders induced by *surface tension* on the other. Burridge shows, e.g., how border (coastal) features such as estuaries tend to engender perpendicular boundaries due to the relative likelihood of social contact (and thus dialectal experience) on the one side of the boundary as opposed to the other. He thus derives predictions about dialect boundaries from physical properties of the space where they are spoken. In more elaborate models the influence of population centers is also studied.

5.5.2   Other Relations

By providing numeric measures of the overall differences between varieties, dialectometry has stimulated various studies on the relations between language variety and other communal properties of human beings.

Manni et al. (2006) investigate whether there is link between genetics and language variation. The authors naturally do not suppose that language users inherit linguistic tendencies genetically, but were interested instead in the question of whether dialects might not persist in families due to the predominance of language learning in the family. It turned out that language variation and genetic make-up – both measured at the level of the municipality – correlated moderately ($r = 0.42$), but that the relationship disappeared when one controlled for the effect of geography, with which both correlate independently. See Manni et al. for further references on this topic.

Falck et al. (2012) investigate the potential influence of dialect (or perhaps cultural identification) on mobility. Their study focuses on mobility, where it was known that people tend to move to places close by – presumably to remain near friends, family, and well-known surroundings. After controlling for this factor, the authors were able to show that, when people move house, they also tend to remain within their dialect area, where the patterns of speech were also familiar.

Given the numeric turn throughout the humanities and social sciences, many further relations could be promising foci of investigation.

5.6   Validation

Computational linguistics has emphasized the need to validate putative means of measuring linguistic features and linguistic differences, so it is perhaps not surprising that early work by computational linguists was the first dialectological work to seek validation for its efforts (Heeringa et al., 2002). As it was early on in computational dialectology, Heeringa et al. (2002) measured the degree to which their clustering results jibed with earlier scholarship in the well-studied case of Dutch dialectology.

Wieling et al. (2009) evaluated several versions of edit distance on the basis of their ability to align phonetic transcriptions (as well as human experts). This is a sensitive task that allowed authors to tease apart the performance of rather similar approaches.

5.6.1   *Human Judgments of Similarity*

As we noted, clustering can be unstable, making it a poor partner in validation efforts. And while comparing one's results to earlier scholarship is indispensable, one does not wish to canonize the earlier work to the degree that computational work can never improve on it. Gooskens and Heeringa (2004) meet both of these objections by comparing edit distance measures of pronunciation differences to dialect speakers' judgments of how similar dialect speech sounded to their own. It was sensible to ask the naive subjects only how similar the speech samples sound to their *own* speech since they had the most experience with this, and since one assumes that dialects function primarily as emblems of geographic identity. Gooskens and Heeringa (2004) also judiciously chose Norway for their experiment, which recommended itself for Norwegians' very accepting attitudes toward dialectal speech. While dialects and accents are frowned upon in many places, Norwegians normally retain their accents even in public speech. The authors were able to show that the computational measure correlated well with speakers' judgments of dissimilarity ($r = 0.67$).

Wieling et al. (2014b) used the more sensitive PMI-based edit distance to measure the strength of foreign accents in American English in the Speech Accent Archive hosted at George Mason University (Weinberger and Kunath, 2011). Although the degree of difference in foreign accents is perhaps not perceived in exactly the same way as the degree of difference in dialect pronunciations, it is likely to be comparable. The subjects in Wieling et al.'s experiment were predominantly linguistically informed listeners, as they had responded to an appeal in the Language Log (http://languagelog.ldc.upenn.edu) to participate as subjects. So these subjects were more discriminating than the untrained participants in Gooskens and Heeringa's (2004) work. Wieling et al. applied a logarithmic transformation to the PMI edit distance in keeping with psychometric custom and obtained a high correlation ($r = 0.81$), which was nearly as high as human performance, measured through the average correlation of individual raters' judgments ($r = 0.84$).

5.6.2   Acoustic Characterizations

A great deal of the work reported on thus far in this chapter involved the automatic analysis of phonetic transcriptions recorded in large dialect atlas projects. In many cases this is the only option available, as sensitive acoustic recordings of the material were simply never made. Tape recorders were unwieldy until the second half of the twentieth century and were for that reason not used on the extensive field trips necessary for data collection.

But many dialectologists are skeptical about the reliance on phonetic transcription, which can vary from transcriber to transcriber. For this reason, but also in order to pursue the computational lines sketched here, it has been important to follow up the transcription-based work with work that does not rely on transcription. Leinonen (2010) therefore applied dialectometric techniques to the SweDia database of dialect recordings (Eriksson, 2004a,b). She first extracted the formants of all the twenty Swedish vowels of the more than thousand speakers using the mean of those formant distances as measures of pronunciation distance. The results were most satisfying, both in confirming the Swedish dialect continuum as well as in demonstrating how dialects have been losing distinctions between speakers forty years apart in age (Leinonen, 2010, figure 7.8, p. 140).

It would clearly be desirable to experiment with more acoustic analyses, but the proper acoustic analysis of consonants is still very difficult (Thomas, 2018).

5.6.3   Articulography

Instead of proceeding from transcriptions (see Section 5.4), or an acoustic characterization of dialects (see Section 5.6.2), a new direction of research in dialectology is focusing on the underlying movements of the tongue and lips.

While the articulation obviously results in the acoustic speech signal, it is not straightforward to infer the precise articulatory trajectories of tongue and lips on the basis of an acoustic analysis. For example, while the first and second formant are frequently assumed to model height and backness of the tongue, this relationship is far from perfect (Rosner and Pickering, 1994; Wieling et al., 2016). Consequently, direct articulatory measurements, such as those that can be made through, e.g., electropalatography, ultrasound tongue imaging, and electromagnetic articulography are sometimes used to study dialect or sociolinguistic variation.

Electropalatography uses a custom-made artificial palate with electrodes, which is able to detect when and where the tongue touches the palate during speech. The drawback of this approach is that each participant requires their own custom-made artificial palate, therefore making this type of research relatively slow and expensive. In addition the position of the tongue when it is not touching the palate is unknown. Ultrasound tongue imaging, by contrast, uses an ultrasound probe positioned below the chin by which a series of images over time are obtained visualizing the shape of the tongue surface. While it is relatively easy to collect data using this approach, the analysis is more complex as image analysis is necessary to process the resulting (grainy) images. Electromagnetic articulography, as a third technique, tracks the movement over time of small sensors attached to the tongue and lips. The advantage of this approach compared to ultrasound tongue imaging is that the analysis is more straightforward (i.e., the positional information is available for each sensor over time), but the disadvantage is that it is more invasive and labor intensive to collect these types of data.

Although these articulatory studies require more effort than simply recording the acoustic signal, there have been some studies mostly including only a limited number of speakers investigating dialect or sociolinguistic varia-tion. For example, Recasens and Espinosa (2007) studied articulatory differ-ences using electropalatography between two Catalan dialects in a sample of ten speakers and found clear articulatory differences regarding the fricatives. Lawson et al. (2011) used ultrasound tongue imaging in a sample of fifteen speakers to show that the /r/ pronunciation in Scottish English was socially stratified. Middle-class speakers generally using bunched articulations, while working-class speakers more frequently used tongue-tip raised variants. More recently, Wieling et al. (2016) used electromagnetic articulography in a sample of forty speakers to show that across the pronunciation of about 100 words, speakers from a dialect in the north of the Netherlands had a more posterior tongue position than those from a more southern dialect.

Particularly, the study of Wieling et al. (2016) continues themes from dialectometry. First by providing aggregate results over a large set of words, rather than focusing on individual sound contrasts. But also due to using a very large data set (due to collecting data over time at a high sampling rate, usually more than 100 Hz) and by using replicable analysis techniques that have also been employed in dialectometry. For example, Wieling et al. (2016) use a non-linear regression technique, generalized additive modeling, which has been employed in dialectometry to model the non-linear geographical patterns of dialect variation (Wieling et al., 2011, 2014a).

5.7   Emerging Opportunities and Issues

We have tried to indicate emerging opportunities and issues in this chapter as we proceeded, but we shall summarize them here and also suggest other areas that we have not treated in depth.

First, we have concentrated on the areas of dialectology that have attracted the most attention from computational linguists. We have therefore said little about morphology and syntax, even though these have attracted some work (Heeringa and Prokić, 2018) and could definitely profit from more.

Second, although we described Séguy's and Goebl's efforts at handling linguistic data at a categorical level, we have not elaborated on the opportunities for extracting such data (e.g., signals of lexical relationships) at length, even though some have been shown to be promising (Nerbonne and Kleiweg, 2007; Szmrecsanyi, 2008) and deserve further attention.

Third, the role of linguistic frequency in detecting affinities is worth more attention. Goebl (1982) has long championed an inverse frequency weighting, regarding similar (or identical) linguistic items that occur infrequently as especially strong evidence of dialect affinity – just as historical linguists also tend to emphasize the significance of unusual shared innovations, albeit in a non-quantitative fashion. Others recommend discounting infrequent linguistic items entirely, regarding them as potential "noise" (Carver, 1987). Nerbonne and Kleiweg (2007) provide evidence for Goebl's position, and Wieling and Montemagni (2015) show that removing infrequent data from analyses worsens their quality, but much too little work has been devoted to this question.

Fourth, the excellent initiatives of Grieve and Burridge presented in Section 5.5.1 clearly deserve further attention. In particular, Burridge promises an explanation of why dialect divisions have the geographic contours they do. It would be interesting to know how much dialect variation can be explained along these lines.

Fifth, as we hinted in Section 5.2, geographic variation is part of a palette of variation types. In spite of some efforts to apply dialectometric techniques to the sociolinguistic question of dialect change (Nerbonne et al., 2013; Valls et al., 2013), there has been little resonance. While this may be related to sociolinguists' focus on individual changes in progress, some work has been at pains to indicate how the aggregate perspective may enrich the usual sociolinguistic one (Wieling et al., 2018). We suspect that computational efforts will likely be fruitful in the study of diastratic variation as well.

Sixth, but most interesting to linguists, would be improvements in the linguistic characterization of the dialect differences that dialectometry so reliably unearths. To what extent can these be subsumed under general characterizations of the sort favored in dialect handbooks? Are there perhaps machine learning techniques that might be brought to bear?

5.8   Conclusions

After identifying the essential research questions in dialectology – namely what's varying and where – this article reviewed computational work to date in dialectology, indicating where progress has been made vis-à-vis those questions. Measures of linguistic proximity have served as the basis for dialectolometry, where notably one was derived from computer science – namely edit distance. Dialectometry has added a number of tools for the investigation of the geographic distribution of linguistic variation, in particular, clustering and multidimensional scaling, and more advanced work is probing geostatistics as well as models inspired by the mathematics of surface tension. Dialectometry has played an important role in enabling studies of the relations between language variation and both genetics and mobility.

We also reviewed efforts at characterizing the linguistic differences among varieties. Computational work has certainly provided means of cataloging such differences exhaustively, and in identifying characteristic elements. We would prefer to have ways of characterizing the differences more insightfully and more concisely, however, and the success in this direction has been modest. We also reviewed efforts at validating the more popular computational measures, a consideration that was certainly inspired by work in computational linguistics. This section closed with remarks on how textually focused work is now branching into the acoustics and the articulation of dialect speech, a further potentially important sort of validation.

We closed with a list of six issues where further progress would be valuable, and where prospects seem promising.

References

Bailey, Guy. 2018. Field interviews in dialectology. Pages 284–299 of: Boberg, Charles, Nerbonne, John, and Watt, Dominic (eds.), *The Handbook of Dialectology*. Hoboken, NJ: Wiley-Blackwell.

Barbiers, Sjef. 2009. Locus and limits of syntactic microvariation. *Lingua*, **119**(11), 1607–1623.

Bolognesi, Roberto, and Heeringa, Wilbert. 2002. De invloed van dominante talen op het lexicon en de fonologie van Sardische dialecten. Pages 45–84 of: Bakker,

Dik, Sanders, Ted, Schoonen, Rob, and van der Wijst, Per (eds.), *Gramma/TTT: Tijdschrift voor taalwetenschap*. Nijmegen: Nijmegen University Press.

Burridge, James. 2017. Spatial evolution of human dialects. *Physical Review X*, **7**(3), 031008.

Carver, Craig M. 1987. *American Regional Dialects: A Word Geography*. Ann Arbor: University of Michigan Press.

Chambers, J. K. 2018. Written dialect surveys. Pages 268–283 of: Boberg, Charles, Nerbonne, John, and Watt, Dominic (eds.), *The Handbook of Dialectology*. Hoboken, NJ: Wiley-Blackwell.

Dolgopolsky, A. B. 1986. A probabilistic hypothesis concerning the oldest relationships among the language families of northern Eurasia. Pages 27–50 of: Shevoroshkin, Vitalij V. (ed.), *Typology, Relationship and Time*. Ann Arbor: Karoma Publisher.

Elspaß, Stephan, and König, Werner (eds.), 2008. *Sprachgeographie digital. Die neue Generation der Sprachatlanten*. Berlin: Walter de Gruyter GmbH & Co. KG.

Embleton, Sheila. 1993. Multidimensional scaling as a dialectometrical technique: Outline of a research project. Pages 267–276 of: Köhler, Reinhard, and Rieger, Burghard (eds.), *Contributions to Quantitative Linguistics*. Dordrecht: Kluwer.

Eriksson, Anders. 2004a. *SweDia 2000: A Swedish Dialect Database*. Department of Linguistics/Institutionen för lingvistik.

Eriksson, Anders. 2004b. SweDia-projektet: dialektforskning i ett jämförande perspektiv. *Folkmålsstudier*, **43**, 11–32.

Falck, Oliver, Heblich, Stephan, Lameli, Alfred, and Südekum, Jens. 2012. Dialects, cultural identity, and economic exchange. *Journal of Urban Economics*, **72**(2-3), 225–239.

Goebl, Hans. 1982. *Dialektometrie: Prinzipien und Methoden des Einsatzes der numerischen Taxonomie im Bereich der Dialektgeographie*. Wien: Österreichische Akademie der Wissenschaften.

Goldman, Jean-Philippe, Leemann, Adrian, Kolly, Marie-José, Hove, Ingrid, Almajai, Ibrahim, Dellwo, Volker, and Moran, Steven. 2014. A crowd-sourcing smartphone application for Swiss German: Putting language documentation in the hands of the users. Pages 3444–3447 of: Calzolari, Nicoletta et al. (ed.), *Proceedings of the Ninth International Conference on Language Resources and Evaluation (LREC'14)*. Reykjavik, Iceland: European Language Resources Association (ELRA).

Gooskens, Charlotte, and Heeringa, Wilbert. 2004. Perceptive evaluation of Levenshtein dialect distance measurements using Norwegian dialect data. *Language Variation and Change*, **16**(3), 189–207.

Grieve, Jack. 2018. Spatial statistics for dialectology. Pages 415–434 of: Boberg, Charles, Nerbonne, John, and Watt, Dominic (eds.), *The Handbook of Dialectology*. Hoboken, NJ: John Wiley & Sons.

Grieve, Jack, Speelman, Dirk, and Geeraerts, Dirk. 2011. A statistical method for the identification and aggregation of regional linguistic variation. *Language Variation and Change*, **23**(2), 193–221.

Heeringa, Wilbert. 2004. Measuring Dialect Pronunciation Differences Using Levenshtein Distance. PhD thesis, University of Groningen, Groningen.

Heeringa, Wilbert, and Nerbonne, John. 2006. De analyse van taalvariatie in het Nederlandse dialectgebied: Methoden en resultaten op basis van lexicon en uitspraak. *Nederlandse Taalkunde*, **11**(3), 218–251.

Heeringa, Wilbert, and Prokić, Jelena. 2018. Computational dialectology. Pages 330–347 of: Boberg, Charles, Nerbonne, John, and Watts, Dominic (eds.), *The Handbook of Dialectology*. Hoboken, NJ: Wiley-Blackwell.

Heeringa, Wilbert, Nerbonne, John, and Kleiweg, Peter. 2002. Validating dialect comparison methods. Pages 445–452 of: Gaul, Wolgang, and Ritter, Gerd (eds.), *Classification, automation, and new media. Proceedings of the 24th conf. of the Gesellschaft für Klassifikation*. Heidelberg: Springer.

Hinskens, Frans. 2018. Dialectology and formal linguistic theory: The blind man and the lame. Pages 88–105 of: Boberg, Charles, Nerbonne, John, and Watt, Dominic (eds.), *The Handbook of Dialectology*. Hoboken, NJ: Wiley-Blackwell.

Jäger, Gerhard. 2013. Phylogenetic inference from word lists using weighted alignment with empirical determined weights. *Language Dynamics and Change*, **3**(2), 245–291.

Jäger, Gerhard. 2015. Support for linguistic macrofamilies from weighted alignment. *Proceedings of the National Academy of Sciences of the United States of America*, **112**(41), 12752–12757.

Kessler, Brett. 1995. Computational dialectology in Irish Gaelic. Pages 60–66 of: *Proceedings of the 7th Conference of the European Chapter of the ACL*. San Francisco: Morgan Kaufmann.

Kleinberg, Jon M. 2004. An impossibility theorem for clustering. Pages 463–470 of: Thrun, Sebastian, and Saul, Lawrence K. and Schölkop, Bernhard (eds.), *Advances in Neural Information Processing Systems 16: Proceedings of the 2003 Conference (NIPS 16)*. Cambridge, MA: MIT Press.

Kretzschmar, William A. 2009. *The Linguistics of Speech*. New York: Cambridge University Press.

Kretzschmar Jr, William A, McDavid, Virginia G, Lerud, Theodore K, and Johnson, Ellen. 1993. *Handbook of the Linguistic Atlas of the Middle and South Atlantic States*. Chicago: University of Chicago Press.

Kruskal, Joseph B., and Wish, Myron. 1978. *Multidimensional Scaling*. Newbury Park, London, New Delhi: Sage Publications.

Labov, William, Ash, Sharon, and Boberg, Charles. 2006a. *The Atlas of North American English: Phonetics, Phonology, and Sound Change*. Berlin, New York: Mouton de Gruyter.

Labov, William, Ash, Sharon, and Boberg, Charles. 2006b. *Atlas of North American English: Phonetics Phonology and Sound Change*. Berlin, New York: Mouton de Gruyter.

Lawson, E., Scobbie, J. M., and Stuart-Smith, J. 2011. The social stratification of tongue shape for postvocalic /r/ in Scottish English. *Journal of Sociolinguistics*, **15**(2), 256–268.

Leinonen, Therese N. 2010. An Acoustic Analysis of Vowel Pronunciation in Swedish Dialects. PhD thesis, Rijksuniversiteit Groningen, Groningen.

Levenshtein, V. I. 1965. Dvoičnye kody s ispravleniem vypadenij, vstavok i zameščenij simbolov. *Doklady Akademij Nauk SSSR*, **163**(4), 845–848.

List, Johann-Mattis. 2012a. LexStat: Automatic detection of cognates in multilingual wordlists. Pages 117–125 of: *Proceedings of the EACL 2012 Joint Workshop of LINGVIS & UNCLH*. Shroudburg, PA: Association for Computational Linguistics.

List, Johann-Mattis. 2012b. SCA: Phonetic alignment based on sound classes. Pages 32–51 of: Slavkovik, Marija, and Lassiter, Dan (eds.), *New Directions in Logic, Language, and Computation*. Berlin, Heidelberg: Springer.

List, Johann-Mattis, Greenhill, Simon, and Forkel, Robert. 2017. *LingPy. A Python library for quantitative tasks in historical linguistics*. Software library maintained at https://doi.org/10.5281/zenodo.1065403.

Llamas, Carmen. 2018. The dialect questionnaire. Pages 253–267 of: Boberg, Charles, Nerbonne, John, and Watt, Dominic (eds.), *The Handbook of Dialectology*. Hoboken, NJ: Wiley-Blackwell.

Macauley, Ronald. 2018. Dialect sampling methods. Pages 241–252 of: Boberg, Charles, Nerbonne, John, and Watt, Dominic (eds.), *The Handbook of Dialectology*. Hoboken, NJ: Wiley-Blackwell.

Manni, Franz, Heeringa, Wilbert, and Nerbonne, John. 2006. To what extent are surnames words? Comparing geographic patterns of surnames and dialect variation in the Netherlands. *Literary and Linguistic Computing*, 21(4), 507–528.

Möller, Robert, and Elspaß, Stephan. 2008. Erhebung dialektgeographischer Daten per Internet: ein Atlasprojekt zur deutschen Alltagssprache. Pages 115–132 of: Elspaß, Stephan, and König, Werner (eds.), *Sprachgeographie digital. Die neue Generation der Sprachatlanten (mit 80 Karten)*. Hildesheim, Zürich, New York: Olms.

Nerbonne, John. 2006. Identifying linguistic structure in aggregate comparison. *Literary and Linguistic Computing*, 21(4), 463–475.

Nerbonne, John. 2009. Data-driven dialectology. *Language and Linguistics Compass*, 3(1), 175–198.

Nerbonne, John. 2015a. Simon Pickl. 2013. Probabilistische Geolinguistik. Geostatistische Analysen lexikalischer Variation in Bayerisch-Schwaben. *Zeitschrift für Rezensionen zur germanistischen Sprachwissenschaft*, 7(1-2), 124–129.

Nerbonne, John. 2015b. Various variation aggregates in the LAMSAS south. Pages 369–382 of: Picone, Michael, and Davis, Catherine (eds.), *New Perspectives on Language Variety in the South: Historical and Contemporary Approaches. (LAVIS III)*. Tuscaloosa: University of Alabama Press.

Nerbonne, John. 2018. Vaulting ambition. Pages 445–468 of: Fuß, Eric Konopka, Marek, Trawiński, Beata, and Waßner, Ulrich H. *Grammar and corpora*. Heidelberg: Heidelberg University Publishing.

Nerbonne, John, Heeringa, Wilbert, and Kleiweg, Peter. 1999. Edit distance and dialect proximity. Pages v–xv of: Sankoff, David, and Kruskal, Joseph (eds.), *Time Warps, String Edits and Macromolecules: The Theory and Practice of Sequence Comparison*. Stanford, CA: CSLI Press.

Nerbonne, John, Heeringa, Wilbert, van den Hout, Eric, van de Kooi, Peter, Otten, Simone, and van de Vis, Willem. 1996. Phonetic distances between Dutch dialects. Pages 185–202 of: Durieux, Gert, Daelemans, Walter, and Gillis, Steven (eds.), *CLIN VI: Proceedings of the Sixth CLIN Meeting*. Antwerp: Centre for Dutch Language and Speech (UIA).

Nerbonne, John, and Kleiweg, Peter. 2007. Toward a Dialectological Yardstick. *Journal of Quantitative Linguistics*, 14(2), 148–166.

Nerbonne, John, Kleiweg, Peter, Manni, Franz, and Heeringa, Wilbert. 2008. Projecting dialect differences to geography: Bootstrapping clustering vs. clustering with noise. Pages 647–654 of: Preisach, Christine, Schmidt-Thieme, Lars, Burkhardt, Hans,

and Decker, Reinhold (eds.), *Data Analysis, Machine Learning, and Applications.*
31st Annual Meeting of the German Classification Society. Berlin: Springer.

Nerbonne, John, and Siedle, Christine. 2005. Dialektklassifikation auf der Grundlage
aggregierter Ausspracheunterschiede. *Zeitschrift für Dialektologie und Linguistik,*
72(2), 129–147.

Nerbonne, John, van Ommen, Sandrien, Gooskens, Charlotte, and Wieling, Martijn.
2013. Measuring socially motivated pronunciation differences. Pages 107–40 of:
Borin, Lars, and Saxena, Anju (eds.), *Approaches to Measuring Linguistic Differences.* Berlin: De Gruyter.

Ng, Andrew Y, and Jordan, Michael I. 2002. On discriminative vs. generative classifiers:
A comparison of logistic regression and naive Bayes. Pages 841–848 of: Becker,
Susanna, Thrun Sebastian, and Obermayer, Klaus (eds.), *Advances in Neural
Information Processing Systems: Proceedings of the 2002 Conference (Vol. 15),*
vol. 14. Cambridge, MA: MIT Press.

Osenova, Petya, Heeringa, Wilbert, and Nerbonne, John. 2009. A quantitative analysis
of Bulgarian dialect pronunciation. *Zeitschrift für Slavische Philologie,* **66**(2),
425–458.

Pickl, Simon. 2013. *Probabilistische Geolinguistik: Geostatistische Analysen lexikalischer Variation in Bayerisch-Schwaben.* Stuttgart: Steiner.

Prokić, Jelena, Çöltekin, Çağri, and Nerbonne, John. 2012. Detecting shibboleths. Pages
72–80 of: *Proceedings of the EACL 2012 Joint Workshop of LINGVIS & UNCLH.*
Shroudsburg, PA: Association for Computational Linguistics.

Prokić, Jelena, and Nerbonne, John. 2008. Recognizing groups among dialects. *International Journal of Humanities and Arts Computing,* **2**, 153–171.

Recasens, Daniel, and Espinosa, Aina. 2007. An electropalatographic and acoustic study
of affricates and fricatives in two Catalan dialects. *Journal of the International
Phonetic Association,* **37**(2), 143–172.

Rosner, Burton S, and Pickering, John B. 1994. *Vowel Perception and Production.*
Oxford University Press.

Scherrer, Yves, Leemann, Adrian, Kolly, Marie-José, and Werlen, Iwar. 2012. *Dialäkt
Äpp – A smartphone application for Swiss German dialects with great scientific
potential.* Lecture at 7th Congress of the International Society for Dialectology
and Geolinguistics (SIDG Congress-Dialect 2.0). Available at https://archive-
ouverte.unige.ch/unige:22817.

Shackleton, Robert. 2010. Quantitative assessment of English-American speech relationships. PhD thesis, Rijksuniversiteit of Groningen.

Szmrecsanyi, Benedikt. 2008. Corpus-based dialectometry: Aggregate morphosyntactic
variability in British English dialects. *International Journal of Humanities and Arts
Computing,* **2**(12), 279–296.

Tabachnick, Barbara G, and Fidell, Linda S. 2012. *Using Multivariate Statistics.*
Boston/Munich: Pearson.

Thomas, Erik R. 2018. Acoustic phonetic dialectlogy. Pages 314–329 of: Boberg,
Charles, Nerbonne, John, and Watt, Dominic (eds.), *The Handbook of Dialectology.*
Hoboken, NJ: Wiley-Blackwell.

Valls, Esteve, Wieling, Martijn, and Nerbonne, John. 2013. Linguistic advergence and
divergence in north-western Catalan: A dialectometric investigation of dialect
leveling and border effects. *Literary and Linguistic Computing,* **28**(1), 119–146.

Van den Berg, Boudewijn L. 2003. Phonology & morphology of Dutch & Frisian dialects in 1.1 million transcriptions, Goeman-Taeldeman-Van Reenen project 1980–1995, Meertens Instituut Electronic Publications in Linguistics 3. Meertens Instituut (CD-ROM), Amsterdam.

Weinberger, Steven H, and Kunath, Stephen A. 2011. The speech accent archive: Towards a typology of English accents. *Language and Computers*, **73**(1), 265–281.

Wichmann, Søren, Müller, André, Velupillai, Viveka, Wett, Annkathrin, Brown, Cecil H., Molochieva, Zarina, Bishoffberger, Julia, Holman, Eric W., Sauppe, Sebastian, Brown, Pamela, Bakker, Dik, List, Johann-Mattis, Egorov, Dmitry, Belyaev, Oleg, Urban, Matthias, Hammarström, Harald, Carrizo, Agustina, Mailhammer, Robert, Geyer, Helen, Beck, David, Korovina, Evgenia, Epps, Pattie, Valenzuela, Pilar, and Grant, Anthony. 2012. *The ASJP Database*. Accessible at https://asjp.clld.org/.

Wieling, Martijn, Bloem, Jelke, Mignella, Kaitlin, Timmermeister, Mona, and Nerbonne, John. 2014b. Measuring foreign accent strength in English. Validating Levenshtein distance as a measure. *Language Dynamics and Change*, **4**(2), 253–269.

Wieling, Martijn, Heeringa, Wilbert, and Nerbonne, John. 2007. An aggregate analysis of pronunciation in the Goeman-Taeldeman-van Reenen-Project data. *Taal en Tongval*, **59**(1), 84–116.

Wieling, Martijn, Margaretha, Eliza, and Nerbonne, John. 2012. Inducing a measure of phonetic similarity from pronunciation variation. *Journal of Phonetics*, **40**(2), 307–314.

Wieling, Martijn, and Montemagni, Simonetta. 2015. Infrequent forms: Noise or not? Pages 215–224 of: Côté, Marie-Héléen, Knooihuizen, Remco, and Nerbonne, John (eds.), *The Future of Dialects*. Berlin: Language Science Press.

Wieling, Martijn, Montemagni, Simonetta, Nerbonne, John, and Baayen, R. Harald. 2014a. Lexical differences between Tuscan dialects and standard Italian: Accounting for geographic and sociodemographic variation using generalized additive mixed modeling. *Language*, **90**(3), 669–692.

Wieling, Martijn, and Nerbonne, John. 2015. Advances in dialectometry. *Annual Review of Linguistics*, **1**, 243–264.

Wieling, Martijn, Nerbonne, John, and Baayen, R. Harald. 2011. Quantitative social dialectology: Explaining linguistic variation geographically and socially. *PLoS ONE*, **6**(9), e23613.

Wieling, Martijn, Prokić, Jelena, and Nerbonne, John. 2009. Evaluating the pairwise string alignment of pronunciations. Pages 26–34 of: *Proceedings of the EACL 2009 Workshop on Language Technology and Resources for Cultural Heritage, Social Sciences, Humanities, and Education (LaTeCH – SHELT&R 2009)*. Shroudsburg, PA: Association for Computational Linguistics.

Wieling, Martijn, Tomaschek, Fabian, Arnold, Denis, Tiede, Mark, Bröker, Franziska, Thiele, Samuel, Wood, Simon N, and Baayen, R Harald. 2016. Investigating dialectal differences using articulography. *Journal of Phonetics*, **59**, 122–143.

Wieling, Martijn, Valls, Esteve, Baayen, R Harald, and Nerbonne, John. 2018. Border effects among Catalan dialects. Pages 71–97 of: Speelman, Dirk, Heylen, Kris, and Geeraerts, Dirk (eds.), *Mixed-Effects Regression Models in Linguistics*. Berlin: Springer.

Part II

Methods and Resources

6   Data Collection and Representation for Similar Languages, Varieties and Dialects

Tanja Samardžić and Nikola Ljubešić

Collections of digital text intended for research – known as *language corpora* – have been used as linguistic data since the pioneering work on the Brown corpus by Francis and Kučera (1967). These data sources can be used for both training natural language processing (NLP) models and linguistic inquiry. Initially compiled for the purpose of the study of language, corpora were not widely used until the early 1990s, when statistical modelling prevailed over rule-based approaches to NLP. Since then, corpora represent fundamental source of training data data for various tasks (Norvig, 2009), but they are also more commonly used in linguistics.

In this chapter, we focus on the issue of representing regional variation in corpora. This issue has recently gained considerable importance in the NLP community, where it used to be common to think of corpora as representing a single, discrete language. For instance, one talks about a corpus of German or a corpus of Hausa. The assumption behind such labels is that languages are discrete entities. This assumption, however, quickly proves too simplistic. A corpus of German might represent just one of multiple varieties of this language, the one used in Germany, for instance, and not those in Austria or Switzerland. Furthermore, a typical corpus of German will contain standard language, which is, in reality, just one of several varieties used by the speakers even within a single, small region, as discussed in more detail in Chapter 3. Given that the performance of NLP tools is known to drop when they are applied on a text that differs from the training examples (Gildea, 2001), more attention needs to be paid to representing variability. This is especially true in the case of regional variation, which can play an important role in tasks such as named entity recognition.

The issue of representing linguistic variation has been addressed in more linguistically oriented corpus research since its beginning. Early corpora were constructed with the goal of representing different facets of language use, with spoken language and different written registers, e.g., fiction, news, textbooks (Burnard, 2007). The fact that data are much more easily available for some categories (e.g., news) than for others (e.g., spoken language) made the corpora largely imbalanced, leading eventually to abandoning the goal of representing actual use. We are now coming back to the issue of representing variation in the context of the change in language use caused by the democratisation of public communication on the internet. Written texts that we need to process are increasingly locally marked and, to a varied degree, spoken-like. At the same time, new, powerful computing techniques allow a novel approach to modelling this variation for the purpose of contemporary end-user NLP tasks, such as sentiment analysis or author profiling. Spoken language, as the most authentic mode of language use, but also the most difficult to represent, is now back in the focus of research. In this context, a new kind of corpora are being created, aiming to represent regional and non-standard varieties of what used to be thought of as a single language.

This chapter presents several solutions to the challenge of representing regional variation and spoken language in corpora. We show how such corpora developed tracking especially the sources of data that have been and can be used for creating such corpora (recorded conversations, computer-mediated communication, locally marked written production). We also describe the best adapted methods used to turn these data sources into properly encoded corpora suitable for NLP and also linguistic research. We show how processing techniques depend on the properties of the chosen data source.

6.1   Representing Language Variability in Corpora

Early work on compiling language corpora aimed at simulating ordinary language exposure by representing functional variation. The famous Brown corpus mentioned above contains 500 samples of different written genres. The British National Corpus, another highly influential resource (Burnard, 2007), includes various written genres too, but also a portion (12 per cent) of transcribed spoken language. The issues of corpus design were widely discussed (Atkins et al., 1992) before the practice moved towards collecting large corpora regardless of the genre. The corpus built in the COBUILD project (Sinclair, 1987) was one of the first to go for the size rather than representativeness, which later became common practice, until the present day.

While functional variation has been addressed in relation to corpus collection from the beginning, regional variation, traditionally studied in the field of dialectology, started to be addressed with corpus-based methodology much later and to a smaller degree.

Automatic quantitative language comparison has been associated with the study of regional variation under the term *dialectometry* since the first quantification of linguistic distance proposed by Séguy (1971). This framework for language comparison, which eventually lead to the development of regionally varied corpora, initially relied on structured data collected through questionnaires. Typically a questionnaire contains a fixed set of items (e.g., lexemes,

Table 6.1 *Traditional structured data format for language comparison*

	$word_1$	$word_2$	$word_3$	...	$word_n$
$site_1$					
$site_2$					
$site_3$					
...					
$site_n$					

sounds) known to vary across a given set of varieties. The versions of the variable items, observed at the level of a word, are then recorded in many observation points and stored in a two-dimension matrix illustrated in Table 6.1. These data frames are then mapped to a vector space and used to calculate linguistic distance between observation sites and to cluster the sites with standard clustering algorithms. This line of research, including the work of Séguy (1971), Goebl (1982, 1984), Nerbonne et al. (1995, 1999), is discussed in more detail in Chapter 5. Here we focus on creating and using text corpora for dialectological comparison.

Introduction of corpus (text) data into the study of regional variation is seen as a way to improve quantitative comparison in two ways. First, corpora contain samples of naturally occurring linguistic production and can thus be used to identify and measure the variation beyond pre-defined word-level variables typically recorded with traditional questionnaires. In this way, measurements are extended to the study of variation in syntactic, pragmatic and discourse phenomena. Second, corpora provide an insight in the frequency of use – that is how much a particular item is used – while structured data record only binary information on whether or not an item is used. The observed or estimated frequency of use is an additional piece of information that can improve explanations of regional variation.

The main disadvantages of corpora as data source for comparing languages are uneven spatial coverage – naturally occurring texts tend to be more con-centrated in particular regions – and sparseness of linguistic phenomena. As a matter of fact, the first dialectological survey of German varieties, famously carried out by Wenker in the nineteenth century, was closer to text than structured data collection. This survey consisted of a number of standard German sentences translated into local varieties. With its spatial coverage, which remains impressive even by the present-day standards, this data set did not provide information about many categories known to vary across regions because most of these categories did not show up in the selected sentences. This is what led, in part, to the development of dialectological questionnaires targeting specific categories of variation.

Unsurprisingly, English was the first language for which regional variation was directly addressed by a corpus compilation project – the International Corpus of English (ICE) (Greenbaum, 1991). Following the sampling methods of the Brown corpus, ICE includes comparable samples of thirteen varieties of English (Canada, East Africa, Great Britain, Hong Kong, India, Ireland and SPICE Ireland, Jamaica, New Zealand, Nigeria, the Philippines, Singapore, Sri Lanka and the United States). Each variety is represented with 500 samples of written or spoken (not for all varieties) language. The association ICAME distributes a similar resource with a few more varieties, but less strictly comparable (Leech and Johansson, 2009). These resources are intended for studying regional variation but on a global scale, which is a rather different notion from what is traditionally understood as dialectology.

Subsequently built data sets for corpus-based study of linguistic variation, discussed in more detail in the following sections of this chapter, increasingly make use of new technologies for drawing samples of spontaneously occurring regionally varied linguistic production. New techniques are proposed to collect the language of the internet, traditional and new, social media, but also to record authentic, ordinary language use. New data sources drive the comparison of similar languages and varieties outside of what is traditionally considered to be dialectology, towards a more comprehensive study of regional variation in language use. This trend fits well the goals of *modern dialectology*, as seen by Chambers and Trudgill (1998) and Britain (2002) (cf. Chapter 5). In the reminder of this chapter, we give an overview of the new collection techniques and the resulting data sets. Our discussion is organised around three types of linguistic variation closely associated to the types of data sources, For a more elaborate overview of the categories of linguistic variation commonly discussed in linguistic literature, we refer the reader to Chapter 1.

6.2   Types of Micro-Variation and the Corresponding Data Collection Procedures

Comparison of similar languages, varieties and dialects has been addressed in the linguistic literature under the common term *micro-variation*.[1] This term can refer to studies in dialectology, which are traditionally associated with the narroow-scale comparison, but also to studies in general linguistics, when the framework involves a narrow-scale comparison (Brandner, 2012).

In this section, we propose a three-way classification of narrow-scale variability and discuss the contemporary techniques used to collect corpora of each variability type. While some existing resources represent multiple types

---

[1] An opposite term, macro-variation, has been used to refer to the comparison of diverse languages on the global scale, performed primarily in the field of typology.

of micro-variation, the techniques used to collect the data depend heavily on the type of variation.

6.2.1   Standard Varieties

The term *standard language* is usually used in contrast to the term *dialect* to refer to the explicitly or implicitly prescribed language used in state institutions (primarily schools) and official media (primarily national newspapers and television), where the content is carefully edited. Standard is usually based on a single or multiple dialects, but it departs from its origins in the process of standardisation. It is not acquired spontaneously, but needs to be studied by all members of the population on a given territory (usually a state).

Formation of standard languages is associated with the formation of national states, mostly in the nineteenth century, but the mapping between standard languages and the states is not of the one-to-one type. A single language can be spread over multiple countries giving rise to multiple standardisations, as in the case of German in Germany versus Switzerland and Austria, Dutch in the Netherlands versus Belgium. An important source of multiple standardisations is the spread of European languages to other continents during the colonisation period, resulting in multiple national varieties of English, Spanish, Portuguese, French and Dutch.

If multiple standardisations are associated with strong political forces or identity issues, they can be taken a step further, giving rise to separate, but mutually understandable languages, as in the case of Scandinavian languages, Czech and Slovak, Bulgarian and Macedonian, or the famous separation between Hindi and Urdu. An especially complex example of such multiple standardisations charged with political and identity issues is the case of the present-day Bosnian, Croatian, Montenegrin and Serbian, which have become separate languages after the split of former Yugoslavia into six independent states during 1990s. Before the split, these four languages constituted a single standard language, Serbo-Croatian, with two standard versions: Croatian (western) and Serbian (eastern). This was a relatively rare example of multiple standardisations of a single language within a state.

Regional variation within the same standard is usually thought to be negligible, but a recent study by Grieve (2016) shows that regional patterns can be detected even in edited text that conforms to the standard. The findings of Grieve (2016) rely on an analysis of regional variation in written and edited American English, represented in the corpus of letters to the editor. The source of data for this corpus are newspaper archives. The corpus includes 251 newspapers published in 244 cities distributed more or less evenly across the territory of the United Sates. It is divided into sub-corpora at the city level (193 metropolitan areas, 29 micropolitan areas, 14 metropolitan divisions, 4 individual counties).

In the remaining of this chapter, we describe data collection procedures for a number of other regionally varied corpora, from early data sets to the contemporary collections.

Data Collection Procedures   An early corpus representing regional variation between two standards is the CONDIV corpus of Dutch varieties (Grondelaers et al., 2000). Its main purpose is to provide data for comparing Netherlandic Dutch and Belgian Dutch. It is a corpus of written texts, including the edited language of news (local and national) and the non-edited language of IRC, one of the first widely used platforms for informal exchange on the internet (this form of communication is today called CMC for computer-mediated communication).

Currently, regionally varied corpora of standard languages tend to be composed of web pages published in specific (top-level) web domains. Most standard varieties do have a corresponding top-level domain, the example among South Slavic languages being .ba for Bosnian, .hr for Croatian, .me for Montenegrin and .rs for Serbian. A similar example for German varieties are .at for Austrian German, .de for Standard German and .ch for Swiss German. For a Romance example, European Portuguese is mostly used .pt while Brazilian Portuguese is covered on .br.

A reasonable assumption is that a significant amount of texts published on these domains is, in fact, written in the corresponding standard variety. Given the (relative) simplicity of collecting large amounts of textual data from top-level domains, this procedure is considered to be the simplest path to a comparable collection of a set of standard varieties. To give an example from crawling the Croatian and Slovenian domains (Ljubešić et al., 2016a), 10.5 per cent of documents on the Croatian web were written in English, while that percentage was 9.88 per cent on the Slovenian web. The percentage of documents written in other languages on both top-level domains is negligible. When it comes to the ratios between similar languages, we can give the example from the Croatian and Serbian top-level domains – the Croatian web contains around 0.3 per cent of documents written in Serbian, while the Serbian web contains around 1.3 per cent of documents written in Croatian (Ljubešić and Klubička, 2014).

The most prominent projects on building web corpora are the WaCky initiative (Baroni et al., 2009), which started the era of building web corpora, the COW corpora initiative (Schäfer and Bildhauer, 2012) focusing primarily on the large European languages, and the TenTen corpora initiative started by the developers of the Sketch Engine tool (Jakubíček et al., 2013), which currently covers both the longest (thirty-four languages) and most diverse (European, Asian, American) list of languages.

Another project that should be mentioned in this brief overview is the CommonCrawl, a project performing crawls over the whole internet for textual data since 2013 with regular data updates. While the amount of data in different languages in this project is significant, the amount of processing needed to extract data from low-density languages questions whether it makes more sense to build top-level domain corpora from scratch.

The technological procedure actually consists of a sequence of operations, the most prominent being: (1) crawling, (2) boilerplate removal, (3) language / variety identification, (4) deduplication and (5) linguistic processing.

The procedure of crawling consists of a process, or series of processes, that retrieve sources of HTML pages from specific URLs, called seed URLs. The content of these pages is searched for new (unknown) URLs, which are then added to the queue of URLs to be retrieved. The crawling procedure is run until one of the stopping criteria is reached: (1) as long as there are URLs in the queue, (2) for a specific amount of time, or (3) until a specified amount of data is collected. While crawling, documents that are not HTML are mostly discarded. The same applies to HTML documents that are below or over given size thresholds. Currently, the most popular crawler for web corpora construction is spiderling (Suchomel and Pomikálek, 2011), part of the Sketch Engine pipeline for building TenTen corpora.

Once a large body of HTML documents are retrieved, the boilerplate removal is run on each of the HTML documents, with the goal of extracting linguistically relevant text, i.e., removing all the HTML mark-up, header, footer information, which we refer to as boilerplate. Most encoding predictors are nowadays based on heuristics, i.e., manually written rules, with the most popular one for web corpus construction being jusText (Pomikálek, 2011), again part of the TenTen pipeline.

Once we have a large body of text extracted from the crawled HTML documents, the language of each document has to be identified. In most cases, language identification is performed at the document level, most frequently using software based on machine learning. One of the most used language identification tools is langid.py (Lui and Baldwin, 2012). Automatic language identification is known to work very well. However, discriminating between similar languages and varieties, which is needed for building regionally varied corpora, typically cannot be performed using standard techniques (Tiedemann and Ljubešić, 2012). For distinguishing varieties, dedicated models have to be used, again based on supervised machine learning. An example tool for discriminating between users tweeting in Bosnian, Croatian, Serbian or Montenegrin is described by Ljubešić and Kranjčić (2015).

Aside from discriminating between different standard varieties, it can be very beneficial to discriminate between standard and non-standard varieties of a single language. This is needed, for instance, if one wants to collect only standard language samples, leaving out all the texts that do not follow strictly a given linguistic norm. For this task, simple heuristics are frequently used, e.g., percentage of words out of vocabulary. However, in this case too, better results are obtained by applying supervised machine learning. One example of discriminating between various linguistic and technical levels of non-standardness of Slovene user-generated content is described in (Ljubešić et al., n.d.). This type of variation is described in more detail in Section 6.2.3.

6.2.2   Dialects: Nonstandard Spoken Language

The term *dialect* is traditionally used to refer to a linguistic variety shared by the population of a given, small, well-delimited territory. The use of this term is, however, evolving and it increasingly includes reference to a less clearly delimited, spontaneously acquired, locally marked variety – in contrast to more clearly territorially delimited, widely used and learned standard. While the interest in automatic processing of dialects is increasing, the extreme variability and the lack of written standard pose considerable problems to the exiting techniques, calling for new approaches.

The use of dialects varies across different territories and is influenced by the standardisation practices on a given territory. French dialects, for instance, are claimed to be considerably levelled (Pooley, 2007), while regional variation is more pronounced in Germany and Italy. The factors that influence the use of dialects can be linguistic, but also cultural and political. Levelling of French dialects, for instance, is usually ascribed to the strong influence of central regulatory institutions. Another factor commonly cited as a cause of abandoning local varieties, for instance in Italy, is the prestige of the language used in national media. Finally, if the standard language is linguistically very similar to a dialect, this might result in the dialect being abandoned.

Dialects tend to be used more if the standard variety used on the same territory is linguistically, but also politically distant. This is the case, for instance, with German dialects in Switzerland. The standard used in public communication in Switzerland is a variety of High German, also used as standard in Germany. This standard is, however, linguistically considerably different from local spoken varieties, to the point that Swiss speakers would not understand the standard without studying it. These circumstances, together with the fact that none of the Swiss cultural centres has a clear prestige, favour the use of dialects and their preservation in everyday communication.

Another case where dialects play a prominent role is Arabic. The name *Arabic* refers, in fact, to a number of dialects usually classified into five prominent types: Egyptian, North African or Maghrebi, Gulf or Arabian Peninsula, Levantine and Modern Standard Arabic (Ali et al., 2016). As evident from the classification, these dialects are spoken on a relatively large territory, spanning across several independent states. They, however, did not go through separate standardisations. Instead, there is a single standard, linguistically distant from all original dialects, that is supposed to be used on the whole territory, but is not systematically enforced. These linguistic and political factors result in strong variability in ordinary language use, where dialects tend to be more in use than the standard.

Data Collection Procedures There are two main sources of dialect corpora: transcriptions of recorded speech and written communication on the internet. In this section, we focus on transcribed speech and leave the discussion on non-standard written language to Section 6.2.3.

One of the first resources targeting the traditional notion of dialectal variation is the Freiburg English Dialect Corpus (Kortmann and Wagner, 2005), which contains transcripts of spoken English in the British Isles. It covers nine dialect areas (Southwest, Southeast, Midlands, North, Scottish Lowlands, Scottish Highlands, Hebrides, Isle of Man, Wales) represented with many recordings taken in different places. Most of the material included in the corpus is recorded and previously (roughly) transcribed in an oral history project. This resource is subsequently used in the development of methods for corpus-based dialectometry (Szmrecsanyi, 2008).

Other examples of transcribed speech corpora of English include the spoken parts of the British National Corpus (Burnard, 2007) and the International Corpus of English (Greenbaum, 1991), already mentioned above, and corpora such as the National Folklore Collection's South Armagh Corpus (NFCSAC) and the Diachronic Electronic Corpus of Tyneside English (DECTE), described by Corrigan (2017).

Beyond English, the Nordic Dialect Corpus[2] represents Scandinavian dialects with transcribed samples of spoken language spanning across the territory of all Nordic countries (Johannessen et al., 2009). Developed by a network of researchers, this corpus gathers different kinds of recordings, transcribed locally using national orthographies (with some phonetic transcription). The transcriptions are aligned to the audio/video sources and linguistically annotated to allow higher-level queries involving word lemmas and part-of-speech.

Similar in composition, but limited to the territory of a single country, is the ArchiMob corpus of spoken Swiss German (Samardžić et al., 2016; Scherrer et al., 2019). It contains transcribed recordings made available through an oral history project conducted by the association Archimob. The recordings included in the corpus (approximately one-tenth of the original videos) are intended to

---

[2] http://tekstlab.uio.no/nota/scandiasyn/

represent different dialects spoken in the German speaking parts of Switzerland. The transcriptions are aligned with the video/audio sources, normalised and tagged with parts of speech. This processing was performed manually for a sample of transcriptions and automatically for the rest.

Finally, spoken Arabic is represented in a popular data set used by Ali et al. (2016) for the experiments in automatic identification of Arabic dialects. This corpus contains recordings from the broadcast news domain and their transcriptions in four dialects (listed earlier) and Modern Standard Arabic. News broadcasts would not be considered dialects in the other listed cases, but in the case of Arabic, this is a representative data source due to the particular relationship between the standard and the dialects sketched above.

What is common to most of the given examples is that the original recordings tend to be produced independently of the corpus creation procedure. Oral history projects prove to be a good resources of data potentially useful for dialect representation. This is due to two main factors. First, the interviews recorded in such projects tend to be semi-conducted, which means that the interviewee is encouraged to speak for a longer time without interruptions. In this way, the recordings contain little overlapping speech, which is hard to transcribe, and often needs to be left out. Second, with a focus on a concrete topic, the attention of the interviewee is drawn away from the linguistic expression itself, allowing access to the authentic language use. Note, however, that a local variety targeted by a dialect corpus is usually not the only variety that the interviewed speaker uses. This variety is mostly used to interact with the members of family or within the circle of close friends. The same speaker is likely to switch to a variety closer to a standard when in a more formal context.

Another important point in common is sound-to-speech alignment, which is produced automatically if transcription is performed using a dedicated tool. However, transcribed data are often found without such alignment, which then needs to be restored in order to allow multimedia queries and training speech-to-text models.

Where the listed corpora differ the most is the choice of writing used for transcription and additional annotation steps. In general, transcriptions can be phonetic (making fine-grained distinctions in sound quality) or orthographic (mapping the sound to a general alphabet). Most of the corpora use orthographic transcription as a rough approximation of the sound, scalable to a large data set. Phonetic transcription is reserved for smaller data sets intended primarily for phonetic research. In the cases where dialects are close to a standard language, orthographic transcription can be performed using the standard writing. However, in the case of distant standard, as in Swiss German and Arabic, the choice of writing becomes complicated and an additional normalisation step is needed.

Dialect corpora also differ in the amount of additional linguistic annotation that they contain, but for the moment, none of them goes beyond part-of-speech tagging.

6.2.3   The Nonedited Language of the Internet

Democratisation of public media that took place with the development of social networks and, more generally, interactive web pages is especially interesting from the point of view of representing micro-variation in language corpora. With the new communication channels, speakers can share information and express their opinions in any language or variety that they find adapted for the occasion. These posts are not edited, and they do not need to conform to the standard prescribed on a given territory. This leads to more variability and, potentially, more authentic linguistic expressions than in edited media. Moreover, this communication remains stored and can be automatically retrieved from web platforms that host it. In this way, internet users create samples of language use suitable for studying micro-variation and training systems for natural language processing.

The non-edited language of the internet represents a large pool of new language samples that allow insight in how language is used in everyday communication. We have already mentioned it in relation with both types of micro-variation, standard language and dialects. Both of the traditionally distinguished modes of language use (registers) are, in fact, present in the non-edited user content on the internet. Speakers interacting through modern communication channels tend to be educated and therefore have mastered the standard language. At the same time, they tend to include regionally marked elements, achieving various expressive and identification effects. The language represented by such corpora is thus placed somewhere between the standard and the dialect, which is exactly the kind of language that is not represented in traditional corpora, but is likely to be the most realistic approximation of the ordinary language use.

An additional advantage of corpora collected from internet platforms is that the language can be associated with other useful information, such as geo-location of the posts, social contacts of the speakers, and rich metadata.

Given the accessibility of non-edited user content on the internet, its scaling potential and richness of the associated data, it is not surprising that corpora of such varieties are increasingly created using constantly evolving techniques.

Data Collection Procedures   We discussed earlier ways of collecting non-standard language from web data in Section 6.2.1 which is mostly available from blogs, forums, user comments and other elements of the Web 2.0. Besides that source of information, there are two main additional sources of such linguistic content. One source consists of social media, such as Twitter, Facebook, Snapchat, Reddit, Instagram, and the other of platforms for instant messaging, e.g., WhatsApp and Viber. While the information from social media can mostly be harvested automatically through APIs (application programming interfaces), the instant messaging data have to be collected directly from users who have participated in the conversations.

To showcase the diversity of the data structures available from APIs of social media, we will describe two social media used most frequently nowadays for collecting linguistic data: Twitter and Facebook.

Twitter currently enables two ways of accessing its data. The first way is the streaming API, which collects a sample of all the data currently being published on the social network. The second way, the search API, enables querying the data published in recent history. The possibility to run it over a prolonged period of time makes the streaming API better suited for collecting large amounts of general Twitter data. The search API, on the other hand, is better for collecting specifically targeted data. The search criteria can include the content of the posts and the language.

The two Twitter APIs can be used (1) directly via the HTTP protocol, (2) via bindings for various programming languages such as Tweepy for Python[3], or (3) via special programs built explicitly for (linguistic) data harvesting such as TweetCat (Ljubešić et al., 2014) or TweetGeo (Ljubešić et al., 2016b).

TweetCat (Ljubešić et al., 2014) enables collecting Twitter data of smaller languages by (1) querying the Search API for high-frequency words specific for the language of interest and (2) performing language identification at the level of a user's timeline once all that users available data are harvested. This user-level approach to language identification is much more reliable than Twitter's own identification, which is performed on each tweet separately and does not distinguish between many languages. An example data set built with TweetCat is a multi-year collection of tweets published in Slovene, a typical case of a language with relatively few speakers (Ljubešić et al., 2017).

TweetGeo (Ljubešić et al., 2016b) is an extension of TweetCat designed to work with the Streaming API for collecting geo-encoded data published in a specific geographic perimeter. This tool enables (1) collecting primarily geo-encoded data from a specific area and (2) performing language identification, if necessary, as a later step. An example data set collected via this method is a large sample of tweets published in the area of Bosnia, Croatia, Montenegro and Serbia in any of the official languages of these four countries, i.e., the BCMS macro-language (Ljubešić et al., 2018).

Apart from the textual content of the posts, Twitter APIs allow collecting some meta-data too. Some of the information potentially available in each tweet

---

[3] http://www.tweepy.org

object is the time stamp, general location of a user, the exact geo-location from which the tweet was sent, number of retweets, the tweet this tweet is a reply to, the user's username, avatar, profile colors, short bio, number of retweets of the user, and the number and list of followers and friends.

The Facebook graph API has a completely different structure. Its social graph consists of nodes (users, pages, groups, posts, comments), edges (connections between various nodes, e.g., a post and its the user who posted it) and fields (metadata on the nodes, e.g., name of a page or birthday of a user). For accessing a node, its identifier has to be known. The API does not give any search or filter functionality on the nodes or fields of the various nodes. The content thus needs to be retrieved before it can be filtered for the desired categories. After accessing a starting node, whose identifier is known, all the posts and the comments to the posts can be collected. Furthermore, publicly available information on each user publishing either the post or the comment can be collected as well. A typical case where one would collect the data using the Facebook graph API is a data set of posts from a page of a newspaper outlet, with the corresponding reactions on each post, and all the comments and reactions to comments, with the available metadata of users posting, commenting, or reacting.

Popular instant messaging services are one more source of data representing the language of the internet. To our knowledge, there are still no automated ways of collecting these data. Instead, data collected through public campaigns, where users are solicited to submit their conversations to a previously prepared location. For example, such campaigns were carried out as part of the projects *What's up, Switzerland*[4] or *sms4science*[5]. The amount of data collected through such campaigns is usually much smaller than in automated retrieval from social media. On the other hand, the advantages of such collection are that (1) the data collection process is more controlled, (2) the copyright issues are resolved by signing a written consent with the authors of the messages and (3) this harvesting method enables collecting additional metadata via questionnaires which might be more trustworthy than the personal metadata available from social media.

6.3   Privacy and Linguistic Micro-Variation

The trade-off between respecting speakers' privacy and representing micro-variation is an important issue affecting all kinds of data sets discussed in this chapter. To share such resources, researchers need to follow contemporary standards regarding metadata and anonymity of the speakers whose language is included in the corpora.

---

[4] www.whatsup-switzerland.ch   [5] www.sms4science.ch

We can distinguish between two major types of data that need to be anonymised when applying data collection techniques described in this chapter: (1) the identity of the author of a textual utterance and (2) the identity of the entities the author is referring to in his or her posts. We term the first anonymisation problem *user anonymisation* and the second *text anonymisation*.

For user anonymisation, the most frequently used approach is pseudoanonymisation, i.e., exchanging the information directly identifying the person (such as its name and birthday) with a numerical identifier which cannot be traced back to the person without the corresponding key. While anonymous, this user is identified in the whole data set with a unique identifier, enabling research in user-dependent phenomena. This anonymisation might be harmed by publishing some metadata, which can open up the data set to potential restoring of the identity of the user (de Montjoye et al., 2015). It is therefore important to carefully gauge the amount of metadata published with the text content.

Text anonymisation is performed in two basic steps (Medlock, 2006): (1) identification of the reference and (2) neutralisation of the reference. For reference identification, natural language processing (NLP) techniques are mostly applied, primarily sequence labelling techniques similar to the task of named entity recognition (Nadeau and Sekine, 2007). In reference neutralisation, we typically distinguish between three levels of neutralisation (Medlock, 2006): (1) removal, where the reference is replaced by a generic reference to any entity, (2) categorisation where the reference is replaced by a generic reference for each type of entity (person, location) and (3) pseudoanonymisation where each reference is replaced with a pseudoidentifier, similar to the most used method for user anonymisation. The last techniques preserves the most specific information, but its use needs to be evaluated against the original goal of the task: anonymity preservation.

6.4   Conclusion

This chapter addressed the issues in representing regional micro-variation in language corpora. We have shown how the goals of representing linguistic variation in language corpora have changed from the early attempts to create representative samples of language use to a renewed interest in micro-variation, relying on new data sources and technology.

We have proposed a three-way classification of the cases of micro-variation that can be represented with text corpora: (1) standard variants (including similar languages), (2) dialects, and (3) non-standard varieties (between dialects and standard). Each of these types of micro-variation, originating from different aspects of language use, calls for a specific approach to data collection, determining the sources of data, but also the techniques applied to turn the collected texts into corpora usable for research and language processing.

References

Ali, Ahmed, Dehak, Najim, Cardinal, Patrick, Khurana, Sameer, Yella, Sree Harsha, Glass, James, Bell, Peter, and Renals, Steve. 2016. Automatic Dialect Detection in Arabic Broadcast Speech. Pages 2934–2938 of: *Interspeech 2016*.

Atkins, Sue, Clear, Jeremy, and Ostler, Nicholas. 1992. Corpus Design Criteria. *Literary and Linguistic Computing*, **7**(1), 1–16.

Baroni, Marco, Bernardini, Silvia, Ferraresi, Adriano, and Zanchetta, Eros. 2009. The WaCky wide web: a collection of very large linguistically processed web-crawled corpora. *Language resources and evaluation*, **43**(3), 209–226.

Brandner, Ellen. 2012. Syntactic Microvariation. *Language and Linguistics Compass*, **6**, 113–130.

Britain, David. 2002. Dialectology. In: Bickerton, David (ed.), *A Web Guide to Teaching and Learning in Languages, Linguistics and Area Studies*. Southampton: Subject Centre for Languages, Linguistics and Area Studies.

Burnard, Lou (ed.). 2007. *Reference Guide for the British National Corpus*. Research Technologies Service at Oxford University Computing Services.

Chambers, J.K., and Trudgill, Peter. 1998. *Dialectology*. Cambridge: Cambridge University Press.

Corrigan, Karen P. 2017. Corpora for Regional and Social Analysis. Pages 105–188 of: Montgomery, Chris, and Moore, Emma (eds.), *Language and a Sense of Place: Studies in Language and Region*. Cambridge University Press.

de Montjoye, Yves-Alexandre, Radaelli, Laura, Singh, Vivek Kumar, and Pentland, Alex "Sandy". 2015. Unique in the shopping mall: On the reidentifiability of credit card metadata. *Science*, **347**(6221), 536–539.

Francis, Nelson, and Kučera, Henry. 1967. *Computational analysis of present-day American English*. Providence: Brown University Press.

Gildea, Daniel. 2001. Corpus Variation and Parser Performance. Pages 167–202 of: *2001 Conference on Empirical Methods in Natural Language Processing (EMNLP)*.

Goebl, Hans. 1982. *Dialektometrie. Prinzipien und Methoden des Einsatzes der numerischen Taxonomie im Bereich der Dialektgeographie*. Wien: Verlag der Österreichischen Akademie der Wissenschaften.

Goebl, Hans. 1984. *Dialektometrische Studien: Anhand italoromanischer, riitoromanischer und galloromanischer Sprachmaterialien aus AIS und ALF. 3 Vol.* Tübingen: Max Niemeyer.

Greenbaum, Sidney. 1991. ICE: the International Corpus of English. **7**(10), 3–7.

Grieve, Jack. 2016. *Regional Variation in Written American English*. Studies in English Language. Cambridge University Press.

Grondelaers, Stefan, Deygers, K, Van Aken, H, Van Den Heede, Vicky, and Speelman, D. 2000. Het CONDIV-corpus geschreven Nederlands. *Nederlandse Taalkunde*, **5**(01), 356–363.

Jakubíček, Miloš, Kilgarriff, Adam, Kovář, Vojtěch, Rychlý, Pavel, and Suchomel, Vít. 2013. The tenten corpus family. Pages 125–127 of: *7th International Corpus Linguistics Conference CL*. Lancaster, United Kingdom: Lancaster University.

Johannessen, Janne Bondi, Priestley, Joel, Hagen, Kristin, Åfarli, Tor Anders, and Øystein Alexander Vangsnes. 2009. The Nordic Dialect Corpus - an Advanced Research Tool. Pages 73–80 of: Jokinen, Kristiina, and Bick, Eckhard (eds.), *Proceedings of the 17th Nordic Conference of Computational Linguistics NODALIDA 2009*. Odense, Denmark: NEALT Proceedings Series Volume 4.

Kortmann, Bernd, and Wagner, Susanne. 2005. The Freiburg English dialect project and corpus. Pages 1–20 of: Kortmann, Bernd, Herrmann, Tanja, Pietsch, Lukas, and Wagner, Susane (eds.), *A Comparative Grammar of British English Dialects: Agreement, Gender, Relative Clauses*. Berlin, New York: Mouton de Gruyter.

Leech, Geoffrey, and Johansson, Stig. 2009. The coming of ICAME. *ICAME Journal*, **33**, 5–20.

Ljubešić, Nikola, and Klubička, Filip. 2014. {bs,hr,sr}WaC – Web corpora of Bosnian, Croatian and Serbian. Pages 29–35 of: *Proceedings of the 9th Web as Corpus Workshop (WaC-9)*. Gothenburg, Sweden: Association for Computational Linguistics.

Ljubešić, Nikola, and Kranjčić, Denis. 2015. Discriminating between closely related languages on twitter. *Informatica*, **39**(1), 1–8.

Ljubešić, Nikola, Fišer, Darja, Erjavec, Tomaž, Čibej, Jaka, Marko, Dafne, Pollak, Senja, and Škrjanec, Iza. Predicting the level of text standardness in user-generated content. Pages 371–378 of: *Proceedings of the International Conference Recent Advances in Natural Language Processing*.

Ljubešić, Nikola, Samardžić, Tanja, and Derungs, Curdin. 2016b. TweetGeo-A Tool for Collecting, Processing and Analysing Geo-encoded Linguistic Data. Pages 3412–3421 of: *Proceedings of COLING 2016, the 26th International Conference on Computational Linguistics: Technical Papers*.

Ljubešić, Nikola, Erjavec, Tomaž, and Fišer, Darja. 2017. *Twitter corpus Janes-Tweet 1.0*. Slovenian language resource repository CLARIN.SI, Ljubljana, Slovenia.

Ljubešić, Nikola, Esplà-Gomis, Miquel, Toral, Antonio, Rojas, Sergio Ortiz, and Klubička, Filip. 2016a. Producing Monolingual and Parallel Web Corpora at the Same Time – SpiderLing and Bitextor's Love Affair. Pages 2949–2956 of: Calzolari, Nicoletta, Choukri, Khalid, Declerck, Thierry, Goggi, Sara, Grobelnik, Marko, Maegaard, Bente, Mariani, Joseph, Mazo, Helene, Moreno, Asuncion, Odijk, Jan, and Piperidis, Stelios (eds.), *Proceedings of the Tenth International Conference on Language Resources and Evaluation (LREC 2016)*. Portorož, Slovenia: European Language Resources Association (ELRA).

Ljubešić, Nikola, Fišer, Darja, and Erjavec, Tomaž. 2014. TweetCaT: A Tool for Building Twitter Corpora of Smaller Languages. Pages 2279–2283 of: *Proceedings of the Ninth International Conference on Language Resources and Evaluation (LREC 14)*.

Ljubešić, Nikola, Miličević Petrović, Maja, and Samardžić, Tanja. 2018. Borders and boundaries in Bosnian, Croatian, Montenegrin and Serbian: Twitter data to the rescue. *Journal of Linguistic Geography*, **6**(2), 100–124.

Lui, Marco, and Baldwin, Timothy. 2012. langid.py: An Off-the-shelf Language Identification Tool. Pages 25–30 of: *Proceedings of the ACL 2012 System Demonstrations*. Jeju Island, Korea: Association for Computational Linguistics.

Medlock, Ben. 2006. An Introduction to NLP-based Textual Anonymisation. Pages 1051–1056 of: *Proceedings of the 5th International Conference on Language Resources and Evaluation (LREC 2006*.

Nadeau, David, and Sekine, Satoshi. 2007. A survey of named entity recognition and classification. *Lingvisticae Investigationes*, **30**(1), 3–26.

Nerbonne, John, Heeringa, Wilbert, van den Hout, Erik, van der Kooi, Peter, Otten, Simone, and van de Vis, Willem. 1995. Phonetic distance between Dutch dialects. Pages 185–202 of: Durieux, Gert, Daelemans, Walter, and Gillis, Steven (eds.),

CLIN VI: Proceedings from the Sixth CLIN Meeting. Antwerpen: Center for Dutch Language and Speech, University of (UIA).

Nerbonne, John, Heeringa, Wilbert, and Kleiweg, Peter. 1999. Edit distance and dialect proximity. Pages 5–15 of: Sankoff, David, and Kruskal, Joseph (eds.), *Time Warps, String Edits and Macromolecules: The Theory and Practice of Sequence Comparison*. Stanford: CSLI.

Norvig, Peter. 2009. Natural Language Corpus Data. Pages 219–243 of: Segaran, Toby, and Hammerbacher, Jeff (eds.), *Beautiful Data: The Stories Behind Elegant Data Solutions*. Beijing: O'Reilly.

Pomikálek, Jan. 2011. *jusText*. LINDAT/CLARIN digital library at the Institute of Formal and Applied Linguistics (ÚFAL), Faculty of Mathematics and Physics, Charles University, Prague, Czech Republic.

Pooley, Tim. 2007. Dialect Levelling in Southern France. *Nottingham French Studies*, **46**(2), 40–63.

Samardžić, Tanja, Scherrer, Yves, and Glaser, Elvira. 2016. ArchiMob – A Corpus of Spoken Swiss German. Pages 4061–4066 of: Calzolari, Nicoletta, Choukri, Khalid, Declerck, Thierry, Goggi, Sara, Grobelnik, Marko, Maegaard, Bente, Mariani, Joseph, Mazo, Helene, Moreno, Asuncion, Odijk, Jan, and Piperidis, Stelios (eds.), *Proceedings of the Tenth International Conference on Language Resources and Evaluation (LREC 2016)*. Portorož, Slovenia: European Language Resources Association (ELRA).

Scherrer, Yves, Samardžić, Tanja, and Glaser, Elvira. 2019. Digitising Swiss German: how to process and study a polycentric spoken language. *Language Resources and Evaluation*, **53**, 735–769.

Schäfer, Roland, and Bildhauer, Felix. 2012. Building Large Corpora from the Web Using a New Efficient Tool Chain. Pages 486–493 of: Calzolari, Nicoletta, Choukri, Khalid, Declerck, Thierry, Doğan, Mehmet Uğur, Maegaard, Bente, Mariani, Joseph, Moreno, Asuncion, Odijk, Jan, and Piperidis, Stelios (eds.), *Proceedings of the Eight International Conference on Language Resources and Evaluation (LREC'12)*. Istanbul, Turkey: European Language Resources Association (ELRA).

Sinclair, John. 1987. *Looking Up: An Account of the COBUILD Project in Lexical Computing*. London: Collins.

Suchomel, Vít, and Pomikálek, Jan. 2011. Practical web crawling for text corpora. Pages 97–108 of: *Proceedings of Recent Advances in Slavonic Natural Language Processing, RASLAN*. Brno, Czech Republic: Masaryk University.

Szmrecsanyi, Benedikt. 2008. Corpus-based Dialectometry: Aggregate Morphosyntactic Variability in British English Dialects. *International Journal of Humanities and Arts Computing*, **2**(1-2), 279–296.

Séguy, Jean. 1971. La relation entre la distance spatiale et la distance lexicale. *Revue de linguistique romane*, **35**, 335–357.

Tiedemann, Jörg, and Ljubešić, Nikola. 2012. Efficient discrimination between closely related languages. *Proceedings of COLING 2012*, 2619–2634.

7   Adaptation of Morphosyntactic Taggers
Cross-lectal and Multilectal Approaches

Yves Scherrer

7.1   Introduction

The topic of this book, "similar languages, varieties, and dialects," encompasses several linguistic and sociolinguistic configurations that call for adapted solutions. Most research in this area approaches these configurations from the angle of data availability and assumes that they show an imbalance of high-resource and low-resource varieties. A popular approach is thus to create models for the high-resource varieties and adapt them in some way to the low-resource varieties, which is facilitated by the posited similarity between the varieties. While such cross-lingual (or more generally, cross-lectal) approaches have been proposed for a range of natural language processing (NLP) tasks such as dependency parsing (see Chapter 8), named-entity recognition, or semantic role labeling, this chapter focuses on the task of morphosyntactic tagging. Morphosyntactic tagging is considered one of the core language technologies (Rehm and Uszkoreit, 2013) and often serves as a pre-annotation layer for higher-level tasks such as parsing. Furthermore, morphosyntactic annotation is useful for corpus-linguistic research as it enables search queries that are independent of the lexical forms, which is especially practical for non-standardized varieties such as dialects.

In this introduction, we present the task of morphosyntactic tagging and the most popular model architectures currently in use (Section 7.1.1), we describe different linguistic and sociolinguistic scenarios and their impact on data availability (Section 7.1.2) and give a general overview of cross-lingual and cross-lectal transfer learning (Section 7.1.3). In the remaining sections, we describe the different families of cross-lingual learning approaches in detail, providing examples of recent research on tagging for similar language varieties.

7.1.1   Morphosyntactic Tagging

Tagging in general refers to any kind of sequence labeling task. In natural language processing, sequences are typically sentences consisting of words, and every word of this sequence is assigned a label out of a predefined set of labels. Morphosyntactic tagging is one of the most prominent sequence labeling tasks, and two flavors – *part-of-speech tagging* and (for lack of a better term) *full morphological tagging* – can be distinguished.

Part-of-speech (POS) tagging refers to the process of assigning a part-of-speech label to each word of a sequence. Part-of-speech labels correspond to the main word classes or syntactic categories, such as noun, verb, adjective, pronoun, adverb, and punctuation. The number of part-of-speech labels varies across different annotation schemes and traditions,[1] but recent work has striven to define a core label set of ten to twenty labels that is as language-independent as possible (Petrov et al., 2012). For part-of-speech tagging, it is common to achieve more than 95 percent of accuracy with the adequate training data, to the point that it has been called a "solved task" (see, e.g., Manning, 2011, for a critical discussion).

In contrast to part-of-speech tagging, full morphological tagging relies on richer tag sets. The tags include, in addition to the main word class, a set of values for morphological features such as gender, number, case, or person, depending on the morphological complexity of the language (Hajič, 2000). As a rule of thumb, the full morphological label should, together with the lemma, enable the unambiguous reconstruction of the inflected word form. Whereas the set of part-of-speech tags is fairly language-independent, the inventory of morphosyntactic tags depends to a large extent on the particular linguistic systems. For instance, not all languages morphologically encode gender, and not all of those that do share the same values of the gender feature. Moreover, the combinatorics of different features results in an explosion of the number of distinct tags seen in a training corpus. For morphologically rich languages, it is common to have tag inventories of more than 1000 distinct elements (Erjavec, 2010). This makes full morphological tagging considerably more difficult than part-of-speech tagging.

Historically, there has not been a clear distinction between part-of-speech tagging and full morphological tagging. One of the most influential tag sets is the Penn Treebank tag set for English (Marcus et al., 1993), which defines forty-five labels. Due to the low complexity of English inflectional morphology, this tag set is sufficient for full morphological tagging of English, as per the definition given. Simultaneous annotation efforts for other languages provided tag sets of similar sizes (an overview is given in Petrov et al., 2012), but these could most often not provide full morphological disambiguation due to the higher morphological complexity of the corresponding languages. It is only with recent work on "universal" annotation that this distinction has been clarified, first through the development of a language-independent

---

[1] For example, there is some debate about whether proper nouns should be labeled differently from common nouns or not, or whether auxiliary verbs should be distinguished from lexical verbs or not (Nivre et al., 2016).

universal part-of-speech tag set (Petrov et al., 2012) and of a unified feature-value inventory for morphological features (Zeman, 2008), and later through the harmonization of the two within the universal dependencies project (Nivre et al., 2016).

Morphosyntactic tagging is a disambiguation task. For those words that occur only with a single label in the training corpus, the prediction is trivial. Depending on the task (part-of-speech tagging or morphological tagging) and the language, the proportion of such unambiguous words is considerable and may exceed 50 percent (Jurafsky and Martin, 2009). Hence, the two main difficulties that a tagger needs to solve are ambiguous words – word forms associated with more than one label in the training corpus –, and unknown words – word forms not encountered at all in the training corpus.

In contrast to other NLP tasks such as parsing, morphological analysis and machine translation, rule-based taggers relying on manually coded (morpho-) syntactic knowledge have never been popular. The few references in that domain use a full-fledged parser internally and restrict its output to the labels assigned to the terminal nodes (e.g., Tapanainen and Voutilainen, 1994; Scherrer, 2008). Tagging as such has typically been viewed as a disambiguation task that is most effectively handled using data-driven methods trained on hand-annotated corpora.

One of the simplest model architectures for tagging is the Hidden Markov Model (HMM), which models sequence labeling as a combination of emission probabilities (the association of tags with words) and transition probabilities (the probabilities of tag sequences). The former generally include some back-off mechanism based on suffix analysis for handling unknown words. Two of the historically most popular taggers, TreeTagger (Schmid, 1994) and TnT (Brants, 2000), are based on a HMM architecture and have been found hard to beat, especially in low-resource scenarios (Plank et al., 2016). Other, more practical reasons for the popularity of these systems include the availability of pre-trained TreeTagger models for a large number of languages, and the fact that TnT – unlike its open-source reimplementation HunPos (Halácsy et al., 2007) – stores the model parameters in plain text files that are easy to modify after training.

Most subsequent work has focused on alternative machine learning algorithms that support more sophisticated feature representations than HMMs. For example, Ratnaparkhi (1996) and Toutanova et al. (2003) use Maximum-Entropy Markov Models instead of HMMs, Giménez and Màrquez (2004) use support vector machine (SVM) classifiers, and Müller et al. (2013) rely on a conditional random fields (CRF) architecture. The latter proved to be especially well suited for large tag sets such as those used in full morphological tagging.

In recent years, tagger architectures based on neural networks have been introduced successfully, following Collobert et al. (2011). The advantage of neural networks lies in the fact that the feature representations (e.g., whether the tagger should focus on suffixes of a certain length, on capitalization, or on particular combinations of words) do not have to be specified explicitly in advance, but are learned directly within the model. Neural network taggers generally use a combination of character-level representations that inform about internal word structure (*character embeddings* or, more precisely, *character-level word embeddings*) and word-level representations that inform about the distributional similarities of words in their sentential context (*word embeddings*). Most neural network taggers use recurrent neural networks, in which the internal states of the network at each word (and at each decision) are connected. Different types of connections, such as long short-term memory (LSTM) or gated recurrent unit (GRU) cells, are available, and connections can be unidirectional (from left to right) or bidirectional. A representative example of such a tagger architecture is described in Plank et al. (2016). Other architectures use convolutional neural networks (CNNs) to represent the input data (e.g., Yu et al., 2017), or add a CRF on top of the output layer to capture the contextual dependencies between adjacent tags (e.g., Lample et al., 2016; Yang and Zhang, 2018).

For full morphological tagging, the question about the representation of complex tags arises. A tag is typically encoded as a sequence of feature-value pairs, and two tags may thus be distinct to several degrees, as in examples (a)–(c):

(a) POS=VERB|Mood=Ind|Number=Sing|Person=3|Tense=Past|VerbForm=Fin
(b) POS=VERB|Mood=Ind|Number=Sing|Person=3|Tense=Pres|VerbForm=Fin
(c) POS=NOUN|Animacy=Anim|Case=Nom|Gender=Masc|Number=Sing

The most straightforward option is to consider each tag string as a distinct entity. Tagging a word thus amounts to picking one tag string among all distinct tag strings seen in the training data. With this option, the same model architectures as for POS-tagging can be used, but it is impossible for the model to learn generalizations about particular features, e.g., that (a) and (b) both represent finite verb forms.

Another option is to model each feature separately. Tagging a word then amounts to picking one value for each feature (absent features are typically given a null value that is removed later) and concatenating them into a tag string. This approach requires changes to the model architecture, but allows the model to generalize better. While most work is based on the first option, Müller et al. (2013) and Pinter et al. (2017) are notable representatives of the second option, the former relying on a CRF model, the latter on a recurrent neural network model. Our own recent experiments (Scherrer and Rabus, 2017; Scherrer et al., 2018; Scherrer and Rabus, 2019) use these two tagging architectures. A related approach has been proposed by Silfverberg and Drobac (2018), who view the tag string as a sequence that is generated one feature at a time.

A recent addition to neural NLP are multi-task models (Ruder, 2017). Such models are trained not only on the main task (part-of-speech or morphological tagging in the present case) but also on some auxiliary task(s). A popular auxiliar task is the prediction of word frequency, following the intuition that low-frequency words have different tag distributions than high-frequency words (Plank et al., 2016). In the case of similar language varieties, it may be useful to train a single tagger model on multiple varieties and include variety identification as an auxiliary task. This allows the tagger to take advantage of the increased training corpus size, but also to learn differences between the varieties. Such an approach has been proposed by Cotterell and Heigold (2017) and has been applied successfully in Scherrer and Rabus (2019).

Different tagging models have been compared in Plank et al. (2016) for part-of-speech tagging, and in Horsmann and Zesch (2017) for finer-grained tag sets that lie somewhere between part-of-speech tagging and full morphological tagging. These comparisons show (1) that neural-network-based taggers generally surpass traditional methods, but only if the training corpora are large enough, and (2) that neural-network-based taggers are especially well suited to tagging problems with large tag sets. However, results have been found to depend a lot on the considered languages and tag sets.

7.1.2   Scenarios

This book intends to offer an overview of NLP methods for similar languages, similar varieties, and dialects. While it is well known that the distinction between a language, a language variety, and a dialect is determined to a large extent by political and sociolinguistic criteria rather than purely linguistic ones (Trudgill, 2000), these criteria often have a direct impact on the usage of the varieties, and therefore on the type of data that are available for computational research (see also Chapter 3).

Similar languages are generally characterized by the fact that each of them has some degree of official recognition (nationally or regionally), is standardized, and can be qualified as *autonomous* or *Ausbau* language (Trudgill, 2004) as a result of its independent cultural status. These attributes are typically lacking for *dialects*: most dialects are not autonomous language varieties, but are dependent on one variety of particular status, which is referred to as their *roofing language*. For example, Swiss German dialects depend on Standard German in the sense that formal written communication in Switzerland is carried out in Standard German, just like Arabic dialects are roofed by standardized pan-Arabic varieties such as Modern Standard Arabic (cf. Chapter 13). In the context of cross-lectal learning, the roofing language is often a natural choice as the high-resource variety for its associated (low-resource) dialects. Moreover, the absence of standardization for dialects also means that pronunciation differences are reflected more easily in writing than in standardized varieties; this greater variability in the textual data poses particular challenges for NLP applications such as tagging.

The relation between dialects and their roofing variety mirrors the relation between different diachronic states of a language and its present-day variety: in most linguistic areas of Europe, orthographic standardization has set in only a few centuries ago (Baddeley and Voeste, 2012), such that earlier stages of written language exhibit the same type of spelling variation that is observed today in dialectal variation. In consequence, methods that have been developed in the context of historical language varieties may also prove useful for the processing of synchronic dialectal varieties.

Similar varieties typically refer to different national or regional varieties of a pluricentric language (Clyne, 1992). Such varieties follow to a large extent the same standardization guidelines. Surprisingly, discussion of such phenomena is almost completely lacking in NLP research, and many data sets do not even specify the variety they represent.[2] The underlying assumptions seem to be that (1) the inter-variety differences are too infrequent to require specific modeling, and that (2) some of the data sets include data from several varieties, such that models trained on these data sets end up being relatively variety-independent. Indeed, in one of the rare studies involving tagging of different national varieties of Spanish (Francom et al., 2014), the authors find that data annotation inconsistencies and register mismatch affect tagging accuracy more than regional variation.

The status of similar languages and varieties as autonomous languages facilitates the collection of textual material for corpus construction, as popular domains and genres such as newspaper text, legal documents, film subtitles, and literary texts are in principle available. This contrasts with dialects that lack official status and therefore see limited written production. This especially holds in situations of *diglossia* (Ferguson, 1959), where the different varieties are used in different functional contexts. As a result, dialect corpora most often contain transcriptions of speech or text from computer-mediated communication, which are fundamentally different from the domains and genres typically found in NLP corpora of standardized varieties (see Chapter 6).

In all scenarios, the overarching question is about how to deal with the variation that occurs in the considered varieties: should it be neutralized so that

---

[2] For example, none of the six English treebanks available in the Universal Dependencies repository (as of June 29, 2018) specifies explicitly which national or regional variety of English it covers, although the data sources and the places of data collection may hint at the regional variety of the data. The same holds for the six French treebanks and the three Spanish treebanks. Only one of the Portuguese treebanks explicitly states that it contains material from both European and Brazilian variants.

simpler, variation-independent models can be built, or should variety-specific models be created? In NLP for historical language varieties, this question has largely been answered in favor of the former approach, using normalization techniques to reduce the massive amounts of variation (see Section 7.3). For related varieties and dialects, both approaches are technically viable, and the answer to this question ultimately lies in the aims of the computational modeling rather than in the technical possibilities.

7.1.3   Cross-lingual and Cross-lectal Learning

In the previous section, we sketched different scenarios, all of which concern sets of closely related language varieties. It is typical of these scenarios that the availability of linguistic resources (in the form of annotated corpora for training) varies widely across the members of such a set. Therefore, the wish may occur to leverage the better-resourced varieties of the set in order to annotate the less-resourced ones. This is the core idea of cross-lectal learning.

It is not always obvious to identify the high-resource and low-resource varieties in a set of closely related varieties. Whereas dialects generally sport fewer resources than their corresponding roofing languages, the resource distributions of pluricentric language varieties often depend on coincidental factors and may even be task dependent. For example, Latin American varieties of Spanish tend to be less rich in NLP resources than European varieties because research has historically been more active on the Iberic peninsula than in Latin America. Danish may be more resourced than Norwegian when it comes to parallel data thanks to Denmark's membership in the European Union and the related translation activities, but Norwegian is currently more resourced in terms of syntactically annotated data than Danish.[3]

We argue here that the similar languages scenarios can often be cast as a low-resource languages problem, for which a number of cross-lingual transfer learning methods have been proposed (Tiedemann and Agić, 2016). The general goal of cross-lingual transfer learning is to create tools for a *low-resource language* (LRL) when training data are only available for a (not necessarily related) *high-resource language* (HRL); in this context, the high-resource language is also referred to as *donor language* or *source language*, and the low-resource language as the *recipient language* or *target language*. Although there seems to be a general consensus that transfer learning methods work better when the involved language varieties are closely related, the majority of the proposed methods aims to be as language-independent as possible and

---

[3] As of June 2018, the http://universaldependencies.org repository contains one Danish corpus with 100,000 words, whereas both varieties of Norwegian, Bokmål and Nynorsk, are represented by corpora with more than 300,000 words.

forgoes the explicit modeling of features that hold only for related varieties (e.g., surface similarities like large number of cognates or structural similarities like word order). Here, we would like to take a different stance and present models that sacrifice language independence for better adaptation to related language varieties.

In the following sections, we present the three main approaches to cross-lingual transfer learning for similar language varieties. The first approach, subsumed under the name *model transfer*, aims at training tagging models directly on annotated HRL data in such a way that they end up being generic enough to be applied without change to a LRL (Section 7.2). The second approach operates on the data level and has consequently been called *data transfer*. Its goal is to make the data of the HRL and LRL look more similar than they actually are, such that a tagger trained on one variety can be applied to the modified version of the data of the other variety (Section 7.3). The most popular flavor of this approach consists in *normalizing* the LRL towards the HRL. The third approach acknowledges the fact that there are different varieties with different properties and thus explicitly aims at building multilingual, or multilectal, models. The underlying assumption is that small amounts of data can be made available even for the low-resource varieties and that these data sets can be combined intelligently with the larger data sets of the high-resource ones (Section 7.4).

7.2   Model Transfer Methods

7.2.1   Plain Model Transfer

One of the most straightforward techniques to tag a LRL when only training data from a related HRL are available is to assume that the two varieties are in fact the same, or at least so similar that they do not require different models. In this case, a tagger is trained exclusively on HRL data and applied directly and without any modification to data from the LRL. While this assumption is too naive in most cases, this approach is often presented as a simple baseline with which more sophisticated approaches are compared. However, most work in the area of similar varieties of pluricentric languages implicitly follows this strategy by assuming that the overlap in the lexicon and in morphosyntactic structures is so high that it is not worth while training distinct taggers for each variety.

In Scherrer (2014), we report plain model transfer baseline results for various West Germanic, West Slavic, and Ibero-Romance languages: a TnT tagger is trained on a HRL and applied without modification to a related LRL. Table 7.1 extends these experiments to a larger set of tagger architectures:

- **TnT** (Brants, 2000): a non-neural, HMM-based tagger that relies on suffix analysis for unknown words;

Table 7.1 *Tagging Accuracies for Systems Trained on the HRL and Tested on the LRL. The data sets are described in Scherrer (2014).*

HRL → LRL	TnT	BTagger	MarMoT	CLSTM
Czech → Polish	66.4%	**69.3%**	67.2%	66.9%
Czech → Slovak	80.6%	81.1%	80.1%	**82.0%**
German → Dutch	24.5%	**32.7%**	25.3%	32.0%
Spanish → Catalan	58.4%	**67.2%**	62.8%	59.1%
Spanish → Aragonese	71.6%	72.7%	72.0%	**73.2%**

- **BTagger** (Gesmundo, 2011): a non-neural perceptron-based tagger based on bidirectional guided learning and semi-automatic feature template extraction;
- **MarMoT** (Müller et al., 2013): a non-neural CRF-based tagger;
- **CLSTM** (Scherrer and Rabus, 2019): a neural tagger using a character-level LSTM to represent words.

The results show that this naive approach can work surprisingly well even in configurations where the HRL and LRL are considered distinct languages (e.g., Czech → Slovak with over 80 percent accuracy, Spanish → Aragonese with over 70 percent accuracy). The success of plain model transfer depends a lot on the type of feature representations used when training the HRL tagger: modern discriminative or neural tagging models such as BTagger or CLSTM provide fair tagging performance even with high out-of-vocabulary rates, thanks to their fine-grained feature representations. The differences are especially striking for language pairs with different spelling conventions such as German → Dutch.

7.2.2   Multi-source Transfer

There are linguistic configurations with a clearly defined low-resource variety, but with several related high-resource varieties, all of which are expected to contribute to various extents to the tagging of the low-resource variety. One such case is Rusyn, a Slavic variety spoken predominantly in Transcarpathian Ukraine, eastern Slovakia, and southeastern Poland, and related most closely to Ukrainian but also to Polish and Slovak. Scherrer and Rabus (2017) train a single tagger on the concatenation of Slovak, Ukrainian, Polish, and Russian data and apply this multilingual tagger directly to Rusyn, achieving 79.2 percent part-of-speech accuracy and 72.0 percent full morphological tagging accuracy, with an out-of-vocabulary (OOV) rate of 26.4 percent. For comparison, the best single-source model is the one trained on Ukrainian, which yields 69.7 percent POS accuracy, 63.4 percent morphology accuracy, and 37.1 percent

OOV rate. An ablation study furthermore showed that in agreement with linguistic knowledge, removing Ukrainian from the multi-source tagger hurts its performance most, whereas the contributions of Polish and Slovak are minor and the Russian corpora do not facilitate Rusyn tagging at all. Follow-up experiments with neural taggers on the same multi-source setup showed improvements of up to 5 percent absolute in terms of full morphological tagging accuracy (Scherrer and Rabus, 2019).

Multi-source transfer approaches must meet two important requirements. First, all source languages need to share the same tag set and annotation conventions. This requirement has become much easier to meet in recent years thanks to the Universal Dependencies project and the related standardized annotation schemes. Second, all languages of the experiment need to share the same script, such that the taggers are able to learn generalizations about subword features (e.g., suffixes) that cover multiple languages. This is not naturally the case in the study cited earlier: Polish and Slovak are written in Latin script, but Rusyn, Ukrainian, and Russian use Cyrillic script. We decided to transliterate the Polish and Slovak data to Cyrillic script, so that no modification would be required for the target language Rusyn.

In simple model transfer approaches, the LRL and HRL words are assumed to be close enough that a sufficient number of HRL features learned by the tagger would fire for the relevant LRL words. By choosing character-level features, such as word prefixes or suffixes, this assumption can be satisfied in many cases. However, it is possible to define the HRL features in such a way that they become more language-independent (this case is called *delexicalization*), or to explicitly convert them to LRL features (*relexicalization*). These two approaches will be presented in the following sections.

7.2.3   *Delexicalization and Cross-lingual Word Embeddings*

Delexicalization was first proposed for dependency parsing (Zeman and Resnik, 2008; McDonald et al., 2011). Common dependency parsers use features based on word forms and part-of-speech tags to predict the dependency relations, and delexicalization simply removes the word form features in order to obtain a language-independent parser, the underlying idea being that the part-of-speech tags – which still need to be predicted in a language-dependent way – provide sufficient information for parsing.

For tagging itself, only the word forms (and parts thereof) are traditionally used as features, and there is no obvious choice of alternative, language-independent features. Yu et al. (2016) have attempted to use several statistics derived from the word forms as language-independent features, such as word length, word frequency, or entropy of the previous and following words, but without much success.

Another delexicalization approach for tagging has been pioneered by Täckström et al. (2012). They cluster all words of the HRL according to their distributional properties and replace the word forms by their cluster numbers in the training data. For example, words like *very, mildly, terribly* would be clustered together in cluster 101, and the tagger would then learn that cluster 101 words should be tagged as adverbs. Using a word-aligned parallel corpus, the cluster numbers are transferred to the LRL corpus, which can then be annotated using the same tagger. For similar language varieties, the association of HRL and LRL clusters could be inferred in a different way than by using a parallel corpus. Word clusters have been used in a similar way by Owoputi et al. (2013) to reduce the out-of-vocabulary rates in informal online conversations, but not in a completely delexicalized manner.

In recent years, vector-based representations of the distributional properties of words (so-called word embeddings) have been used with success in various NLP tasks. The approach of Täckström et al. (2012) can be adapted easily by replacing the cluster numbers with word embedding vectors. In order for this approach to work in a cross-lingual way, the word embeddings of the HRL and LRL need to be in the same multidimensional space. This is generally not the case, as word embeddings are typically inferred separately for each language, using large unannotated corpora such as Wikipedia dumps or web crawls (see Chapter 6). There is a large (and still growing) amount of research on how to project word embeddings of several languages into a common space (for overviews, see Upadhyay et al., 2016; Ruder et al., 2019). A typical approach is to use a seed dictionary to find a linear transformation that projects the vectors of one language into the space of the other language such that the words end up as close as possible to their translational equivalents defined in the dictionary. An application to POS-tagging has been presented in Zhang et al. (2016).

A bottleneck of this approach is that the embeddings have to be trained on large amounts of raw data, typically containing millions of words. For low-resource varieties such as dialects or similar varieties, this requirement is unrealistic. For example, Magistry et al. (2019) train cross-lingual word embeddings for three French regional languages – Alsatian, Occitan, and Picard – in view of using them for part-of-speech tagging. They show that embeddings trained on corpora containing one to two million words are not able to yield taggers that are competitive with much simpler adaptation strategies.

The current trend in cross-lingual embeddings research seems to be to relax the seed dictionary requirement as much as possible, to the point that no attention is paid to the existence of cognates and otherwise identical words (e.g., Artetxe et al., 2017), which however occur massively in similar languages. One notable exception is Sharoff (2018), who infers Levenshtein distance weights from the seed dictionary of related languages and uses this weighted Levenshtein distance to optimize the mapping between monolingual embeddings.

Another issue that is often overlooked concerns the fact that the projection of multilingual word embeddings into a single space works reliably only if the corpora used to train them are comparable in terms of domains and genres (Søgaard et al., 2018). This requirement can be difficult to satisfy in the configurations of interest here, in particular with dialects, whose domains of usage are inherently different from the ones of the respective roofing languages.

7.2.4   Relexicalization

A more traditional approach to model transfer assumes that the features of the HRL tagger are actual word forms or subword features (as opposed to numerical representations like embeddings) and can be modified after training. For example, the HRL word forms in a trained tagging model can be replaced by LRL equivalents extracted from a bilingual dictionary, yielding a LRL tagger. This approach works well with traditional tagger architectures such as HMMs, where emission and transition probabilities can be modified separately, according to the linguistic requirements.

The pioneering work in this domain is Feldman et al. (2006), who replace the emission probabilities of a HRL tagger by a lexicon generated independently from a morphological generator of the LRL. In related work (Scherrer, 2014; Scherrer and Sagot, 2014), we adapted the relexicalization approach to similar language varieties by building bilingual dictionaries in an unsupervised way, taking advantage of the prevalence of cognates, similar word forms and phrases. We then "translated" the HRL emission parameters using this dictionary. With this approach, we obtained error reduction rates between 36.2 and 73.7 percent for seven West Germanic, West Slavic, and Ibero-Romance languages. Whether it is easier to induce a bilingual dictionary or to create or adapt a morphological generator for the target language depends on the actual linguistic configuration.

The transition probabilities are often considered to be stable across related languages, but Babych and Sharoff (2016) propose a method to rewrite these parameters as well, which can be useful if the tag sets are not identical across languages. While the delexicalization method with cross-lingual word embeddings tends to work better under laboratory conditions, the relexicalization method can still be competitive thanks to its lower and easier-to-satisfy data requirements.

7.3   Normalization and Other Data Transfer Methods

Tagging text of a low-resource variety does not necessarily require building a tagger for that variety. Instead, one could translate the LRL text to the HRL and tag it with an off-the-shelf HRL tagger. This strategy has encountered considerable success in the area of historical language processing. In these cases, taggers are readily available for the standardized modern variety (the HRL), but not for the historical varieties for which documents need to be annotated (the LRLs). Thus, the chosen solution has been the following:

1. Train a tagger for the modern variety.
2. Create a *normalization* (or *modernization*) system that converts historical text into modern text.
3. Convert the historical data set to the modern variety and annotate it with the modern tagger.
4. Revert the modernized word forms to the original ones, keeping the annotations.

In this scenario, normalization has two crucial benefits: (1) it eliminates the requirement for annotated training data of the low-resource variety by enabling the use of a high-resource variety tagger, and (2) it reduces the amount of spelling variation in the low-resource variety to a level that is manageable by standard taggers, diminishing the out-of-vocabulary rates.

Historical varieties, just like dialectal varieties, exhibit large amounts of spelling variation. In both situations, it makes sense to forgo creating taggers specifically designed to deal with such variation and rather reduce the variation by means of some independent normalization method.

7.3.1   Normalization Methods

Text normalization – whether applied to historical varieties, dialectal varieties or user-generated content on social media – can be seen as a typical instance of the noisy channel model (see Koehn, 2010): the observed spellings are "corrupted" variants of the standardized spellings, which have to be reconstructed. Normalization methods therefore typically rely on a channel model and a language model. The channel model defines what types of spelling changes are allowed, and the language model specifies what strings are correct standardized spellings.

One instance of such a model has been presented by Pettersson et al. (2013a). Their aim is to approximately match historical words in a modern-language lexicon, measuring similarity with Levenshtein distance. In this case, Levenshtein distance figures as the channel model, and the lexicon is used as the language model. This method is completely unsupervised in the sense that it does not require any parallel data (word pairs) and uses a language-independent similarity measure. If parallel data are available, these can be used to adapt the weights of a weighted edit distance measure, as in Mann and Yarowsky (2001) for closely related languages, Scherrer (2007) for dialects, or Pettersson et al. (2013a) for historical varieties. Reffle (2011) and Etxeberria et al. (2019) propose to learn weighted finite-state transducers instead of simpler edit-distance-based models.

Bollmann (2012) presents a method for automatically extracting context-sensitive rewrite rules from a parallel corpus. These rules are then used as the channel model, either on their own or in conjunction with a language model consisting of a reference lexicon of the standardized variety. A combination of approaches is used in the VARD 2 normalization system (Rayson et al., 2007; Baron and Rayson, 2008), which views text normalization as a particular case of spellchecking. It relies on a lexicon of known variants, a set of letter replacement rules, phonetic matching, and edit distance.

Statistical machine translation systems also follow the noisy channel metaphor (Koehn, 2010). In particular, Vilar et al. (2007) and Tiedemann (2009) proposed character-level statistical machine translation (CSMT) as an alternative approach to translating words between closely related languages. Character-level SMT is different from standard (i.e., word-level) SMT in that, instead of translating words occurring in sentence pairs, it translates characters occurring in word pairs. CSMT has been successfully applied to translation between closely related languages (Tiedemann, 2009), standardization of user-generated content (De Clercq et al., 2013; Ljubešić et al., 2014; Ljubešić et al., 2016) and normalization of historical words (Pettersson et al., 2013b; Sánchez-Martínez et al., 2013; Pettersson et al., 2014; Scherrer and Erjavec, 2016).

Scherrer and Erjavec (2016) present a bootstrapping approach that allows CSMT to be used without parallel training data: they generate noisy parallel data with the unsupervised Levenshtein model of Pettersson et al. (2013a) and train the CSMT model on these noisy data. CSMT successfully regularizes the model, leading to better normalization than with the Levenshtein-based model alone.

All of these methods normalize each word independently without looking at the sentential context. This setup has been viewed as sufficient, on one hand, because the varieties in question generally do not exhibit much syntactic variation and, on the other hand, because the main goal of normalization is not to produce fluent modern-language text, but rather to provide glossing intended to improve corpus search, linguistic analysis, and, last but not least, automatic annotation such as morphosyntactic tagging (Gotscharek et al., 2009; Samardzić et al., 2016).

Nevertheless, context can be useful for disambiguating ambiguous spellings and to account for phonological effects at word boundaries that affect spelling. Ljubešić et al. (2016) and Scherrer and Ljubešić (2016) extend the scope of the CSMT model to entire segments (utterances or sentences) and obtain improvements for historical, dialectal, and social media data, depending on the level of ambiguity present in the data.[4]

As the machine translation community moves from statistical to neural models, neural-network based normalization models have also started to appear. Bollmann and Søgaard (2016) are the first to our knowledge to use neural networks for historical spelling normalization. They train a bidirectional LSTM on character-aligned word pairs; alignment is performed using iterated Levenshtein alignment, but their method outperforms previous work (Bollmann, 2012) only in a multi-task setting where training data with different spelling characteristics are included. Korchagina (2017) uses a character-level neural machine translation framework that obviates the need for preliminary character alignment. Tang et al. (2018) compare various neural machine translation architectures and basic translation units (single characters or pre-segmented character sequences) on the task of word-by-word spelling normalization in five languages; neural models outperform CSMT models in two out of five languages, but no clear winning parameter setting was found. Lusetti et al. (2018) present a neural normalization method that includes external language models and find improvements over comparable CSMT models.

At the moment – and unlike in general machine translation – neural normalization models do not clearly outperform statistical ones (Bollmann, 2019). I see two main reasons for this. First, normalization models are generally characterized by rather simple channel models and heavy reliance on language models, but neural translation models typically provide more powerful channel models at the expense of an explicit language model. Second, the generally small training data sizes do not favor the more data-hungry neural models either.

It should be noted that normalization as a task may encounter resistance for political or sociolinguistic reasons, in particular in the context of minority languages. Typically, some language varieties have been involved in long identitary struggles to emphasize their (cultural and linguistic) difference from a majority language, and the last thing that the main actors of these struggles want to see is to have it reduced to that majority language by some normalization procedure, even though that might be the most adapted approach from a technological point of view. The relation between contemporary language varieties is often more ideologically charged than the relation between different diachronic states of a language.

---

[4] Sentence-level normalization systems have an important drawback, namely that it is difficult to retrieve the word boundaries, especially if the inputs and outputs have different numbers of tokens. To this end, the work cited here uses a specifically designed re-alignment script that is based on the phrase alignment information output by the CSMT system and a set of heuristics. This script is included in a larger set of scripts designed to simplify the use of CSMT systems: https://github.com/clarinsi/csmtiser.

7.3.2   Normalization as a Preprocessing Step for Tagging

The usefulness of normalization for tagging has been demonstrated in various case studies. For example, Scherrer and Erjavec (2016) applied a modern Slovene tagger to unnormalized or normalized historical Slovene and showed that normalization indeed improved tagging accuracy by up to 40 percent absolute, depending on the normalization setting and the time period. However, a supervised tagger directly trained on manually annotated historical data always outperformed the normalization-based taggers. Obviously, in many situations, training a supervised tagger is not a viable option due to the lack of annotated training data.

The CLIN27 shared task on historical text modernization (Tjong Kim Sang et al., 2017) also included an evaluation of part-of-speech tagging: the same modern Dutch tagger was applied to the unnormalized text, the texts normalized with one of the submitted systems, and the manually normalized text. While the unnormalized data yielded a tagging accuracy of 70.9 percent and an OOV rate of 40.7 percent, the best submitted normalization system obtained an accuracy of 85.6 percent, reducing the OOV rate to 14.8 percent. For comparison, the manually normalized data resulted in an accuracy of 87.5 percent and an OOV rate of 9.3 percent. The detailed results also show that normalization performance and tagging performance are not necessarily correlated: for example, the Bochum system was ranked first on the normalization task (on par with two other systems), but performed much worse on the tagging task. The OOV rates suggest that the Bochum system did a good job on normalizing rare words, but was less successful with frequent words.

If the goal of normalization lies merely in tagging, it can be sufficient to focus on normalizing frequent words and let the unknown word module of the HRL tagger deal with the rare words. In their case study, Bernhard and Ligozat (2013) focus on tagging Alsatian, a German variety spoken in the Alsace region of France, using a tagger trained on Standard German. They manually create a normalization dictionary that relates the 107 most frequent Alsatian word types to their Standard German equivalents, leaving all other Alsatian words untouched. This minimalistic normalization improves tagging accuracy by 11 to 33 percent absolute, depending on the text genre and tagging algorithm used.

A study by Bollmann (2013) further illustrates the impact of normalization quality on tagging. He trained four normalization models using 100, 250, 500, and 1000 word pairs respectively, and created four normalized variants of the test corpus, which were then annotated with a tagger of the normalized variety. While each step yielded additional improvements in tagging accuracy, the biggest increases were seen with the first 100 or 250 word pairs.

In some cases, a normalization approach may be in competition with a supervised tagging approach. Samardžić et al. (2016) discuss two scenarios for tagging transcriptions of Swiss German dialects (cf. also Chapter 6). The supervised option relies on a collection of part-of-speech annotated Swiss German texts from various written sources (Hollenstein and Aepli, 2014). This corpus is rather small (73,000 tokens) and differs in genre (written news data and literature versus transcribed speech), but contains the same dialectal varieties as the target texts. The normalization approach uses a Standard German tagger trained on TüBa-D/S, an annotated corpus of spontaneous dialogues conducted in Standard German (360,000 tokens). In this case, the text genre matches, but the normalization of the dialectal data to Standard German may introduce additional errors. The first option slightly outperformed the second one, indicating that using less training data from a non-matching genre in the same variety can give better results than using more data from a matching genre in a different variety together with normalization. However, the test data normalization approach is sufficiently competitive to provide a viable approach if training data of the same variety are too scarce.

Recent experiments on the same data set (Scherrer et al., 2019) show that a combination of both approaches may be most promising: adding the normalized forms as additional features to the supervised tagger (in the training set as well as in the test set) increased tagging accuracy by up to 10 percent absolute. In turn, the gains obtained with sentence-level normalization suggests that better knowledge of the syntactic structure, e.g., in the form of POS-tags, may be helpful for normalization. An interesting strand for future research will thus be to jointly learn normalization and tagging. This would, however, require at least minimal amounts of training data for both tasks.

7.3.3   *Annotation Projection*

A different variant of data transfer techniques is called *annotation projection*, and has been introduced by Yarowksy and Ngai (2001). It requires two resources: a tagger of the source language (or an annotated corpus from which it can be trained) and a parallel corpus relating the source with the target language. The source side of the parallel corpus is annotated with the existing tagger, and the labels are projected to the target side using word alignment links produced by an alignment tool. The resulting annotated target corpus can then serve as training data for a target tagger.

On the surface, this approach looks rather simple, but complications arise through word alignment errors, as well as many-to-one and one-to-many alignments. Yarowksy and Ngai (2001) introduce simple heuristics to reduce such noise, and follow-up work by Das and Petrov (2011) and Duong et al. (2013) provides interesting extensions. However, none of these works specifically address configurations with similar languages.

A multilingual extension has been introduced by Agić et al. (2015). They argue that the reliance on a single source language, in most cases English, is not optimal, and that multiple source languages can be used for projection by means of massively multilingual parallel corpora, such as the Bible. For a given target language, they project annotations from all available source corpora and use simple majority voting to resolve ambiguities. They also provide an optional second retraining step, in which low-resource taggers (such as those obtained at the end of the majority voting step) are included to guide the annotations of another low-resource language. This second step could be helpful in scenarios where several low-resource languages are related among each other, but no related high-resource language is available.

Annotation projection is not a particularly popular choice for configurations involving closely related varieties, mainly because large parallel corpora can be hard to find: for instance, parallel corpora involving a dialect and its corresponding standard variety are not naturally available, as dialects do not have official status and speakers are generally fluent in both varieties, obviating the need for translations.

One exception is the work of Aepli et al. (2014), who use a similar approach as Agić et al. (2015) to create a full morphological tagger for Macedonian using majority voting from the related languages Bulgarian, Czech, Slovene, and Serbian as well as from English. Their full tagging setup is somewhat more complicated and allows different morphological features to be inferred from different sets of source languages. The voting process is also guided by partial tagging information for Macedonian. The authors obtain an overall tagging accuracy of 88 percent, which is close to state-of-the-art performance for full tagging of morphologically rich languages (for contemporary results, see, e.g., Müller et al., 2013).

7.3.4   Training Data Translation

Tiedemann et al. (2014) introduce yet another variant of data transfer that relies on the same resources as annotation projection, namely an annotated corpus of the source language and a parallel corpus relating the source with the target language. Instead of annotating the parallel corpus, they use the parallel corpus to train a machine translation system (from source to target language) and use that system to translate the annotated source corpus to the target language, keeping the annotations intact.

Tiedemann et al. (2014) mention two inherent advantages of training data translation compared to annotation projection. First, instead of using an external word alignment tool that can add errors, the translation process and word alignment are intrinsically linked, at least in statistical machine translation models.

As a result, training data translation contains one step less, and thus fewer chances of accumulating errors. Second, (statistical) machine translation tends to produce more literal translations than the human translations in parallel texts usually are, which reduces the amount of misalignments. The choice between annotation projection and training data translation may also be guided by the target domain: if the annotated source corpus matches the target domain better, then training data translation should be preferred, and if the parallel corpus is closer to the target domain, annotation projection may be the better choice.

In any case, this approach suffers from the same data availability constraints as annotation projection and is thus of limited use for the closely related language scenarios. Moreover, it requires translation from the HRL to the LRL. This translation direction is unintuitive for a scenario where the former is standardized and the latter is not: it corresponds to "un-normalization" and hence to the introduction of noise during the translation process.

Nevertheless, Boujelbane et al. (2014) provide an example of this approach: they translate a Modern Standard Arabic (MSA) part-of-speech annotated corpus to Tunisian dialect (TD) and train a tagger on the resulting TD data. The translation model is not trained on a large parallel corpus, but mostly relies on a dictionary and a set of hand-written morphosyntactic translation rules. They improve tagging accuracy by 15 percent absolute compared to applying an MSA tagger directly to TD.

7.4   Tagger Adaptation and Multilingual Models

The approaches presented in this section make the assumption that no training data annotated with part-of-speech (or morphological) tags is available for the target variety, but that other types of data (raw text for training word embeddings, parallel corpora for training normalization systems, bilingual dictionaries, etc.) can be used instead. However, in many cases, at least small amounts of annotated data of the target variety can be made available. In this section, we review some approaches that take advantage of these types of data.

7.4.1   *From Domain Adaptation to Language Adaptation*

Mismatches in text genre or domain have caused problems in NLP research for a long time: the situation is common where the annotated training data stems from a particular domain (most often newswire) but the trained model is supposed to be applied with high accuracy to data of a different domain (e.g., tweets, biomedical documents, or speech transcripts). Algorithms for resolving such mismatches have been researched in the area called *domain adaptation*. The typical domain adaptation scenario involves a large annotated "out-of-domain" training corpus and a small annotated "in-domain" corpus, and the goal of the learning algorithm is to learn general knowledge about the language from the out-of-domain data and complement it with domain-specific knowledge from the in-domain data (e.g., Daumé III, 2007). Domain adaptation can also be done in a semi-supervised fashion, where the in-domain corpus is not annotated (e.g., Kübler and Baucom, 2011). The domain adaptation problem can be reformulated as a language adaptation problem if the involved languages are very similar.

For example, Jørgensen et al. (2016) create a tagger for African American Vernacular English (AAVE) tweets using domain adaptation strategies. They start by training a tagger on a large, non-AAVE-specific Twitter corpus and add domain-specific information like word embeddings, unlabeled in-domain data, and tag dictionaries extracted from the web. They also make use of a strategy called *self-training*: self-training consists in annotating unlabeled data using an imperfect tagging method, correcting the annotations in some way, and adding the corrected data to the training set of a second tagger, which will hopefully perform better than the initial imperfect one. A variety of methods can be used for the correction step, e.g., majority voting from different taggers (Kübler and Baucom, 2011; Aepli et al., 2014) or annotation projection (Duong et al., 2013).

Another option that is frequently employed in the context of neural network models is *curriculum training* or *fine-tuning*. Here, a model is trained in two phases, first on out-of-domain data and second on in-domain data. The motivation of this approach is that the small in-domain data set should not be "wasted" for learning the generic properties of the language in question. This approach could well be applied to tagging of low-resource varieties, but we are not aware of any such work.

7.4.2   Multilingual and Multilectal Models

We have already alluded to the possibility of using multiple source languages for tagging a different target language (Section 7.2.2). This idea can be combined with domain adaptation if small amounts of annotated target language data are added into the multilingual model, as suggested by Cotterell and Heigold (2017).

Multilingual – or multilectal – models can be trained in a completely language-agnostic way, i.e., by making the model believe that all training instances stem from the same language. This may work reasonably well if the involved languages are indeed very similar, but multilectal models generally work better if they are given information about the language variety of each training instance. When using neural network architectures, there are essentially two options for providing language information. The first option is to add a *language label* at the beginning (and/or at the end) of each sentence, as if it were an additional word (a). This information will be passed along successive states of the neural network and can influence the tagging decisions. The second option is a multi-task learning scenario, in which the model is trained to predict the language labels added on the output side (b). In this scenario, one may think of the language label as an additional morphological feature *Lang* that is appended to the tag of each word of the training data. By forcing the model to predict the language variety of each word, it can learn some generalizations about the interactions of morphosyntactic tags and language varieties.

(a)	⟨EN⟩	I	am	a	student	⟨EN⟩
	NA	PRON	VERB	DET	NOUN	NA

(b)	I	am	a	student
	PRON|Lang=EN	VERB|Lang=EN	DET|Lang=EN	NOUN|Lang=EN

The crucial difference between these two options is their behavior at test time. With option (a), the language labels need to be specified in the input. With option (b), the input does not need to be modified, as the language labels are generated by the model. This option can therefore be used when the test data cannot be unambiguously assigned a language label.

With both options, the neural network tagger will build internal, vector-based representations of the language labels. By mapping these representations to a low-dimensional space, one can visualize the "landscape" of language varieties as it has been inferred by the tagger. Östling and Tiedemann (2017) present an example of such work, using language modelling instead of tagging as the underlying task.

Multilectal models are particularly well suited for situations where several target language varieties are to be supported. It would be interesting to apply this approach to complex dialect landscapes whose varieties are known to be distinct, but not distinct enough to warrant completely independent models.

7.5   Conclusions

The goal of this chapter was to give a high-level overview of different approaches to tagging similar language varieties. If sufficient manually annotated training data are available, one may obviously attempt to create distinct tagging models for each language variety. On the opposite, one may also attempt to create a single tagging model for all varieties, using all available training data without distinction. However, most linguistic configurations call for some intermediate approach, whenever the variety for which training data are available is not the same as the variety for which a tagger is needed. For such scenarios, a range of cross-lingual learning techniques have been developed, but most of them adopt a broader scope in the sense that they do not assume any etymological relation between the involved language varieties. Also, some of these techniques have been developed with other tasks such as parsing in mind. We have striven to present the different approaches, giving examples from morphosyntactic tagging tasks and closely related language settings.

Two opposing trends can be seen in recent work. One aims at reducing inter-linguistic variation, e.g., by using normalization systems, such that traditional tagging algorithms can continue to be applied. The other one aims at embracing variation to create taggers that intrinsically handle data with internal variation, as witnessed by the increasing use of character-level features and vector-based word representations. While the most popular approach has without doubt been the one based on normalization, a slow shift towards the second type of models can be perceived, although examples of their application to similar language settings are still scarce. In both approaches however, the internal states of the models (of the normalization model in the former, or of the tagging model in the latter) can give rise to linguistic interpretations about the relationship between the modeled language varieties. Tagging of similar languages can thus be much more than just a particular application of a decade-old sequence labeling task.

References

Aepli, Noëmi, von Waldenfels, Ruprecht, and Samardžić, Tanja. 2014. Part-of-speech tag disambiguation by cross-linguistic majority vote. Pages 76–84 of: *Proceedings of the First Workshop on Applying NLP Tools to Similar Languages, Varieties and Dialects*.

Agić, Željko, Hovy, Dirk, and Søgaard, Anders. 2015. If all you have is a bit of the Bible: Learning POS taggers for truly low-resource languages. Pages 268–272 of: *Proceedings of the 53rd Annual Meeting of the Association for Computational Linguistics and the 7th International Joint Conference on Natural Language Processing*.

Artetxe, Mikel, Labaka, Gorka, and Agirre, Eneko. 2017. Learning bilingual word embeddings with (almost) no bilingual data. Pages 451–462 of: *Proceedings of the 55th Annual Meeting of the Association for Computational Linguistics (Volume 1: Long Papers)*.

Babych, Bogdan, and Sharoff, Serge. 2016. Ukrainian part-of-speech tagger for hybrid MT: Rapid induction of morphological disambiguation resources from a closely related language. Pages 1–12 of: *Proceedings of the Fifth Workshop on Hybrid Approaches to Translation (HyTra), European Association for Machine Translation (EAMT)*.

Baddeley, Susan, and Voeste, Anja (eds.). 2012. *Orthographies in Early Modern Europe*. Berlin, Boston: De Gruyter Mouton.

Baron, Alistair, and Rayson, Paul. 2008. VARD 2: A tool for dealing with spelling variation in historical corpora. Pages 1–15 of: *Proceedings of the Postgraduate Conference in Corpus Linguistics*. Birmingham, UK: Aston University.

Bernhard, Delphine, and Ligozat, Anne-Laure. 2013. Hassle-free POS-tagging for the Alsatian dialects. Pages 85–92 of: Zampieri, Marcos, and Diwersy, Sascha (eds.), *Non-Standard Data Sources in Corpus Based-Research*. ZSM Studien. Shaker.

Bollmann, Marcel. 2012. (Semi-)automatic normalization of historical texts using distance measures and the Norma tool. Pages 3–14 of: *Proceedings of the Second Workshop on Annotation of Corpora for Research in the Humanities (ACRH-2)*.

Bollmann, Marcel. 2013. POS tagging for historical texts with sparse training data. Pages 11–18 of: *Proceedings of the 7th Linguistic Annotation Workshop and Interoperability with Discourse*.

Bollmann, Marcel. 2019. A large-scale comparison of historical text normalization systems. Pages 3885–3898 of: *Proceedings of the 2019 Conference of the North American Chapter of the Association for Computational Linguistics: Human Language Technologies*.

Bollmann, Marcel, and Søgaard, Anders. 2016. Improving historical spelling normalization with bi-directional LSTMs and multi-task learning. Pages 131–139 of: *Proceedings of COLING 2016, the 26th International Conference on Computational Linguistics*.

Boujelbane, Rahma, Mallek, Mariem, Ellouze, Mariem, and Belguith, Lamia Hadrich. 2014. Fine-grained POS tagging of spoken Tunisian dialect corpora. Pages 59–62 of: Métais, Elisabeth, Roche, Mathieu, and Teisseire, Maguelonne (eds.), *Natural Language Processing and Information Systems*. Basel, Switzerland: Springer.

Brants, Thorsten. 2000. TnT – A statistical part-of-speech tagger. Pages 224–231 of: *Proceedings of the Sixth Conference on Applied Natural Language Processing*.

Clyne, Michael G. (ed.). 1992. *Pluricentric Languages: Differing Norms in Different Nations*. Contributions to the Sociology of Language, no. 62. Berlin, New York: Mouton de Gruyter.

Collobert, Ronan, Weston, Jason, Bottou, Léon, Karlen, Michael, Kavukcuoglu, Koray, and Kuksa, Pavel. 2011. Natural language processing (almost) from scratch. *Journal of Machine Learning Research*, **12**, 2493–2537.

Cotterell, Ryan, and Heigold, Georg. 2017. Cross-lingual character-level neural morphological tagging. Pages 748–759 of: *Proceedings of the 2017 Conference on Empirical Methods in Natural Language Processing*.

Das, Dipanjan, and Petrov, Slav. 2011. Unsupervised part-of-speech tagging with bilingual graph-based projections. Pages 600–609 of: *Proceedings of the 49th Annual Meeting of the Association for Computational Linguistics: Human Language Technologies*.

Daumé III, Hal. 2007. Frustratingly easy domain adaptation. Pages 256–263 of: *Proceedings of the 45th Annual Meeting of the Association of Computational Linguistics*.

De Clercq, Orphée, Desmet, Bart, Schulz, Sarah, Lefever, Els, and Hoste, Véronique. 2013. Normalization of Dutch user-generated content. Pages 179–188 of: *Proceedings of RANLP 2013*.

Duong, Long, Cook, Paul, Bird, Steven, and Pecina, Pavel. 2013. Simpler unsupervised POS tagging with bilingual projections. Pages 634–639 of: *Proceedings of the 51st Annual Meeting of the Association for Computational Linguistics*.

Erjavec, Tomaž. 2010. MULTEXT-East version 4: Multilingual morphosyntactic specifications, lexicons and corpora. In: *Proceedings of the Seventh International Conference on Language Resources and Evaluation (LREC'10)*. Valletta, Malta: European Language Resources Association (ELRA).

Etxeberria, Izaskun, Alegria, Iñaki, and Uria, Larraitz. 2019. Weighted finite-state transducers for normalization of historical texts. *Natural Language Engineering*, **25**(2), 307–321.

Feldman, Anna, Hana, Jirka, and Brew, Chris. 2006. A cross-language approach to rapid creation of new morphosyntactically annotated resources. Pages 549–554 of: *Proceedings of the Fifth International Conference on Language Resources and Evaluation (LREC 2006)*. European Language Resources Association (ELRA).

Ferguson, Charles A. 1959. Diglossia. *Word*, **15**(2), 325–340.

Francom, Jerid, Hulden, Mans, and Ussishkin, Adam. 2014. ACTIV-ES: A comparable, cross-dialect corpus of "everyday" Spanish from Argentina, Mexico, and Spain. Pages 1733–1737 of: *Proceedings of the Ninth International Conference on Language Resources and Evaluation (LREC'14)*. Reykjavik, Iceland: European Language Resources Association (ELRA).

Gesmundo, Andrea. 2011. Bidirectional sequence classification for tagging tasks with guided learning. In: *Actes de la 18e conference sur le Traitement Automatique des Langues Naturelles*.

Giménez, Jesús, and Màrquez, Lluís. 2004. SVMTool: A general POS tagger generator based on support vector machines. Pages 43–46 of: *Proceedings of the Fourth International Conference on Language Resources and Evaluation (LREC 2004)*. Lisbon, Portugal: European Language Resources Association (ELRA).

Gotscharek, Annette, Neumann, Andreas, Reffle, Ulrich, Ringlstetter, Christoph, and Schulz, Klaus U. 2009. Enabling information retrieval on historical document collections: The role of matching procedures and special lexica. Pages 69–76 of: *Proceedings of The Third Workshop on Analytics for Noisy Unstructured Text Data (AND'09)*.

Hajič, Jan. 2000. Morphological tagging: Data vs. dictionaries. In: *Proceedings of the 1st North American Chapter of the Association for Computational Linguistics Conference (NAACL 2000)*.

Halácsy, Péter, Kornai, András, and Oravecz, Csaba. 2007. HunPos – An open source trigram tagger. Pages 209–212 of: *Proceedings of the 45th Annual Meeting of the Association for Computational Linguistics, Companion Volume: Demo and Poster Sessions*.

Hollenstein, Nora, and Aepli, Noëmi. 2014. Compilation of a Swiss German dialect corpus and its application to PoS tagging. In: *Proceedings of the First Workshop on Applying NLP Tools to Similar Languages, Varieties and Dialects (VarDial)*.

Horsmann, Tobias, and Zesch, Torsten. 2017. Do LSTMs really work so well for PoS tagging? – A replication study. Pages 727–736 of: *Proceedings of the 2017 Conference on Empirical Methods in Natural Language Processing*.

Jørgensen, Anna, Hovy, Dirk, and Søgaard, Anders. 2016. Learning a POS tagger for AAVE-like language. Pages 1115–1120 of: *Proceedings of the 2016 Conference of the North American Chapter of the Association for Computational Linguistics: Human Language Technologies*.

Jurafsky, Daniel, and Martin, James H. 2009. *Speech and Language Processing: An Introduction to Natural Language Processing, Speech Recognition, and Computational Linguistics*. 2nd edn. Upper Saddle River, NJ, USA: Prentice-Hall.

Koehn, Philipp. 2010. *Statistical Machine Translation*. Cambridge, UK: Cambridge University Press.

Korchagina, Natalia. 2017. Normalizing medieval German texts: From rules to deep learning. Pages 12–17 of: *Proceedings of the NoDaLiDa 2017 Workshop on Processing Historical Language.*

Kübler, Sandra, and Baucom, Eric. 2011. Fast domain adaptation for part of speech tagging for dialogues. Pages 41–48 of: *Proceedings of the International Conference Recent Advances in Natural Language Processing 2011.*

Lample, Guillaume, Ballesteros, Miguel, Subramanian, Sandeep, Kawakami, Kazuya, and Dyer, Chris. 2016. Neural architectures for named entity recognition. Pages 260–270 of: *Proceedings of the 2016 Conference of the North American Chapter of the Association for Computational Linguistics: Human Language Technologies.* San Diego, CA: Association for Computational Linguistics.

Ljubešić, Nikola, Erjavec, Tomaž, and Fišer, Darja. 2014. Standardizing tweets with character-level machine translation. Pages 164–175 of: *Proceedings of CICLing 2014.* Lecture Notes in Computer Science. Kathmandu, Nepal: Springer.

Ljubešić, Nikola, Zupan, Katja, Fišer, Darja, and Erjavec, Tomaž. 2016. Normalising Slovene data: Historical texts vs. user-generated content. Pages 146–155 of: *Proceedings of the 13th Conference on Natural Language Processing (KONVENS 2016).*

Lusetti, Massimo, Ruzsics, Tatyana, Göhring, Anne, Samardžić, Tanja, and Stark, Elisabeth. 2018. Encoder-decoder methods for text normalization. Pages 18–28 of: *Proceedings of the Fifth Workshop on NLP for Similar Languages, Varieties and Dialects (VarDial 2018).* Association for Computational Linguistics.

Magistry, Pierre, Ligozat, Anne-Laure, and Rosset, Sophie. 2019. Exploiting languages proximity for part-of-speech tagging of three French regional languages. *Language Resources and Evaluation*, **53**, 865–888.

Mann, Gideon S., and Yarowsky, David. 2001. Multipath translation lexicon induction via bridge languages. Pages 151–158 of: *Proceedings of NAACL 2001.*

Manning, Christopher D. 2011. Part-of-speech tagging from 97% to 100%: Is it time for some linguistics? Pages 171–189 of: Gelbukh, Alexander (ed.), *Proceedings of the 12th International Conference on Computational Linguistics and Intelligent Text Processing (CICLing 2011).* Lecture Notes in Computer Science, no. 6608. Berlin/Heidelberg, Germany: Springer.

Marcus, Mitchell P., Santorini, Beatrice, and Marcinkiewicz, Mary Ann. 1993. Building a large annotated corpus of English: The Penn treebank. *Computational Linguistics*, **2**(19), 313–330.

McDonald, Ryan, Petrov, Slav, and Hall, Keith. 2011. Multi-source transfer of delexicalized dependency parsers. Pages 62–72 of: *Proceedings of the 2011 Conference on Empirical Methods in Natural Language Processing.*

Müller, Thomas, Schmid, Helmut, and Schütze, Hinrich. 2013. Efficient higher-order CRFs for morphological tagging. Pages 322–332 of: *Proceedings of the 2013 Conference on Empirical Methods in Natural Language Processing.*

Nivre, Joakim, de Marneffe, Marie-Catherine, Ginter, Filip, Goldberg, Yoav, Hajič, Jan, Manning, Christopher D., McDonald, Ryan, Petrov, Slav, Pyysalo, Sampo, Silveira, Natalia, Tsarfaty, Reut, and Zeman, Daniel. 2016. Universal Dependencies v1: A multilingual treebank collection. In: *Proceedings of the Tenth International Conference on Language Resources and Evaluation (LREC 2016).* Portorož, Slovenia: European Language Resources Association (ELRA).

Östling, Robert, and Tiedemann, Jörg. 2017. Continuous multilinguality with language vectors. Pages 644–649 of: *Proceedings of the 15th Conference of the European Chapter of the Association for Computational Linguistics: Volume 2, Short Papers.*

Owoputi, Olutobi, O'Connor, Brendan, Dyer, Chris, Gimpel, Kevin, Schneider, Nathan, and Smith, Noah A. 2013. Improved part-of-speech tagging for online conversational text with word clusters. Pages 380–390 of: *Proceedings of the 2013 Conference of the North American Chapter of the Association for Computational Linguistics: Human Language Technologies.*

Petrov, Slav, Das, Dipanjan, and McDonald, Ryan. 2012. A universal part-of-speech tagset. In: *Proceedings of the Eight International Conference on Language Resources and Evaluation (LREC'12).* Istanbul, Turkey: European Language Resources Association (ELRA).

Pettersson, Eva, Megyesi, Beáta B., and Nivre, Joakim. 2013a. Normalisation of historical text using context-sensitive weighted Levenshtein distance and compound splitting. Pages 163–179 of: *Proceedings of the 19th Nordic Conference of Computational Linguistics (Nodalida 2013).*

Pettersson, Eva, Megyesi, Beáta B., and Tiedemann, Jörg. 2013b. An SMT approach to automatic annotation of historical text. Pages 54–69 of: *Proceedings of the Nodalida Workshop on Computational Historical Linguistics.*

Pettersson, Eva, Megyesi, Beáta B., and Nivre, Joakim. 2014. A multilingual evaluation of three spelling normalisation methods for historical text. Pages 32–41 of: *Proceedings of the 8th Workshop on Language Technology for Cultural Heritage, Social Sciences, and Humanities (LaTeCH).*

Pinter, Yuval, Guthrie, Robert, and Eisenstein, Jacob. 2017. Mimicking word embeddings using subword RNNs. Pages 102–112 of: *Proceedings of the 2017 Conference on Empirical Methods in Natural Language Processing.*

Plank, Barbara, Søgaard, Anders, and Goldberg, Yoav. 2016. Multilingual part-of-speech tagging with bidirectional long short-term memory models and auxiliary loss. Pages 412–418 of: *Proceedings of the 54th Annual Meeting of the Association for Computational Linguistics.*

Ratnaparkhi, Adwait. 1996. A maximum entropy model for part-of-speech tagging. Pages 133–142 of: *Proceedings of the Conference on Empirical Methods in Natural Language Processing.*

Rayson, Paul, Archer, Dawn, Baron, Alistair, and Smith, Nick. 2007. Tagging historical corpora – The problem of spelling variation. In: *Proceedings of Digital Historical Corpora, Dagstuhl-Seminar 06491.* Wadern, Germany: International Conference and Research Center for Computer Science, Schloss Dagstuhl.

Reffle, Ulrich. 2011. Efficiently generating correction suggestions for garbled tokens of historical language. *Natural Language Engineering*, **17**, 265–282.

Rehm, Georg, and Uszkoreit, Hans (eds.). 2013. *Strategic Research Agenda for Multilingual Europe 2020.* Berlin/Heidelberg, Germany: Springer.

Ruder, Sebastian. 2017. An overview of multi-task learning in deep neural networks. *arXiv e-prints*, arXiv:1706.05098.

Ruder, Sebastian, Vulić, Ivan, and Søgaard, Anders. 2019. A survey of cross-lingual word embedding models. *Journal of Artificial Intelligence Research*, **65**, 569–631.

Samardzić, Tanja, Scherrer, Yves, and Glaser, Elvira. 2016. ArchiMob – A corpus of spoken Swiss German. Pages 4061–4066 of: *Proceedings of the Tenth International*

Conference on Language Resources and Evaluation (LREC 2016). European Language Resources Association (ELRA).

Sánchez-Martínez, Felipe, Martínez-Sempere, Isabel, Ivars-Ribes, Xavier, and Carrasco, Rafael C. 2013. *An open diachronic corpus of historical Spanish: annotation criteria and automatic modernisation of spelling.* Research Report. Departament de Llenguatges i Sistemes Informàtics, Universitat d'Alacant, Alicante.

Scherrer, Yves. 2007. Adaptive string distance measures for bilingual dialect lexicon induction. Pages 55–60 of: *Proceedings of the ACL 2007 Student Research Workshop.*

Scherrer, Yves. 2008. Part-of-speech tagging with a symbolic full parser: Using the TIGER treebank to evaluate Fips. Pages 16–23 of: *Proceedings of the Workshop on Parsing German.*

Scherrer, Yves. 2014. Unsupervised adaptation of supervised part-of-speech taggers for closely related languages. Pages 30–38 of: *Proceedings of the First Workshop on Applying NLP Tools to Similar Languages, Varieties and Dialects.*

Scherrer, Yves, and Erjavec, Tomaž. 2016. Modernising historical Slovene words. *Natural Language Engineering*, **6**(22), 881–905.

Scherrer, Yves, and Ljubešić, Nikola. 2016. Automatic normalisation of the Swiss German ArchiMob corpus using character-level machine translation. Pages 248–255 of: *Proceedings of the 13th Conference on Natural Language Processing (KONVENS 2016).*

Scherrer, Yves, and Rabus, Achim. 2017. Multi-source morphosyntactic tagging for spoken Rusyn. Pages 84–92 of: *Proceedings of the Fourth Workshop on NLP for Similar Languages, Varieties and Dialects (VarDial).*

Scherrer, Yves, and Rabus, Achim. 2019. Neural morphosyntactic tagging for Rusyn. *Natural Language Engineering*, **25**(5), 633–650.

Scherrer, Yves, and Sagot, Benoît. 2014. A language-independent and fully unsupervised approach to lexicon induction and part-of-speech tagging for closely related languages. Pages 502–508 of: *Proceedings of the Ninth International Conference on Language Resources and Evaluation (LREC'14).* Reykjavik, Iceland: European Language Resources Association (ELRA).

Scherrer, Yves, Mocken, Susanne, and Rabus, Achim. 2018. New developments in tagging pre-modern orthodox Slavic texts. *Scripta & e-Scripta*, **18**, 9–34.

Scherrer, Yves, Samardžić, Tanja, and Glaser, Elvira. 2019. Digitising Swiss German: How to process and study a polycentric spoken language. *Language Resources and Evaluation*, **53**, 735–769.

Schmid, Helmut. 1994. Probabilistic part-of-speech tagging using decision trees. In: *Proceedings of International Conference on New Methods in Language Processing.*

Sharoff, Serge. 2018. Language adaptation experiments via cross-lingual embeddings for related languages. Pages 844–849 of: *Proceedings of the Eleventh International Conference on Language Resources and Evaluation (LREC 2018).* Miyazaki, Japan: European Language Resources Association (ELRA).

Silfverberg, Miikka, and Drobac, Senka. 2018. Sub-label dependencies for neural morphological tagging – The joint submission of University of Colorado and University of Helsinki for VarDial 2018. Pages 37–45 of: *Proceedings of the Fifth Workshop on NLP for Similar Languages, Varieties and Dialects (VarDial 2018).*

Søgaard, Anders, Ruder, Sebastian, and Vulić, Ivan. 2018. On the limitations of unsupervised bilingual dictionary induction. Pages 778–788 of: *Proceedings of the 56th Annual Meeting of the Association for Computational Linguistics (Volume 1: Long Papers)*.

Täckström, Oscar, McDonald, Ryan, and Uszkoreit, Jakob. 2012. Cross-lingual word clusters for direct transfer of linguistic structure. Pages 477–487 of: *Proceedings of the 2012 Conference of the North American Chapter of the Association for Computational Linguistics: Human Language Technologies*.

Tang, Gongbo, Cap, Fabienne, Pettersson, Eva, and Nivre, Joakim. 2018. An evaluation of neural machine translation models on historical spelling normalization. Pages 1320–1331 of: *Proceedings of COLING 2018, the 27th International Conference on Computational Linguistics*.

Tapanainen, Pasi, and Voutilainen, Atro. 1994. Tagging accurately – Don't guess if you know. Pages 47–52 of: *Proceedings of the Fourth Conference on Applied Natural Language Processing*.

Tiedemann, Jörg. 2009. Character-based PSMT for closely related languages. Pages 12–19 of: *Proceedings of EAMT 2009*.

Tiedemann, Jörg, and Agić, Željko. 2016. Synthetic treebanking for cross-lingual dependency parsing. *Journal of Artificial Intelligence Research*, **55**, 209–248.

Tiedemann, Jörg, Agić, Željko, and Nivre, Joakim. 2014. Treebank translation for cross-lingual parser induction. Pages 130–140 of: *Proceedings of the Eighteenth Conference on Computational Natural Language Learning*.

Tjong Kim Sang, Erik, Bollmann, Marcel, Boschker, Remko, Casacuberta, Francisco, Dietz, Feike, Dipper, Stefanie, Domingo, Miguel, van der Goot, Rob, van Koppen, Marjo, Ljubešić, Nikola, Östling, Robert, Petran, Florian, Pettersson, Eva, Scherrer, Yves, Schraagen, Marijn, Sevens, Leen, Tiedemann, Jörg, Vanallemeersch, Tom, and Zervanou, Kalliopi. 2017. The CLIN27 shared task: Translating historical text to contemporary language for improving automatic linguistic annotation. *Computational Linguistics in the Netherlands Journal*, **7**, 53–64.

Toutanova, Kristina, Klein, Dan, Manning, Christopher D., and Singer, Yoram. 2003. Feature-rich part-of-speech tagging with a cyclic dependency network. Pages 173–180 of: *Proceedings of the 2003 Conference of the North American Chapter of the Association for Computational Linguistics on Human Language Technology (NAACL 2003)*.

Trudgill, Peter. 2000. *Sociolinguistics: An Introduction to Language and Society*. London: Penguin Books.

Trudgill, Peter. 2004. Glocalisation and the Ausbau sociolinguistics of modern Europe. Pages 35–49 of: Duszak, A., and Okulska, U. (eds.), *Speaking from the Margin: Global English from a European Perspective*. Frankfurt: Peter Lang.

Upadhyay, Shyam, Faruqui, Manaal, Dyer, Chris, and Roth, Dan. 2016. Cross-lingual models of word embeddings: An empirical comparison. Pages 1661–1670 of: *Proceedings of the 54th Annual Meeting of the Association for Computational Linguistics (Volume 1: Long Papers)*.

Vilar, David, Peter, Jan-Thorsten, and Ney, Hermann. 2007. Can we translate letters? Pages 33–39 of: *Proceedings of the Second Workshop on Statistical Machine Translation*.

Yang, Jie, and Zhang, Yue. 2018. NCRF++: An open-source neural sequence labeling toolkit. Pages 74–79 of: *Proceedings of ACL 2018, System Demonstrations*.

Yarowksy, David, and Ngai, Grace. 2001. Inducing multilingual POS taggers and NP bracketers via robust projection across aligned corpora. Pages 200–207 of: *Proceedings of NAACL 2001*.

Yu, Xiang, Falenska, Agnieszka, and Vu, Ngoc Thang. 2017. A general-purpose tagger with convolutional neural networks. Pages 124–129 of: *Proceedings of the First Workshop on Subword and Character Level Models in NLP*.

Yu, Zhiwei, Mareček, David, Žabokrtský, Zdeněk, and Zeman, Daniel. 2016. If you even don't have a bit of Bible: Learning delexicalized POS taggers. In: *Proceedings of the Tenth International Conference on Language Resources and Evaluation (LREC 2016)*. European Language Resources Association (ELRA).

Zeman, Daniel. 2008. Reusable tagset conversion using tagset drivers. In: *Proceedings of the Sixth International Conference on Language Resources and Evaluation (LREC'08)*. Marrakech, Morocco: European Language Resources Association (ELRA).

Zeman, Daniel, and Resnik, Philip. 2008. Cross-language parser adaptation between related languages. Pages 35–42 of: *Proceedings of the IJCNLP-08 Workshop on NLP for Less Privileged Languages*.

Zhang, Yuan, Gaddy, David, Barzilay, Regina, and Jaakkola, Tommi. 2016. Ten pairs to tag – Multilingual POS tagging via coarse mapping between embeddings. Pages 1307–1317 of: *Proceedings of the 2016 Conference of the North American Chapter of the Association for Computational Linguistics: Human Language Technologies*.

8 Sharing Dependency Parsers between Similar Languages

Željko Agić

8.1 Introduction

8.1.1 The Great Language Divide

From web search to speech recognition or machine translation, language technology today improves the way we humans communicate at the largest scale. This technology owes its success to supervised machine learning, whereby models such as dependency parsers or neural machine translators are built from human-annotated or otherwise curated data. As such curation is costly, it creates a divide: While the world speaks around 7,000 languages, there is some basic language technology support for not over 100 languages (Nivre et al., 2016). Even more so, all languages but English are under-resourced to some degree, including the European ones that typically do have some basic processing tools such as part-of-speech taggers or dependency parsers (Rehm and Uszkoreit, 2012). The resource divide between the languages put forth a crucial challenge for language technology: How to scale beyond the 1 percent resource-rich languages and offer basic technology to the 99 percent? To create language technology without manually annotated data is at the focal point of *cross-lingual transfer learning.*

8.1.2 "Robin Hood" Language Technology

Central to cross-lingual learning is the dichotomy between resource-rich *source languages* and low-resource *target languages*: We seek to transfer existing models from the sources to the targets. But: How can an English tagger ever hope to annotate Punjabi texts for parts of speech, or a Danish parser to yield syntactic dependencies on top of Albanian sentences? Surely not without adaptation. Thus, cross-lingual learning is essentially the study of adaptation of source-language models to fit target languages. Like Robin Hood, cross-lingual learning is taking resources from the rich and giving to the poor languages, but in a win–win scenario where the rich still get to keep their technology. We can

Work in part done while at the IT University of Copenhagen, Denmark.

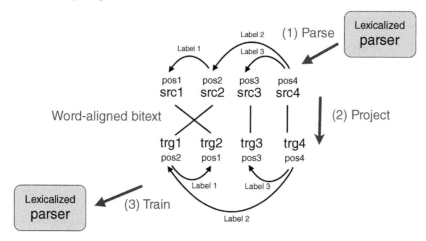

Figure 8.1 An illustration of annotation projection for dependency parsing, by Tiedemann and Agić (2016).

identify two main strands of cross-lingual work. In my listing, I focus exclusively on the basic language technology task of parsing sentences for syntactic dependency trees, or in short, dependency parsing (Kübler et al., 2009).

Annotation Projection: The key ingredient of these approaches are parallel corpora of text that spans multiple source and target languages. Since sentence and word alignments are unsupervised, relatively reliable mappings of sentences and words between the languages come for free. The challenge is then to project the source-side annotations into the target words and sentences. Once the annotations are projected, one can train whatever dedicated model on top of them for the target language. The procedure is depicted in Figure 8.1.

Seeded by Yarowsky et al. (2001), the basic idea of annotation projection has seen many refinements over the years, especially for dependency parsing, from Hwa et al. (2005), who featured English and Chinese only, Tiedemann and Agić (2016), who used machine translation to first create the target language texts and then project the dependency trees, to Agić et al. (2016), who yield hundreds of parsers in one go. The latter also propose that only using the most massively multilingual parallel texts such as the Bible provides a fair test bed for the most severely under-resourced languages and that gathering projections from multiple sources into multiple targets offers substantial gains.

Projecting annotations from multiple sources generally requires a more elaborate approach to arrive at target-language dependency trees, which typically features an accumulation phase, whereby the source contributions are collected,

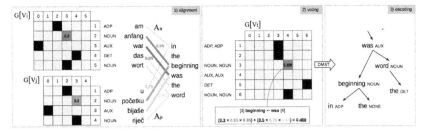

Figure 8.2 An illustration of annotation projection from two source sentences into one target sentence for parts of speech and syntactic dependencies, by Agić et al. (2016). Each source edge contributes weights to the target dependency graph $G[V_t]$ which is then decoded into a dependency tree by a maximum spanning tree algorithm. The edge weights come from tagger and parser confidences, sentence and word alignment probabilities, and are possibly further constrained through some model of language similarity.

and a decoding phase, where the final target tree is decided as in Figure 8.2. Schlichtkrull and Søgaard (2017) later show that postponing the decoding by making neural parsers learn from projected graphs instead of decoded trees yields even higher accuracies.

Annotation projection has historically produced the most accurate target-languages parser, e.g., the work by Ma and Xia (2014) or Rasooli and Collins (2015). Other work suggested that coupling the projection of related tasks, such as part-of-speech tagging and dependency parsing, offers further gains, as per Johannsen et al. (2016).

Model Transfer: As the age-long linguistic debate goes, while languages are abundant with differences, they do also share certain universalities. In its most basic form, model transfer relies on such common, albeit impoverished, feature representations. For example, if we agree that a dependency parser can learn to attach parts of speech instead of actual words, and if we agree on a common part-of-speech representation across many languages, then any parser can parse any language. This is the essence of delexicalized parsing, as depicted by Figure 8.3: We train a source parser on parts of speech and syntactic dependencies, and then run that model on target sequences of parts of speech to produce new dependencies.

The seed idea is due to Zeman and Resnik (2008) who shared parsers between Danish and Swedish, but it was popularized by the seminal works of McDonald et al. (2011) and Søgaard (2011). They also independently suggested multiple sources of delexicalized parsers. These ideas were further built on by impactful work in selective feature sharing by Naseem et al. (2012) and Zhang and

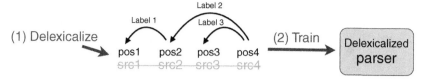

Figure 8.3 An illustration of delexicalized transfer for dependency parsing, by Tiedemann and Agić (2016).

Barzilay (2015). Another crucial aspect of this line of work are the cross-linguistically uniform feature representations, in this case, parts of speech. The first widely adopted universal representation was by Petrov et al. (2011), which then evolved via McDonald et al. (2013) into the Universal Dependencies treebanks (Nivre et al., 2016). McDonald et al. (2013) were also crucial in exposing the need for uniform representations in cross-lingual evaluation: We can reliably measure the performance of cross-lingual dependency parsers only if the training and test data are uniform in their representations of syntax across languages.

8.1.3   *The Yield and the Lessons Learned*

Recent years have marked great success for cross-lingual learning for dependency parsing: We now know how to produce workable parsers for hundreds of languages, even in one go, and we know what conditions make these parsers thrive. Transfer learning for low-resource dependency parsing continues to be a vibrant field of research in the brave new neural world, whereby multilingual distributed word representations offer even richer opportunities to adapt and transfer source-side models (Ammar et al., 2016) without relying on just uniform parts of speech as a rather impoverished multilingual model.

The Proxy Fallacy: Yet, with great power comes great responsibility, and cross-lingual parsing is not without its caveats. As McDonald et al. (2013) have shown, we must have uniform syntactic representations to reliably compare cross-lingual parsers across languages. The flip side of their argument is: We can evaluate only if annotated test data exist. However, true low-resource languages as targets of our research are, well, low-resource: they don't come bundled with manually annotated test data. For this reason, by and large, empirical work in cross-lingual parsing simulates low-resource scenarios and instead evaluates for resource-rich languages. That way, the bias creeps in through, e.g., the choice of parallel corpora: Typically research uses Europarl, which is near-perfectly tokenized and aligned, huge at more than 2 million sentences per language pair, but it covers only 21 languages of the European Union, all of which already have dedicated data to train dependency parsers.

How are Europarl-based cross-lingual parsers representative of low-resource languages such as Punjabi, Hausa, Tigrinya? Yet, how do we address this rhetorical inquiry if there are simply no test data for Punjabi and the like? I call this *the proxy fallacy*, and I posit that cross-lingual learning needs to address its concern in order to progress to true feasibility in the future.

The Absence of Breadth: Consider a dependency parsing experiment with annotation projection from multiple sources. What does it require? At the least, a parallel corpus that features multiple source and target languages, data to train monolingual source parsers, and data to evaluate cross-lingual target parsers at the end of projection. This is a list of constraints, and constraints typically reduce experiment breadth. As a result, typical papers in the field of language technology predominantly experiment with English only (Bender, 2013), and those in cross-lingual learning rarely go above a dozen, the proxy fallacy is thriving (Agić et al., 2015). Mielke (2016) even implies that the average number of languages per paper is not changing much over the years either.

What then happens when even the work on cross-lingual learning does not employ multilingual breadth and, at the same time, space constraints delineate our publications? We are necessarily left with too few languages in the experiments to truly understand what happens in the extremes of language similarity, when source and target languages are either very similar or very far apart.

8.1.4   What of the Other Extreme of Similarity?

How well does a delexicalized transfer parser perform when it parses Danish or Czech, if we know that it was trained on English annotated data? Similarly, if dependency trees are projected from English into Danish and Czech via a parallel corpus, how accurate are the cross-lingual parsers trained on the two respective portions?

Typology and Transfer: Following the key work of McDonald et al. (2013), we now know that linguistic similarity plays an important role in cross-lingual transfer. As a general rule, any given method of cross-lingual parsing will work better if the languages are more related. The intuition is clear, at least. For example, if the only information source for a delexicalized parser is sequences of part-of-speech tags at training time, it will obviously perform better if it parses similar sequences at runtime. As these tag sequences in turn capture word order, such training consequentially builds parsers that favor related word orders. In a similar vein, if dependency trees are algorithmically projected from source to target sentences, the procedure will have an inherently harder time working with more complex word alignment patterns.

The frame of mind regarding similarity and transfer presented above has ushered in a large body of work in devising various models of linguistic typology and exploiting them in cross-lingual parsing and beyond, all of which has been surveyed extensively by O'Horan et al. (2016), Bender (2016), and Ponti et al. (2018). Essentially, from a bird's-eye view, the work in modeling typological relations for cross-lingual parsing deals with promoting the similarities, while suppressing the differences, with the ultimate goal of bringing the sources and targets closer together. For example, a transfer parser for Croatian may benefit from sharing morphological properties with Czech and word order with Slovenian, and thus the transfer should weigh these features higher than the others.

A Change in Viewpoints: Inherent in the relation between typology and transfer is their separation in the form of language agnosticism. In language technology we boast the assumed language independence of our learning algorithms. The data determines the language, in what some researchers also boldly state is simply linguistic naivety (Bender, 2009). In that sense, most research keeps cross-lingual parsing methods unchanged with respect to the source–target pairs; typically, we do not adapt or change the method itself, we simply observe how it fares in relation to the change in language similarity. Even more so, cross-lingual learning tends to care more for the case of extreme differences, since arguably that tests the approaches more thoroughly. Basically, as we know that the performance of a method is bound to deteriorate with increased dissimilarity, we are curious to uncover its breaking point.

Here, I posit a change in perspective: Instead of keeping the cross-lingual transfer methods monolithic, and focusing on the extreme of dissimilarity, what if we look at the other end of the spectrum and highlight the similarity? In specific, are there cases of similarity that warrant entirely different cross-lingual transfer models, and if yes, what are these models and how do they compare to the more generic ones? For better or for worse, what I find is that our field is only now beginning to uncover answers to these exciting questions.

8.2   A New Hope? Notable Exceptions

How do we efficiently generate parsers for low-resource target languages that have closely related languages in the list of fortunate well-resourced sources? I proceed to give a somewhat cursory account of the work in transferring parsers between similar languages.

8.2.1   A Slightly Biased Account of the Early Days

What I call the early days of sharing parsers between related languages also mirrors the early days of cross-lingual parsing: the era before the emergence of

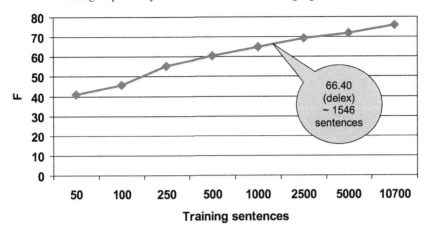

Figure 8.4 The famous learning curve from Zeman and Resnik (2008). The learning curve shows the point at which human annotation surpasses delexicalization is at 1,546 hand-annotated training instances. Such a number of instances is typically out of reach for true low-resource languages.

uniform syntactic representations by McDonald et al. (2013) and the Universal Dependencies movement that followed in their footsteps (Nivre et al., 2016).

To start off, as an interesting historical point, the work by Zeman and Resnik (2008) as instigators of delexicalization in transfer parsing in fact features two closely related languages, Danish and Swedish. In a non-trivial effort, they make uniform the morphosyntactic representations between the two treebanks. Their experiment proceeds to show that simple delexicalization is worth approximately 1,600 manually annotated sentences in parsing accuracy for Danish (see Figure 8.4). As future work will reveal in the years that followed Zeman and Resnik (2008), this rather high gain is indicative of close relatedness, because delexicalization is shown to be worth much less on average, and especially across more distant groups of languages. I am also compelled to note at this point that the non-trivial work in treebank uniformization for multilingual parsing between many formalisms has remained one forte of Zeman and colleagues throughout the past decade (Zeman, 2008; Zeman et al., 2014). At times undoubtedly unrewarding, this work has been instrumental in pushing the frontiers of cross-lingual parsing in the pre-uniformity era.

On the margins of language technology mainstream, other research featured parser transfer within specific groups of languages. One such example is my own collaborative work with South Slavic languages, where we sought to attain better parsing for Croatian and Slovene through treebank sharing, while at the same time transferring these improved parsers to a then severely low-resource Serbian language. We first experimented with dictionary-based "translation" of

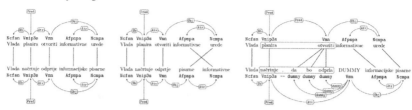

Figure 8.5 The machine translation-based annotation projection sharing strategies by Agić et al. (2014). From left to right, Croatian is translated into Slovene via character-based translation without reordering, word-based translation with reordering, and full-blown phrase-based machine translation. Annotation projection follows the translation step, and is based on the refinement of Hwa et al. (2005) by Tiedemann (2014). Note that without reordering the annotation projection step is here trivial, as the dependency trees are simply copied over to the target sentence.

a Slovene treebank into Croatian (Agić et al., 2012), and then with uniform test sets to evaluate various standard cross-lingual methods (Agić et al., 2014), such as direct transfer, annotation projection, and synthetic treebanking via machine translation following Tiedemann et al. (2014). Our work found that contrary to the more elaborate needs of more distant languages, simplest approaches worked best for this specific South Slavic languages: Character- and word-based machine translation was consistently better than phrase-based in annotation projection, and simple delexicalized transfer offered scores comparable to Zeman and Resnik (2008). In essence, very simple adaptations such as vocabulary interventions were sufficient to yield workable parsers in the target languages. We later expand on this work in the Universal Dependencies realm by cross-lingually parsing Serbian using Croatian training data with no interventions whatsoever, i.e., we simply parse Serbian test data using a fully lexicalized Croatian parser (Agić and Ljubešić, 2015). While this particular result does yield a practically usable dependency parser for Serbian, it also makes implications on the arbitrariness of extra-linguistic constraints imposed within certain language continuums, whereby the dependency parser does not seem to care much about such delimitations, and offers uninterrupted good performance instead.

The findings that are presented above are further confirmed by Garcia et al. (2018), who use the lessons learned in cross-lingual parsing of Romance languages to construct a new Universal Dependencies treebank for Galician. They proceed to show that delexicalization has limited, if any gains when languages are very closely related, and they also show that sharing source-language treebanks matches the scores of between 10 and 20,000 tokens of annotated in-language data, which is aligned with the original result by Zeman and Resnik (2008).

Beyond these highlighted contribution, there is very little work to be found on sharing dependency parsers between similar languages in the period before McDonald et al. (2013), save for the fact that their own experiments featured aspects of relatedness as well. Namely, as the first uniform treebanks featured resource-rich languages, the experiments would always feature parser sharing at least within and between Germanic and Romance languages, for better or for worse. This bias also holds true to their prior work on multi-source delexicalized transfer (McDonald et al., 2011).

8.2.2   What Changed with Universal Dependencies?

In my view, the Universal Dependencies collaboration is one of the most important movements in current language technology. Its first version appeared in 2015 and featured ten dependency treebanks (Nivre et al., 2016). By the latter release in July 2018, it now boasts 122 treebanks, all fully annotated for parts of speech, morphology, and syntactic dependencies, making it arguably the biggest and the most useful manually annotated multilingual resource in our field.

With Universal Dependencies at hand, we can now experiment with more than seventy languages across diverse language families, in the vein of the work on multilingual tagging work by Plank et al. (2016) or the exploration of parsing metrics by Nivre and Fang (2017). Is there voluminous work in parsing closely related languages in the yield of Universal Dependencies, then? While a more precise answer is complex, as it has to do with the pace of adoption for new resources in scientific research, from a bird's eye view, at this point in time, I am compelled to conclude that it has not: There are still but a handful of research units that problematize close relatedness in parsing. Yet, there is something stirring in this landscape as of very recently: most notably, an actual shared task in dependency parsing of closely related languages and a general move towards charting out the complex interactions between language technology and linguistic typology.

8.2.3   The VarDial Shared Tasks

Only very recently have we seen the first coordinated focused effort in cross-lingual parsing aimed specifically on closely related languages: the VarDial shared task by Zampieri et al. (2017). The task featured three target languages: Croatian, Norwegian, and Slovak. The respective designated source languages were Danish and Swedish for Norwegian, Slovene for Croatian, and Czech for Slovak. The task enforced realistic preprocessing, and made available some seed parallel data for all source–target language pairs (Tiedemann, 2012). Baselines and upper bounds were provided by the organizers: non-adapted

LAS	Croatian	Norwegian	Slovak
CUNI	60.70	70.21	78.12
Helsinki-CLP	57.98	68.60	73.14
tubasfs	55.20	65.62	64.05

UAS	Croatian	Norwegian	Slovak
CUNI	69.73	77.13	84.92
Helsinki-CLP	69.57	76.77	82.87
tubasfs	75.61	74.61	73.16

Figure 8.6 The results of the VarDial 2017 campaign in cross-lingual dependency parsing for closely related languages by Zampieri et al. (2017). Most notably, the scores are rather high, up to the point of practical usability in downstream applications, by contrast to work on truly low-resource languages where scores are easily 15–20 points lower in realistic test setups (Agić et al., 2016). The discrepancy between UAS and LAS score differences for the two top systems is due to additional label normalization that the top system includes, which in turn indicates via UAS scores that all three systems were more or less of comparable perfomance.

source models, delexicalized transfer parsers, and fully supervised in-language models. All data are based on Universal Dependencies.

Three teams participated in the task (Çöltekin and Rama, 2017; Rosa et al., 2017; Tiedemann, 2017). Two systems suggested to use word-based translation similar to Agić et al. (2014) from Figure 8.5, while the third system involved a mix of treebank translation and subsequent annotation projection following Tiedemann et al. (2014). The submission record modest improvements over the baseline for Croatian (2–7 points in labeled attachment) and more substantial for Norwegian (over 10 points). Most notably, the two top submissions for Slovak score above the monolingual upper bound, likely due to the very large amount of training data that is available for Czech as its source language.

As stated by Zampieri et al. (2017) in their findings, such results strongly indicate that practically usable parsers are attainable if the low-resource target languages are fortunate enough to have closely related and well-resourced cousins. This important finding is not highlighted enough in the standard cross-lingual parsing literature, where exclusive focus is on extreme dissimilarity instead.

The previous decade has witnessed markedly venerable shared tasks in monolingual data-driven dependency parsing: CoNLL 2006-2007 (Buchholz and Marsi, 2006; Nivre et al., 2007). These tasks have significantly advanced the field towards practicable language-agnostic dependency parsers, and they have also promoted useful dependency treebanks for 17 languages, many of which are still in use today, either for legacy purposes of backward compatibility, or revamped as contributions to Universal Dependencies. Taking this admirable example as inspiration, one can only hope for wider adoption of the VarDial shared task in parsing related languages in the future. What we need is simply more multilingual data and more system submissions.

8.2.4   Some Best Practices

There is a small but notable portion of work in cross-lingual parser selection for low-resource languages that is of relevance to relatedness in parsing. Given a target language, the task is to select the optimal delexicalized transfer parser for that language from a pool of sources. For example, Rosa and Žabokrtský (2015a) explore the Kullback–Leibler divergence of part-of-speech sequences between the input data and the treebank training data to select optimal parsers, and further, Rosa and Žabokrtský (2015b) use such metrics as weights in voting dependency trees from edge graphs created by parsing the same target sentences by multiple source parsers similar to Sagae and Lavie (2006). This idea is further explored by Agić et al. (2017), who relax the similarity constraint so as to not compare test sets, but individual input sentences instead. Most notably, Agić et al. (2017) find that there is a discrepancy between what the best parser is on test set and on sentence level: Figure 8.7 indicates that for nearly 30 percent test sentences over 26 languages, the best parse comes from a delexicalized parser that is not ranked best on the entire test set of that respective language. This result is important for the downstream utilization of cross-lingual dependency

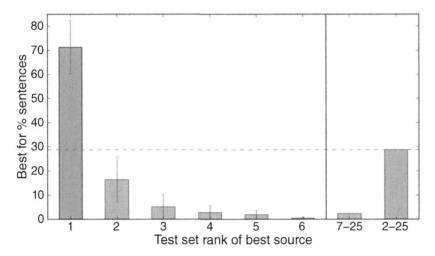

Figure 8.7 Agić et al. (2017) shows that the optimal single-source delexical-ized transfer parser should not be selected per language (or per test set), but rather per sentence as the minimal input unit for a parser. The figure illustrates that around 30 percent sentences over 26 test languages get a suboptimal parse through test set-level parser selection.

parsers. Out there "in the wild" we do not parse languages, we parse streams of running text, and it seems that what works for test sets does not necessarily work best for the individual sentences!

A recent contribution by Rosa (2018), who also contributed the best system in the VarDial 2017 shared task, lists the best practices in bootstrapping cross-lingual parsers for low-resource languages via annotation projection. The proposal especially emphasizes the use of linguistic similarity metrics such as KL divergence, hard-coded linguistic features such as the now-ubiquitous WALS data (Dryer et al., 2005), and the like. Further thorough exploration needs to particularly emphasize closely related languages so as to bring forth a set of similar recommendations that go beyond the confines of annotation projection and other general cross-lingual learning methods for bootstrapping parsers.

8.3   To Conclude: A Glimpse of the Future

"The End of the Beginning." Instead of a decisive conclusion, I offer an observation. To paraphrase Churchill: In its entirety, the field of cross-lingual transfer learning is arguably far from the beginning of its end, but perhaps it is now closing in on the end of its beginning. We now have uniform data sets for basic syntactic processing tasks across more than seventy languages (120 data sets) and counting, and advanced generic learning machinery in the form of deep neural networks to facilitate learning between languages, tasks, or both (Kaiser et al., 2017). The stage is set for a new phase of advancements in transferring models between source and target languages.

In a similar vein, the research in adapting and sharing parsers between similar languages is still in its early days. The contributions are too few, and by and large, they do not scratch deep beneath the surface of standard cross-lingual parsing: What we have seen thus far are mainly lighter adaptations of the well-known approaches to annotation projection or delexicalized transfer. The most notable findings have been to not delexicalize at all or to employ lighter transformations in form of character-level translation or word reordering. The only shared task to highlight similar languages offered a limited range of data sets and has left but a small footprint on the field due to limited participation: There were three target languages and as many submitted systems.

Yet, I predict a bright future to the challenge of porting parsers between similar languages, whether to enable a low-resource language, or to enrich and robustify already existing monolingual parsers through cross-lingual support (de Lhoneux et al., 2018). Research in closely related languages can benefit, or even make targeted contributions to the pool of resources in Universal Dependencies to extend the experiment scope and to get informed feedback from larger scale work on cross-lingual parsing.

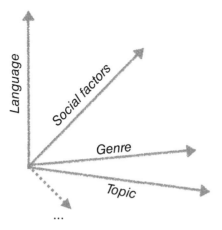

Figure 8.8 Plank (2016) proposes that linguistic datasets all sample from a variety space, which is in turn conditioned by latent factors such as demographics, language or dialect, topic or genre. The notion of variety is introduced so as to avoid the use of *domain* as an inherently overloaded term. Plank further discusses the historically opportunistic nature of such sampling, which spawned the newswire bias in language technology.

I wrap up the article with a few notes on what the future research directions in parsing similar languages may be.

Learning in a Variety Space: To share in the view of Plank (2016) (see Figure 8.8), I envision research in cross-lingual dependency parsing that transcends the traditional hard separations between domains, languages, demographic properties, and other extra-linguistic features. Such research would assume that in language technology research we always sample from a possibly infinite variety space that is jointly conditioned on all the listed factors, and that truly robust language technology should thus learn integral models to address in a principled way the multiple sources of adversity incurred by the many forms that similarity or diversity may take. One obvious suspect to investigate in the immediate future is multilingual and multi-task learning, where different tasks for different languages would inform one another to mutual benefit.

Approximate Evaluation: Cross-lingual learning is at an evaluation impasse, since we lack the test data in true low-resource languages to empirically assess the models we produce. For this reason, I see approximate evaluation of dependency parsers (and language technology in general) of vital importance for the future development of cross-lingual methods. Namely, if we can reliably, up to some epsilon, approximate the true test set scores of dependency parsers without using hand-annotated data, we can push one step closer to plotting cross-lingual parsing accuracies on world maps instead of cramming them in twenty-row tables at best. Should a compromise be made between approximate evaluation and evaluation by proxy, I argue that the choice should be made that maximizes the number of languages spanned by the experiment. At this point I am aware of only a few contributions to this important topic. Gulordava and Merlo (2016) perform a large-scale study of parsability over synthetic treebank data by controlling for dependency length and word order variability. Agić et al. (2017) show how to use translated tag dictionaries of only 100 entries to reliably approximate the true test set scores of cross-lingual part of speech taggers.

Synthetic Data: There is recent exciting work with generating synthetic data in delexicalized transfer parsing by Wang and Eisner (2018). Such synthetic data can then be treated as artificial languages that fall within different parts of the similarity spectrum with regards to real human languages from, say, Universal Dependencies. Wang and Eisner (2018) pose the question: What if the closest source for a given target language is still too far away? They propose to stochastically permute the constituents of existing treebanks so that they better resemble the target language. This general principle can be applied in training parsers, as the proposed system does push delexicalized parsing beyond baseline scores and into competitive space (see Figure 8.9), but it can also find uses in approximate evaluation.

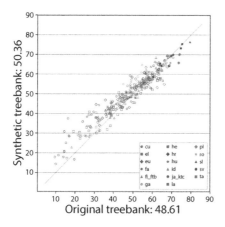

Figure 8.9 Wang and Eisner (2018) show the benefits of generating synthetic treebanks by permuting the existing sources so as to resemble the target sequences of parts of speech. In this figure from their paper on 337 language pairs, they show significant improvements in attachment scores in favor of synthetic source languages. This is strong evidence that if similarity is not already there in our human-annotated data, we can make the data fit the target languages by stochastic permutations.

References

Agić, Željko, Hovy, Dirk, and Søgaard, Anders. 2015. If all you have is a bit of the Bible: Learning POS taggers for truly low-resource languages. Pages 268–272 of: *ACL*.

Agić, Željko, and Ljubešić, Nikola. 2015. Universal Dependencies for Croatian (that work for Serbian, too). Pages 1–8 of: *BSNLP*.

Agić, Željko, Merkler, Danijela, and Berovic, Daša. 2012. Slovene-Croatian treebank transfer using bilingual lexicon improves Croatian dependency parsing. Pages 5–9 of: *IS-LTC*.

Agić, Željko, Tiedemann, Jörg, Dobrovoljc, Kaja, Krek, Simon, Merkler, Danijela, and Može, Sara. 2014. Cross-lingual dependency parsing of related languages with rich morphosyntactic tagsets. Pages 13–24 of: *EMNLP 2014 Workshop on Language Technology for Closely Related Languages and Language Variants*.

Agić, Željko, Johannsen, Anders, Plank, Barbara, Martínez Alonso, Héctor, Schluter, Natalie, and Søgaard, Anders. 2016. Multilingual projection for parsing truly low-resource languages. *TACL*, **4**, 301–312.

Agić, Željko, Plank, Barbara, and Søgaard, Anders. 2017. Cross-lingual tagger evaluation without test data. In: *EACL*.

Ammar, Waleed, Mulcaire, George, Ballesteros, Miguel, Dyer, Chris, and Smith, Noah A. 2016. Many languages, one parser. *TACL*, **4**, 431–444.

Bender, Emily M. 2009. Linguistically naïve!= language independent: Why NLP needs linguistic typology. Pages 26–32 of: *EACL*. Association for Computational Linguistics.

Bender, Emily M. 2013. *Linguistic Fundamentals for Natural Language Processing: 100 Essentials from Morphology and Syntax*. Morgan & Claypool Publishers.

Bender, Emily M. 2016. Linguistic typology in natural language processing. *Linguistic Typology*, **20**(3), 645–660.

Buchholz, Sabine, and Marsi, Erwin. 2006. CoNLL-X shared task on multilingual dependency parsing. Pages 149–164 of: *CONLL*.

Çöltekin, Çağrı, and Rama, Taraka. 2017. Tübingen system in VarDial 2017 shared task: experiments with language identification and cross-lingual parsing. Pages 146–155 of: *VarDial*.

de Lhoneux, Miryam, Bjerva, Johannes, Augenstein, Isabelle, and Søgaard, Anders. 2018. Parameter sharing between dependency parsers for related languages. *arXiv preprint arXiv:1808.09055*.

Dryer, Matthew S, Gil, David, Comrie, Bernard, Jung, Hagen, Schmidt, Claudia, et al. 2005. The world atlas of language structures.

Garcia, Marcos, Gómez-Rodríguez, Carlos, and Alonso, Miguel A. 2018. New treebank or repurposed? On the feasibility of cross-lingual parsing of Romance languages with Universal Dependencies. *Natural Language Engineering*, **24**(1), 91–122.

Gulordava, Gulordava, and Merlo, Paola. 2016. Multilingual dependency parsing evaluation: A large scale analysis of word order properties using artificial data. *TACL*, **4**, 343–356.

Hwa, Rebecca, Resnik, Philip, Weinberg, Amy, Cabezas, Clara, and Kolak, Okan. 2005. Bootstrapping parsers via syntactic projection across parallel texts. *Natural language engineering*, **11**(3), 311–325.

Johannsen, Anders, Agić, Željko, and Søgaard, Anders. 2016. Joint part-of-speech and dependency projection from multiple sources. Pages 561–566 of: *ACL*.

Kaiser, Lukasz, Gomez, Aidan N, Shazeer, Noam, Vaswani, Ashish, Parmar, Niki, Jones, Llion, and Uszkoreit, Jakob. 2017. One model to learn them all. *arXiv preprint arXiv:1706.05137.*

Kübler, Sandra, McDonald, Ryan, and Nivre, Joakim. 2009. *Dependency Parsing.* Morgan & Claypool Publishers.

Ma, Xuezhe, and Xia, Fei. 2014. Unsupervised dependency parsing with transferring distribution via parallel guidance and entropy regularization. Pages 1337–1348 of: *ACL.*

McDonald, Ryan, Petrov, Slav, and Hall, Keith. 2011. Multi-source transfer of delexicalized dependency parsers. Pages 62–72 of: *EMNLP.*

McDonald, Ryan, Nivre, Joakim, Quirmbach-Brundage, Yvonne, Goldberg, Yoav, Das, Dipanjan, Ganchev, Kuzman, Hall, Keith, Petrov, Slav, Zhang, Hao, Täckström, Oscar, Bedini, Claudia, Bertomeu Castelló, Núria, and Lee, Jungmee. 2013. Universal dependency annotation for multilingual parsing. Pages 92–97 of: *ACL.*

Mielke, Sebastian J. 2016. *Language diversity in ACL 2004–2016.* https://sjmielke.com/acl-language-diversity.htm.

Naseem, Tahira, Barzilay, Regina, and Globerson, Amir. 2012. Selective sharing for multilingual dependency parsing. Pages 629–637 of: *ACL.*

Nivre, Joakim, and Fang, Chiao-Ting. 2017. Universal dependency evaluation. Pages 86–95 of: *UDW.*

Nivre, Joakim, Hall, Johan, Kübler, Sandra, McDonald, Ryan, Nilsson, Jens, Riedel, Sebastian, and Yuret, Deniz. 2007. The CoNLL 2007 shared task on dependency parsing. Pages 915–932 of: *EMNLP–CoNLL.*

Nivre, Joakim, de Marneffe, Marie-Catherine, Ginter, Filip, Goldberg, Yoav, Hajič Jan, Manning, Christopher D, McDonald, Ryan, Petrov, Slav, Pyysalo, Sampo, Silveira, Natalia, et al. 2016. Universal dependencies v1: A multilingual treebank collection. Pages 1659–1666 of: *LREC 2016.*

O'Horan, Helen, Berzak, Yevgeni, Vulić, Ivan, Reichart, Roi, and Korhonen, Anna. 2016. Survey on the use of typological information in natural language processing. *arXiv preprint arXiv:1610.03349.*

Petrov, Slav, Das, Dipanjan, and McDonald, Ryan. 2011. A universal part-of-speech tagset. *arXiv preprint arXiv:1104.2086.*

Plank, Barbara. 2016. What to do about non-standard (or non-canonical) language in NLP. *arXiv preprint arXiv:1608.07836.*

Plank, Barbara, Søgaard, Anders, and Goldberg, Yoav. 2016. Multilingual part-of-speech tagging with bidirectional long short-term memory models and auxiliary loss. *arXiv preprint arXiv:1604.05529.*

Ponti, Edoardo Maria, O'Horan, Helen, Berzak, Yevgeni, Vulić, Ivan, Reichart, Roi, Poibeau, Thierry, Shutova, Ekaterina, and Korhonen, Anna. 2018. Modeling language variation and universals: A survey on typological linguistics for natural language processing. *arXiv preprint arXiv:1807.00914.*

Rasooli, Mohammad Sadegh, and Collins, Michael. 2015. Density-driven cross-lingual transfer of dependency parsers. Pages 328–338 of: *EMNLP.*

Rehm, Georg, and Uszkoreit, Hans. 2012. *META-NET White Paper Series: Europe's Languages in the digital age.* Springer, Heidelberg.

Rosa, Rudolf. 2018. *Discovering the Structure of Natural Language Sentences by Semi-Supervised Methods.* Charles University.

Rosa, Rudolf, Zeman, Daniel, Mareček, David, and Žabokrtskỳ, Zdeněk. 2017. Slavic forest, Norwegian wood. Pages 210–219 of: *VarDial*.

Rosa, Rudolf, and Žabokrtský, Zdeněk. 2015a. KLcpos3 - A language similarity measure for delexicalized parser transfer. Pages 243–249 of: *ACL*.

Rosa, Rudolf, and Žabokrtský, Zdeněk. 2015b. MSTParser Model Interpolation for Multi-source Delexicalized Transfer. Pages 71–75 of: *IWPT*.

Sagae, Kenji, and Lavie, Alon. 2006. Parser combination by reparsing. Pages 129–132 of: *NAACL*.

Schlichtkrull, Michael Sejr, and Søgaard, Anders. 2017. Cross-lingual dependency parsing with late decoding for truly low-resource languages. *arXiv preprint arXiv:1701.01623*.

Søgaard, Anders. 2011. Data point selection for cross-language adaptation of dependency parsers. Pages 682–686 of: *ACL*.

Tiedemann, Jörg. 2012. Parallel data, tools and interfaces in OPUS. Pages 2214–2218 of: *LREC*, vol. 2012.

Tiedemann, Jörg. 2014. Rediscovering annotation projection for cross-lingual parser induction. Pages 1854–1864 of: *COLING*.

Tiedemann, Jörg. 2017. Cross-Lingual dependency parsing for closely related languages-Helsinki's submission to VarDial 2017. *arXiv preprint arXiv: 1708.05719*.

Tiedemann, Jörg, and Agić, Željko. 2016. Synthetic treebanking for cross-lingual dependency parsing. *Journal of Artificial Intelligence Research*, **55**, 209–248.

Tiedemann, Jörg, Agić, Željko, and Nivre, Joakim. 2014. Treebank translation for cross-lingual parser induction. Pages 130–140 of: *CoNLL*.

Wang, Dingquan, and Eisner, Jason. 2018. Synthetic data made to order: The case of parsing. Page 1325–1337 of: *EMNLP*.

Yarowsky, David, Ngai, Grace, and Wicentowski, Richard. 2001. Inducing multilingual text analysis tools via robust projection across aligned corpora. Pages 1–8 of: *Proceedings of the first international conference on Human language technology research*. Association for Computational Linguistics.

Zampieri, Marcos, Malmasi, Shervin, Ljubešić, Nikola, Nakov, Preslav, Ali, Ahmed, Tiedemann, Jörg, Scherrer, Yves, and Aepli, Noëmi. 2017. Findings of the VarDial Evaluation Campaign 2017. Pages 1–15 of: *VarDial*. Valencia, Spain: Association for Computational Linguistics.

Zeman, Daniel. 2008. Reusable tagset conversion using tagset drivers. Pages 28–30 of: *LREC*, vol. 2008.

Zeman, Daniel, and Resnik, Philip. 2008. Cross-language parser adaptation between related languages. Pages 35–42 of: *IJCNLP*.

Zeman, Daniel, Dušek, Ondřej, Mareček, David, Popel, Martin, Ramasamy, Loganathan, Štěpánek, Jan, Žabokrtskỳ, Zdeněk, and Hajič, Jan. 2014. HamleDT: Harmonized multi-language dependency treebank. *Language Resources and Evaluation*, **48**(4), 601–637.

Zhang, Yuan, and Barzilay, Regina. 2015. Hierarchical low-rank tensors for multilingual transfer parsing. Pages 1857–1867 of: *EMNLP*.

Part III

Applications and Language Specific Issues

9   Dialect and Similar Language Identification

Marcos Zampieri

9.1   Introduction

Automatic language identification, or simply language identification, is "the task of determining the natural language that a document or part thereof is written in" (Jauhiainen et al., 2019a). It consists of the application of computational methods to identify the language in texts, speech, and sign language. In this chapter, I focus on the identification of languages in texts, an important first step in many natural language processing (NLP) pipelines.

There are a number of situations in which the language(s) of a document is/are unknown. Language identification is important, for example, for machine translation (MT) systems in cases in which the source language of a document is unknown. It is also important in information retrieval (IR) systems. For example, English terms are used in a number of languages in various domains, but only documents written in a particular language are relevant for a given search. Finally, several popular software tools (e.g., text processors such as Microsoft Word) contain important built-in language identification modules.

As discussed in Jauhiainen et al. (2019a), in the early 2000s, language identification in texts was regarded by many as a solved task (McNamee, 2005). Statistical *n*-gram-based systems are able to achieve very high performance in identifying a small set of (often unrelated) languages (e.g., Finnish and Japanese) in text collections containing medium to large standard monolingual texts such as newspaper articles. With the widespread availability of user-generated content on the internet, and microblogging in particular, attention has shifted to more challenging scenarios in which the performance of language identification systems is still far from perfect. This includes discriminating between similar languages (e.g., Malay and Indonesian or Croatian and Serbian)

I would like to thank the Cambridge University Press editorial team for all the support provided during the preparation of this manuscript.

I further thank my fellow DSL shared task co-organizers who helped with designing and running the shared tasks presented in this chapter.

This chapter has some overlap with the content of the DSL shared tasks reports, referred to in this paper, and my PhD thesis (Zampieri, 2016).

(Ranaivo-Malançon, 2006; Ljubešić et al., 2007) and between standard national language varieties (e.g., Brazilian and European Portuguese or British and American English) (Lui and Cook, 2013; Zampieri et al., 2016) or dialects (e.g., the many dialects of Arabic) (Sadat et al., 2014; Tillmann et al., 2014) and iden-tifying the languages in multilingual documents (Nguyen and Dogruoz, 2014), in very short and nonstandard documents (e.g., tweets) (Tromp and Pechnizkiy, 2012), and in documents containing code switching (Solorio et al., 2014).

Given these challenging scenarios, we (Zampieri et al., 2015a) outlined the four main current research directions in language identification:

1. Increase the coverage of language identification systems from a few dozen languages to several hundred languages or, in a few cases, more than a thousand languages. Brown (2013, 2014) – for example, developed language identification systems to identify more than 1,000 languages.
2. Improve the performance of language identification systems across differ-ent domains and text types. The language used in tweets, for example, is very different from the language used in newspaper texts. To perform well across multiple domains, language identification systems should be able to recognize language features that are domain/text type independent as explored in Lui and Baldwin (2012).
3. Handle nonstandard texts. As discussed, state-of-the-art language identifi-cation systems achieve very high performance on language identification in standard contemporary texts, but the same is not true for other text types such as very short texts like tweets (Zubiaga et al., 2015), texts containing code switching (Solorio et al., 2014), and historical manuscripts (Jauhiainen et al., 2019b).
4. Discriminate between very similar languages, language varieties, and dialects (Sadat et al., 2014; Tillmann et al., 2014). This can provide useful information for applications such as machine translation and information retrieval, which may benefit from training systems on variety/dialect specific data, and geolocation prediction, systems which often rely on language/dialect features.

This chapter provides a concise overview of language identification with a special focus on the last research direction: language identification applied to language varieties, dialects, and similar languages. It takes into account the findings of the shared tasks organized within the scope of the workshops on NLP for Similar Language, Varieties, and Dialects (VarDial). The shared tasks at VarDial provide participants with benchmark data sets on multiple languages, dialects, text types, and domains which allow participants to compare the performance of language identification systems in a variety of scenarios. Two of these competitions are presented in more detail in this chapter.

The distinction between dialects, language varieties, and similar languages is extensively discussed in other chapters of this volume both from a (socio-) linguistic and computational perspective. This chapter, however, does not draw a line between dialects, (standard national) language varieties, and similar languages. This is on purpose as the challenges faced by language identification systems in processing, for example, Brazilian and European Portuguese, Croatian and Serbian, or Arabic dialects, are identical. Finally, in this chapter, I use the term *language variety* as a synonym for *standard national language varieties* of pluricentric languages (as in Clyne (1992)) such as Brazilian and European Portuguese or British and American English. Other language varieties, such as those related to style and register variation, are therefore outside the scope of this chapter.

9.2   A Supervised Text Classification Problem

Automatic language identification is most commonly approached using supervised text classification. Text classification methods are popular in NLP and are applied not only to language identification but also to many other applications (e.g., spam detection). It is defined as "the task of automatically sorting a set of documents into categories (or classes, or topics) from a predefined set" (Sebastiani, 2005). Classes are represented by a finite set of labels. In language identification, documents are texts whose language is unknown and the labels are the set of languages (or language varieties or dialects) that the system is trained to recognize.

The most common type of classification used in language identification is multi\class single-label classification, which allows only one label from a finite sent of n labels to be attributed to each instance. The language of a text can be either Spanish or German or English or Japanese, but not two or more of them at the same time. The term *single-label* is used in contrast to *multilabel classification*, which allows more than one label to be attributed to each instance. Language identification applied to multilingual documents may be modeled as a multilabel classification problem allowing more than label (language) to be attributed to each instance (text). In this chapter, however, single-label classification is discussed.

Given a set of documents written in different languages, a language identification system will implement the following main steps (Lui, 2014).

1. Data representation: select a text representation (e.g., characters, words, or a combination of the two).
2. Language modeling: calculate or derive a model from documents known to be written in each language.

3. Classification function: define a function that best represents the similarity between a document and each language model.
4. Prediction or output: compute the highest-scoring model to determine the language of the document.

There have been several types of feature representations used in language identification, many of them presented in this chapter. Character-based representations are the most popular and generally regarded to be the form of text representation that result in the best language identification performance. Among the first attempts to use character n-grams in language identification are Beesley (1988) and Dunning (1994). The interested reader can find comprehensive accounts on the history of language identification in the recent survey published by Jauhiainen et al. (2019a) and in the PhD thesis by Lui (2014).

9.3   Collecting Data

One of the main challenges of developing high-performing language identification systems for similar languages, language varieties, and dialects is the lack of suitable corpora available for varieties and dialects.[1] The case of dialects is the most challenging one as dialects are per se non-standard and only marginally used in printed media, resulting in very limited availability of books and newspapers for almost all dialects. There are a few strategies that have been used to address this challenge such as producing text data by transcribing speech, either manually as in the ArchiMob corpus for (Swiss) German dialects (Samardžić et al., 2016), or automatically using automatic speech recognition (ASR) systems as in Ali et al. (2016) for Arabic dialects. Social media is another interesting and popular way to obtain dialect text data, as described in Cotterell and Callison-Burch (2014), who used Twitter to collect data for Arabic dialects.

Each national variety of a language (e.g., British and American English) possess its own written standard, which may differ in several linguistic features and in spelling conventions (e.g., *neighbour* in the United Kingdom versus *neighbor* in the United States). Most books, magazines, and newspapers reflect these differences making them suitable data sources for most language varieties. As presented in Section 9.3.1, one example of journalistic corpus for language varieties is the DSL Corpus Collection (DSLCC) (Tan et al., 2014), which contains data collected from multiple newspapers from each country to diminish the topical and stylistic biases intrinsic to any newspaper. Other popular data sources used in NLP such as the Wikipedia, on the other hand, are not suited for the same purpose as it disregards language varieties. Wikipedia is

---

[1] The challenges of data collection and representation for similar languages, varieties, and dialects are discussed in detail in Chapter 6 of this volume.

a collaborative resource that allows speakers of multiple language varieties as well as nonnative speakers to contribute to the same article(s) available in a single English, Portuguese, or Spanish Wikipedia.[2] Finally, movie and TV subtitles have also successfully been used as data sources for Dutch and Flemish (van der Lee and van den Bosch, 2017; Zampieri et al., 2018) and in related NLP applications, such as machine translation between Brazilian and European Portuguese (Costa-jussà et al., 2018).

9.3.1   The DSL Corpus Collection

One of the most widely used data sets for similar language and language variety identification is the aforementioned Discriminating between Similar Languages Corpus Collection (Tan et al., 2014). The DSLCC is a collection of journalistic texts retrieved from (pre-)existing corpora, originally compiled for the first DSL shared task organized in 2014.[3] The DSLCC has been used in all subsequent DSL shared tasks. Five versions have been released so far and are freely available for the research community, the DSLCC v1.0, v2.0, v2.1, v3.0, and v4.0. The sources used to collect the texts included in the DSLCC are the SETimes Corpus (Tyers and Alperen, 2010) (available at OPUS (Tiedemann, 2012)), HC Corpora (Christensen, 2014), and Leipzig Corpora Collection (Biemann et al., 2007). Journalistic texts were used under the assumption that they are the most accurate representation of the contemporary written standard of a language.

Versions 1.0 and 2.0 of the DSLCC contain 18,000 randomly sampled training instances and 2,000 development instances for each language or language variety. For testing, DSLCC v1.0 contains 1,000 test instances for each language or variety, v2.0 contains 2,000 test instances divided into test set A (original texts) and test set B (texts with most named entities removed). The DSLCC v2.1 does not contain a test partition because it was compiled for the purpose of a qualitative study (unshared task) and not a quantitative one. This impacts the number of articles in Macanese Portuguese and Mexican Spanish. Text excerpts included in the DSLCC v1.0 have a minimum 20 tokens each without an upper limit. The number of texts and tokens per language in the DSLCC v1.0 is presented in Table 9.1.

Finally, text excerpts included in the DSLCC v2.0 and v2.1 contain a minimum of 20 tokens and a maximum of 100 tokens making the task more challenging. The number of texts and tokens per language in the DSLCC v2.0 and v2.1 is presented in Table 9.2.

---

[2] Notable exceptions are the "Simple English" Wikipedia which, as the name suggests, contains simplified English and a few (small) dialect Wikipedias.
[3] See http://ttg.uni-saarland.de/resources/DSLCC.

Table 9.1 *DSLCC v1.0: Language Groups*

Group	Language/Variety	Code	Documents	Tokens
A	Bosnian	*bs*	21,000	152,305
	Croatian	*hr*	21,000	151,502
	Serbian	*sr*	21,000	148,852
B	Indonesian	*id*	21,000	147,050
	Malay	*my*	21,000	145,258
C	Czech	*cz*	21,000	155,202
	Slovene	*sk*	21,000	152,052
D	Brazilian Portuguese	*pt-BR*	21,000	155,258
	European Portuguese	*pt-PT*	21,000	154,255
E	Argentine Spanish	*es-AR*	21,000	146,852
	Castilian Spanish	*es-ES*	21,000	147,800

Table 9.2 *DSLCC v2.0 and v2.1: Languages Grouped by Similarity*

Language/Variety	Code	Documents	Tokens
Bosnian	*bs*	22,000	130,509
Croatian	*hr*	22,000	129,985
Serbian	*sr*	22,000	132,585
Indonesian	*id*	22,000	115,250
Malay	*my*	22,000	118,784
Czech	*cz*	22,000	120,585
Slovak	*sk*	22,000	122,009
Brazilian Portuguese	*pt-BR*	22,000	130,585
European Portuguese	*pt-PT*	22,000	131,998
Macanese Portuguese	*pt-MO*	20,000	110,587
Argentine Spanish	*es-AR*	22,000	128,777
Castilian Spanish	*es-ES*	22,000	128,150
Mexican Spanish	*es-MX*	20,000	109,522
Bulgarian	*bg*	22,000	129,586
Macedonian	*mk*	22,000	130,963
Others	*xx*	22,000	131,020

9.4   Competitions

Shared tasks are important in NLP as they provide standardized evaluation metrics and benchmark data for various tasks and applications (Nissim et al., 2017). There have been a few shared tasks organized on dialect, similar language, and language variety identification in recent years such as the PAN lab 2017 at CLEF (Pardo et al., 2017), which featured dialects and varieties of Arabic, English, Spanish, and Portuguese. The most popular venue for such competitions is the aforementioned VarDial workshop, which is co-located yearly with international NLP conferences. Since VarDial's first edition in 2014, shared tasks on various topics related to language variation have been organized jointly with the workshop. The multilingual DSL shared task has been organized from 2014 to 2017 along with many other competitions on identifying varieties and dialects of Arabic, Romanian, Dutch, and Indo-Aryan langauges, to name a few.

In the next sections I briefly present and discuss the findings of two of the four editions of the DSL shared tasks organized in 2014 and 2015 within the scope of the VarDial workshop.

9.4.1   DSL Shared Task 2014

The DSL shared task 2014 (Zampieri et al., 2014) was, to the best of my knowledge, the first language identification competition to focus on discriminating between similar languages and language varieties.[4] The data used in this competition are the DSLCC v1.0. The DSL shared task 2014 attracted twenty-two teams from different countries, eight submitted their final results, and five wrote system description papers describing their systems.

Participants could choose to participate in any of the following two tracks:

- **Closed submission:** Using only the DSLCC v1.0 for training.
- **Open submission:** Using any data set for training.

Two teams compiled data sets to participate in the open submission track. All other teams used only the DSLCC v1.0 competing in the closed submission track. The five top performing teams in the closed submission track submitted system description papers: NRC-CNRC, RAE, UMich, UniMelb-NLP, and QMUL.

The NRC-CNRC team (Goutte et al., 2014) proposed a two-stage classification system that first predicts the language group followed by the language or language variety of each text. This two-stage approach proved to very effective. It was used by other teams in the DSL 2014 and replicated by several teams in subsequent editions of the DSL shared task. In NRC-CNRC's system, the language group is identified using a probabilistic classifier and within each group, the languages or language varieties are identified using linear SVM classifiers. The RAE team (Porta and Sancho, 2014) also used a two-stage classifier to identify first the language group and then the language or language variety of each text. The system uses a maximum entropy (MaxEnt) classifier

---

[4] For a comprehensive evaluation of the DSL 2014 and 2015 see Goutte et al. (2016).

with word *n*-grams, characters *n*-grams, and a list of tokens containing words that are exclusive to a language or variety. The UniMelb-NLP team (Lui et al., 2014) also proposed a two-stage approach similar to the NRC-CNRC and RAE teams. UniMelb-NLP tested different kinds of text representations, including delexicalized representations using a universal POS tagger. The team used the popular off-the-shelf *langid.py* (Lui and Baldwin, 2012), a general-purpose language identification tool that relies on information gain (IG) to select the best features for classification.

The UMich team (King et al., 2014) approached the task using words and characters as features applying IG, a parallel text feature selection, and manual feature selection to select the best features in the system. UMich used naive Bayes, logistic regression, and SVM as classifiers. The QMUL team (Purver, 2014) also used words and characters as features and a linear SVM classifier.

Table 9.3 presents the results obtained by the eight teams that submitted their results for the closed submission track, the five aforementioned systems plus the three teams that did not submit system descriptions: LIRA, UDE ,and CLCG. Results are presented in terms of macro average *F*-score and accuracy and ranked according to accuracy.

The performance of five teams (NRC-CNRC, RAE, UMich, UniMelb-NLP, and QMUL) is higher than 90 percent accuracy. Similar studies published on discriminating similar languages and language varieties on other data sets report similar performance level (Tiedemann and Ljubešić, 2012; Lui and Cook, 2013). Three teams obtained substantially lower scores ranging from 45.33 percent to 76.64 percent accuracy.

Table 9.4 shows the performance of systems in discriminating each language within groups A to E in terms of accuracy. Teams are sorted alphabetically and the best score per language group is displayed in bold.

Table 9.3 *DSL Shared Task 2014: Closed Submission Results in an Eleven-Class Classification Setting Using the DSLCC v1.0 (Zampieri et al., 2014)*

Team	Macro-avg. *F*-score	Accuracy
NRC-CNRC	0.957	0.957
RAE	0.947	0.947
UMich	0.932	0.932
UniMelb-NLP	0.918	0.918
QMUL	0.925	0.906
LIRA	0.721	0.766
UDE	0.657	0.681
CLCG	0.405	0.453

Table 9.4 *DSL Shared Task 2014: Performance for Language Groups in the Closed Submission in an Eleven-Class Classification Setting (Zampieri et al., 2014)*

	CLCG	LIRA	NRC-CNRC	QMUL	RAE	UDE	UMich	UniMelb-NLP
A	0.338	0.333	**0.936**	0.879	0.919	0.785	0.919	0.915
B	0.503	0.982	**0.996**	0.935	0.994	0.892	0.992	0.972
C	0.500	**1.000**	**1.000**	0.962	**1.000**	0.493	0.999	**1.000**
D	0.496	0.892	**0.956**	0.905	0.948	0.493	0.926	0.896
E	0.503	0.843	**0.910**	0.865	0.888	0.694	0.876	0.807

The top six teams obtained results above 90 percent accuracy for groups B (Malay and Indonesian) and C (Czech and Slovak). Half of the teams obtained perfect performance on Czech and Slovak texts, suggesting that texts from these two languages are not as similar as imagined when the DSLCC was compiled.

Discriminating between Bosnian, Croatian, and Serbian proved to be a very challenging task, as discussed in Ljubešić et al. (2007); Tiedemann (2014), and others. The best result for this group was obtained by the NRC-CNRC team, 93.5 percent accuracy. The language groups containing texts written in varieties of the same language – namely D (Portuguese) and E (Spanish) – were the most difficult to discriminate.

As discussed earlier, compiling language variety corpora is a challenge as popular language resources such as Wikipedia are not suited for this task. Given the difficulties in compiling suitable corpora, only two teams, UniMelb-NLP and UMich, compiled external language resources and submitted results for the open submission track. UniMelb-NLP obtained 0.880 and UMich achieved 0.859 accuracy, indicating that the use of external data sources does not necessarily increase performance in this shared task. This has probably to do with the influence of the domain and text types in this task, as discussed in Lui and Baldwin (2012) and Lui and Cook (2013).

9.5   DSL Shared Task 2015

The second edition of the DSL shared task was organized in 2015 (Zampieri et al., 2015b).[5] There was a slight increase in participation, evidencing the interest of the NLP community in this topic. Twenty-four enrolled to participate in the DSL 2015; ten of them submitted predictions, and seven system description papers were written and published in the VarDial proceedings.

---

[5] See http://ttg.uni-saarland.de/lt4vardial2015/index.html.

The DSLCC v2.0. and v2.1. have been compiled and released to participants who could choose to participate in any of the two following tracks:

- **Closed submission:** Using only the DSLCC v2.0.
- **Open submission:** Using any data set, including the DSLCC v2.0. Using the DSLCC v1.0 also makes a submission open.

Two test sets were released in the DSL 2015:

- **Test Set A:** Includes original texts retrieved from newspapers.
- **Test Set B:** Includes texts retrieved from newspapers with most capitalized named entities (NEs) substituted by placeholders.

The substitution of most NEs with placeholders was carried out to decrease topic bias in classification and to evaluate the extent to which NEs influence systems' performance. It is common for Argentinian Spanish texts, for example, to have words like *Argentina* or *Buenos Aires* in a much higher frequency than texts from Spain, whereas texts from Spain are much more likely to contain words like *Madrid* or *Barcelona*.

The teams participating in the DSL 2015 challenge used various features and classifier combinations, taking advantage of the experience acquired with the DSL 2014. The BOBICEV team (Bobicev, 2015) used prediction by partial matching (PPM), a technique based on conditional probabilities of the upcoming character given one or more previous characters. The BRUniBP team (Ács et al., 2015) approached the task using a two-stage system, replicating the approach proposed by the highest performing teams in the DSL 2014, using a MaxEnt classifier. To discriminate between the language groups, BRUniBP used a set of 100,000 keywords as features. To discriminate the languages within each group, character *n*-grams, word *n*-grams, TF-IDF score, and stopwords were used as features.

The MAC team (Malmasi and Dras, 2015) used an ensemble of linear SVM classifiers. As features, the MAC team used character *n*-grams (up to 6-grams), word unigrams, and word bigrams. The MMS team (Zampieri et al., 2015a) combined TF-IDF weighting and an SVM classifier, which previously had achieved high performance in native language identification (Gebre et al., 2013). The NLEL team (Fabra-Boluda et al., 2015) used a naive Bayes classifier trained as a two-stage classifier in the open submission and a single multiclass classifier in the closed submission. The NRC team (Goutte and Léger, 2015) included members of the NRC-CNRC team, the best performing team in the DSL 2014 closed submission track. NRC tested a variation of their two-stage classification system used in 2014.

The PRHLT team (Franco-Salvador et al., 2015) was another team to use a two-stage approach in the DSL 2015. The use of word and sentence vectors, which back in 2015 was a relatively new trend in NLP, was the main novelty of their approach. Finally, the SUKI team (Jauhiainen et al., 2015a) used token-based backoff, which was previously applied to general-purpose language identification by Jauhiainen et al. (2015b). Different types of token representation (e.g., space-delimited tokens and lowercase tokens) and character n-grams (from 1 to 8) were used as features.

The results obtained by the nine teams who submitted their runs to the closed submission track on test set A (original texts) are shown in Table 9.5 in terms of accuracy.

The best result was obtained by the MAC team scoring 95.54 percent accuracy, followed closely by MMS and NRC, both achieving 95.24 percent accuracy. The results for test set B (off-domain, tweets) are shown in Table 9.6,

Table 9.5 *DSL Shared Task 2015:
Closed Submission Results for Test Set
A in a Fourteen-Class Classification
Setting (Zampieri et al., 2015b)*

Team	Accuracy
MAC	95.54
MMS*	95.24
NRC	95.24
SUKI	94.67
BOBICEV	94.14
BRUNIBP	93.66
PRHLT	92.74
INRIA	83.91
NLEL	64.04

Table 9.6 *DSL Shared Task 2015:
Closed Submission Results for Test Set
B in a Fourteen-Class Classification
Setting (Zampieri et al., 2015b)*

Team	Accuracy
MAC	94.01
SUKI	93.02
NRC	93.01
MMS*	92.78
BOBICEV	92.22
PRHLT	90.80
NLEL	62.78

Table 9.7 *DSL Shared Task 2015:*
Open Submission Results for Test Set
A in a Fourteen-Class Classification
Setting (Zampieri et al., 2015b)

Team	Accuracy
NRC	95.65
NLEL	91.84
OSEVAL	76.17

Table 9.8 *DSL Shared Task 2015:*
Open Submission Results for Test Set
B in a Fourteen-Class Classification
Setting (Zampieri et al., 2015b)

Team	Accuracy
NRC	93.41
NLEL	89.56
OSEVAL	75.30

where an expected drop in accuracy with respect to the results obtained on test set A can be observed The MAC team performed best in test set B, achieving 94.01 percent accuracy, followed by SUKI and NRC with 93.02 percent and 93.01 percent, respectively.

Next, I present the results of the open submission track. Only three teams participated in this track: NRC, NLEL, and OSEVAL. Their results are presented in Table 9.7. It is worth noting that, unlike the DSL shared task in 2014, when all open submission results scored substantially lower than closed submission ones, two out of the three teams that participated in the open submission, NRC and NLEL, achieved better accuracy in the open submission than in the closed one on test set A. This is likely due to the availability of in-domain data (the DSLCC v1.0), a training corpus of the same kind as the DSLCC v2.0.

Table 9.8 presents the open submission results for test set B. An improvement in performance compared to the closed submission on test set B was observed for NLEL and NRC.

9.6   Conclusion and Future Perspectives

This chapter presented a brief overview of automatic language identification, an important task in many NLP pipelines. Language identification is far from a solved task, with four main research directions outlined in Zampieri et al.

(2015a). In this chapter, I present previous studies on the identification of similar languages, varieties, and dialects, a well-known challenge in language identification.

Competitions and shared tasks are vital to create resources and evaluate methods in NLP; therefore, in this chapter, I focused on two editions of the DSL shared tasks organized in 2014 and 2015, which featured texts from several groups of similar languages (such as Czech and Slovak) and language varieties (such as Brazilian and European Portuguese). I presented the data collected for these competitions (the DSLCC) and discussed the results obtained by the participants. According to the results of these shared tasks, machine learning classifiers such as SVMs trained on character and word n-grams deliver state-of-the-art performance for this task.

Apart from a brief mention about the use of word vectors by one of the teams that participated in the DSL 2015, deep learning methods have not been discussed in this chapter. Deep learning methods are considered state-of-the-art in many NLP tasks, outperforming "classical" machine learning classifiers such as SVMs, which probably makes the reader wonder about the performance of more up-to-date NLP methods applied to similar language and dialect identification. On this matter, the VarDial shared task reports from 2014 to 2018 (Zampieri et al., 2014, 2015a; Malmasi et al., 2016; Zampieri et al., 2017, 2018), which present the results of multiple shared tasks on the topic, indicate that deep learning methods do not outperform traditional machine learning models (see Medvedeva et al. (2017) for a discussion). More recently, however, in the 2019 Cuneiform Language Identification (CLI) shared task at VarDial (Zampieri et al., 2019), featuring multiple historical dialects of two languages written in Cuneiform script (Sumerian and Akkadian), one system (Bernier-Colborne et al., 2019) achieved the best performance in the competition using BERT (Devlin et al., 2018). This suggests that BERT-based methods may be able to outperform traditional machine learning methods in other dialect/language identification scenarios. Nevertheless, more research on the performance of BERT and related methods for similar languages and dialect identification must be carried out to support this claim.

References

Ács, Judit, Grad-Gyenge, László, and de Rezende Oliveira, Thiago Bruno Rodrigues. 2015. A Two-level Classifier for Discriminating Similar Languages. In: *Proceedings of LT4VarDial*.

Ali, Ahmed, Dehak, Najim, Cardinal, Patrick, Khurana, Sameer, Yella, Sree Harsha, Glass, James, Bell, Peter, and Renals, Steve. 2016. Automatic Dialect Detection in Arabic Broadcast Speech. In: *Proceedings of INTERSPEECH*.

Beesley, Kenneth. 1988. Language Identifier: A Computer Program for Automatic Natural-Language Identification of On-line Text. Pages 57, 54 of: *Proceedings of the Annual Conference of the American Translators Association*.

Bernier-Colborne, Gabriel, Goutte, Cyril, and Léger, Serge. 2019. Improving Cuneiform Language Identification with BERT. Pages 17–25 of: *Proceedings of the Sixth Workshop on NLP for Similar Languages, Varieties and Dialects.*

Biemann, Chris, Heyer, Gerhard, Quasthoff, Uwe, and Richter, Matthias. 2007. The Leipzig Corpora Collection-Monolingual Corpora of Standard Size. In: *Proceedings of Corpus Linguistics.*

Bobicev, Victoria. 2015. Discriminating between Similar Languages Using PPM. In: *Proceedings of the LT4VarDial Workshop (LT4VarDial).*

Brown, Ralf. 2013. Selecting and Weighting *n*-Grams to Identify 1100 Languages. Pages 519–526 of: *Proceedings of the 16th International Conference on Text Speech and Dialogue (TSD2013), Lecture Notes in Artificial Intelligence (LNAI 8082).*

Brown, Ralf. 2014. Non-linear Mapping for Improved Identification of 1300+ Languages. In: *Proceedings of EMNLP.*

Christensen, Hans. 2014. *HC corpora.* www.corpora.heliohost.org.

Clyne, Michael. 1992. *Pluricentric Languages: Different Norms in Different Nations.*

Costa-jussà, Marta R, Zampieri, Marcos, and Pal, Santanu. 2018. A Neural Approach to Language Variety Translation. Pages 275–282 of: *Proceedings of the Fifth Workshop on NLP for Similar Languages, Varieties and Dialects (VarDial 2018).*

Cotterell, Ryan, and Callison-Burch, Chris. 2014. A Multi-dialect, Multi-genre Corpus of Informal Written Arabic. In: *Proceedings LREC.*

Devlin, Jacob, Chang, Ming-Wei, Lee, Kenton, and Toutanova, Kristina. 2018. Bert: Pretraining of Deep Bidirectional Transformers for Language Understanding. *arXiv preprint arXiv:1810.04805.*

Dunning, Ted. 1994. *Statistical Identification of Language.* Technical Report, Computing Research Lab - New Mexico State University.

Fabra-Boluda, Raül, Rangel, Francisco, and Rosso, Paolo. 2015. NLEL UPV Autoritas Participation at Discrimination between Similar Languages (DSL) 2015 Shared Task. In: *Proceedings of the LT4VarDial Workshop (LT4VarDial).*

Franco-Salvador, Marc, Rosso, Paolo, and Rangel, Francisco. 2015. Distributed Representations of Words and Documents for Discriminating Similar Languages. In: *Proceedings of the LT4VarDial Workshop (LT4VarDial).*

Gebre, Binyam Gebrekidan, Zampieri, Marcos, Wittenburg, Peter, and Heskes, Tom. 2013. Improving Native Language Identification with TF-IDF Weighting. In: *Proceedings of the BEA workshop.*

Goutte, Cyril, and Léger, Serge. 2015. Experiments in Discriminating Similar Languages. In: *Proceedings of the LT4VarDial Workshop (LT4VarDial).*

Goutte, Cyril, Léger, Serge, and Carpuat, Marine. 2014. The NRC System for Discriminating Similar Languages. In: *Proceedings of the VarDial Workshop (VarDial).*

Goutte, Cyril, Leger, Serge, Malmasi, Shervin and Zampieri, Marcos. 2016. Discriminating Similar Languages: Evaluations and Explorations. In: *Proceedings of Language Resources and Evaluation.*

Jauhiainen, Tommi, Jauhiainen, Heidi, Alstola, Tero, and Lindén, Krister. 2019b. Language and Dialect Identification of Cuneiform Texts. Pages 89–98 of: *Proceedings of the Sixth Workshop on NLP for Similar Languages, Varieties and Dialects.*

Jauhiainen, Tommi, Jauhiainen, Heidi, and Lindén, Krister. 2015a. Discriminating Similar Languages with Token-based Backoff. In: *Proceedings of VarDial.*

Jauhiainen, Tommi, Lindén, Krister, and Jauhiainen, Heidi. 2015b. Language Set Identification in Noisy Synthetic Multilingual Documents. Pages 633–643 of: *Proceedings of CICLING. CICLING* '15.

Jauhiainen, Tommi, Lui, Marco, Zampieri, Marcos, Baldwin, Timothy, and Lindén, Krister. 2019a. Automatic Language Identification in Texts: A Survey. *Journal of Artificial Intelligence Research.*

King, Ben, Radev, Dragomir, and Abney, Steven. 2014. Experiments in Sentence Language Identification with Groups of Similar Languages. In: *Proceedings of the VarDial Workshop (VarDial).*

Ljubešić, Nikola, Mikelic, Nives, and Boras, Damir. 2007. Language Identification: How to Distinguish Similar Languages? In: *Proceedings of ITI.*

Lui, Marco. 2014. Generalized Language Identification. Ph thesis, University of Melbourne.

Lui, Marco, and Baldwin, Timothy. 2012. Langid.Py: An Off-the-shelf Language Identification Tool. Pages 25–30 of: *Proceedings of the ACL 2012 System Demonstrations.* ACL '12.

Lui, Marco, and Cook, Paul. 2013. Classifying English Documents by National Dialect. In: *Proceedings of ALTA.*

Lui, Marco, Letcher, Ned, Adams, Oliver, Duong, Long, Cook, Paul, and Baldwin, Timothy. 2014. Exploring Methods and Resources for Discriminating Similar Languages. In: *Proceedings of VarDial.*

Malmasi, Shervin, and Dras, Mark. 2015. Language Identification using Classifier Ensembles. In: *Proceedings of the VarDial Workshop (VarDial).*

Malmasi, Shervin, Zampieri, Marcos, Ljubešić, Nikola, Nakov, Preslav, Ali, Ahmed, and Tiedemann, Jörg. 2016. Discriminating between Similar Languages and Arabic Dialect Identification: A Report on the Third DSL Shared Task. In: *Proceedings of VarDial.*

McNamee, Paul. 2005. Language Identification: A Solved Problem Suitable for Undergraduate Instruction. *Journal of Computing Sciences in Colleges,* **20**(3), 94–101.

Medvedeva, Maria, Kroon, Martin, and Plank, Barbara. 2017. When Sparse Traditional Models Outperform Dense Neural Networks: the Curious Case of Discriminating between Similar Languages. In: *Proceedings of the VarDial Workshop (VarDial).*

Nguyen, Dong, and Dogruoz, A. Seza. 2014. Word Level Language Identification in Online Multilingual Communication. In: *Proceedings of EMNLP.*

Nissim, Malvina, Abzianidze, Lasha, Evang, Kilian, van der Goot, Rob, Haagsma, Hessel, Plank, Barbara, and Wieling, Martijn. 2017. Sharing Is Caring: The Future of Shared Tasks. *Computational Linguistics,* **43**(4), 897–904.

Pardo, Francisco Manuel Rangel, Rosso, Paolo, Potthast, Martin, and Stein, Benno. 2017. Overview of the 5th Author Profiling Task at PAN 2017: Gender and Language Variety Identification in Twitter. In: *CLEF (Working Notes).*

Porta, Jordi, and Sancho, José-Luis. 2014. Using Maximum Entropy Models to Discriminate between Similar Languages and Varieties. In: *Proceedings of the VarDial Workshop (VarDial).*

Purver, Matthew. 2014. A Simple Baseline for Discriminating Similar Language. In: *Proceedings of VarDial Workshop.*

Ranaivo-Malançon, Bali. 2006. Automatic Identification of Close Languages - Case Study: Malay and Indonesian. *ECTI Transactions on Computer and Information Technology*, **2**, 126–134.

Sadat, Fatiha, Kazemi, Farnazeh, and Farzindar, Atefeh. 2014. Automatic Identification of Arabic Language Varieties and Dialects in Social Media. Pages 22–27 of: *Proceedings of the Second Workshop on Natural Language Processing for Social Media*. SocialNLP '14.

Samardžić, Tanja, Scherrer, Yves, and Glaser, Elvira. 2016. ArchiMob – A Corpus of Spoken Swiss German. In: *Proceedings of LREC*.

Sebastiani, Fabrizio. 2005. Text Categorization. Pages 109–129 of: *Text Mining and Its Applications to Intelligence, CRM and Knowledge Management*.

Solorio, Thamar, Blair, Elizabeth, Maharjan, Suraj, Bethard, Steven, Diab, Mona, Ghoneim, Mahmoud, Hawwari, Abdelati, AlGhamdi, Fahad, Hirschberg, Julia, Chang, Alison, and Fung, Pascale. 2014. Overview for the First Shared Task on Language Identification in Code-Switched Data. In: *Proceedings of the CodeSwitch Workshop*.

Tan, Liling, Zampieri, Marcos, Ljubešić, Nikola, and Tiedemann, Jörg. 2014. Merging Comparable Data Sources for the Discrimination of Similar Languages: The DSL Corpus Collection. In: *Proceedings of BUCC*.

Tiedemann, Jörg. 2012. Parallel Data, Tools and Interfaces in OPUS. In: *Proceedings of LREC*.

Tiedemann, Jörg. 2014. Rediscovering Annotation Projection for Cross-Lingual Parser Induction. In: *Proceedings of COLING*.

Tiedemann, Jörg, and Ljubešić, Nikola. 2012. Efficient Discrimination Between Closely Related Languages. Pages 2619–2634 of: *Proceedings of the 24th International Conference on Computational Linguistics*. COLING '12.

Tillmann, Christoph, Mansour, Saab, and Al-Onaizan, Yaser. 2014. Improved Sentence-Level Arabic Dialect Classification. In: *Proceedings of the VarDial Workshop (VarDial)*.

Tromp, Erik, and Pechnizkiy, Mykola. 2012. Graph-Based n-Gram Language Identification on Short Texts. Pages 27–34 of: *Proceedings of the Twentieth Belgian Dutch Conference on Machine Learning (Benelearn 2011)*.

Tyers, Francis, and Alperen, Murat Serdar. 2010. South-East European Times: A Parallel Corpus of Balkan Languages. In: *Proceedings of the LREC workshop on Exploitation of multilingual resources and tools for Central and (South) Eastern European Languages*.

van der Lee, Chris, and van den Bosch, Antal. 2017. Exploring Lexical and Syntactic Features for Language Variety Identification. In: *Proceedings of the Fourth Workshop on NLP for Similar Languages, Varieties and Dialects (VarDial)*.

Zampieri, Marcos. 2016. Pluricentric Languages: Automatic Identification and Linguistic Variation. Ph thesis, Saarland University.

Zampieri, Marcos, Gebre, Binyam Gebrekidan, Costa, Hernani, and van Genabith, Josef. 2015a. Comparing Approaches to the Identification of Similar Languages. In: *Proceedings of the VarDial Workshop (LT4VarDial)*.

Zampieri, Marcos, Malmasi, Shervin, Ljubešić, Nikola, Nakov, Preslav, Ali, Ahmed, Tiedemann, Jörg, Scherrer, Yves, and Aepli, Noëmi. 2017. Findings of the VarDial Evaluation Campaign 2017. In: *Proceedings of VarDial*.

Zampieri, Marcos, Malmasi, Shervin, Nakov, Preslav, Ali, Ahmed, Shon, Suwon, Glass, James, Scherrer, Yves, Samardžić, Tanja, Ljubešić, Nikola, Tiedemann, Jörg, van der Lee, Chris, Grondelaers, Stefan, Oostdijk, Nelleke, Speelman, Dirk, van den Bosch, Antal, Kumar, Ritesh, Lahiri, Bornini, and Jain, Mayank. 2018. Language Identification and Morphosyntactic Tagging: The Second VarDial Evaluation Campaign. Pages 1–17 of: *Proceedings of the Fifth Workshop on NLP for Similar Languages, Varieties and Dialects (VarDial 2018)*. Association for Computational Linguistics.

Zampieri, Marcos, Malmasi, Shervin, Scherrer, Yves, Samardžić, Tanja, Tyers, Francis, Silfverberg, Miikka, Klyueva, Natalia, Pan, Tung-Le, Huang, Chu-Ren, Ionescu, Radu Tudor, Butnaru, Andrei, and Jauhiainen, Tommi. 2019. A Report on the Third VarDial Evaluation Campaign. In: *Proceedings of VarDial*. Association for Computational Linguistics.

Zampieri, Marcos, Malmasi, Shervin, Sulea, Octavia-Maria, and Dinu, Liviu P. 2016. A Computational Approach to the Study of Portuguese Newspapers Published in Macau. Pages 47–51 of: *Proceedings of Workshop on Natural Language Processing Meets Journalism (NLPMJ)*.

Zampieri, Marcos, Tan, Liling, Ljubešić, Nikola, and Tiedemann, Jörg. 2014. A Report on the DSL Shared Task 2014. In: *Proceedings of VarDial*.

Zampieri, Marcos, Tan, Liling, Ljubešić, Nikola, Tiedemann, Jörg, and Nakov, Preslav. 2015b. Overview of the DSL Shared Task 2015. In: *Proceedings of the LT4VarDial Workshop (LT4VarDial)*.

Zubiaga, Arkaitz, San Vicente, Iñaki, Gamallo, Pablo, Pichel, José Ramom, Alegria, Iñaki, Aranberri, Nora, Ezeiza, Aitzol, and Fresno, Víctor. 2015. TweetLID: A Benchmark for Tweet Language Identification. *Language Resources and Evaluation*, 1–38.

10 Dialect Variation on Social Media

Dong Nguyen

10.1 Introduction

Social media has changed our daily lives: We share our thoughts, opinions, and news using social media and connect with people throughout the world. Social media has also radically changed a variety of research disciplines: It is both *massive* – we can now study potentially millions of people – and *microscopic* – we can carry out analyses at the level of individual interactions (Golder and Macy, 2014). Rather than relying on self-reports or elicited data, we can now observe *language in use* at scale in a variety of social contexts. The availability of social media data has been one of the driving factors of the emerging area of *computational sociolinguistics* (Nguyen et al., 2016).

There is no "single" online language variety (Herring and Androutsopoulos, 2015). Instead, we find a multitude of linguistic varieties and styles in social media, even within a single social media platform. Still, the informal nature of social media platforms means that language in social media is often closer to everyday speech than the language typically found in many other data sources, such as newspapers. Social media is therefore a rich resource to study regional and social variation in language. Here are two tweets from public Twitter accounts, one by Virgin Media and one by Cara Delevingne, an international model:

> virginmedia: *Nice one bruv! Here if you need us. ^MK*

> Caradelevingne: *Soo excited 2announce my first Novel titled*
> *Mirror Mirror!Pre order on Amazon!!Can't*
> *wait 2share story with you all!* [link]

The tweet posted from the Virgin Media account involves an interaction with a customer. The language is informal, perhaps to connect with the customer. We find an instance of *bruv*, an address term that has featured in a sociolinguistic

This work was supported by The Alan Turing Institute under the EPSRC grant EP/N510129/1 through an Alan Turing Institute Fellowship (TU/A/000006). Bo Wang and Maria Liakata are thanked for help with accessing the Twitter data.

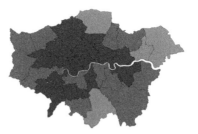

(a) *Pants* versus *trousers* in England

(b) Standard *were* versus nonstandard *was* in London

Figure 10.1 Geotagged tweets, May–August 2014

study (Kerswill, 2013). The tweet posted by the supermodel is a promotional tweet, with orthographic variation (e.g., *soo* instead of *so* and *2* instead of *to*) and spacing and punctuation that automatic tools would be challenged by.

Patterns in language variation become more salient when we aggregate across a larger number of tweets, for example to study regional patterns. Figure 10.1a shows the relative frequencies of *pants* and *trousers* in England based on geo-tagged Twitter data from May–August 2014.[1] *Pants* has a higher usage in the north west of England, which matches the pattern observed through fieldwork carried out by undergraduate students of linguistics and English language at the University of Manchester.[2]

We can also zoom in on a particular region, for example London. London has been of interest in sociolinguistic studies, because of its multicultural character and the emergence of Multicultural London English. Cheshire and Fox (2009) studied the *was* versus *were* variation in London by analyzing speech of adolescents and elderly speakers in the multicultural inner London area (Hackney) and in a less diverse outer London area (Havering). The use of nonstandard *was* in standard *were* contexts was higher in outer London adolescents compared to inner London adolescents. A similar trend is observed on Twitter (Figure 10.1b), by comparing the use of nonstandard *was* (*we was, you was, they was*) to standard *were* (*we were, you were, they were*). Standard *were* has a higher occurrence in inner London.

The scale of social media data makes it possible to study rare phenomena, such as specific syntactic constructions or lexical variants. Furthermore, infor-mation on interaction patterns makes it possible to jointly analyze geographical variation with a variety of social factors, for example, how linguistic choices relate to someone's online conversation partner. However, there are also many

---

[1] Part of a larger data set collected for UK election passive polling and analysis (Wang et al., 2017a,b).

[2] See http://projects.alc.manchester.ac.uk/ukdialectmaps/lexical-variation/trousers/.

challenges: Social media data need to be repurposed – social media platforms were not designed to study dialect variation – and processing language in social media can be challenging because many NLP tools are not robust to linguistic variation.

This chapter focuses on geographical dialect variation in social media from the perspective of computational linguistics, but it also draws from sociolinguistics and dialectology (see also Chapter 5) to identify fruitful future research directions. First, I'll discuss opportunities and challenges that social media offers for analyzing dialects (Section 10.2). I'll then discuss the processing of social media data (Section 10.3) and computational studies on geographical variation in social media (Section 10.4). The chapter concludes with a future outlook (Section 10.5).

10.2   Social Media for Dialect Research

This section discusses aspects of using social media for dialect research.

Unobtrusive Observation of Language Everyday speech, for example when you are talking to your family or close friends, is of particular interest in the study of dialect. However, capturing everyday speech is difficult. Questionnaires have been fundamental to collect dialect data. For example, a question might be "What do you call this plant."[3] However, the way the questions are phrased, or the interaction with the researcher could influence the responses given. Furthermore, questionnaires usually do not support fine-grained measurements regarding the frequency of use of a certain variable and the analysis of *intraspeaker* variation, for example, how the choice for a particular variant depends on the situational context. Observations and sociolinguistic interviews are also frequently used to collect data, but here the presence of the observer or the interviewer could again influence the language.

One of the key advantages of using social media for research is that it allows unobtrusive observation of language and behavior (Salganik, 2017). As Golder and Macy (2014, p. 133) point out: "the social pressures and normative constraints on individuals are exerted by their peers rather than by the researchers." Social media allows us to study how language is *used* in a variety of social contexts. Moreover, language and social behavior are recorded *in real time*, and there is no need to specify beforehand which items are of interest, in contrast to questionnaires.

Social Media Users Traditional dialectology has focused on so-called NORMs, i.e. non-mobile, old, rural men (Chambers and Trudgill, 1998, p. 29),

---

[3] See Llamas (2018) for a discussion on questionnaires for dialect research.

because they were believed to be more conservative in their speech. However, from about the 1960s attention has shifted from rural areas to urban areas and widened to a variety of social groups. With social media, we often have data about both rural and urban areas. The use of social media means a radical shift away from NORMs as the target population. In a 2018 report by PEW Research on social media use by Americans,[4] 88% of eighteen- to twenty-nine-year-olds indicated that they use any form of social media. This declines to only 37% of Americans aged sixty-five and older. As another example, in a study focused on Dutch Twitter users (Nguyen et al., 2013), a fine-grained manual annotation effort revealed a heavily skewed distribution toward younger users. Furthermore, only 5 out of 2,709 users (excluding profiles for which no annotations could be obtained) were annotated as *retired*. Moreover, in social media not all accounts belong to an individual, but sometimes accounts represent organisations, fake people and bots.

When studying sociolinguistic variation in social media, *demographic information* about the users is often important to understand demographic biases in the data and how language varies across social groups. For example, in Nguyen et al. (2013), there were more females among the younger age category, but more males among the older age categories. When studying how language varies across demographic groups, it is important to control for these unbalanced gender distributions. Unfortunately, in many cases (almost) no demographic information is available. Different approaches have therefore been explored to derive demographic information, such as automatically inferring demographics from language use (see Nguyen et al. (2016) for an overview), combining location-tagged data with census data (Jacobo et al., 2018; Jørgensen et al., 2015) and deriving demographics from names (Bamman et al., 2014b). A limitation of these approaches is that classifications are imposed on users, rather than asking the users themselves, which can be especially problematic when it involves variables like gender and ethnicity. Androutsopoulos (2013) mentions the alternative of moving away from sociodemographic categories and focusing on participant roles (e.g., admin, novice).

Critical for studying dialect variation in social media is location information. Social media content sometimes comes with fine-grained location information, such as GPS coordinates, and many studies rely on geo-tagged content alone. However, this is often only a small fraction of the number of posts produced. Studies sometimes estimate a "home location" for social media users, for example, based on the location of the first tweet (Eisenstein et al., 2010), or by using the most frequent location (Jacobo et al., 2018). Such aggregations, however, lose information about mobility patterns of users.

---

[4] www.pewinternet.org/2018/03/01/social-media-use-in-2018/.

Extracting locations from profile information has also been explored. For the data set used in Nguyen et al. (2015), my collaborator Dolf Trieschnigg collected a data set focused on two Dutch provinces (Limburg and Friesland). Users were mapped to locations based on the text provided in the location field in their profiles. However, this turned out to be nontrivial. For example, users who lived in the city of Leeuwarden, the provincial capital of Friesland (the Netherlands), provided strings like *Leeuwarden*; *Leeuwarden, The Netherlands*; and *Leeuwarden, Friesland*. However, a long tail of profile locations occurred only once in our data, such as *leeuwarden de gekste* "leeuwarden the craziest"; *leeuwarden# freeceland*; *LeeuwardenCity (L)*; and *Leeuwarden & Barcelona*.

Sampling In many cases a study involves selecting a sample from the data. Sampling approaches include random sampling, by time period, by individuals/group, event, or by convenience (Herring, 2004). To analyze geographical variation in language using computational approaches, some studies have selected tweets or users based on geotags (Eisenstein et al., 2010), based on profile information (Nguyen et al., 2015), by searching for specific key words (Doyle, 2014; Jones, 2015), and by searching for specific hash tags (Shoemark et al., 2017). However, sampling approaches can introduce biases. For example, Pavalanathan and Eisenstein (2015b) found that GPS-tagged tweets were more often written by young people and women, in comparison to tweets with self-reported locations.

Operationalisation of Concepts The use of social media sometimes requires adapting operationalisations of concepts developed on other domains. An example is the concept of *audience*. The influence of audience on a speaker's style has been widely studied in sociolinguistics, for example, using the framework of audience design (Bell, 1984). We tend to speak differently when talking to our boss as opposed to when talking to a close friend. However, in many social media platforms, e.g., Twitter, multiple audiences (e.g., friends, colleagues) are collapsed into a single context. While the audience is potentially limitless, users do often imagine an audience when writing messages, and they may target messages to different audiences (Marwick and boyd, 2011). This means that when we want to apply a framework such as audience design to a social media context, we need to rethink how we operationalize audience (Androutsopoulos, 2014; Nguyen et al., 2015; Pavalanathan and Eisenstein, 2015a). For example, studies on Twitter and audience used the presence of hashtags and user mentions as proxies for the target audience (Nguyen et al., 2015; Pavalanathan and Eisenstein, 2015a). Messages with hashtags were assumed to target a broader audience, while messages with user mentions were assumed to target smaller audiences.

As another example, the units of analysis in social media do not always correspond to traditional units of analysis. For instance, posts are not one-to-one comparable to utterances or turns (Androutsopoulos, 2013). Similarly, looking at code-switching patterns may involve different units of analysis compared to studies on spoken data that have focused on analyzing turns or sentences.

Ethical Concerns The use of social media also raises various ethical concerns. Social media has been particularly attractive because of its perceived public nature. While many platforms offer a binary choice regarding visibility (public versus private posts), in reality privacy is not a binary notion but highly contextual and situational (Zook et al., 2017). In other words, there is a difference between what is legal,[5] and norms and expectations regarding privacy and the use of such data. Ethical concerns surround not only the collection of data but also how such content is quoted in research output (Williams et al., 2017) and how the data are made available to other researchers.

10.3   Processing Data

Processing language in social media using automatic tools can be challenging. Many NLP tools have been developed on nonsocial media data, like newswire texts, and they might work less well for social media. Adapting and/or designing NLP tools for social media can require quite some effort. For example, taggers designed for social media often include special tags for hashtags, @mentions and emoticons. To illustrate this, Table 10.1 shows two tweets tagged by the ARK Twitter Part-of-Speech (POS) tagger (Owoputi et al., 2013). A "compound tag" is used to handle cases such as *lemme* (let me).

Multilingual social media users sometimes use multiple languages in a single social media post, presenting another challenge to NLP tools. Although most NLP tools assume that the input text is written in a single language, there is an increasing interest in developing NLP tools for code-switched texts (e.g., Bhat et al. (2018)). Fine-grained language identification at the word level (Nguyen and Doğruöz, 2013) can be a useful step in processing code-switched texts.

Studies have found that the performance of NLP tools can vary based on the sociodemographic background of authors. Hovy and Søgaard (2015) observed performance differences in regard to the age of the authors when the POS tagger was trained on texts from newspapers, and Jørgensen et al. (2015) found that POS taggers are more likely to make mistakes on African American Vernacular English (AAVE) sentences compared to non-AAVE sentences. Furthermore, Blodgett et al. (2016) found that messages from African Americans were more

---

[5] For example, Williams et al. (2017) point out that users consent that their public tweets will be made available to third parties.

Table 10.1 *Assigned POS Tags by the Tool from Owoputi et al. (2013)*

Nice	A	adjective	Yes	!	interjection
one	$	numeral	!	,	punctuation
bruv	N	common noun	Lemme	L	nominal +
!	,	interjection			verbal,
Here	R	adverb			verbal +
		pre- or postposition,			nominal
		or subordinating	know	V	verb
if	P	conjunction	what	O	pronoun
you	O	pronoun	u	O	pronoun
need	V	verb	think	V	verb
us	O	pronoun	:)	E	emoticon
.	,	punctuation	#digitalart	#	hashtag
		other abbreviations,			
		foreign words,			
		possessive endings,			
MK	G	symbols, garbage			

likely to be erroneously classified as non-English by automatic language identification systems. Such disparities in performance can have ethical implications: Texts produced by certain social groups may be wrongly analyzed, or even excluded, from a variety of social media analyses.

The difficulty of processing language in social media also affects the analysis of linguistic variation. Computational approaches have mostly focused on lexical (e.g., *pants* versus *trousers*) and orthographic (e.g., *going* versus *goin*) variation. Analyzing syntactic variation typically requires the use of a tagger. For example, in a study on African American English in Twitter, Blodgett et al. (2016) analyzed habitual *be* by tagging tweets with the ARK Twitter POS tagger (Owoputi et al., 2013) and searching for O-be-V and O-b-V sequences. A workaround is to search for lexical patterns instead that instantiate a syntactic variation of interest. For example, Doyle (2014) analyzed the occurrence of *needs done* (need + past participle) and *might could* (double modals). However, this would limit the analysis to specific strings.

10.4   Patterns in Social Media

The use of certain words or grammatical constructions can reveal where someone is from. There is a large body of work on text-based geocoding: Given a text, automatically predict the location of the user or message. These geocoding approaches sometimes identify dialect features (e.g., Rahimi et al. (2017)), but it is usually not their primary aim. For example, toponyms are useful features for these tasks, but they are usually not of interest for research on dialect variation. Work in this area is, therefore, not discussed here, but the interested reader is referred to Melo and Martins (2016) for an extensive overview.

This section focuses on the analysis of dialect variation. There is a lot of variety in the type of analyses that have been carried out, from analyzing individual linguistic features (e.g., usage of *yinz*) or alternations (e.g., usage of *soda* versus *pop* versus *coke*) to automatically discovering dialect regions. Section 10.4.1 discusses how findings from social media data have been compared to more conventional sources. Next, Section 10.4.2 looks at analyzing dialect variation at different linguistic levels.

10.4.1   Comparison against Other Sources

Findings from social media data have been compared against conventional sources in several ways, and so far they generally seem to match them quite well. Small differences are expected, of course, as there are often differences in demographics, the time period of data collection, and the type of variation studied (many studies using conventional sources focus on phonological variation).

One can compare individual patterns in social media against conventional sources. For example, Doyle (2014) studied syntactic patterns in US-geotagged tweets and found high correlations with patterns in the *Atlas of North American English* and the *Harvard Dialect Survey*. Individual patterns are sometimes aggregated to discover dialect regions, which can then in turn also be compared against previous sociolinguistic studies. For example, Huang et al. (2016) found that regions identified in Twitter were broadly similar to regions identified in previous studies based on phonetic variation. Some computational methods can be used to automatically identify dialect terms. These terms can also be evaluated by comparing against conventional sources. However, one should keep in mind that these conventional sources might not cover all relevant terms, for example, they might miss dialect terms specific to online language. The neural network approach by Rahimi et al. (2017) enables retrieving the k-nearest terms given the name of a region. They compared the identified terms to dialect terms in the DAREDS data set, a data set the authors created based on the *Dictionary of American Regional English* (DARE).

10.4.2   Analyzing Variation

Most studies so far have focused on lexical variation or variation that can be captured using lexical patterns. Eisenstein et al. (2010) proposed a topic model that incorporates topics and regions as latent variables to model lexical variation. They found that dialect regions were characterized by various dialect words, locallyspecific abbreviations and named entities. Huang et al. (2016)

take an approach that is more common in conventional dialect studies by looking at lexical alternations: different ways of saying the same thing, such as *automobile* versus *car* and *holiday* versus *vacation*, so that topic is controlled for. Using statistical testing with methods such as Global Moran's I, they identified lexical alternations that exhibited significant spatial autocorrelation in a large corpus of geotagged tweets from the United States. Rahimi et al. (2017) proposed a neural network approach with one hidden layer to predict the location of a user given tweets. The locations (latitude/longitudes coordinates) are discretized using k-d tree leaf nodes or k-means. The model also learns an embedding of the terms this way, which can be used to detect dialectal terms.

Many studies on dialect are based on speech data and focus on phonological variation. In contrast, with social media the focus has been on written data. Orthographic variation therefore provides an interesting opportunity to bring different strands of research together. Language in social media tends to be closer to spoken language, and Eisenstein (2015) suggests a strong connection between orthographic and phonological variation. He finds that orthographic variation is sensitive to phonological and grammatical contexts and mirrors to some extent patterns in speech. However, the link between orthography and phonology is complex. The pronunciation of a word is not always obvious from its spelling. Jones (2015) gives examples of this and points out that one has to be careful when using written social media data alone to make claims about phonology.

Jones (2015) studied regional patterns in AAVE by analyzing nonstandard spellings on Twitter linked to six phonological phenomena, such as glottal stops and nasal assimilation. He found that the identified dialect regions aligned with patterns of movement during the Great Migrations. Jørgensen et al. (2015) also focused on AAVE. They studied three phonological features based on how they are manifestated as orthographic variations on Twitter (e.g., *brotha* versus *brother*). The orthographic variations were correlated with demographic variables obtained from census data as well as with geographical variables.

Grammatical variation has received less attention so far, possibly because of challenges related to parsing Twitter data. Grammatical variation has been analyzed using POS taggers as well as by searching for specific strings. Stewart (2014) analyzed African American English syntax in US-geotagged tweets. Regular expressions and two different part-of-speech taggers were used to find patterns such as habitual *be* and copula deletion. Doyle (2014) searched for strings like *needs done* (need + past participle) and *might could* (double modals) and found strong correlations with existing dialect sources. Haddican and Johnson (2012) studied regional effects on the English particle verb alternation using both acceptability judgments and a Twitter study. To collect Twitter data, they searched for specific strings (*turn on the light* versus *turn the light on* and variations). They found no regional effects in the United Kingdom, but they did find trans-Atlantic differences (United Kingdom and Ireland versus the United States and Canada). Jacobo et al. (2018) analyzed a large French Twitter corpus. Among the variables studied, they looked at the omission of the French negative particle *ne*, which is considered optional in spoken French but obligatory in writing. They found that in the north of France there was a higher use of nonstandard language.

There is also geographical variation at the semantic level. Word embeddings, which represent words as low-dimensional vectors (e.g., 100 dimensions), are effective approaches to capture the meaning of words and therefore to study semantic variation. Bamman et al. (2014a) present an extension of the skip-gram model to learn how the meaning of words varies geographically. While the skip-gram model has a single embedding matrix with embedding vectors for each word, the model proposed by Bamman et al. learns a global embedding matrix as well as additional matrices for different contexts, which in their study were the geographical states in the United States. These context-specific embeddings capture how the global representation should shift for specific contexts (e.g., when the word is used in Kansas). Based on a large geotagged Twitter corpus, their model learned that *wicked* in Kansas is close to terms like *evil*, *pure* and *gods*. And that in contrast, *wicked* in Massachusetts is most similar to intensifiers like *super*, *ridiculously* and *insanely*.

10.5   Future Outlook

This chapter concludes by discussing several open research directions.

Bottom-Up Discovery of Features So far, most studies have focused on linguistic features that are selected based on intuition, manual inspection, or findings from previous studies on dialect. This is in fact similar to when using questionnaires, for which the researcher has to specify target items beforehand. However, the scale of social media also supports bottom-up *discovery* of linguistic features. Approaches to automatically identify variables that exhibit geographical variation tend to identify many proper nouns (Nguyen and Eisenstein, 2017; Pavalanathan and Eisenstein, 2015a; Rahimi et al., 2017), such as names of cities, regions, and companies. Additional filtering is therefore necessary to find the ones that are meaningful for sociolinguistic analyses. The next step would be identifying alternations. For example, Shoemark et al. (2017) manually selected variables for which users can produce either a Standard English or Scottish variant. Combining methods to identify variables that exhibit geographical variation (Nguyen and Eisenstein, 2017) with methods to identify lexical variants (Gouws et al., 2011) could be interesting to explore.

Geographical *and* Social Factors In both sociolinguistics and dialectology, geographical variation has often been studied separately from social variation (Britain, 2010). However, the integration of social factors, such as sociodemographic variables and social network structures, is increasingly receiving more attention (Kristiansen, 2018; Wieling et al., 2011). Social media affords studying language use in a variety of social settings. The availability of information about social network structures, conversation partners, etc., supports a further integration of social aspects in the study of dialects. Examples of this include work on audience design (Nguyen et al., 2015) and work on combining sociodemographic factors with geographical variation (Jacobo et al., 2018). For example, Nguyen et al. (2015) studied the use of two minority languages in the Netherlands. Tweets directed to larger audiences were more often written in Dutch, while within conversations users often switched to the minority languages. Recent studies have looked at the relation between sociolinguistic variation and political views in the context of the Scottish Independence referendum (Shoemark et al., 2017) and in the context of the Catalonian referendum (Stewart et al., 2018). Finally, social factors could also be integrated in analyses on how innovations spread (Eisenstein et al., 2014).

Level of Analysis and Treatment of Place So far, most work in computational linguistics has focused on broad patterns of geographical variation, e.g., across the whole of the Netherlands (Nguyen and Eisenstein, 2017), or across the whole of the United States (Doyle, 2014; Eisenstein et al., 2010; Huang et al., 2016). Less work has focused on variation in specific regions or cities. The scale of the data and the fine-grained location information allow us to study geographical patterns – quantitatively – on a detailed level, such as neighborhoods in urban cores. A challenge when zooming in on such levels is that for some fine-grained levels the data might become too sparse in certain areas. Further work could also explore more socially constructed approaches toward space (Johnstone, 2004) (for example, the view that being Texan is culturally defined rather than geographically defined). The study by Cocos and Callison-Burch (2017) is a first step in this direction. They explore modeling language with respect to attributes of a location (e.g., residential land use, movie theater) instead of absolute physical locations and use this as context when training word embeddings.

Dialect Perception Perception studies make up a core part of sociolinguistic research, but using computational methods to study the social values that people place on linguistic forms is an underexplored area. Rymes and Leone-Pizzighella (2018) motivate that Web 2.0 enables studying processes through which linguistic forms gain social value and demonstrate this with a qualitative analysis of YouTube comments of videos taking part in the accent competition.

The scale of social media allows studying such processes quantitatively over time. Work in this space could also draw from recent studies on fairness and how computational methods encode social biases (Garg et al., 2018).

Variation *and* Change Social media also provides the opportunity to study language change across space and time. For example, Eisenstein et al. (2014) analyzed patterns in diffusion of linguistic change over the United States. Geographical proximity and population size were important factors, but the study also found that demographic similarity (especially in regard to race) played a central role. There has been more work on language change and social media, e.g., Grieve et al. (2017) studied the emergence of new words, but this study focused only on the diachronic dimension. A challenge is teasing apart true language change from confounding factors, especially since social media data are generated in an uncontrolled setting. For example, the population of a social media platform need not stay the same, e.g., younger users might migrate to another platform over time.

Multiple Platforms, Multiple Modalities Social media studies usually focus on a *single* data source, e.g., Twitter, Facebook, or YouTube. However, different social media platforms have different mechanisms shaping language use and behavior. Research that compares patterns across different social media platforms would thus support more robust interpretations of the findings and help us answer questions about generalizability. Furthermore, social media also allows us to extend our focus to other modalities, like speech or video, which could shed further light on the relation between phonological and orthographic variation.

References

Androutsopoulos, Jannis. 2013. Online data collection. Pages 236–249 of: Mallinson, Christine, Childs, Becky, and Herk, Gerard Van (eds.), *Data Collection in Sociolinguistics: Methods and Applications*. Routledge.

Androutsopoulos, Jannis. 2014. Languaging when contexts collapse: Audience design in social networking. *Discourse, Context & Media*, **4–5**, 62–73.

Bamman, David, Dyer, Chris, and Smith, Noah A. 2014a. Distributed representations of geographically situated language. Pages 828–834 of: *Proceedings of the 52nd Annual Meeting of the Association for Computational Linguistics, Volume 2: Short Papers.*

Bamman, David, Eisenstein, Jacob, and Schnoebelen, Tyler. 2014b. Gender identity and lexical variation in social media. *Journal of Sociolinguistics*, **18**(2), 135–160.

Bell, Allan. 1984. Language style as audience design. *Language in Society*, **13**(2), 145–204.

Bhat, Irshad, Bhat, Riyaz A., Shrivastava, Manish, and Sharma, Dipti. 2018. Universal dependency parsing for Hindi-English code-switching. Pages 987–998 of: *Proceedings of the 2018 Conference of the North American Chapter of the Association for Computational Linguistics: Human Language Technologies, Volume 1: Long Papers.*

Blodgett, Su Lin, Green, Lisa, and O'Connor, Brendan. 2016. Demographic dialectal variation in social media: A case study of African-American English. Pages 1119–1130 of: *Proceedings of the 2016 Conference on Empirical Methods in Natural Language Processing.*

Britain, David. 2010. *An International Handbook of Linguistic Variation.* Handbooks of Linguistics and Communication Science, no. 30. Mouton de Gruyter. Pages 142–163.

Chambers, Jack K., and Trudgill, Peter. 1998. *Dialectology.* Cambridge University Press.

Cheshire, Jenny, and Fox, Sue. 2009. Was/were variation: A perspective from London. *Language Variation and Change,* **21**(1), 1–38.

Cocos, Anne, and Callison-Burch, Chris. 2017. The language of place: Semantic value from geospatial context. Pages 99–104 of: *Proceedings of the 15th Conference of the European Chapter of the Association for Computational Linguistics, Volume 2, Short Papers.*

Doyle, Gabriel. 2014. Mapping dialectal variation by querying social media. Pages 98–106 of: *Proceedings of the 14th Conference of the European Chapter of the Association for Computational Linguistics.*

Eisenstein, Jacob. 2015. Systematic patterning in phonologically-motivated orthographic variation. *Journal of Sociolinguistics,* **19**(2), 161–188.

Eisenstein, Jacob, O'Connor, Brendan, Smith, Noah A., and Xing, Eric P. 2010. A latent variable model for geographic lexical variation. Pages 1277–1287 of: *Proceedings of the 2010 Conference on Empirical Methods in Natural Language Processing.*

Eisenstein, Jacob, O'Connor, Brendan, Smith, Noah A., and Xing, Eric P. 2014. Diffusion of lexical change in social media. *PLoS ONE,* **9**(11), e113114.

Garg, Nikhil, Schiebinger, Londa, Jurafsky, Dan, and Zou, James. 2018. Word embeddings quantify 100 years of gender and ethnic stereotypes. *Proceedings of the National Academy of Sciences,* **115**(16), E3635–E3644.

Golder, Scott A., and Macy, Michael W. 2014. Digital footprints: Opportunities and challenges for online social research. *Annual Review of Sociology,* **40**(1), 129–152.

Gouws, Stephan, Hovy, Dirk, and Metzler, Donald. 2011. Unsupervised mining of lexical variants from noisy text. Pages 82–90 of: *Proceedings of the First workshop on Unsupervised Learning in NLP.*

Grieve, Jack, Nini, Andrea, and Guo, Diansheng. 2017. Analyzing lexical emergence in Modern American English online. *English Language and Linguistics,* **21**(1), 99–127.

Haddican, Bill, and Johnson, Daniel Ezra. 2012. Effects on the particle verb alternation across English dialects. *University of Pennsylvania Working Papers in Linguistics,* **18**(2), 5.

Herring, Susan C. 2004. *Designing for virtual communities in the service of learning.* Cambridge University Press. Pages 338–376.

Herring, Susan C, and Androutsopoulos, Jannis. 2015. *The Handbook of Discourse Analysis.* Wiley. Pages 127–151.

Hovy, Dirk, and Søgaard, Anders. 2015. Tagging performance correlates with author age. Pages 483–488 of: *Proceedings of the 53rd Annual Meeting of the Association for Computational Linguistics and the 7th International Joint Conference on Natural Language Processing, Volume 2: Short Papers.*

Huang, Yuan, Guo, Diansheng, Kasakoff, Alice, and Grieve, Jack. 2016. Understanding U.S. regional linguistic variation with Twitter data analysis. *Computers, Environment and Urban Systems*, **59**, 244–255.

Jacobo, Levy Abitbol, Karsai, Márton, Magué, Jean-Philippe, Chevrot, Jean-Pierre, and Fleury, Eric. 2018. Socioeconomic dependencies of linguistic patterns in Twitter: A multivariate analysis. Pages 1125–1134 of: *Proceedings of the 2018 World Wide Web Conference WWW '18.*

Johnstone, Barbara. 2004. *Sociolinguistic Variation: Critical Reflections.* Oxford University Press. Pages 65–83.

Jones, Taylor. 2015. Toward a description of African American vernacular English dialect regions using "Black Twitter". *American Speech*, **90**(4), 403–440.

Jørgensen, Anna Katrine, Hovy, Dirk, and Søgaard, Anders. 2015. Challenges of studying and processing dialects in social media. Pages 9–18 of: *Proceedings of the Workshop on Noisy User-Generated Text.*

Kerswill, Paul. 2013. *Space in Language and Linguistics: Geographical, Interactional, and Cognitive Perspectives.* Walter de Gruyter. Pages 128–164.

Kristiansen, Tore. 2018. *The Handbook of Dialectology.* Wiley-Blackwell. Pages 106–122.

Llamas, Carmen. 2018. *The Handbook of Dialectology.* Wiley-Blackwell. Pages 253–267.

Marwick, Alice E., and boyd, danah. 2011. I tweet honestly, I tweet passionately: Twitter users, context collapse, and the imagined audience. *New Media & Society*, **13**(1), 114–133.

Melo, Fernando, and Martins, Bruno. 2016. Automated geocoding of textual documents: A survey of current approaches. *Transactions in GIS*, **21**(1), 3–38.

Nguyen, Dong, and Doğruöz, A. Seza. 2013. Word level language identification in online multilingual communication. Pages 857–862 of: *Proceedings of the 2013 Conference on Empirical Methods in Natural Language Processing.*

Nguyen, Dong, and Eisenstein, Jacob. 2017. A kernel independence test for geographical language variation. *Computational Linguistics*, **43**(3), 567–592.

Nguyen, Dong, Gravel, Rilana, Trieschnigg, Dolf, and Meder, Theo. 2013. "How old do you think I am?" A study of language and age in Twitter. Pages 439–448 of: *Proceedings of the Seventh International AAAI Conference on Weblogs and Social Media.*

Nguyen, Dong, Trieschnigg, Dolf, and Cornips, Leonie. 2015. Audience and the use of minority languages on Twitter. Pages 666–669 of: *Proceedings of the Ninth International AAAI Conference on Web and Social Media.*

Nguyen, Dong, Doğruöz, A. Seza, Rosé, Carolyn P., and de Jong, Franciska. 2016. Computational sociolinguistics: A survey. *Computational Linguistics*, **42**(3), 537–593.

Owoputi, Olutobi, O'Connor, Brendan, Dyer, Chris, Gimpel, Kevin, Schneider, Nathan, and Smith, Noah A. 2013. Improved part-of-speech tagging for online conversational text with word clusters. Pages 380–390 of: *Proceedings of the 2013 Conference of the North American Chapter of the Association for Computational Linguistics: Human Language Technologies.*

Pavalanathan, Umashanthi, and Eisenstein, Jacob. 2015a. Audience-modulated variation in online social media. *American Speech*, **90**(2), 187–213.

Pavalanathan, Umashanthi, and Eisenstein, Jacob. 2015b. Confounds and consequences in geotagged Twitter data. Pages 2138–2148 of: *Proceedings of the 2015 Conference on Empirical Methods in Natural Language Processing*.

Rahimi, Afshin, Cohn, Trevor, and Baldwin, Timothy. 2017. A neural model for user geolocation and lexical dialectology. Pages 209–216 of: *Proceedings of the 55th Annual Meeting of the Association for Computational Linguistics, Volume 2: Short Papers*.

Rymes, Betsy, and Leone-Pizzighella, Andrea. 2018. YouTube-based accent challenge narratives: Web 2.0 as a context for studying the social value of accent. *International Journal of the Sociology of Language*, **2018**(250), 137–163.

Salganik, Matthew J. 2017. *Bit by Bit: Social Research in the Digital Age*. Princeton University Press.

Shoemark, Philippa, Sur, Debnil, Shrimpton, Luke, Murray, Iain, and Goldwater, Sharon. 2017. Aye or naw, whit dae ye hink? Scottish independence and linguistic identity on social media. Pages 1239–1248 of: *Proceedings of the 15th Conference of the European Chapter of the Association for Computational Linguistics: Volume 1, Long Papers*, vol. 1.

Stewart, Ian. 2014. Now we stronger than ever: African-American English syntax in Twitter. Pages 31–37 of: *Proceedings of the Student Research Workshop at the 14th Conference of the European Chapter of the Association for Computational Linguistics*.

Stewart, Ian, Pinter, Yuval, and Eisenstein, Jacob. 2018. Sí o no, què penses? Catalonian independence and linguistic identity on social media. In: *Proceedings of the North American Chapter of the Association for Computational Linguistics (NAACL)*.

Wang, Bo, Liakata, Maria, Zubiaga, Arkaitz, and Procter, Rob. 2017a. TDParse: Multi-target-specific sentiment recognition on Twitter. Pages 483–493 of: *Proceedings of the 15th Conference of the European Chapter of the Association for Computational Linguistics: Volume 1, Long Papers*.

Wang, Bo, Liakata, Maria, Tsakalidis, Adam, Georgakopoulos Kolaitis, Spiros, Papadopoulos, Symeon, Apostolidis, Lazaros, Zubiaga, Arkaitz, Procter, Rob, and Kompatsiaris, Yiannis. 2017b. TOTEMSS: Topic-based, Temporal Sentiment Summarisation for Twitter. Pages 21–24 of: *Proceedings of the IJCNLP 2017, System Demonstrations*.

Wieling, Martijn, Nerbonne, John, and Baayen, R. Harald. 2011. Quantitative social dialectology: Explaining linguistic variation geographically and socially. *PLOS ONE*, **6**(9), 1–14.

Williams, Matthew L, Burnap, Pete, and Sloan, Luke. 2017. Towards an ethical framework for publishing Twitter data in social research: Taking into account users' views, online context and algorithmic estimation. *Sociology*, **51**(6), 1149–1168.

Zook, Matthew, Barocas, Solon, boyd, danah, Crawford, Kate, Keller, Emily, Gangadharan, Seeta Peña, Goodman, Alyssa, Hollander, Rachelle, Koenig, Barbara A., Metcalf, Jacob, Narayanan, Arvind, Nelson, Alondra, and Pasquale, Frank. 2017. Ten simple rules for responsible big data research. *PLOS Computational Biology*, **13**(3), 1–10.

11 Machine Translation between Similar Languages

Preslav Nakov and Jörg Tiedemann

11.1 Introduction

Translation between similar languages is commonly considered to be unnecessary and less interesting from an academic and commercial point of view. Closely related languages are often mutually intelligible and translation is too expensive and time-consuming to perform. However, the situation is far from trivial and this chapter sheds some light on approaches that have been proposed to automate the process to make it feasible to support fast and accurate translations between languages that seem very similar at first sight, but whose differences reflect important parts of the cultural identity of their speakers.

A typical case is that there is some dominating language and a number of closely related languages with fewer speakers and resources (see Figure 11.1). A good reason for the focus on machine translation (MT) between such languages is the extended support of low-resource languages to reduce linguistic discrimination. Besides this aspect, MT has other benefits, such as the cost-efficient adaptation of tools to new languages from closely related high-resource languages. Related languages can also function as a pivot in MT to other less-similar languages, and they can be used for annotation transfer or model adaptation. Furthermore, the strong relationship between similar languages can be used to build more powerful multilingual natural language processing (NLP) models with higher coverage.

11.2 Models and Approaches

The similarity between closely related languages enables low-level techniques and simplifying assumptions that are not possible for less similar languages. Closely related languages share many aspects of syntactic structure and typically exhibit a strong lexical overlap due to tight etymological connections. This leads to less expressed divergences in word order and lexical semantics, which greatly supports the ability of a machine translation system to capture the proper mapping from one language to another.

The machine translation approaches can be classified into different classes and a typical distinction is between hand-crafted rule-based systems and

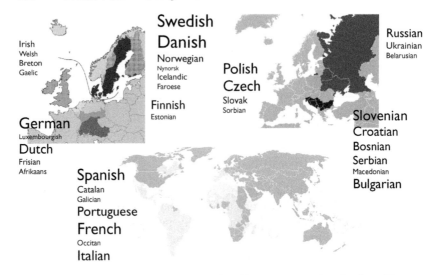

Figure 11.1 Groups of closely related languages are often dominated by one or a few high-resource languages and a number of languages with little or no NLP support. (Images from Wikipedia. The font size is for illustration and is not based on real statistics.)

data-driven models. Hand-crafted systems typically include manually derived linguistic rules that perform source language analysis, cross-lingual transfer, and target language generation (the classical transfer-based model). An expert is needed to write such rules and their effectiveness is tested in real-world data. Data-driven models apply learning algorithms to find abstractions for a given task, e.g., translation between natural languages.

These models have a number of free parameters that need to be learned from data, and in the case of translation those are human translations. Hence, data-driven MT is typically based in the field of supervised machine learning, and models span from example-based machine translation over statistical machine translation (SMT) to neural machine translation (NMT). We leave out example-based MT in our descriptions, but we will focus on statistical machine translation.

Figure 11.2 illustrates the basic steps for the different approaches on a very schematic level. Transfer models commonly apply a pipeline with three independent steps of analysis, transfer, and generation. This is a common approach for hand-crafted systems (Forcada et al., 2011). Statistical MT systems model a direct mapping between the source and the target based on some kind of segmentation and a probabilistic search strategy (Koehn, 2010). This is often decomposed into different components, as illustrated in Figure 11.3. Neural machine translation is typically based on an encoder–decoder with a semantic

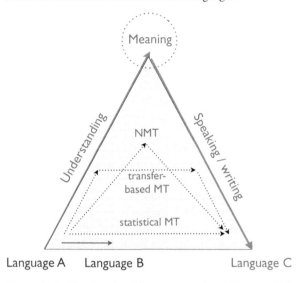

Figure 11.2 Closely related languages and machine translation in relation to the Vauquois triangle of translation. Translating between the closely related languages *A* and *B* may not need the same level of abstraction as translating from *A* to *C*.

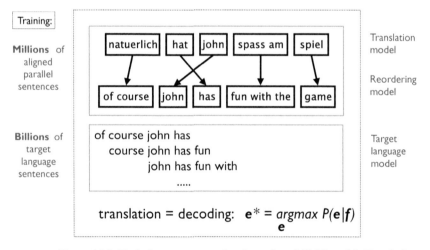

Figure 11.3 Typical components of a phrase-based SMT model. Translation refers to a probabilistic decoding according to a weighted combination of scores coming from the various components.

vector representation in the middle: first, the source-language input sentence is encoded into a vector or a sequence of vectors, and then a target-language translation is generated from that representation (Sutskever et al., 2014).

All but neural MTs are basically symbolic methods that use discrete rules for the translation process. However, statistical MT applies probabilistic parameters learned from data, whereas hand-crafted systems typically include manually defined (and linguistically motivated) preference rules when searching for translation hypotheses.

The translation between closely related languages is special in the way that it does not always require full understanding of the input to produce proper output in the target language due to the semantic similarity between the languages. This fact is the reason why less abstract models, such as statistical MT, are very successful in that case. In Figure 11.2, the intuition is illustrated by the distance that needs to be captured by a direct SMT model compared to an encoder–decoder model that needs to find proper semantic abstractions. Furthermore, hand-crafted rule-based systems may come in handy as well because very general rules (of a low level of abstraction) can be sufficient to make proper mappings between closely related languages. Complicated restructuring and semantic interpretation is not necessary in most cases, and experts are capable of writing high-coverage rules.

Figure 11.4 shows some examples from different language pairs that demonstrate that closely related languages are often structurally very similar, which greatly facilitates the process of machine translation between them.

Catalan - Spanish

Oko, comprova l'equip.
Oko, comprueba el equipo.

No hi ha constellació en la distància Visual.
No hay constelación en la distancia Visual.

Cap explosió estelar.
Ninguna explosión estelar.

Bosnian - Macedonian

Kako znate da se radi o jednoj životinji?
Како знете дека се работи за животно?

Ni ja ne verujem u zmajeve...
И јас не верувам во змејови ...

Danish - Norwegian

Du ser forfærdelig ud.
- Du ser forferdelig ut.

Du kunnei det mindste have barberet dig.
Du kunne i det minste ha barbert deg.

Icelandic - Swedish

Barnið er dáið.
Barnet är dött.

Hann andaði aðeins í smástund.
Han andades bara en kort stund.

Svo andaði hann ekki meira.
Han andades aldrig igen.

Figure 11.4 Examples of movie subtitle translations between closely related languages (in the same and in different alphabets).

There are certainly a number of important challenges, e.g., the use of different writing systems and conventions, differences in morphology, the risk of false friends and divergent language evolution due to different language contact situations. Nevertheless, those differences are often consistent and can reliably be detected from limited training data.

11.3   Character-Level Machine Translation

Let us take as an example Macedonian and Bulgarian, which are closely related languages as illustrated in Figure 11.5. The language similarity and the regularities in morphological variation and spelling conventions between them motivate the application of character-level translation models. The idea is to generalize from translation models over word sequences to the translation of character sequences.

Applying SMT to characters instead of words is straightforward (Vilar et al., 2007; Tiedemann, 2012a). The sentences are simply treated as sequences of characters, as shown in Figure 11.6. Phrase translation tables become translation tables of (arbitrary) character sequences (up to a certain pre-defined

MK:	што е тоа ?
BG:	какво е това ?
MK:	држете се цврсто .
BG:	дръжте се здраво .
MK:	никогаш не сум преспала цела сезона
BG:	никога не съм спала цял сезон
MK:	ова нешто е неверојатно !
BG:	това нещо е удивително !
MK:	состаноков е завршен .
BG:	край на срещата .

Figure 11.5 Example sentences (tokenized, lowercased) from movie subtitles in Macedonian and Bulgarian.

MK:	што е тоа ?
BG:	какво е това ?
MK:	ш т о _ е _ т о а _ ?
BG:	к а к в о _ е _ т о в а _ ?

Figure 11.6 Preparing data for character-based translation. Space characters require special treatment to preserve them in the data. Here, we simply convert them to underscores assuming that this character is not overloaded with other semantics.

maximum length), and language models model character n-grams instead of word n-grams.

11.3.1   Training Character-Level SMT Models

Phrase-based SMT needs a translation model, which is trained on a parallel sentence-aligned corpus, known as *bitext*, and a target language model, which is trained on monolingual target-language text.

Training character-level language models is straightforward using the available tools for n-gram language modeling and preparing the data as depicted in Figure 11.6. Due to the reduced vocabulary (considering characters instead of words), we can easily train a model of higher order. This is also necessary in order to capture the larger context needed to avoid the generation of non-word sequences.

Training a translation model involves aligning the bitext at the word level. Certainly, it is possible to align characters with the same standard models and tools that are commonly used for word-based models (Vogel et al., 1996; Och and Ney, 2003; Dyer et al., 2013). However, word alignment algorithms were not designed for aligning characters, and thus their context-independent lexical and distortion parameters do not fit well for the character alignment task.

There are various character-level alignment algorithms developed for transliteration and character-to-phoneme translation (Damper et al., 2005; Durrani et al., 2010). Such methods are commonly based on finite-state transducers and edit-distance operations (Ristad and Yianilos, 1998). These context-independent low-level operations perform character-by-character transformations, but are also insufficient as the differences between closely related languages go beyond transliteration. There are extensions of the transducer models that introduce many-to-many alignments for character transformations (Jiampojamarn et al., 2007), but even those are limited to context-independent edit operations.

The vocabulary in the character alignment task is extremely small, which makes the expressive power of lexical translation parameters less effective. Yet, it is possible to make use of the expressive power of word alignment models by adjusting the *data*, so that contextual information is included in the lexical items that are to be aligned. Considering character n-grams instead of single characters achieves this without changing the task of creating a character-level alignment (Nakov and Tiedemann, 2012; Tiedemann, 2012a; Tiedemann and Nakov, 2013).

For example, using character bigrams as shown in Figure 11.7 increases the size of the vocabulary of the Bulgarian side of a training bitext of 100k sentences from 101 single characters to 1,893 character bigrams. A comparison of vocabulary sizes for a Macedonian–Bulgarian training bitext is given in Table 11.1.

Table 11.1 *Vocabulary size of character-level alignment models and the corresponding word-level model.*

	Macedonian	Bulgarian
single characters	99	101
character bigrams	1,851	1,893
character trigrams	13,794	14,305
words	41,816	30,927

Table 11.2 *Examples from a character-level phrase table (without scores): may cover words and phrases.*

Macedonian	Bulgarian
_ д е к а _ т о j _	_ , ч е _ т о й _
_ с о _ т о j _	_ с _ т о я _
а в м е _	а х м е _
а в м е _ д а _	а х м е _ д а _
а в м е _ в о _	а х м е _ в _
_ в е р у в а м _	_ в я р в а м _
у в а м _ , _ д е к а _	в а м _ , _ ч е _

original:
МК: навистина ?
BG: наистина ?

bigrams:
МК: на ав ви ис ст ти ин на а_ _? ?_
BG: на аи ис ст ти ин на а_ _? ?_

trigrams:
МК: нав ави вис ист сти тин ина на_ а_? _?_ ?__
BG: наи аис ист сти тин ина на_ а_? _?_ ?__

Figure 11.7 Preparing a bitext of *n*-grams for character alignment.

The result of character *n*-gram alignments can be directly mapped to a single character alignment that we will need for the extraction of character-level phrase tables. Each bigram represents the position of its initial character. Adding spaces at the end of each sentence ensures that we have as many bigrams as single characters.

Next, the parameters of the log-linear SMT model need to be tuned. This is commonly done using minimum error rate training (Och, 2003) to optimize for BLEU (bilingual evaluation understudy) (Papineni et al., 2002), or a similar evaluation measure. Computing BLEU scores over matching character sequences does not make much sense, especially if the n-gram size is limited to small values of n (usually 4 or less). Therefore, there is a need to post-process the n-best lists of machine translations of the development data in each step, and then to calculate the usual word-based BLEU score. This ensures that the parameters are optimized towards a well-performing SMT output of surface strings.

One drawback of character-based SMT models is their inability to model long-distance word reorderings. However, this should not be a major limitation, as we do not expect large syntactic divergence between closely related languages. Another issue is that the sentences become longer in the sense of longer sequences that need to be translated. This causes an overhead at decoding time for the SMT system, which should be considered. It could also cause problems for word alignment tools, some of which struggle to handle sequences longer than a certain maximal length.

In the following, we present the results of experiments with Macedonian–Bulgarian using data from the OpenSubtitle corpus, which is part of the OPUS collection (Tiedemann, 2012b): 102k parallel sentences (10M words) for training, 10k for tuning, and 10k for testing.

The results are shown in Table 11.3. The word-based baseline is 31.10 in terms of BLEU. In the next group of experiments, we can see that standard character-level SMT (c1), i.e., simply treating characters as separate words, performs slightly better (+0.39 BLEU) than word-level SMT. However, changing MERT (minimum error rate training) to tune for word-level as opposed to character-level BLEU as in (c2) yields another +0.79 of BLEU points of improvement. Finally, using bigram-based character alignments yields further improvement of +0.43 BLEU (and trigram-based character alignment is worse than bigram-based).

Table 11.3 **Macedonian–Bulgarian translation.** *Superscripts show absolute improvement over the word-level baseline (w1).*

MK→BG		BLEU %	NIST	TER	METEOR
Word-level SMT					
w1	SMT baseline	**31.10**	6.56	50.72	70.53
Character-level SMT					
c1	Char-aligned, char-BLEU-tuned	**31.49**$^{(+0.39)}$	6.58	50.27	71.10
c1	Char-aligned, word-BLEU-tuned	**32.28**$^{(+1.18)}$	6.70	49.70	71.35
c2	Bigram-aligned, word-BLEU-tuned	**32.71**$^{(+1.61)}$	6.77	49.23	71.65
	Trigram-aligned, word-BLEU-tuned	32.07$^{(+0.97)}$	6.68	49.82	71.21

The success of the character-based SMT models raises at least two additional questions: (1) How much data are necessary for training reasonable character-level translation models that are still better than a standard word-level model trained on the same data? (2) How strongly related should the languages be so that it is beneficial to use SMT at the character level?

We investigated the first question by using increasing amounts of training data. For comparability, we kept the model parameters fixed, and we used the best character-based model. The top-left plot in Figure 11.8 shows the learning curves for word- and character-level models for Macedonian–Bulgarian. We can see that the character-level models clearly outperform the word-level ones for the small amounts of training data that we have: the abstraction at the character level is much stronger and yields more robust models.

Figure 11.8 also shows the learning curves for three additional South–Slavic language pairs. We can see that the character-level models make sense with small data sets. They outperform word-level models at least until around 100,000 sentence pairs of training data.

Certainly, language relatedness has an impact on the effectiveness of character-level SMT. The difference between character- and word-level models

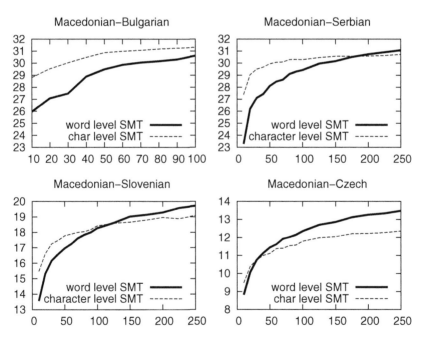

Figure 11.8 BLEU for word- and character-level SMT models for varying sizes of parallel training data (in thousands of sentence pairs).

shows that Slovenian is not the most appropriate choice for character-level SMT due to its weaker relation to Macedonian.

Furthermore, we can see that the performance of character-level models levels out at some point and standard word-level models surpass them with an almost linear increase in MT quality up to the point we have considered in the training procedures. Looking at Czech, we can see that character-level models are competitive for very small data sets only, but their performance is so low that they are practically useless. In general, translation is more difficult for more distant languages; this is also the case for word-level models.

11.4   Closely Related Languages as MT Pivots

Data-driven machine translation systems, which dominate the field of machine translation today, are easy to build and offer competitive performance in terms of translation quality. Unfortunately, training such systems requires large parallel corpora of sentences and their translations, which are not available for most language pairs and textual domains. As a result, building an SMT system to translate directly between two languages is often not possible. A common solution to this problem is to use an intermediate, or *pivot* language to bridge the gap.

A typical approach is a *cascaded translation* model using two independent steps of translating from the source to the pivot and then from the pivot to the target language. A special, and in fact very common, case is where the pivot language is closely related to the source language (see Figure 11.9), which makes it possible to train useful systems on much smaller bitexts using *character-level translation* models. This is the case we will consider in the following, using the example of translating Macedonian to English via related languages, primarily Bulgarian.

SMT using pivot languages has been investigated in a number of studies. For example, Cohn and Lapata (2007) used *triangulation* techniques to combine phrase tables. The lexical weights in such an approach can be estimated by bridging word alignments (Wu and Wang, 2007; Bertoldi et al., 2008). Cascaded translation approaches via pivot languages were used by various researchers (de Gispert and Mariño, 2006; Koehn et al., 2009; Wu and Wang, 2009). Several techniques were compared in (de Gispert and Mariño, 2006; Wu and Wang, 2009; Utiyama and Isahara, 2007). Pivot languages can also be used for paraphrasing and lexical adaptation (Bannard and Callison-Burch, 2005; Crego et al., 2010). In the following, we will explore the special case of pivot translation when the pivot language is closely related to the source language.

Table 11.4 shows statistics about the OPUS data we use. We further use 10k parallel sentence pairs for tuning and another 10k for evaluation.

Table 11.4 *Size of the data sets.*

Data Set	# Sentences	# Words
MK-EN	160K	1.1M
MK-BG	102K	0.65M
BG-EN	10M	76M
MK-mono	536K	4M
BG-mono	16M	136M
EN-mono	43M	435M

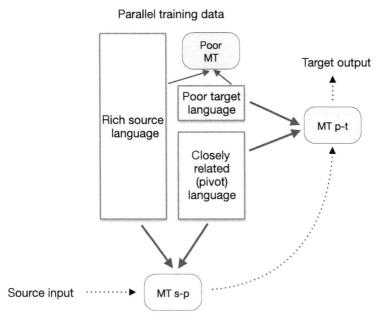

Figure 11.9 Pivot-based machine translation using closely related languages as a means to bridge the lack of parallel training data for direct translation.

11.4.1   Cascaded Pivot Translation

We base our translations on the individually trained translation models for the source (Macedonian) to the pivot language (Bulgarian) and for the pivot language to the final target language (English, in our case). As proposed by Tiedemann (2012a), we rerank k-best (we set k to 10) translations to find the best hypothesis for each test sentence.

Table 11.5 *Evaluating cascaded translation: Macedonian to English, pivoting via Bulgarian.*

	BLEU	NIST	TER	METEOR
Model	**Individually Tuned**			
Word-level pivot	22.48	5.46	64.11	47.77
Char-level pivot	25.67	5.91	60.45	54.61
Word+char+MK-EN	25.00	5.86	61.47	50.19
Model	**Globally Tuned**			
Word-level pivot	23.38	5.44	64.33	48.31
Char-level pivot	25.73	5.81	61.91	52.47
Word+char+MK-EN	26.36	5.92	60.85	53.39

We can just apply the models tuned for the individual translation tasks, which is suboptimal. Thus, we also introduce a global tuning approach, where we generate k-best lists for the combined cascaded translation model, and we tune the corresponding end-to-end weights using MERT (Och, 2003) or Pairwise Ranking Optimization (PRO) (Hopkins and May, 2011). We set the size of the k-best lists to 20 in both steps to keep the size manageable, with $20 \times 20 = 400$ hypotheses per sentence.

Another option is to combine (1) the direct translation model, (2) the word-level pivot model, and (3) the character-level pivot model. Using the three translation paths (direct translation, word-level pivot, and character-level pivot), we obtain an extended set of parameters covering five individual systems. Again, we have the option to throw them all in one k-best reranking system or to use global tuning.

Table 11.5 summarizes the results of the cascaded translation models. We can see that the character-level model adds significantly to the performance of the cascaded model compared to the entirely word-level one. Combining the two together with direct translation path yields further improvements, but only when global tuning is used.

11.4.2   Synthetic Training Data

Another possibility to make use of pivot languages is to create synthetic training data. For example, we can translate the Bulgarian side of our large Bulgarian–English training bitext to Macedonian, thus ending up with "Macedonian"–English training data.

Table 11.6 shows the evaluation results for such an experiment. Experiments with word-level and character-level SMT are shown in rows 1 and 2, respectively. The result from the model trained on a concatenation of synthetic bitexts

Table 11.6 *Macedonian–English translation using synthetic data (by translating X–EN to MK–EN) using different pivot languages: Bulgarian (BG), Serbian (SR), Slovenian (SL), and Czech (CZ).*

Model	BLEU	NIST	TER	METEOR
BG word-syn.	26.01	5.82	61.49	50.31
BG char-syn.	28.17	6.17	58.97	55.27
BG w+c-syn.	28.62	6.25	58.52	55.75
BG w+c-syn.+MK-EN	29.11	6.30	58.27	56.64
SR word-syn.	25.39	5.72	63.26	41.15
SR char-syn.	27.25	6.14	60.31	47.32
SR w+c-syn.	29.05	6.29	59.73	49.18
SR w+c-syn.+MK-EN	30.39	6.51	58.08	50.91
SL word-syn.	24.78	5.58	64.04	39.34
SL char-syn.	24.03	5.67	63.11	44.76
SL w+c-syn.	27.30	6.11	60.46	47.69
SL w+c-syn.+MK-EN	28.42	6.26	59.57	49.06
CZ word-syn.	26.48	5.83	62.52	41.02
CZ char-syn.	23.74	5.51	64.96	44.96
CZ w+c-syn.	28.03	6.08	61.12	48.41
CZ w+c-syn.+MK-EN	29.24	6.29	59.39	49.60
ALL-syn.	36.25	7.24	53.06	61.74
ALL-syn.+MK-EN	**36.69**	**7.28**	**52.83**	**62.26**

is shown in the third row. Finally, we also added the original MK–EN bitext to the combination (shown on row 4). We can see from the top four rows that using synthetic data outperforms cascaded translation by 2–3 BLEU points absolute. Here again, the character-level model is much more valuable than the word-level one.

One huge advantage of using syhthetic training data over the cascaded approaches that we presented earlier is the reduced decoding time. With synthetic data, the system behaves like a traditional phrase-based SMT system. The only large-scale effort is the translation of the training corpus, but this needs to be done only once and can easily be performed off-line in a distributed setup.

11.4.3 Other Pivot Languages

An important question is what kinds of languages are useful for pivot-based translation. To address this question, we generated translations of our Macedonian–English data set but this time via Serbian, Slovene, and Czech. We used synthetic training data based on translation models trained on subsets of

Table 11.7 *English-Macedonian translation (BLEU) using synthetic data via various pivot languages.*

Model	Word-level	Char-level	Combined
baseline EN-MK	22.03	–	–
synthetic EN-MK (Bulgarian)	23.01	**24.33**	24.03
synthetic EN-MK (Serbian)	25.23	25.01	**25.76**
synthetic EN-MK (Czech)	23.85	22.85	**25.03**
all data sets	–	–	**30.63**

100,000 sentence pairs in order to make the results comparable to the Bulgarian case. The pivot–English data are comparable for Slovene and Serbian (one million sentence pairs) and almost double the size for Czech (1.9 million).

Table 11.6 shows results for all pivot languages: Bulgarian, Serbian, Slovenian, and Czech. We can see that Serbian, which is geographically adjacent to Macedonian, performs similarly to Bulgarian, which is also adjacent, while Slovenian, which is farther away and not adjacent to any of the above, performs worse. Note that with a Slovenian pivot, the character-level model performs worse than the word-level model.

This suggests that the differences between Slovenian and Macedonian are not that much at the subword level but mostly at the word level. This is even more evident for Czech, which is geographically farther away and which also belongs to a different Slavic subgroup. Note, however, that we had much more training data for Czech–English, which explains the strong overall performance of its word-level model.

Overall, we have seen that as the relatedness between the source and the pivot language decreases, so does the utility of the character-level model. However, in all cases the character-level model helps when combined with the word-level one, yielding 1.5–4 BLEU points of absolute improvement. Moreover, using all four pivots yields a boost of seven additional BLEU points over the best single pivot.

Table 11.7 confirms the same success also in the reverse translation direction: from English to Macedonian. We can see sizable improvements by combining various types of synthetic training data derived from models that translate between closely related languages.

11.4.4 Manual Evaluation

Finally, we performed manual evaluation of the word-level, the character-level, and the combined systems for translating from Macedonian to English using Bulgarian. We asked three speakers of Macedonian and Bulgarian to rank the

Table 11.8 *Comparing word-level and character-level BLEU to human judgments for Macedonian–English using Bulgarian: global pivoting vs. synthetic data (see Tables 11.5 and 11.6).*

Model	Word BLEU	Char BLEU	Avg. Rank	">" Score	Untranslated Words
Reference	—	—	1.57	0.73	—
Baseline	22.33	50.83	3.37	0.25	4,959
Word-pivot	23.38	53.26	2.81	0.42	3,144
Char-pivot	25.73	56.00	2.51	0.52	1,841
Comb-pivot	26.36	56.39	2.63	0.46	1,491
Word-synth.	26.01	55.59	2.77	0.43	3,258
Char-synth.	28.17	58.21	2.31	0.58	1,818
Comb-synth.	28.62	58.53	2.11	0.65	1,712

English output from the eight anonymized systems given the Macedonian input; we used 100 test sentences for this.

The results are shown in Table 11.8. Column 4 shows the *average rank* for each system, and column 5 shows the *">" score* as defined by Callison-Burch et al. (2012): the number of times a given system was judged to be strictly better than the rest divided by the frequency it was judged strictly better or strictly worse than the rest. We further include word- and character-level BLEU, and the number of untranslated words.

We calculated Cohen's kappas (Cohen, 1960) of 0.87, 0.86, and 0.83 between the pairs of judges, following the procedure in Callison-Burch et al. (2012). This corresponds to almost perfect agreement (Landis and Koch, 1977), probably due to the short length of the subtitles, which allows for few differences in translation and simplifies ranking.

The individual human judgments (not shown to save space) correlate perfectly in terms of relative ranking of (1) the three pivoting systems and (2) the three synthetic data systems. Moreover, the individual and the overall human judgments also correlate well with the BLEU scores on (1) and (2), with one notable exception: humans ranked *char-pivot* higher than *comb-pivot*, while word- and char-BLEU switched their ranks. A closer investigation found that this is probably due to length: the hypothesis/reference ratio for *char-pivot* is 1.006, while for *comb-pivot* it is 1.016. In contrast, for *char-synth.* it is 1.006, while for *comb-synth.* it is 1.002. It has been shown (Nakov et al., 2012) that the closer this ratio gets to 1, the better the BLEU score is expected to be. Note also that word-BLEU and char-BLEU correlate perfectly on (1) and (2), which is probably due to tuning the two systems for word-BLEU.

Interestingly, the BLEU-based rankings of the systems inside (1) and (2) perfectly correlate with the number of untranslated words. Note the robustness of the character-level models: they reduce the number of untranslated words by more than 40%. Having untranslated words in the final English translation could be annoying since they are in Cyrillic, but more importantly, they could contain information that is critical for a human, or even for the SMT system, without which it could not generate a good translation for the remaining words in the sentence. This is especially true for content-baring long, low-frequency words. For example, the inability to translate the Macedonian лутам ('I am angry') yields "You don' лутам." instead of "I'm not mad at you."

Character models are very robust with respect to unknown morphological forms, e.g., a word-level model would not translate развеселам, yielding "I'm trying to make a развеселам.", while a character-level model will transform it to the Bulgarian развеселя, thus allowing the fluent "I'm trying to cheer you up." Note that this transformation does not have to pick the correct Bulgarian form, e.g., развеселя is a conjugated verb, but it is translated as an infinitive in English. Moreover, character-level models are very robust to typos, and concatenated or wrongly split words, which are quite common in movie subtitles.

11.5   Bitext Combination

One simple way to make use of a bitext for a resource-rich language that is related to a resource-poor language is to combine them. This could work as related languages tend to have (1) similar word order and syntax, and, more importantly, (2) overlapping vocabulary, and (3) similar spelling. Consider Spanish and Portuguese as an example (and let us pretend that Portuguese is resource-poor, which it is not), and let us look at Article 1 of the Universal Declaration of Human Rights:[1]

- **Spanish:** *Todos los seres humanos nacen libres e iguales en dignidad y derechos y, dotados como están de razón y conciencia, deben comportarse fraternalmente los unos con los otros.*

- **Portuguese:** *Todos os seres humanos nascem livres e iguais em dignidade e em direitos. Dotados de razão e de consciência, devem agir uns para com os outros em espírito de fraternidade.*

The exact word-level overlap is only 17%. Still, there is some overlap at the level of short phrases too. Spanish and Portuguese share about 90% of their vocabulary, and thus the observed level of overlap may appear to be

---

[1]   All human beings are born free and equal in dignity and rights. They are endowed with reason and conscience and should act towards one another in a spirit of brotherhood. (English)

surprisingly low. The reason is that many cognates between the two languages exhibit minor spelling variations. These variations can stem from different rules of orthography, e.g., *senhor* versus *señor* in Portuguese and Spanish, but they can also be due to genuine phonological differences. For example, the Portuguese suffix *-ção* corresponds to the Spanish suffix *-ción*, e.g., *evolução* versus *evolución*. Similar systematic differences exist for verb endings like *-ou* versus *-ó* (for third person singular, simple past tense), e.g., *visitou* versus *visitó*, or *-ei* versus *-é* (for first person singular, simple past tense), e.g., *visitei* versus *visité*. There are also occasional differences that apply to a particular word only, e.g., *dizer* versus *decir*, *Mário* versus *Mario*, and *Maria* versus *María*.

Going back to our example, if we ignore the spelling variations between the cognates in the two languages, the overlap jumps significantly:

- **Portuguese (cognates transliterated to Spanish):**
  Todos los seres humanos nacen libres e iguales en dignidad y en derechos. Dotados de razón y de conciencia, deben agir unos para con los otros en espírito de fraternidad.

All words in this sentence are Spanish, and most of the differences from the official Spanish version above are due to different word choice by the translator; in fact, the sentence can become fluent Spanish if *agir unos par* is changed to *comportarse los unos con*.

This vocabulary overlap (especially after transliteration) means that the resource-rich auxiliary language can be used as a source of translation options for words that cannot be translated with the resources available for the resource-poor language. In actual text, the vocabulary overlap might extend from individual words to short phrases (especially if the resource-rich languages has been transliterated to look like the resource-poor one), which means that translations of whole phrases could potentially be reused between related languages. Moreover, the vocabulary overlap and the similarity in word order can be used to improve the word alignments for the resource-poor language by biasing the word alignment process with additional sentence pairs from the resource-rich language. One can take advantage of all these opportunities: (1) improve the word alignments for the resource-poor language, (2) further augment it with additional translation options, and (3) take care of potential spelling differences through appropriate transliteration.

Concatenating Bitexts. One can simply concatenate the bitexts for X_1–Y and X_2–Y into one large bitext and use it to train an SMT system. This offers several potential benefits.

First, it can yield improved word alignments for the sentences that came from the X_1–Y bitext, e.g., since the additional sentences can provide new contexts for the rare words in that bitext, thus potentially improving their alignments, which in turn could yield better phrase pairs. Rare words are known to serve as "garbage collectors" (Brown et al., 1993) in the IBM word alignment models.

Namely, a rare source word tends to align to many target language words rather than allowing them to stay unaligned or to align to other source words. See (Graca et al., 2010) for a more detailed discussion and examples.

Second, it can provide new source-language side translation options, thus increasing the lexical coverage and reducing the number of unknown words at translation time; it can also provide new useful non-compositional phrases on the source-language side, thus yielding more fluent translation output. Third, it can offer new target-language side phrases for known source phrases, which could improve fluency by providing more translation options for the language model (LM) to choose from. Fourth, inappropriate phrases including words from X_2 that do not exist in X_1 will be effectively ignored at translation time since they could not possibly match the input, while inappropriate new target-language translations still have the chance to be filtered out by the language model.

However, simple concatenation can be problematic. First, when concatenating the small bitext for X_1–Y with the much larger one for X_2–Y, the latter will dominate during word alignment and phrase extraction, thus hugely influencing both lexical and phrase translation probabilities, which can yield poor performance. This can be counter-acted by repeating the small bitext several times so that the large one does not dominate. Second, since the bitexts are merged mechanically, there is no way to distinguish between phrases extracted from the bitext for X_1–Y from those coming from the bitext for X_2–Y. The former are for the target language pair and thus probably should be preferred, while using the latter should be avoided since they might contain inappropriate translations for some words from X_1. For example, a phrase pair from the Indonesian–English bitext could (correctly) translate *polisi* as *police*, while one from the Malay–English bitext could (correctly for Malay, but inappropriately for Indonesian) translate it as *policy*. This is because the Malay word *polisi* and the Indonesian word *polisi* are false friends.

Combining Phrase Tables. Another way of making use of the additional bitext for X_2–Y in order to train an improved phrase-based SMT system for $X_1 \rightarrow Y$ is to build separate phrase tables from X_1–Y and X_2–Y, which can then be (1) used together, e.g., as alternative decoding paths; (2) merged, e.g., using one or more extra features to indicate the bitext each phrase came from; or (3) interpolated, e.g., using simple linear interpolation.

Building two separate phrase tables offers several advantages. First, the preferable phrases from the bitext for X_1–Y are clearly distinguished from (or given a higher weight in the linear interpolation compared to) the potentially riskier ones from the X_2–Y bitext. Second, the lexical and the phrase translation probabilities are combined in a principled manner. Third, using an X_2–Y bitext that is much larger than that for X_1–Y is not problematic any more. Fourth, as with bitext merging, there are many additional source- and target-language phrases, which offer new translation options.

On the negative side, the opportunity is lost to obtain improved word alignments for the sentences in the X_1–Y bitext.

Getting the Best of Both Worlds. Taking into account the potential advantages and disadvantages of the above two general strategies, Nakov and Ng (2009) proposed an approach that tries to get the best from each of them: (1) improved word alignments for X_1–Y, by biasing the word alignment process using additional sentence pairs from X_2–Y, and (2) increased lexical coverage, by using additional phrase pairs that the X_2–Y bitext can provide. The combined method can be described as follows:

1. First, build a balanced bitext B_{rep}, which consists of the X_1–Y bitext repeated k times followed by one copy of the X_2–Y bitext. The number k is to be chosen so that X_2–Y makes about 50% of the sentence pairs. Then, generate word alignments for B_{rep}, and truncate them, keeping word alignments for only one copy of the X_1–Y bitext. Finally, use these word alignments to extract phrases, and build a phrase table T_{rep_trunc}.
2. Build a bitext B_{cat} that is a simple concatenation of the bitexts for X_1–Y and X_2–Y. Generate word alignments for B_{cat}, extract phrases, and build a phrase table T_{cat}.
3. Generate a merged phrase table by combining T_{rep_trunc} and T_{cat}. The merging gives priority to T_{rep_trunc} and uses extra features, indicating the origin of each entry in the combined phrase table.

Table 11.9 shows the experimental results when using 160K of *pt-en* data to improve Spanish→English SMT. Overall, among the different bitext

Table 11.9 *Improving Spanish→English SMT using 160K additional* **pt–en** *sentence pairs. The first column contains the number of original (es–en) sentence pairs, and the second column shows whether transliteration was used.*

es–en	Tran.	Baseline	Interpol.	Merge	Concat×1	Concat×k	Comb.
10K	no	22.87	23.73	23.60	23.54	23.83	**23.98**
	yes	22.87	25.22	25.16	25.26	25.42	**25.73**
20K	no	24.71	25.02	25.32	25.19	25.29	**25.65**
	yes	24.71	26.07	26.04	26.16	26.18	**26.36**
40K	no	25.80	26.15	26.24	25.92	25.99	**26.49**
	yes	25.80	26.43	26.64	26.78	26.93	**26.95**
80K	no	27.08	27.04	27.02	27.23	27.09	**27.30**
	yes	27.08	27.42	27.29	27.26	27.53	**27.49**
160K	no	27.90	27.72	27.95	27.83	27.83	**28.05**
	yes	27.90	28.13	28.17	28.14	28.14	**28.16**

combination strategies, the **combined** method performs best, followed by **concat**×*k* and **merge**, which are very close in performance. See (Nakov and Ng, 2009, 2012) for further discussion.

11.6   Language Adaptation

In many cases, it might be important to adapt the resource-rich language to make it even closer to the closely related resource-poor one. We have seen that transliteration and the use of synthetic data can help a lot for the case of Spanish and Portuguese. However, this might be of limited utility for other languages, for which more sophisticated adaptation techniques might be needed.

Let us take Malay and Indonesian as an example. Malay (aka *Bahasa Malaysia*) and Indonesian (aka *Bahasa Indonesia*) are closely related Astronesian languages, with about 180 million speakers combined. Malay is official in Malaysia, Singapore, and Brunei, and Indonesian is the national language of Indonesia. The two languages are mutually intelligible, but they differ in orthography/pronunciation and vocabulary.

Malay and Indonesian use a unified spelling system based on the Latin alphabet, but they exhibit occasional differences in orthography due to diverging pronunciation, e.g., *kerana* versus *karena* (because) and *Inggeris* versus *Inggris* (English) in Malay and Indonesian, respectively. More rarely, the differences are historical, e.g., *wang* versus *uang* (money). There are also some differences in name spellings, e.g., Indonesian sometimes uses Dutch spelling, e.g., *Soeharto* versus *Suharto*.

The two languages differ more substantially in vocabulary, mostly because of loan words, where Malay typically follows the English pronunciation, while Indonesian tends to follow Dutch, e.g., *televisyen* versus *televisi*, *Julai* versus *Juli*, and *Jordan* versus *Yordania*. For words of Latin origin that end on *-y* in English, Malay uses *-i*, while Indonesian uses *-as*, e.g., *universiti* versus *universitas*, *kualiti* versus *kualitas*.

While there are many cognates between the two languages, there are also some *false friends*, which are words identically spelled but with different meanings in the two languages. For example, *polisi* means *policy* in Malay but *police* in Indonesian. There are also many partial cognates, e.g., *nanti* means both *will* (future tense marker) and *later* in Malay but only *later* in Indonesian. As a result, fluent Malay and fluent Indonesian can differ substantially.

Consider again Article 1 of the Universal Declaration of Human Rights:

- *Semua* manusia *dilahirkan* bebas *dan* samarata dari segi kemuliaan *dan hak-hak*. *Mereka* mempunyai pemikiran *dan* perasaan *hati* *dan* hendaklah bertindak di antara *satu sama lain* dengan *semangat persaudaraan*. (Malay)

Table 11.10 ***Cosine similarities between some pairs of languages:*** *calculated on the Universal Declaration of Human Rights using tokens, and filtering out punctuation symbols.*

Language pairs	Cosine similarity
Malay–Indonesian	0.802
Portuguese–Spanish	0.475
Bulgarian–Macedonian	0.302
French–English	0.033
Spanish–English	0.031
Indonesian–English	0.002
Malay–English	0.001

- *Semua* orang *dilahirkan* merdeka *dan* mempunyai martabat *dan hak-hak* yang sama. *Mereka* dikaruniai akal *dan hati* nurani *dan* hendaknya bergaul *satu sama lain* dalam *semangat persaudaraan.* (Indonesian)

There is only 50% overlap at the word level, but the actual vocabulary overlap is much higher, e.g., there is only one word in the Malay text that does not exist in Indonesian: *samarata* (equal). Other differences are due to the use of different morphological forms, for example, *hendaklah* vs. *hendaknya* (conscience), derivational variants of *hendak* (want).

The similarity between a pair of languages can be quatified by calculated the cosine similarity between them, e.g., based on the full text of the Universal Declaration of Human Rights.[2] The results are shown in Table 11.10.

We can see that the average similarity between English and {Indonesian, Malay, French, Spanish} is 0.001–0.033, while for closely related language pairs it ranges from 0.302 to 0.802. Of course, this cosine calculation compares surface word overlap only and does not take minor morphological variants into consideration. Yet, it gives an idea about the relative proximity between the languages.

Of course, word choice in translation is often a matter of taste. A native speaker of Indonesian asked to adapt the Malay version to Indonesian while preserving as many words as possible, would produce the following result (Wang et al., 2016):

- *Semua manusia dilahirkan bebas dan* mempunyai martabat *dan hak-hak* yang sama. *Mereka mempunyai pemikiran dan perasaan dan hendaklah* bergaul *satu sama lain* dalam *semangat persaudaraan.* (Indonesian)

---

[2] www.ohchr.org/EN/UDHR/Pages/SearchByLang.aspx

Obtaining this latter version from the original Malay text requires three kinds of word-level operations:

- Deletion of *dari*, *segi*, and *hati*;
- Insertion of *yang* and *sama*;
- Substitution of *samarata* with *mempunyai*, *kemuliaan* with *martabat*, and *dengan* with *dalam*.

It further requires a phrase-level substitution of *bertindak di antara* with *bergaul*. Moreover, there are other potentially useful operations, e.g., a correct translation for the Malay *samarata* can be obtained by splitting it into the Indonesian sequence *sama rata*.

Note that word substitutions are enough in many cases, e.g., they are all that is needed to adapt the following Malay sentence to the Indonesian version below:

- *KDNK Malaysia dijangka cecah 8 peratus pada tahun 2010.* (Malay)
- *PDB Malaysia akan mencapai 8 persen pada tahun 2010.* (Indonesian)
- *Malaysia's GDP is expected to reach 8 percent in 2010.* (English)

Based on these observations, we can design an adaptation algorithm. Suppose we have (1) a small bitext for a resource-poor source language S_1 (e.g., Indonesian) and some target language T (e.g., English), and (2) a large bitext for a related resource-rich source language S_2 (e.g., Malay) and the same target language T. Then we can use pivoting over T to learn word-level and phrase-level paraphrases, as has been previoysly proposed in (Bannard and Callison-Burch, 2005; Callison-Burch et al., 2006), as well as cross-lingual morphological variants between the resource-poor and the resource-rich languages, S_1 and S_2, as shown in Figure 11.10. Subsequently, these learned paraphrases can be

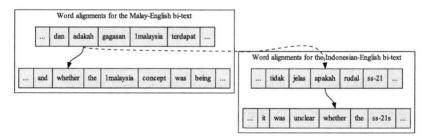

Figure 11.10 Example of word-level paraphrase induction by pivoting over English. The Malay word *adakah* is aligned to the English word *whether* in the Malay–English bitext (shown with solid arcs). The Indonesian word *apakah* is aligned to the same English word *whether* in the Indonesian–English bitext. Thus, *apakah* is a potential translation option for *adakah* (the link between these words is indicated by a dashed arc).

Table 11.11 *The 10-best "Indonesian"-like sentence paraphrases extracted from the confusion network in Figure 11.11. According to a native Indonesian speaker, options 1 and 3 are perfect adaptations, options 2 and 5 have a wrong word order, and the rest are grammatical but not perfect.*

Rank				"Indonesian" Sentence
1	pdb	malaysia	akan	mencapai 8 persen pada tahun 2010 .
2	pdb	malaysia	untuk	mencapai 8 persen pada tahun 2010 .
3	pdb	malaysia	diperkirakan	mencapai 8 persen pada tahun 2010 .
4	maka	malaysia	akan	mencapai 8 persen pada tahun 2010 .
5	maka	malaysia	untuk	mencapai 8 persen pada tahun 2010 .
6	pdb	malaysia	dapat	mencapai 8 persen pada tahun 2010 .
7	maka	malaysia	diperkirakan	mencapai 8 persen pada tahun 2010 .
8	sebesar	malaysia	akan	mencapai 8 persen pada tahun 2010 .
9	pdb	malaysia	diharapkan	mencapai 8 persen pada tahun 2010 .
10	pdb	malaysia	ini	mencapai 8 persen pada tahun 2010 .

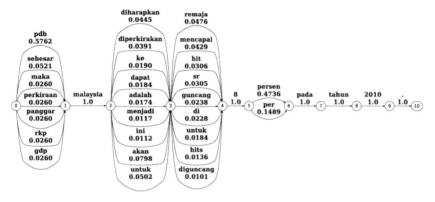

Figure 11.11 Indonesian confusion network for the Malay sentence "KDNK Malaysia dijangka cecah 8 peratus pada tahun 2010." The arcs with scores below 0.01 are omitted, and the words that exist in Indonesian are not paraphrased (for better readability).

used to adapt (the source side of) the large bitext for S_2–T, so that it looks more like S_1. This can be done by generating a lattice of possible transformations of S_2 (Malay), as shown in Figure 11.11, which is then to be rescored using a large language model for S_1 (Indonesian), as shown in Table 11.11. See (Wang et al., 2012) for more details.

Alternatively, we can use a specialized decoder as described by Wang et al. (2016), which performs a sequence of transformations of S_2 that make it each time closer to S_1. The search starts from the initial hypothesis, which is then

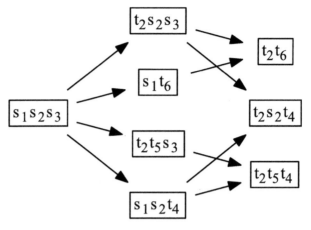

Figure 11.12 **Specialized decoder:** An example search tree for the input sentence $s_1s_2s_3$, given the following phrase-pair translation options: $\{(s_1, t_2),$ $(s_1s_2, t_2t_5), (s_2s_3, t_6), (s_3, t_4)\}$, where s_i and t_j are source and target words.

expanded by replacing a source phrase with a target phrase using one phrase pair from the translation options; then, the process continues recursively with each of the newly produced hypotheses, as shown in Figure 11.12.

The decoder makes use of the following hypothesis producers:

- *Word-level mapping*, e.g., replace *peratus* by *persen*.
- *Phrase-level mapping*, e.g., replace *dijangka cecah* by *akan mencapai"*.
- *Cross-lingual morphological mapping*, e.g., replace *meringkaskan* by the cross-language morphological variant *meringkas*.

Note that the hypotheses here are complete sentences,[3] which allows the decoder to assess the quality of a hypothesis based on a log-linear model with *sentence-level* feature functions:

- Counts: total number of modifications that a given hypothesis producer has made;
- Indonesian language model score;
- Number of tokens in the hypothesis;

---

[3] Beam-search decoders used for statistical machine translation, such as the phrase-based Moses decoder (Koehn et al., 2007), typically work with partial hypotheses, and thus cannot make use of sentence-level features. A notable exception is the Docent decoder (Hardmeier et al., 2013), which performs document-level decoding by making local changes starting from a document-level translation.

Table 11.12 *Improving Indonesian–English MT using Malay adapted to look like Indonesian. Vertically are shown different kinds of adaptation, while horizontally we have different ways to combine the IN–EN bitext with the adapted ML–EN bitext.*

	Model	Concat×1	Concat×k	Comb.
	IN-EN	18.67		
(i)	*IN-EN + ML-EN*	18.49	19.79	20.10
(ii)	*IN-EN + ML-EN:CN-words*	20.60	21.15	21.05
(iii)	*IN-EN + ML-EN:CN-phrases*	21.01	21.31	20.98
(iv)	*IN-EN + ML-EN:Specialized decoder*	21.33	21.42	21.08
	System combination: (i)+(ii)+(iii)+(iv)	**21.74**	**21.81**	**22.03**

- Malay word penalty: number of Malay words in the hypothesis, which are identified using bigram counts from the Indonesian language model;
- Word-level mappings: summation of the logarithms of all conditional probabilities used so far;
- Phrase-level mappings: summation of the logarithms of one of the four probabilities in the pivoted phrase table, i.e., forward/reverse phrase translation probability and forward/reverse lexical weighting probability;
- Cross-lingual morphological mapping: summation of the logarithms of all morphological variant mapping scores.

Table 11.12 shows evaluation results using the specialized decoder vs. using a confusion network with word-level and phrase-level adaptation to produce an "Indonesian"–English bitext from a Malay–English bitext vs. no adaptation at all. Horizontally, the table shows the results for using different ways to combine the Indonesian–English bitext with the adapted "Indonesian"–English bitext. The last line shows the results for system combination of the systems from the previous lines. We can see that the adaptation approaches (2)–(4) yield 1–3 points of absolute improvement in terms of BLEU over the non-adapted combination (1), and up to 4.5 points over using Indonesian–English only. The specialized decoder (4) is slightly better than the confusion network adaptation approaches (2)–(3), and system combination yields 0.5–1 points of absolute improvement over using the specialized decoder only. See (Wang et al., 2016) for further details about these experiments.

11.7   Other Approaches

Rule-Based Approaches. In pre-statistical NLP research, machine translation between related languages was handled using word-for-word translation and manual language-specific rules that take care of the necessary morphological and syntactic transformations. This was tried for a number of language pairs such as Czech–Slovak (Hajič et al., 2000), Czech–Russian (Bemova et al., 1988), Turkish–Crimean Tatar (Altintas and Cicekli, 2002), Irish–Scottish Gaelic (Scannell, 2006), Punjabi–Hindi (Josan and Lehal, 2008), Levantine/Egyptian/Iraqi/Gulf–Standard Arabic (Salloum and Habash, 2012), and Cantonese–Mandarin (Zhang, 1998). The Apertium machine translation platform (Corbí-Bellot et al., 2005) used bilingual dictionaries and manual rules to translate between a number of related Romance languages such as Spanish–Catalan, Spanish–Galician, Occitan–Catalan, and Portuguese–Spanish (Armentano-Oller et al., 2006). Apertium also supports some very small languages such as the Aranese variety of Occitan (Forcada, 2006). There has been also work on rule-based MT using related language *pairs*, e.g., improving Norwegian–English using Danish–English (Bick and Nygaard, 2007). Finally, there have been rule-based MT systems for translating from English to American sign language (Zhao et al., 2000).

Neural Approaches. The word embedding revolution of 2013 had an immediate impact on MT, as word embeddings proved helpful for translating between related languages (Mikolov et al., 2013). The subsequent Neural Machine Translation (NMT) revolution of 2014 (Bahdanau et al., 2015; Cho et al., 2014; Sutskever et al., 2014) yielded seq2seq models that enabled easy translation between a number of languages, including many-to-many and zero-shot translation (Johnson et al., 2017; Aharoni et al., 2019), proving to be especially effective for related languages. It has been further shown that NMT outperforms phrase-based SMT for closely related language varieties such as European–Brazilian Portuguese (Costa-jussà et al., 2018). NMT also allowed for an easy transfer from a resource-rich "parent" language pair such as Uzbek–English to a related resource-poor "child" language pair such as Turkish–English or Uyghur–English (Nguyen and Chiang, 2017) by simply pre-training on the "parent" pair and then training on the "child" pair, using a form of transfer learning originally proposed in (Zoph et al., 2016). In 2017, along came the Transformer variant (Vaswani et al., 2017) of NMT, yielding improvements over seq2seq, e.g., for Romanian–Italian and Dutch–German in bilingual, multilingual and zero-shot NMT setups (Lakew et al., 2018).

11.8   Applications and Future Directions

Machine translation between related languages can enable other technologies by bridging the gap between resource-rich and resource-poor languages. The techniques that we discussed herein can also be used for other tasks such as text normalization or lexical knowledge extraction.

Annotation projection and transfer learning are popular approaches for adapting language tools and resources to new languages. These techniques are

Table 11.13 *Labeled attachment scores for cross-lingual dependency parsers tested on the target language (Croatian, Norwegian, Slovak) and trained with annotated resources in related source languages (Slovenian, Czech and Danish/Swedish, respectively).*

LAS	Croatian	Norwegian	Slovak
Supervised	73.37	81.77	71.41
Delexicalized	50.05	58.13	53.87
MT-based	60.70	70.21	78.12

especially successful in the case of closely related languages. A wide variety of approaches have been proposed in the literature to bootstrap linguistic resources and tools for new languages by re-using information from existing data sets in other languages. These range from projecting annotated data through bilingual corpora using automatic alignment (annotation projection) or data translation to model adaptation and transfer learning (Tiedemann and Agić, 2016). An example application is cross-lingual dependency parsing that has been widely studied and the Fourth Workshop on NLP for Similar Languages, Varieties and Dialects, VarDial'2017, which featured a shared task on that topic with a focus on closely related languages (Zampieri et al., 2017).[4]

The evaluation results reveal that the automatic translation of the annotated data sets is surprisingly effective when training dependency parsers for related languages. Table 11.13 highlights the main findings from the evaluation campaign. The MT-based parsers outperform the delexicalized baselines by a large margin and come close to the supervised models and even surpass them in the case of Slovak. The latter outcome is amazing and further stresses the value of cross-lingual transfer between related languages in situations with highly skewed language resources.

Annotation projection and model transfer have been applied successfully to many other tasks such as part-of-speech tagging and semantic role labelling (Täckström et al., 2013; Van der Plas et al., 2014; Wang and Manning, 2014; Agić et al., 2015; Tiedemann and van der Plas, 2016; Scherrer et al., 2018). Another area of applications is related to text normalization. Language variants, socialects, e.g., social media and historical texts, can be easily normalized using machine translation, which is often applied at the character level (Pettersson et al., 2013; Ljubešić et al., 2014; Scherrer and Erjavec, 2016; Tjong Kim Sang et al., 2017; Hämäläinen et al., 2019). The normalized texts can then be passed through standard text processing tools.

---

[4] See http://bitbucket.org/hy-crossNLP/vardial2017/src/master/

Another recent trend in transfer learning is to train multilingual models. Moving away from treating languages and language pairs in isolation, such models make use of the relationships between languages to pick up additional information from multilingual data (Ammar et al., 2016). In neural machine translation, various approaches to training multilingual models have been proposed (Johnson et al., 2017; Lakew et al., 2018; Aharoni et al., 2019). The general idea is to share parameters between different languages in order to learn from all of them in a multitask training setup. Moreover, it is common to share subword-level vocabularies with tied embeddings, an approach which is particularly useful for closely related languages. More recently, there has been a lot of research interest in building cross-language word embeddings (Lample et al., 2018) or even representations for entire sentences (Joty et al., 2017; Artetxe and Schwenk, 2018; Lample and Conneau, 2019) without the need for parallel bitexts. The interested reader can read more in a recent book on the topic (Søgaard et al., 2019).

Yet another direction is the inclusion of different modalities. Spoken language variants are likely to be the next challenge to be tackled in language technology in connection with proper domain adaptation and language grounding. The importance of training data is still apparent and new techniques for data augmentation and distillation are currently being developed in order to overcome the lack of data in the target language of interest. The experience from treating closely related languages and language variants can pave the way for additional methods for the generation of synthetic data sets that reflect natural variation that needs to be modelled.

We believe that the future will show significant advances in multilingual and multimodal models that will more easily adapt to new domains and linguistic variations.

11.9   Conclusions

This chapter has provided an overview of machine translation techniques for similar languages based on case studies that illustrated the use of such methods. We emphasized data-driven techniques and statistical machine translation as an efficient way of mapping between languages that share important linguistic properties. The strong structural relationship between similar languages makes it possible to run machine translation effectively at the character level. In this way, data sets can be combined with minimal or no adaptation, thus enabling the transfer of knowledge from one language to another. We further discussed the use of pivot-based translation, synthetic data and other adaptation techniques that help to increase the support of low-resource languages. Bootstrapping linguistic resources and tools is also possible through automatic translation between related languages. Furthermore, we mentioned the connection between translation tasks and text normalization, which has its application in domain adaptation and diachronic work. Finally, we also briefly outlined the development of multilingual models that integrate languages into single systems, building on the continuum of languages for improved transfer learning. These models in connection with the integration of non-textual modalities are likely to revolutionize the field of language technology in the near future.

References

Agić, Željko, Hovy, Dirk, and Søgaard, Anders. 2015. If all you have is a bit of the Bible: learning POS taggers for truly low-resource languages. Pages 268–272 of: *Proceedings of the 53rd Annual Meeting of the Association for Computational Linguistics and the 7th International Joint Conference on Natural Language Processing*. ACL-IJCNLP '15.

Aharoni, Roee, Johnson, Melvin, and Firat, Orhan. 2019. Massively multilingual neural machine translation. Pages 3874–3884 of: *Proceedings of the 2019 Conference of the North American Chapter of the Association for Computational Linguistics*. NAACL-HLT '19.

Altintas, Kemal, and Cicekli, Ilyas. 2002. A machine translation system between a pair of closely related languages. Pages 192–196 of: *Proceedings of the 17th International Symposium on Computer and Information Sciences*. ISCIS '02.

Ammar, Waleed, Mulcaire, George, Ballesteros, Miguel, Dyer, Chris, and Smith, Noah A. 2016. Many languages, one parser. *Transactions of the Association for Computational Linguistics*, **4**, 431–444.

Armentano-Oller, Carme, Carrasco, Rafael C., Corbí-Bellot, Antonio M., Forcada, Mikel L., Ginestí-Rosell, Mireia, Ortiz-Rojas, Sergio, Pérez-Ortiz, Juan Antonio, Ramírez-Sánchez, Gema, Sánchez-Martínez, Felipe, and Scalco, Miriam A. 2006. Open-source Portuguese-Spanish machine translation. Pages 50–59 of: *Proceedings of the 7th International Workshop on Computational Processing of the Portuguese Language*. PROPOR '06.

Artetxe, Mikel, and Schwenk, Holger. 2018. Massively multilingual sentence embeddings for zero-shot cross-lingual transfer and beyond. *CoRR*, **abs/1812.10464**.

Bahdanau, Dzmitry, Cho, Kyunghyun, and Bengio, Yoshua. 2015. Neural machine translation by jointly learning to align and translate. In: *Proceedings of the 3rd International Conference on Learning Representations*. ICLR '15.

Bannard, Colin, and Callison-Burch, Chris. 2005. Paraphrasing with bilingual parallel corpora. Pages 597–604 of: *Proceedings of the 43rd Annual Meeting of the Association for Computational Linguistics*. ACL '05.

Bemova, Alevtina, Oliva, Karel, and Panevova, Jarmila. 1988. Some problems of machine translation between closely related languages. In: *Proceedings of the International Conference on Computational Linguistics*. COLING '88.

Bertoldi, Nicola, Barbaiani, Madalina, Federico, Marcello, and Cattoni, Roldano. 2008. Phrase-based statistical machine translation with pivot languages. Pages 143–149 of: *Proceedings of the International Workshop on Spoken Language Translation*. IWSLT '08.

Bick, Eckhard, and Nygaard, Lars. 2007. Using Danish as a CG interlingua: a wide-coverage Norwegian-English machine translation system. Pages 21–28 of: *Proceedings of the 16th Nordic Conference of Computational Linguistics.* NODALIDA '07.

Brown, Peter F., Della Pietra, Stephen A., Della Pietra, Vincent J., Goldsmith, Meredith J., Hajic, Jan, Mercer, Robert L., and Mohanty, Surya. 1993. But dictionaries are data too. Pages 202–205 of: *Proceedings of the workshop on Human Language Technology.* HLT '93.

Callison-Burch, Chris, Koehn, Philipp, and Osborne, Miles. 2006. Improved statistical machine translation using paraphrases. Pages 17–24 of: *Proceedings of the Conference on Human Language Technology Conference of the North American Chapter of the Association for Computational Linguistics.* HLT-NAACL '06.

Callison-Burch, Chris, Koehn, Philipp, Monz, Christof, Post, Matt, Soricut, Radu, and Specia, Lucia. 2012. Findings of the 2012 Workshop on Statistical Machine Translation. Pages 10–51 of: *Proceedings of the 7th Workshop on Statistical Machine Translation.* WMT '12.

Cho, Kyunghyun, van Merriënboer, Bart, Gulcehre, Caglar, Bahdanau, Dzmitry, Bougares, Fethi, Schwenk, Holger, and Bengio, Yoshua. 2014. Learning phrase representations using RNN encoder–decoder for statistical machine translation. Pages 1724–1734 of: *Proceedings of the 2014 Conference on Empirical Methods in Natural Language Processing.* EMNLP '14.

Cohen, Jacob. 1960. A coefficient of agreement for nominal scales. *Educational and Psychological Measurement*, **20**(1), 37–46.

Cohn, Trevor, and Lapata, Mirella. 2007. Machine translation by triangulation: making effective use of multi-parallel corpora. Pages 728–735 of: *Proceedings of the 45th Annual Meeting of the Association for Computational Linguistics.* ACL '07.

Corbí-Bellot, Antonio M., Forcada, Mikel L., Ortiz-Rojas, Sergio, Pérez-Ortiz, Juan Antonio, Ramírez-Sánchez, Gema, Sánchez-Martínez, Felipe, Alegria, Iñaki, Mayor, Aingeru, and Sarasola, Kepa. 2005. An open-source shallow-transfer machine translation engine for the Romance languages of Spain. Pages 79–86 of: *Proceedings of the Tenth Conference of the European Association for Machine Translation.* EAMT '05.

Costa-jussà, Marta R., Zampieri, Marcos, and Pal, Santanu. 2018. A neural approach to language variety translation. Pages 275–282 of: *Proceedings of the Fifth Workshop on NLP for Similar Languages, Varieties and Dialects.* VarDial '18.

Crego, Josep Maria, Max, Aurélien, and Yvon, François. 2010. Local lexical adaptation in machine translation through triangulation: SMT helping SMT. Pages 232–240 of: *Proceedings of the 23rd International Conference on Computational Linguistics.* COLING '10.

Damper, R. I., Marchand, Y., Marsters, J-D. S., and Bazin, A. I. 2005. Aligning text and phonemes for speech technology applications using an EM-like algorithm. *International Journal of Speech Technology*, **8**(2), 149–162.

de Gispert, A., and Mariño, J.B. 2006. Catalan-English statistical machine translation without parallel corpus: bridging through Spanish. Pages 65–68 of: *Proceedings of the 5th Workshop on Strategies for developing Machine Translation for Minority Languages.* SALTMIL '06.

Durrani, Nadir, Sajjad, Hassan, Fraser, Alexander, and Schmid, Helmut. 2010. Hindi-to-Urdu machine translation through transliteration. Pages 465–474 of: *Proceedings of the 48th Annual Meeting of the Association for Computational Linguistics.* ACL '10.

Dyer, Chris, Chahuneau, Victor, and Smith, Noah A. 2013. A simple, fast, and effective reparameterization of IBM model 2. Pages 644–648 of: *Proceedings of the 2013 Conference of the North American Chapter of the Association for Computational Linguistics: Human Language Technologies.* NAACL-HLT '13.

Forcada, Mikel L. 2006. Open-source machine translation: an opportunity for minor languages. In: *Proceedings of the LREC'06 Workshop on Strategies for Developing Machine Translation for Minority Languages.*

Forcada, Mikel L., Ginestí-Rosell, Mireia, Nordfalk, Jacob, O'Regan, Jim, Ortiz-Rojas, Sergio, Pérez-Ortiz, Juan Antonio, Sánchez-Martínez, Felipe, Ramírez-Sánchez, Gema, and Tyers, Francis M. 2011. Apertium: a free/open-source platform for rule-based machine translation. *Machine Translation*, **25**(2), 127–144.

Graca, Joao, Ganchev, Kuzman, and Taskar, Ben. 2010. Learning tractable word alignment models with complex constraints. *Computational linguistics*, **36**, 481–504.

Hajič, Jan, Hric, Jan, and Kuboň, Vladislav. 2000. Machine translation of very close languages. Pages 7–12 of: *Proceedings of the 6th Conference on Applied Natural Language Processing.* ANLP '00.

Hämäläinen, Mika, Säily, Tanja, Rueter, Jack, Tiedemann, Jörg, and Mäkelä, Eetu. 2019. Revisiting NMT for normalization of early English letters. Pages 71–75 of: *Proceedings of the 3rd Joint SIGHUM Workshop on Computational Linguistics for Cultural Heritage, Social Sciences, Humanities and Literature.*

Hardmeier, Christian, Stymne, Sara, Tiedemann, Jörg, and Nivre, Joakim. 2013. Docent: a document-level decoder for phrase-based statistical machine translation. Pages 193–198 of: *Proceedings of the 51st Annual Meeting of the Association for Computational Linguistics: System Demonstrations.* ACL '13.

Hopkins, Mark, and May, Jonathan. 2011. Tuning as ranking. Pages 1352–1362 of: *Proceedings of the 8th Conference on Empirical Methods in Natural Language Processing.* EMNLP '11.

Jiampojamarn, Sittichai, Kondrak, Grzegorz, and Sherif, Tarek. 2007. Applying many-to-many alignments and hidden Markov models to letter-to-phoneme conversion. Pages 372–379 of: *Proceedings of the Conference of the North American Chapter of the Association for Computational Linguistics.* NAACL-HLT '07.

Johnson, Melvin, Schuster, Mike, Le, Quoc V., Krikun, Maxim, Wu, Yonghui, Chen, Zhifeng, Thorat, Nikhil, Viégas, Fernanda, Wattenberg, Martin, Corrado, Greg, Hughes, Macduff, and Dean, Jeffrey. 2017. Google's multilingual neural machine translation system: enabling zero-shot translation. *Transactions of the Association for Computational Linguistics*, **5**, 339–351.

Josan, Gurpreet Singh, and Lehal, Gurpreet Singh. 2008. A Punjabi to Hindi machine translation system. Pages 157–160 of: *Proceedings of the 22nd International Conference on on Computational Linguistics.* COLING '08.

Joty, Shafiq, Nakov, Preslav, Màrquez, Lluís, and Jaradat, Israa. 2017. Cross-language learning with adversarial neural networks. Pages 226–237 of: *Proceedings of the 21st Conference on Computational Natural Language Learning.* CoNLL '17.

Koehn, Philipp. 2010. *Statistical Machine Translation*. New York: Cambridge University Press.

Koehn, Philipp, Hoang, Hieu, Birch, Alexandra, Callison-Burch, Chris, Federico, Marcello, Bertoldi, Nicola, Cowan, Brooke, Shen, Wade, Moran, Christine, Zens, Richard, Dyer, Chris, Bojar, Ondrej, Constantin, Alexandra, and Herbst, Evan. 2007. Moses: open source toolkit for statistical machine translation. Pages 177–180 of: *Proceedings of the Annual Meeting of the Association for Computational Linguistics*. ACL'07.

Koehn, Philipp, Birch, Alexandra, and Steinberger, Ralf. 2009. 462 Machine translation systems for Europe. Pages 65–72 of: *Proceedings of MT Summit XII*.

Lakew, Surafel Melaku, Cettolo, Mauro, and Federico, Marcello. 2018. A comparison of transformer and recurrent neural networks on multilingual neural machine translation. Pages 641–652 of: *Proceedings of the 27th International Conference on Computational Linguistics*. COLING '18.

Lample, Guillaume, and Conneau, Alexis. 2019. Cross-lingual language model pretraining. *CoRR*, **abs/1901.07291**.

Lample, Guillaume, Conneau, Alexis, Ranzato, Marc'Aurelio, Denoyer, Ludovic, and Jégou, Hervé. 2018. Word translation without parallel data. In: *Proceedings of the 6th International Conference on Learning Representations*. ICLR '18.

Landis, Richard, and Koch, Gary. 1977. The measurement of observer agreement for categorical data. *Biometrics*, **33**(1), 159–74.

Ljubešić, Nikola, Erjavec, Tomaž, and Fišer, Darja. 2014. Standardizing tweets with character-level machine translation. Pages 164–175 of: *International Conference on Intelligent Text Processing and Computational Linguistics*. CICLING '14.

Mikolov, Tomas, Le, Quoc V., and Sutskever, Ilya. 2013. Exploiting similarities among languages for machine translation. *CoRR*, **abs/1309.4168**.

Nakov, Preslav, and Ng, Hwee Tou. 2009. Improved statistical machine translation for resource-poor languages using related resource-rich languages. Pages 1358–1367 of: *Proceedings of the 2009 Conference on Empirical Methods in Natural Language Processing*. EMNLP '09.

Nakov, Preslav, and Ng, Hwee Tou. 2012. Improving statistical machine translation for a resource-poor language using related resource-rich languages. *Journal of Artificial Intelligence Research*, **44**, 179–222.

Nakov, Preslav, and Tiedemann, Jörg. 2012. Combining word-level and character-level models for machine translation between closely-related languages. Pages 301–305 of: *Proceedings of the 50th Annual Meeting of the Association for Computational Linguistics*. ACL '12.

Nakov, Preslav, Guzman, Francisco, and Vogel, Stephan. 2012. Optimizing for sentence-level BLEU+1 yields short translations. Pages 1979–1994 of: *Proceedings of the 24th International Conference on Computational Linguistics*. COLING '12.

Nguyen, Toan Q., and Chiang, David. 2017. Transfer learning across low-resource, related languages for neural machine translation. Pages 296–301 of: *Proceedings of the Eighth International Joint Conference on Natural Language Processing*. IJCNLP '17.

Och, Franz Josef. 2003. Minimum error rate training in statistical machine translation. Pages 160–167 of: *Proceedings of the 41st Annual Meeting of the Association for Computational Linguistics*. ACL '03.

Och, Franz Josef, and Ney, Hermann. 2003. A systematic comparison of various statistical alignment models. *Computational Linguistics*, **29**(1), 19–51.

Papineni, Kishore, Roukos, Salim, Ward, Todd, and Zhu, Wei-Jing. 2002. BLEU: a method for automatic evaluation of machine translation. Pages 311–318 of: *Proceedings of the 40th Annual Meeting of the Association for Computational Linguistics*.

Pettersson, Eva, Megyesi, Beáta B., and Tiedemann, Jörg. 2013 (May). An SMT approach to automatic annotation of historical text. Pages 54–69 of: *Proceedings of the NoDaLiDa Workshop on Computational Historical Linguistics*.

Ristad, Eric Sven, and Yianilos, Peter N. 1998. Learning string edit distance. *IEEE Transactions on Pattern Recognition and Machine Intelligence*, **20**(5), 522–532.

Salloum, Wael, and Habash, Nizar. 2012. Elissa: a dialectal to standard Arabic machine translation system. Pages 385–392 of: *Proceedings of COLING 2012: Demonstration Papers*. COLING '12.

Scannell, Kevin. 2006. Machine translation for closely related language pairs. Pages 103–108 of: *Proceedings of the LREC 2006 Workshop on Strategies for Developing Machine Translation for Minority Languages*.

Scherrer, Yves, and Erjavec, Tomaž. 2016. Modernising historical Slovene words. *Natural Language Engineering*, **22**(6), 881–905.

Scherrer, Yves, Mocken, Susanne, and Rabus, Achim. 2018. New developments in tagging pre-modern Orthodox Slavic texts. *Scripta & e-Scripta: The Journal of Interdisciplinar Mediaeval Studies*, **18**, 9–34.

Søgaard, Anders, Vulic, Ivan, Ruder, Sebastian, and Faruqui, Manaal. 2019. *Cross-Lingual Word Embeddings*. Synthesis Lectures on Human Language Technologies. San Rafael: Morgan & Claypool Publishers.

Sutskever, Ilya, Vinyals, Oriol, and Le, Quoc V. 2014. Sequence to sequence learning with neural networks. Pages 3104–3112 of: *Proceedings of the 27th International Conference on Neural Information Processing System*. NIPS'14.

Täckström, Oscar, Das, Dipanjan, Petrov, Slav, McDonald, Ryan, and Nivre, Joakim. 2013. Token and type constraints for cross-lingual part-of-speech tagging. *Transactions of the Association for Computational Linguistics*, **1**, 1–12.

Tiedemann, Jörg. 2012a. Character-based pivot translation for under-resourced languages and domains. Pages 141–151 of: *Proceedings of the 13th Conference of the European Chapter of the Association for Computational Linguistics*. EACL '12.

Tiedemann, Jörg. 2012b. Parallel data, tools and interfaces in OPUS. Pages 2214–2218 of: *Proceedings of the Eighth International Conference on Language Resources and Evaluation*. LREC '12.

Tiedemann, Jörg, and Agić, Zeljko. 2016. Synthetic treebanking for cross-lingual dependency parsing. *Journal of Artificial Intelligence Research*, **55**, 209–248.

Tiedemann, Jörg, and Nakov, Preslav. 2013. Analyzing the use of character-level translation with sparse and noisy datasets. Pages 676–684 of: *Proceedings of the International Conference Recent Advances in Natural Language Processing*. RANLP '13.

Tiedemann, Jörg, and van der Plas, Lonneke. 2016. Bootstrapping a dependency parser for Maltese - a real-world test case. In: Weiling, Martijn, Kroon, Martin, Noord, Gertjan Van, and Bouma, Gosse (eds), *From Semantics to Dialectometry: Festschrift in Honour of John Nerbonne*. Tributes, vol. 32. London: College Publications.

Tjong Kim Sang, Erik, Bollman, Marcel, Boschker, Remko, Casacuberta, Francisco, Dietz, FM, Dipper, Stefanie, Domingo, Miguel, van der Goot, Rob, van Koppen, JM, Ljubešić, Nikola, Östling, Robert, Petran, Florian, Pettersson, Eva, Scherrer, Yves, Schraagen, M.P., Sevens, Leen, Tiedeman, Jörg, Vanallemeersch, Tom, and Zervanou, K. 2017. The CLIN27 shared task: translating historical text to contemporary language for improving automatic linguistic annotation. *Computational Linguistics in the Netherlands Journal*, **7**, 53–64.

Utiyama, Masao, and Isahara, Hitoshi. 2007. A comparison of pivot methods for phrase-based statistical machine translation. Pages 484–491 of: *Proceedings of the Conference of the North American Chapter of the Association for Computational Linguistics: Human Language Technologies*. NAACL-HLT '07.

Van der Plas, Lonneke, Apidianaki, Marianna, and Chen, Chenhua. 2014. Global methods for cross-lingual semantic role and predicate labelling. Pages 1279–1290 of: *Proceedings of the 25th International Conference on Computational Linguistics*. COLING '14.

Vaswani, Ashish, Shazeer, Noam, Parmar, Niki, Uszkoreit, Jakob, Jones, Llion, Gomez, Aidan N., Kaiser, Lukasz, and Polosukhin, Illia. 2017. Attention is all you need. Pages 5998–6008 of: *Proceedings of the Annual Conference on Neural Information Processing Systems*. NIPS '17.

Vilar, David, Peter, Jan-T., and Ney, Hermann. 2007. Can we translate letters? Pages 33–39 of: *Proceedings of the Second Workshop on Statistical Machine Translation*. StatMT '07.

Vogel, Stephan, Ney, Hermann, and Tillmann, Christoph. 1996. HMM-based word alignment in statistical translation. Pages 836–841 of: *Proceedings of the 16th conference on Computational linguistics*. COLING '96.

Wang, Mengqiu, and Manning, Christopher D. 2014. Cross-lingual projected expectation regularization for weakly supervised learning. *Transactions of the Association for Computational Linguistics*, **2**, 55–66.

Wang, Pidong, Nakov, Preslav, and Ng, Hwee Tou. 2012. Source language adaptation for resource-poor machine translation. Pages 286–296 of: *Proceedings of the 2012 Joint Conference on Empirical Methods in Natural Language Processing and Computational Natural Language Learning*. EMNLP-CoNLL '12.

Wang, Pidong, Nakov, Preslav, and Ng, Hwee Tou. 2016. Source language adaptation approaches for resource-poor machine translation. *Computational Linguistics*, **42**(2), 277–306.

Wu, Hua, and Wang, Haifeng. 2007. Pivot language approach for phrase-based statistical machine translation. Pages 856–863 of: *Proceedings of the 45th Annual Meeting of the Association of Computational Linguistics*. ACL '07.

Wu, Hua, and Wang, Haifeng. 2009. Revisiting pivot language approach for machine translation. Pages 154–162 of: *Proceedings of the Joint Conference of the Annual Meeting of the ACL and the International Joint Conference on Natural Language Processing*. ACL-IJCNLP '09.

Zampieri, Marcos, Malmasi, Shervin, Ljubešić, Nikola, Nakov, Preslav, Ali, Ahmed, Tiedemann, Jörg, Scherrer, Yves, and Aepli, Noëmi. 2017. Findings of the VarDial Evaluation Campaign 2017. Pages 1–15 of: *Proceedings of the Fourth Workshop on NLP for Similar Languages, Varieties and Dialects*. VarDial '17.

Zhang, Xiaoheng. 1998. Dialect MT: a case study between Cantonese and Mandarin. Pages 1460–1464 of: *Proceedings of the 17th International Conference on Computational Linguistics*. COLING '98.

Zhao, Liwei, Kipper, Karin, Schuler, William, Vogler, Christian, Badler, Norman I., and Palmer, Martha. 2000. A machine translation system from English to American Sign Language. Pages 54–67 of: *Proceedings of the 4th Conference of the Association for Machine Translation in the Americas on Envisioning Machine Translation in the Information Future*. AMTA '00.

Zoph, Barret, Yuret, Deniz, May, Jonathan, and Knight, Kevin. 2016. Transfer learning for low-resource neural machine translation. Pages 1568–1575 of: *Proceedings of the 2016 Conference on Empirical Methods in Natural Language Processing*. EMNLP '16.

12 Automatic Spoken Dialect Identification

Pedro A. Torres-Carrasquillo and Bengt J. Borgström

12.1 Introduction

In this chapter, the topic of spoken dialect identification is addressed. Spoken dialect identification is typically considered as a special case of language identification and is defined as the process of identifying a variation within a given language class or family of languages given a spoken utterance. The literature has broadly classified a number of cases as dialect identification. Although the most common case is that defined above, there are a number of related tasks that are sometimes termed as dialect identification. For example in the 2009 National Institute of Standards and Technology (NIST) Language Recognition Evaluation (LRE) (LRE, 2009), the ability of systems to identify "language pairs" was considered. A particularly interesting case was the task of discriminating between Hindi and Urdu. The community tends to accept the definition of these two as languages and not as dialects. However, there is some debate about where the line needs to be defined between language classes and dialects or language subclasses. This case illustrates some of the difficulties in the machine learning community on how to address the dialect identification problem.

A second issue that illustrates the challenges faced by the community is the lack of clearly labeled data. The lack of appropriately labeled data is probably the single most important reason for the lack of extensive research in the area of dialect identification. This issue is exacerbated in the era of data hungry

DISTRIBUTION STATEMENT A. Approved for public release. Distribution is unlimited.
This material is based upon work supported by the Department of Defense under Air Force Contract No. FA8702-15-D-0001. Any opinions, findings, conclusions or recommendations expressed in this material are those of the author(s) and do not necessarily reflect the views of the Department of Defense.

deep learning approaches. As an example, also in a previous LRE, another task that has been addressed is the identification of Spanish dialects. The Spanish dialect task focused on discriminating between, Spanish as spoken in Spain and other Spanish variations mainly spoken in Central and South America and the Caribbean. In this task it is particularly interesting that although these two main classes are probably distinguishable, it is also true that for each of these two broad classes many dialectical "sub-classes" exist. To expand on this idea, a dialect task could be set up between the Spanish spoken in the islands of Puerto Rico and the Dominican Republic. This distinction is also true for most of the variations of Spanish spoken through South American and the different regions in Spain. It is not surprising to expect that the variations within some of these classes may be more or less significant depending on the specific sub-classes/variations addressed and that the amount of data needed by modern systems increases when these variations are very subtle. In the specific example of this Spanish task all the data came from approximately 80 30-minute conversations which is likely too little for current state-of-the-art approaches.

In the remaining of this chapter some background material is provided, describing previous work on dialect/language identification including a view of the development of these systems over the last two decades ranging from phonetic based systems to acoustic systems. Section 12.3 describes some of the available data resources followed by a description of the current state-of-the-art systems in Section 12.4. Section 12.5 presents a high-level description of NIST standardized evaluations and the role of these evaluations in the dialect recognition community and Section 12.6 presents a description of some of the challenges in this area as the community moves forward.

12.2   Background

Dialect identification is usually considered within two general contexts. First, dialect identification, along with some of its related tasks can be useful for general information finding and filtering. In this case, the automatic system is tasked with identifying a specific dialect from among large number of classes. This set of classes can be either a set of dialects within a number of language classes (Mexican Spanish vs Argentinian Spanish vs Mandarin) or can be conditioned to find the dialect variation within members of the same language (Mexican Spanish vs Argentinian Spanish).

A second general set of applications for which the dialect identification is used, is pre-processing for automatic systems consumption. In this case, the dialect identification system can be used as a precursor for a, usually larger, automatic system such as automatic speech recognition (ASR). In the case where enough data are available for each dialect of interest, the ASR system

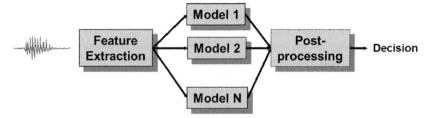

Figure 12.1 Canonical architecture for a spoken dialect identification system.

can be trained either directly or bootstrapped from the language of interest and result in improved performance.

The canonical architecture for a canonical language/dialect identification system is shown in Figure 12.1. A LID/DID system usually consists of a feature extraction stage, where speech samples are converted to salient features. The features of choice are typically based on the spectrum of the speech signal or related to either some linguistic or rhythm unit. The second common stage employed in these systems is the model stage. During training phase, a number (usually > 100s) of labelled samples are used to create a model representing the class (dialect) of interest. During testing, the model created during the training phase is employed to compute some measure of similarity between the incoming speech and the set of models available. Finally, the highest likelihood model is chosen. This final decision can be based on the raw likelihoods or an optional additional stage may be employed to perform the final decision.

12.2.1   Cues for identification

There is vast literature on the potential set of cues used by humans and machines to be able to discriminate language and dialect classes. Although an in-depth description of these is beyond the scope of this chapter, a brief summary that serves as the motivation for the automatic systems to be described is included below.

- **Phonology/phonetic content**: The phonetic inventory of a dialect provides information about the differences across the different classes of interest. Additionally the sequence of phonetic events, phonotactics, observed across the dialects of interest provides information that can be exploited to discriminate dialects.
- **High-level lexicon**: The words and lexicon across dialect can also provide discriminative information within different dialects.
- **Pronunciation**: The fine-level pronunciation structure is also a cue used by humans and machines that can aid the identification of dialects. The fine detail

in this acoustic structure is exploited by "acoustic systems" to discriminate dialects, specifically in cepstral based systems.

• **Rhythm**: The intonation (stress), pitch differences, duration and general rhythm patterns are also a set of cues used to separate dialect differences.

In the section that follows, specific systems developed using the general set of cues described above are described.

12.2.2   Dialect discrimination systems

There exist two major categories of scientific work in the literature for the automatic dialect identification. First, techniques adopted from the more general case of language identification (derivative approaches). In this case, a technique is developed to conduct dialect identification by extending a language identification approach without any major changes other than the training data used for each class of interest. This category seems to dominate the automatic dialect identification systems, possibly due to the broader appeal in the community of the more general language identification problem. A second category of approaches is also found in the literature focused on approaches developed directly for the problem of dialect identification rather than an extension of a language identification approach. Systems developed under each of these categories are described below.

12.2.3   LID approaches

Beginning in the 1990s, many approaches have been developed for the language identification task and used directly on the dialect identification task. These language identification approaches include techniques dealing with phonotactic modeling, acoustic modeling and more recently sub-space approaches.

Phonotactic approaches   Phonotactic modeling relies on considering the phonetic inventory of a language and the temporal sequence of these phonetic units to classify languages. For example, Zissman (Zissman and Singer, 1994) describes the phonetic sequence in the German work spiel and the English word shpeel. In the case of the German pronunciation the phonemic sequence is expected to be /SH P IY L/ while the expected English sequence begins with the sequence /SH P/. This is an example of a common sequence in one language (German) that occurs infrequently in another language (English). This kind or realization is the core information that is exploited by phonotactic approaches. The core algorithm developed to exploit the phonotactic technique is known as "Phone Recognition Followed by Language Modeling".

A particular instantiation of this work, also by Zissman (Zissman, 1996), is the algorithm termed "Parallel Phone Recognition Followed by Language

Modeling" (PPRLM). The PPRLM algorithm extends the PRLM technique to produced alternative sequences given a single language phone recognition stage and produce language likelihoods for each language of interest and each language recognition stage. To clarify the concept a two-language PPRLM system, say English and Spanish, incoming speech is "tokenized" into a sequence of phones using the phone inventory for the language the tokenizer is trained on. A language model is used to consider the sequences observed for the target language of interest. A large amount of work is this area is available in the literature, particularly the work by Zissman (Zissman and Singer, 1994; Zissman, 1996) and Navratil (Navrátil and Zuhlke, 1997; Biadsy et al., 2010) among others. One item to highlight on these systems is that the language of the tokenizer is completely independent from the target languages of interest. For example, an English tokenizer can be used to discriminate between multiple Arabic dialects.

The PPRLM framework has been extended by a number of people to address the dialect problem. Biadsy (Biadsy et al., 2010) applies the PRLM technique to the task of classifying Arabic dialects into five classes: Gulf, Iraqi, Levantine, Egyptian and Maghrebi. In this work, the work by Zissman on PPRLM is employed by using 6 tokenizers in parallel to discriminate among the five Arabic classes above.

Many extension of the core PRLM framework had been proposed over the years for the language identification task, an extension than was proposed for the dialect identification task was the work by Akbacak (Akbacak et al., 2011). In this work, the PRLM framework is used in conjunction with a number of ASR improvements and the language model component also modified beyond the conventional n-gram approach. The resulting system was used to classify Arabic dialects.

Acoustic approaches   Gaussian mixture models (GMMs) had been extensively used for speaker recognition through most of the 1990s and early 200s with great success (Reynolds and Rose, 1995; Reynolds et al., 2000). The concepts developed for speaker recognition had been used for language identification with modest success until the work by Torres-Carrasquillo (Torres-Carrasquillo et al., 2002) combined the GMM approach with a different feature extraction approach, shifted-delta-cepstral coefficients (Bielefeld, 1994), where additional timing information is spanned beyond the conventional time frame. Additionally, the incorporation of ASR techniques, specifically discriminative training (Burget et al., 2006) of GMMs also provided excellent results on these systems. A brief description of the GMM systems is shown below.

In a GMM system, a GMM is trained for each dialect of interest under the assumption that the finer acoustic detail of sounds specific to each dialect and the frequency of these sounds will allow to discriminate each language. The model trained for each language uses the Gaussian relationship in (1), where the model parameters $\{w_k, \mu_k, \Sigma_k\}$ are trained using the expectation-maximization algorithm to best fit model to the frame-based observations for each language of interest. A particular extension directly transferred from the speaker recognition world is the universal background model (UBM) approach. The UBM in speaker recognition systems was motivated mainly for two reasons. First, the UBM allowed for fast scoring of the speaker models by complete scoring the UBM against all mixtures but only partially scoring each of the individual speaker models. A second motivation for the UBM concept in speaker recognition is to obtain more robust models by using the UBM as a backoff strategy given the "small" amount of observations usually available for a speaker of interest. In the case of language and dialect recognition, the second motivation is not applicable as the amount of data available to train a model is usually in the order of hours if not tens of hours. The speed off motivation, although not as critical given the amount of models to be scored is small (< 10) compared to 100s of speaker models, does result in faster recognition rates without loss in performance.

Another extension of GMMs to the dialect identification task is that performed by Lei (Lei and Hansen, 2010). In this work the GMM approach is combined with a frame selection technique to try to emphasize more discriminative frames in the set of feature frames on which to focus the training and testing. The motivation for this work comes from the expectation that differences in dialect are likely to be very subtle compared to the acoustic differences across languages and that focusing on these, hopefully, more discriminative frames should enhance performance.

Another class of acoustic systems, that became popular in the 2000s was the support vector machine (SVM). The SVMs (Burges, 1998) were a popular approach in machine learning that was able to produce excellent performance in the speaker recognition community and once again was extended into the language/dialect recognition problem (Campbell et al., 2006). In the case of SVMs The pool of frames obtained for the incoming speech stream were converted into a fixed-length large dimensional vector and used to represent the dialect of interest. The SVM were important and this stage for two reasons. First, the performance of the SVM system was on the same level as the GMM approaches and resulted in additional performance increases when combined with the GMM approaches. Secondly, the SVM approaches were extended by using GMMs as the high-dimensional representation component and served as a precursor of the sub-space approaches that have dominated the language/dialect recognition community until the present.

12.2.4   Non-LID Approaches

In contrast to the approaches described in the previous section, the systems described in this section focus on approaches that have been developed for performing dialect identification but are not necessarily an extension of work previously used for language identification.

An approach that seems to have more traction in the literature for dialect identification compared to language identification is the use of prosody. Barkat (Barkat et al., 1999) uses prosody based information for baseline perceptual studies of discriminability among Arabic dialects. Biadsy (Biadsy et al., 2009) incorporated some of the insight provided by Barkat and proposed an Arabic dialect system that used prosodic and rhythmic information as complementary features to a phonotactic approach.

Hamdi (Hamdi-Sultan et al., 2004) had also looked at various prosody and rhythm sources of information to assess discriminability among Arabic dialects. The proposed approach in this case relied on studying basic statistics about the vocalic and consonant components of the Arabic dialects on the study.

Recently a number of machine learning approaches have been applied to the dialect identification problem without necessarily been developed for language identification task. Approaches based on deep neural networks, combination of classifiers and other emerging technologies are beginning to show as solutions to the dialect identification problem.

It is not surprising that the vast majority of the work in the literature dealing with automatic dialect identification is derivative work from the work on language identification. It is not entirely clear whether this is a by-product of the size of the community that is interested on the dialect identification problem or a lack of resources available or even a combination of these and possible other factors. The resources available, particularly data sets, will be address in the next section.

12.3   Resources for Dialect Identification

In most research communities, the interest and amount of work conducted in an area is directly proportional to two main factors. The availability of funding to pursue the research and, more critically in the age of deep neural networks, the resources available to validate and test improvements usually in the form of large amounts of data with a good portion of the available data including truth markings.

In this section, the attempt is to provide a reasonable sample of the data available in addition to the authors assessment of some of the issues related to these resources. The datasets presented will provide the initial source reference for the datasets when possible and attempt to cover a diverse set of the dialect sets available in the literature. One point that maybe important is that in some cases the datasets described are shown as results has been shown in the literature multiple times over the years, however it is not clear to the authors that some of

Table 12.1 *Summary of popular spoken dialect identification data sets.*

Dataset	Source/Key Publication	Speech Type	Speakers	Task(s) Supported
Miami Corpus	Zissman (Zissman et al., 1996)	Spontaneous Read	~ 100 Cuban ~ 50 Peruvian ~ 40 Columbian	• Cuban vs. Peruvian
CallFriend Corpus	LDC (LDC, 1996)	Spontaneous	60/class	• American English (Southern vs. Non-Southern) • Mandarin (Mainland vs. Taiwanese) • Spanish (Caribbean vs. Non-Caribbean)
Accents British Isles	D'Arcy (D'Arcy et al., 2004)	Read	300 Speakers	• 13/15 class discrimination
Arabic Classes	Hansen (Lei and Hansen, 2010)	Conversational	500 Speakers	• Arabic classes: United Arab Emirates, Egyptian, Iraqi, Palestinian and Syrian
LRE2011 Arabic	NIST (LRE, 2011)	Conversational Broadcast News	100s of Speakers	• Arabic classes: Iraqi, Levantine, Maghrebi, Classes Modern Standard Arabic
LRE2015	NIST (LRE, 2015)	Conversational Broadcast News	100s of Speakers	• Arabic classes: Egyptian, Iraqi, Levantine, Maghrebi, Modern Standard Arabic • Spanish classes: Caribbean, European, Latin American • Chinese classes: Cantonese, Mandarin, Min, Wu
Arabic Maghrebi	Nour-Eddine (Nour-Eddine, 2015)	TV shows Movies	500 Speakers	• Arabic Maghrebi classes: Moroccan, Oranian, Algiersian, Constantinian, Tunisian
Arabic Algerian	Bougrine (Bougrine et al., 2018)	Internal collection Radio TV Broadcast	< 100 Speakers	• Arabic Algerian classes: Oran, Algiers, Laghouat, Adrar, Bousaada, Djelfa
Chinese Classes	Hansen (Lei and Hansen, 2010)	Not Known	450 Speakers	• Chinese classes: Mandarin, Cantonese and Xiang

these datasets are publicly available for community research but are still deemed important for the community to know about their existence. Table 12.1 provides a summary of the data sets described below.

Miami Corpus   The Miami Corpus (Zissman et al., 1996) is a collection of Spanish speakers collected in the city of Miami in Florida in the United States. The set was collected in the mid-1990s and contains Spanish speakers from more than 10 Spanish speaking countries although the numbers are too low for most of these countries except Cuba, Peru and possibly Colombia. The set has been used by multiple researchers over the years to support the task of differentiating Cuban and Peruvian dialects of Spanish.

CallFriend Corpus   The CallFriend corpus (LDC, 1996) was originally collected to support the NNIST-LRE effort. The corpus contained 12
language classes and 3 dialect classes within 3 of the languages supported
(English, Mandarin, Spanish). The dialect component of the corpus can be
used to support three tasks. The three dialect tasks are: American English
(Non-Southern vs Southern), Mandarin (Mainland vs Taiwanese) and Spanish
(Caribbean vs Non-Caribbean). The Spanish dialect task is the one task that may
seem somewhat atypical. In this case, the Caribbean class is mainly composed
of Spanish from Puerto Rico and the Dominican Republic while the non-
Caribbean class includes many of the remaining Spanish classes including
European (Spain), Mexico, and South American countries. The corpus consists
of telephone calls between people known to each other and the typical call lasted
about 30 minutes.

Accents of the British Isles (ABI) corpus   The ABI corpus (D'Arcy
et al., 2004) is a collection of speech data composed of 15 regional accents
of British English. This corpus has been used for dialect identification work
(Ferragne and Pellegrino, 2007) and for other related studies such as impact
on other speech processing systems (D'Arcy and Russell, 2008). The corpus
consists of nearly 300 speakers divided across the different variations. The
recordings consisted of read material of prompted text. The total amount of
speech recorded was near 100 hours of speech.

Arabic and Chinese Data Sets   Two sets of languages and dialects
seem to be the most commonly used for system validation in the literature.
In both of these cases there are a large number of publications that address
discrimination of the language classes spoken in China and the Arabic speaking
countries. One similarity for these two languages is that although in many
cases these include both language subclasses and dialects, most papers dealing
with these classes refer to the problem as dialect classification whether the
dialect problem is the one mainly been addressed or the language sub-classes
is addressed. For the purpose of this chapter the data sets are included as
been of interest to the community aside from the issue of dialects vs language
subclasses.

Arabic and Chinese classes (Hansen)   Hansen (Lei and Hansen,
2010) has work on the Arabic and Chinese sub-classes classification task.
Although the details about the origination of the dataset are not referred to, the
Arabic dataset used includes Arabic classes from United Arab Emirates, Egypt,
Iraq, Palestine and Syria. For each class there are 100 gender-balanced speakers
collected. The speakers are given seed topics and complete two recording
sessions on two of the potential topics. The amount of speech collected in
most cases is on the range of 5–10 minutes. Hansen also works in the paper

on the Chinese sub-classes task. The language sub-classes included in this set are Mandarin, Cantonese, and Xiang. As mentioned above, these are usually not considered dialects but language sub-classes but are likely relevant to the general community working on the dialect/language classes discrimination task. In this set, nearly 450 speakers including both males and females are available with speech data collected in the range 4–8 minutes. Additional details on the collection are not disclosed.

NIST-LRE 2011 data set   The NIST-LRE 2011 (LRE, 2011) campaign included a set of Arabic classes within its general task. In this case the Arabic classes included Iraqi, Levantine, Maghrebi and Modern Standard Arabic (MSA). In this evaluation the data included two main sources: conversational telephone speech and broadcast news. The broadcast news set usually included narrowband segments extracted from the broadcast, usually field reporting. The set includes a fair balance between genders and is usually available in terms of the segments used for the evaluation protocol but the full-length segment or program references for the broadcasts can be obtained.

NIST-LRE 2015 data set   The NIST-LRE 2015 (LRE, 2015) campaign featured three dialect/language classes discrimination tasks. The three discrimination tasks included Arabic classes, Chinese classes and a somewhat unusual tasks that required discrimination between Portuguese and a number of Spanish classes. The Arabic task included five classes: Egyptian, Iraqi, Levantine, Maghrebi and Modern Standard Arabic. The Chinese task included four classes: Cantonese, Mandarin, Min and Wu. The Iberian task included four classes: Portuguese, Caribbean, European, and Latin American Spanish. For the Iberian task the subset of Spanish classes is likely of high interest. The data for these three tasks, as in the 2011 campaign, included both conversational and broadcast news with a fair gender diversity. As in the previous datasets used for LRE campaigns, the Caribbean data set was mainly composed of the Caribbean islands of Puerto Rico and Dominican Republic. The previously defined non-Caribbean Spanish has been split between European (Spain) and Latin American Spanish. The Latin American Spanish includes a diverse representation of Spanish speaking countries along with second language Spanish speakers.

Appen and LDC Arabic datasets   Biadsy (Biadsy and Hirschberg, 2009) uses a data set of corpora collected by Appen and LDC to create a set suitable for dialect identification. The data set consists of four Arabic classes: Gulf, Iraqi, Egyptian, and Levantine. The Appen component of this set includes Gulf Arabic and Iraqi Arabic. The LDC subset includes CallHome and CallFriend Egyptian (previously described), and the conversational telephone Levantine Fisher set. Each of these sets contain 100s of speakers from about

400 speakers from the CallHome/CallFriend combination to about 1300 speakers in the Fisher set. The amount of data collected for the conversations in this data set range from about a minimum of 5 minutes to about 30 minutes. The sets include both genders although not necessarily well balanced. One issue that is unclear for this data set is whether there are specific channel effect that make the dialect identification process easier.

Arabic Dialects (Maghrebi)   Nour-Eddine (Nour-Eddine, 2015) used a data set collected from found sources to conduct Arabic dialect identification for classes of Maghrebi Arabic. Specifically, the corpus used in this work include five dialect classes of Arabic Maghrebi: Moroccan, Oranian, Algiersian, Constantinian and Tunisian. The sources for these five classes included broadcast shows and movies which represent a very particular kind of acoustic conditions. The set included about a 100 speakers and about 50 hours per dialect class. There is no information available about the gender balance of this set or how the shows and movies used were selected.

Arabic Dialects (Algerian)   Bourgrine (Bougrine et al., 2018) conducted experiments of variations of Algerian Arabic. In this set, six Algerian Arabic classes are included: Oran, Algiers, Laghouat, Adrar, Bousaada and Djelfa. There are two sources of data used in this collection. The first source is a collection conducted internally by the authors that included guided narration, short phrases and short reading excerpts. The second source of data is extracted from radio and TV broadcasts. The amount of speech collected and the gender information is not cleared.

12.3.1   Summary of Data Sets

In this section, a survey of datasets available in the literature is presented. Although certainly other datasets are available most of those data sets are either not as popular in the literature or small for most viable automatic dialect recognition research. There are a number of issues that can be considered problematic when discussing data suitable for dialect identification research. First, the lack of consistent definitions between language sub-classes, dialects and accents can make it very difficult to get the community on the same page. A second issue that is likely going to be more critical in the future is that of the amount of data available for most corpora. In the age of deep neural networks the emerging algorithms consistently employ very large amounts of data. For many speech processing algorithms thousands of hours of speech are needed with a fair amount of those set including substantial truth markings. A third potential issue is the lack of a spearheading application that relies on the use of dialect identification. This lack of a core application likely results in weakened community interest and a lack of resources driving issues such as the limited amounts of data available for research.

12.4   State of the Art

12.4.1   Subspace Approaches to Language Recognition

Traditional approaches to spoken language recognition include phonotactic and acoustic-phonetic systems. In both cases, languages can be modeled as high-dimensional embeddings. For example, the *bag of sounds* framework estimates the histogram of the phonetic distribution in a speech sample, and compares this vector to the known phonotactic behavior of different languages (Li and Ma, 2005; Li et al., 2006). In GMM-based acoustic-phonetic approaches, GMM mixture means are concatenated to form supervectors, which are compared to known language models (Torres-Carrasquillo et al., 2002). Various other types of language recognition systems also represent the language-dependent properties of speech in high-dimensional embeddings. In these cases, language classification requires the calculation of similarity scores between large vectors. Subspace modeling tools such as SVMs and Factor Analysis (FA) enable efficient processing in high-dimensional spaces, and allow similarity scores to focus on discriminative language-dependent information while de-emphasizing nuisance attributes.

Support Vector Machines   SVMs represent a low-complexity solution for comparing vectors in high dimensions. They utilize kernels to calculate vector similarity scores, and can be trained efficiently in a discriminative manner (Burges, 1998). Specifically, in the context of language recognition, separate *one-versue-all* SVMs are typically trained to detect each of N individual languages. In (Li and Ma, 2005; Li et al., 2006), SVMs were used for language classification with histograms of phonetic distributions. In (Zhai et al., 2006), language n-grams were instead used as features, and in (Campbell et al., 2006) SVMs were applied to GMM-based supervectors. SVMs allow for a variety of parametric kernels to be used during classification. In (Li and Ma, 2005; Li et al., 2006; Zhai et al., 2006), linear kernels were utilized, and no significant performance benefits were observed with more complex kernels. In other work, SVM kernels were designed to approximate information theoretic divergence measures. In (Campbell et al., 2006), a kernal based on the Kullback-Leibler (KL) divergence between GMM-based supervectors was proposed, and this idea was extended to include GMM covariance matrices in (Campbell et al., 2008). A kernel based on the Bhattacharyya Distance was proposed in (You et al., 2008) and (You et al., 2009).

Factor Analysis   Another method for efficiently comparing vectors in high dimensions is factor analysis, which builds on the assumption that the variability of interest inhabits a small subspace. Factor analysis yielded significant performance benefits when applied to modeling GMM-based supervectors in speaker verification. Specifically, Joint Factor Analysis (JFA) modeled speaker and channel variability in separate subspaces (Kenny, 2005; Vogt et al., 2005; Kenny et al., 2007), and allowed vector similarity scores to be calculated as statistical measures (Glembek et al., 2009). Efficient probabilistic methods exist for training the JFA model, even in resource-constrained scenarios (Vogt and Sridharan, 2008). The success of JFA in speaker recognition motivated similar approaches to be applied to language recognition, leading to feature-space Latent Factor Analysis (fLFA). In fLFA, channel variability is assumed to inhabit a subspace of the overall acoustic feature space, and features are compensated via projection into the complement of the channel space (Castaldo et al., 2007; Hubeika et al., 2008). In (Campbell, 2008), feature-space Nuisance Attribute Projection (fNAP) was proposed for language recognition, which similarly removes an approximated channel term from the input acoustic features. However, fNAP is trained in a discriminative manner, as opposed to fLFA which is typically trained using statistical approaches.

Although JFA achieved significant success in speaker recognition, it proved difficult to separately model speaker and channel variability in the high-dimensional supervector space. An alternative was proposed in (Dehak et al., 2011a), where factor analysis was applied to model the total variability of GMM-based supervectors. The maximum a posteriori (MAP) estimate of the latent factor was extracted to efficiently capture speaker and channel variability in a low-dimensional space. Referred to as the *i-vector*, this embedding allowed for sophisticated modeling and scoring techniques due to its small size. Following work in speaker recognition, the i-vector framework was successfully applied to language recognition in (Dehak et al., 2011b; Martinez et al., 2011). In (D'Haro et al., 2012), the i-vector framework was alternatively used to model phonotactic embeddings.

One of the main benefits to using i-vectors for language recognition was that it allows for efficient classification in a low-dimensional space. For example, multi-class logistic regression was used to calculate language posterior probabilities (Brummer and Van Leeuwen, 2006). Another method for language classification with i-vectors was a Gaussian Backend (GB). In this technique, individual languages were modeled as separate Gaussian distributions, and class posterior probabilities were derived in a straight-forward manner using a Bayesian approach (Zissman, 1996). In the general case, this results in a quadratic classifier. However, if the covariance matrices of individual languages are tied, it leads to a linear classifier. The GB can be trained as a generative model, or in a discriminative manner (Hubeika et al., 2008; McCree, 2014), and has become the standard method for language recognition with i-vectors.

12.4.2   Deep Learning Approaches to Language Recognition

For many years, the state of the art in language recognition relied on the use of i-vectors (Martinez et al., 2011; Dehak et al., 2011b). Borrowed from the speaker recognition field (Dehak et al., 2011a), i-vectors were extracted as low-dimensional embeddings based on a generative model which captured the short-time acoustic patterns of spoken language. Language posterior probabilities for an input signal were then typically estimated using a GB, which could be trained in either a generative or discriminative manner (Penagarikano et al., 2012).

Recently, the successful application of deep neural networks to speech and speaker recognition (Hinton et al., 2012; Lei et al., 2014b; Richardson et al., 2015; Snyder et al., 2018) has inspired an abundance of deep learning approaches to language recognition. Many of these have leveraged the impressive performance of i-vector-based systems by utilizing deep neural networks to improve the i-vector framework. Others have exploited deep learning to design discriminative embeddings or train end-to-end recognition systems.

Using DNNs within the I-vector Framework   Initial efforts to exploit the modeling capacity of deep neural networks within language recognition were aimed at improving the i-vector framework. A fundamental step of i-vector extraction is modeling the short-time acoustic patterns of spoken language with a GMM (Dehak et al., 2011a). Traditionally, this GMM was trained in a fully unsupervised manner. In (Lei et al., 2014a), a phonetically-aware GMM was instead proposed. A deep neural network was first trained to classify short-time acoustic features by their phonetic label. The output posterior probabilities were then used during the expectation step of GMM training to cluster short-time acoustic features by phonetic context, so that the mixtures of the GMM carried phonetic meaning. Phonetically-aware GMMs provided significant improvements in robustness for language recognition (Lei et al., 2014a; Richardson et al., 2015).

An alternative way in which the i-vector framework was improved via deep neural networks was with bottleneck features (BNFs). Traditionally, short-time features for language recognition, such as Shifted Delta Cesptra Coefficients (Torres-Carrasquillo et al., 2002), were hand-crafted to capture acoustic information relevant to spoken language. In (Song et al., 2013), a deep neural network was trained to predict phonetic classes from short-time spectral features, and the network was configured to include a narrow bottleneck layer.

In this way, the network learned to capture short-time information relevant to phonetic classification in the low-dimensional bottleneck layer, and this embedding could then be used as input to the i-vector extraction process. Many variants of this approach have since been proposed. In (Matejka et al., 2014), BNFs were stacked with conventional spectral features to exploit their complementary nature. A convolutional neural network (CNN) was used in (Ganapathy et al., 2014) to improve the robustness of the BNF extractor. In (Fér et al., 2015), multilingual BNFs were proposed, in which separate sub-networks were trained to classify phonetic content from different languages. Overall, the ability to discriminatively train BNFs as nonlinear embeddings have yielded significant performance improvements for language recognition across a variety of tasks and conditions, relative to hand-crafted spectral features.

Finally, deep learning has been used to predict language classes based on i-vectors. Traditionally, classification within the i-vector framework was performed using a GB. In such systems, languages were typically modeled as Gaussian distributions with a shared covariance matrix, leading to a linear classifier, and could be trained either in a generative or discriminative manner (Penagarikano et al., 2012). In (Matějka et al., 2012) and (McLaren et al., 2013), DNNs were instead used to directly perform language classification based on input i-vectors, leading to performance improvements. DNN-based i-vector classification was further explored in (Yu et al., 2016; Sun et al., 2016; Shon et al., 2016; Ranjan et al., 2016), as part of the NIST 2015 I-vector Challenge (Greenberg et al., 2014).

End-to-end Recognition Systems   Instead of using deep learning to improve the i-vector framework, many efforts explored end-to-end architectures for language recognition. (Lopez-Moreno et al., 2014) proposed a system which directly predicted language classes from short-time spectral features using a feed-forward DNN, and achieved significant performance benefits relative to i-vector-based recognition. In (Gonzalez-Dominguez et al., 2014), this work was extended to utilize a Long Short-Term Memory (LSTM) architecture, allowing for better modeling of the dynamic patterns in spoken language. CNNs were used in (Lozano-Diez et al., 2015) as part of end-to-end recognition, in order to improve system robustness, particularly for short-duration signals. Finally, in (Geng et al., 2016), an Attention-Based Recurrent Neural Network (RNN) was applied, allowing the network to focus on the more discriminative information. (Trong et al., 2016) offers a comprehensive comparative study on various neural network architectures for end-to-end language recognition.

Discriminatively Trained Language Embeddings   While end-to-end systems can provide significant performance improvements in spoken language recognition relative to i-vector-based systems, training such systems can prove difficult since they require vast data sets and can be prone to model over-fitting. To overcome these hurdles, discriminatively trained language embeddings were pursued as a method by which to exploit the high modeling capacity of DNNs while avoiding the overfitting tendencies of end-to-end systems. In (Lozano-Diez et al., 2018a) and (Lozano-Diez et al., 2018b), an end-to-end language recognition system was first trained, wherein the DNN architecture included bi-directional LSTM (BLSTM) layers, and utterance-level statistics were summarized via mean and standard deviation pooling layers. Fully-connected layers located after the pooling layers were then extracted as language embeddings, and classified using conventional GBs. (Snyder et al., 2018) continued the exploration into language embeddings by using a time-delay neural network (TDNN) architecture, and showing the benefit of data augmentation while training the embedding extractor. In (Gelly and Gauvain, 2017), the cost function used to train the original end-to-end system was improved by including an angular proximity term. In (Brummer et al., 2018) and (Villalba et al., 2018), discriminative embeddings were extended to include probabilisitc motivation, and performance improvements were observed for some tasks. Overall, the use of language embeddings has been shown to generally outperform fully end-to-end language recognition systems, which is speculated to be due to the difficulty encountered when the training the latter (Villalba et al., 2018; Snyder et al., 2018).

12.5 Standarized Evaluations and Recent Performance

12.5.1 Standarized Evaluations

NIST has conducted periodical evaluations on technologies that have a direct impact on the dialect identification task. Particularly the evaluations conducted for speaker recognition and language identification have direct impact on the development and progress in the field of dialect identification. In this section details are provided about the NIST evaluation process and the impact,directly or indirectly, those evaluations have on the dialect identification community. The history of the broad set of speech evaluations conducted by NIST have been described over the years in multiple publications. For example Martin (Martin and Garofolo, 2007), describes the motivation and history of the main speech related applications. Later on Przybocki (Przybocki and Martin, 2004; Przybocki et al., 2006), describes the early history of the speaker recognition evaluations. Although deeper details can be found in those publications, for the dialect identification community the main reasons that these evaluations are relevant are as follows:

- **Cross pollination**: Techniques developed for both speaker and language recognition have consistently crossed into the leading techniques for dialect recognition. More specifically, techniques developed for the popular research area of speaker recognition are typically transferred to the area of language recognition and in turn to the dialect recognition arena. Techniques previously described in this chapter such as GMMs, SVMs, i-vector and x-vector approaches have all reached popularity in the speaker recognition community before been exploited for language and dialect recognition.

- **Common data set**: The NIST evaluation data sets have consistently become the de facto standards in many speech communities allowing for comparison of results among researchers. Many researchers can attest the challenge involved in assessing the quality of the techniques developed and published in the literature when the data sets used are either proprietary or used in non-standard ways. The availability of the NIST data sets that are made available through evaluation participation has allowed researchers, in many cases, to overcome this challenge of comparing the approaches developed.
- **Common metric**: Similarly to the case of standardized data sets, the use of metrics utilized for the NiSt evaluations have allowed the community to make system comparison on a common metric rather than metrics of choice by each particular research team.
- **Interesting and challenging set**: The final advantage that is observed as a byproduct of standardized evaluations is the evolution of the data as the performance obtained is improved. It is a common situation on these evaluations that, although the task is basically fixed, the data is data conditions are continuously modified to address real world needs. A simple example of this situation is the progression from early evaluations away from conversational telephone speech captured on land line to a majority of the data these days consisting of speech collected over mobile phones.

The description presented in this section has centered on the general advantages of standardized evaluations using the NIST evaluations as a particular example. There are other evaluations available in the literature but those seem to generate fewer citations and not as popular in this research community. Table 12.2 summarizes the dialect tasks included as part of the two most recent LREs.

12.5.2 *NIST-LRE 2017 Language Sub-classes and Dialect Performance*

As stated throughout this chapter, the work in this field covers the spectrum from dialect identification to accent recognition and language varieties. Tables 12.3–12.6 show the performance of a single x-vector, current state of the art, system on the tasks described earlier and conducted on the NIST-LRE 2017 campaign. The performance of the system is shown as closed-set accuracy.

The tables shown demonstrate the performance across a variety of classification tasks on different language sub-classes and dialects. Analysis of these results is sometimes difficult as usually insight of the languages is needed

Table 12.2 *Dialect Classes on 2015 and 2017 NIST LREs.*

Evaluation	Dialect Classes
LRE2015	· Arabic classes: Egyptian, Iraqi, Levantine, Maghrebi, Modern Standard Arabic · Spanish classes: Caribbean, European, Latin American · Chinese classes: Cantonese, Mandarin, Min, Wu
LRE2017	· Arabic classes: Egyptian, Iraqi, Levantine, Maghrebi · Chinese classes: Mandarin, Min · English classes: British, General American · Iberian classes: Caribbean, European, Latin American, Brazilian Portuguese

Table 12.3 *Arabic Classes*

	Egyptian	Iraqi	Levantine	Maghrebi
Egyptian	2313	141	50	87
Iraqi	124	1688	111	167
Levantine	75	212	1700	201
Maghrebi	62	247	134	2034

Table 12.4 *English Classes*

	British	American
British	249	12
American	120	1536

Table 12.5 *Iberian Classes*

	Portuguese	Caribbean Spanish	European Spanish	Latin American Spanish
Portuguese	1464	15	14	49
Caribbean Spanish	62	1012	55	792
European Spanish	36	251	1838	750
Latin American Spanish	41	188	167	1517

beyond what is available. In the cases shown here, and for which limited expertise is available, informal discussions with native speakers agree with the confusions observed. In the cases of the English and Spanish classification tasks, the performance observed on the British versus American English classes is pretty high and as expected. A few more observations can be done for

Table 12.6 *Chinese Classes*

	Mandarin	Min
Mandarin	1636	79
Min	78	1078

the Iberian classification task. First, the small amount of confusions observed between Portuguese and the different Spanish classes is expected and further analysis is needed to get additional insight into what is causing those errors. For the case of the confusions among the different Spanish classes the one interesting result that needs further consideration is the confusion observed among Caribbean and Latin American Spanish. In the opinion of the authors, this is a reasonable confusion but the one striking detail is the issue that many true Caribbean Spanish utterances are confused as Latin American utterances but the converse is not true. Extensive analysis is underway to assess the current weaknesses on these tasks but in the past issues such as mislabeled data and non-nativeness have commonly been a major part of the confusions.

12.6   Challenges and Future Outlook

In this chapter, dialect identification has been addressed. As discussed, dialect identification is usually discussed in the context of language identification and considered as a special case of language identification. A large amount of the literature tends to focus as extending language identification algorithms for the dialect identification task with little or no modifications to the underlying language identification systems. There are a number of ways that dialect identification could become more important in the future and a few of these ideas are discussed below.

- **Lead application**: Dialect identification is faced with the difficult challenge of a critical application that enables broader interest and resources to be devolved to dialect recognition research. Consistently, most of the applications for dialect identification are in the realm of data filtering and triage, or as preprocessing stages for further automatic processing. Either one of these applications may be losing steam as the end users keep finding potential ways around addressing dialect. For example, as large amounts of data are available enough coverage of speech recognition systems the need to use divide and conquer approaches to obtain improved performance may be reduced. Additionally, the reduce cost of computation may also reduce the need for dialect recognition as a pre-processing stage as it may be possible to shift the burden to some extent to the additional hardware. Other application could be envisioned such using dialect as a component of speaker recognition systems but this kind of applications are still periphery applications that are unlikely to drive a new wave of interest in this area.

- **Inconsistent and limited resources**: This issue is intimately related to the critical application need described earlier. As limited monetary resource are available the ability to address the need for data is not addressed, this in turn reduces the possibility to develop large, consistent corpora that would enable more research using advanced systems. Potentially, astute uses of available data are possible but it is not clear if those breakthrough alternatives are been developed. Going forward the dialect identification community needs to address these issues and figure out creative ways to use current data and how to extend the current resources in a data hungry and truth constrained environment.

References

LRE (2009). NIST language recognition evaluation. https://www.nist.gov/itl/iad/mig/language-recognition.

LRE (2011). NIST 2011 language recognition evaluation. https://www.nist.gov/itl/iad/mig/language-recognition.

LRE (2015). NIST 2015 language recognition evaluation. https://www.nist.gov/itl/iad/mig/language-recognition.

Akbacak, M., Vergyri, D., Stolcke, A., Scheffer, N., and Mandal, A. (2011). Effective arabic dialect classification using diverse phonotactic models. In *Annual Conference of the International Speech Communication Association*.

Barkat, M., Ohala, J. J., and Pellegrino, F. (1999). Prosody as a distinctive feature for the discrimination of arabic dialects. In *Eurospeech*.

Biadsy, F. and Hirschberg, J. (2009). Using prosody and phonotactics in arabic dialect identification. In *Annual Conference of the International Speech Communication Association*.

Biadsy, F., Hirschberg, J., and Habash, N. (2009). Spoken arabic dialect identification using phonotactic modeling. In *Proceedings of the EACL 2009 Workshop on Computational Approaches to Semitic Languages*, pages 53–61. Association for Computational Linguistics.

Biadsy, F., Soltau, H., Mangu, L., Navratil, J., and Hirschberg, J. B. (2010). Discriminative phonotactics for dialect recognition using context-dependent phone classifiers. In *Odyssey: The Speaker and Language, Recognition Workshop*.

Bielefeld, B. (1994). Language identification using shifted delta cepstrum. In *Annual Speech Research Symposium*.

Bougrine, S., Cherroun, H., and Ziadi, D. (2018). Prosody-based spoken algerian arabic dialect identification. *Procedia Computer Science*, 128:9–17.

Brummer, N., Silnova, A., Burget, L., and Stafylakis, T. (2018). Gaussian meta-embeddings for efficient scoring of a heavy-tailed plda model. *arXiv preprint arXiv:1802.09777*.

Brummer, N. and Van Leeuwen, D. A. (2006). On calibration of language recognition scores. In *Odyssey: The Speaker and Language Recognition Workshop*, pages 1–8. IEEE.

Burges, C. J. (1998). A tutorial on support vector machines for pattern recognition. *Data mining and knowledge discovery*, 2(2):121–167.

Burget, L., Matejka, P., and Cernocky, J. (2006). Discriminative training techniques for acoustic language identification. In *Proceedings of the IEEE International Conference on Acoustics Speech and Signal Processing*, volume 1, pages I–I. IEEE.

Campbell, W. M. (2008). A covariance kernel for svm language recognition. In *Proceedings of the IEEE International Conference on Acoustics Speech and Signal Processing*, pages 4141–4144. IEEE.

Campbell, W. M., Campbell, J. P., Reynolds, D. A., Singer, E., and Torres-Carrasquillo, P. A. (2006). Support vector machines for speaker and language recognition. *Computer Speech & Language*, 20(2–3):210–229.

Campbell, W. M., Sturim, D. E., Torres-Carrasquillo, P. A., and Reynolds, D. A. (2008). A comparison of subspace feature-domain methods for language recognition. In *Annual Conference of the International Speech Communication Association*.

Castaldo, F., Colibro, D., Dalmasso, E., Laface, P., and Vair, C. (2007). Compensation of nuisance factors for speaker and language recognition. *IEEE Transactions on Audio, Speech, and Language Processing*, 15(7):1969–1978.

D'Arcy, S. and Russell, M. J. (2008). Experiments with the abi (accents of the british isles) speech corpus. In *Annual Conference of the International Speech Communication Association*.

D'Arcy, S. M., Russell, M. J., Browning, S. R., and Tomlinson, M. J. (2004). The accents of the british isles (abi) corpus. In *Proceedings of MIDL Workshop*.

Dehak, N., Kenny, P. J., Dehak, R., Dumouchel, P., and Ouellet, P. (2011a). Front-end factor analysis for speaker verification. *IEEE Transactions on Audio, Speech, and Language Processing*, 19(4):788–798.

Dehak, N., Torres-Carrasquillo, P. A., Reynolds, D., and Dehak, R. (2011b). Language recognition via i-vectors and dimensionality reduction. In *Annual Conference of the International Speech Communication Association*.

D'Haro, L. F., Glembek, O., Plchot, O., Matějka, P., Soufifar, M., Cordoba, R., and Černocký, J. (2012). Phonotactic language recognition using i-vectors and phoneme posteriogram counts. In *Annual Conference of the International Speech Communication Association*.

Fér, R., Matějka, P., Grézl, F., Plchot, O., and Černocký, J. (2015). Multilingual bottleneck features for language recognition. In *Annual Conference of the International Speech Communication Association*.

Ferragne, E. and Pellegrino, F. (2007). Automatic dialect identification: A study of british english. In *Speaker Classification II*, pages 243–257. Springer.

Ganapathy, S., Han, K., Thomas, S., Omar, M., Segbroeck, M. V., and Narayanan, S. S. (2014). Robust language identification using convolutional neural network features. In *Annual Conference of the International Speech Communication Association*.

Gelly, G. and Gauvain, J.-L. (2017). Spoken language identification using lstm-based angular proximity. In *Annual Conference of the International Speech Communication Association*, pages 2566–2570.

Geng, W., Wang, W., Zhao, Y., Cai, X., Xu, B., Xinyuan, C., et al. (2016). End-to-end language identification using attention-based recurrent neural networks. In *Annual Conference of the International Speech Communication Association*.

Glembek, O., Burget, L., Dehak, N., Brummer, N., and Kenny, P. (2009). Comparison of scoring methods used in speaker recognition with joint factor analysis. In *Proceedings of the IEEE International Conference on Acoustics Speech and Signal Processing*, pages 4057–4060. IEEE.

Gonzalez-Dominguez, J., Lopez-Moreno, I., Sak, H., Gonzalez-Rodriguez, J., and Moreno, P. J. (2014). Automatic language identification using long short-term memory recurrent neural networks. In *Annual Conference of the International Speech Communication Association*.

Greenberg, C. S., Bansé, D., Doddington, G. R., Garcia-Romero, D., Godfrey, J. J., Kinnunen, T., Martin, A. F., McCree, A., Przybocki, M., and Reynolds, D. A. (2014). The nist 2014 speaker recognition i-vector machine learning challenge. In *Odyssey: The Speaker and Language, Recognition Workshop*, pages 224–230.

Hamdi-Sultan, R., Barkat-Defradas, M., Ferragne, E., and Pellegrino, F. (2004). Speech timing and rhythmic structure in arabic dialects: a comparison of two approaches. In *Annual Conference of the International Speech Communication Association*, pages 1613–1616.

Hinton, G., Deng, L., Yu, D., Dahl, G., Mohamed, A.-r., Jaitly, N., Senior, A., Vanhoucke, V., Nguyen, P., Kingsbury, B., et al. (2012). Deep neural networks for acoustic modeling in speech recognition. *IEEE Signal Processing Magazine*, 29.

Hubeika, V., Burget, L., Matějka, P., and Schwarz, P. (2008). Discriminative training and channel compensation for acoustic language recognition. In *Annual Conference of the International Speech Communication Association*.

Kenny, P. (2005). Joint factor analysis of speaker and session variability: Theory and algorithms. *CRIM, Montreal,(Report) CRIM-06/08-13*, 14:28–29.

Kenny, P., Boulianne, G., Ouellet, P., and Dumouchel, P. (2007). Joint factor analysis versus eigenchannels in speaker recognition. *IEEE Transactions on Audio, Speech, and Language Processing*, 15(4):1435–1447.

LDC (1996). Callfriend corpus. http://www.ldc.upenn/ldc/about/callfriend.html.

Lei, Y., Ferrer, L., Lawson, A., McLaren, M., and Scheffer, N. (2014a). Application of convolutional neural networks to language identification in noisy conditions. In *Odyssey: The Speaker and Language, Recognition Workshop*, pages 1–8. ISCA.

Lei, Y. and Hansen, J. H. (2010). Dialect classification via text-independent training and testing for arabic, spanish, and chinese. *IEEE Transactions on Audio, Speech, and Language Processing*, 19(1):85–96.

Lei, Y., Scheffer, N., Ferrer, L., and McLaren, M. (2014b). A novel scheme for speaker recognition using a phonetically-aware deep neural network. In *Proceedings of the IEEE International Conference on Acoustics Speech and Signal Processing*, pages 1695–1699. IEEE.

Li, H. and Ma, B. (2005). A phonotactic language model for spoken language identification. In *Proceedings of the 43rd Annual Meeting on Association for Computational Linguistics*, pages 515–522.

Li, H., Ma, B., and Lee, C.-H. (2006). A vector space modeling approach to spoken language identification. *IEEE Transactions on Audio, Speech, and Language Processing*, 15(1):271–284.

Lopez-Moreno, I., Gonzalez-Dominguez, J., Plchot, O., Martinez, D., Gonzalez-Rodriguez, J., and Moreno, P. (2014). Automatic language identification using deep neural networks. In *Proceedings of the IEEE International Conference on Acoustics Speech and Signal Processing*, pages 5337–5341. IEEE.

Lozano-Diez, A., Plchot, O., Matejka, P., and Gonzalez-Rodriguez, J. (2018a). Dnn based embeddings for language recognition. In *Proceedings of the IEEE International Conference on Acoustics Speech and Signal Processing*, pages 5184–5188. IEEE.

Lozano-Diez, A., Plchot, O., Matejka, P., Novotnỳ, O., and Gonzalez-Rodriguez, J. (2018b). Analysis of dnn-based embeddings for language recognition on the nist lre 2017. In *Odyssey: The Speaker and Language, Recognition Workshop*.

Lozano-Diez, A., Zazo-Candil, R., Gonzalez-Dominguez, J., Toledano, D. T., and Gonzalez-Rodriguez, J. (2015). An end-to-end approach to language identification in short utterances using convolutional neural networks. In *Annual Conference of the International Speech Communication Association*.

Martin, A. F. and Garofolo, J. S. (2007). Nist speech processing evaluations: Lvcsr, speaker recognition, language recognition. In *2007 IEEE Workshop on Signal Processing Applications for Public Security and Forensics*, pages 1–7.

Martinez, D., Plchot, O., Burget, L., Glembek, O., and Matějka, P. (2011). Language recognition in ivectors space. In *Annual Conference of the International Speech Communication Association*.

Matějka, P., Plchot, O., Soufifar, M., Glembek, O., D'haro Enríquez, L. F., Veselỳ, K., Grézl, F., Ma, J., Matsoukas, S., and Dehak, N. (2012). Patrol team language identification system for darpa rats p1 evaluation. In *Annual Conference of the International Speech Communication Association*.

Matejka, P., Zhang, L., Ng, T., Mallidi, H. S., Glembek, O., Ma, J., and Zhang, B. (2014). Neural network bottleneck features for language identification. *Odyssey: The Speaker and Language, Recognition Workshop*, pages 299–304.

McCree, A. (2014). Multiclass discriminative training of i-vector language recognition. In *Odyssey: The Speaker and Language Recognition Workshop*, pages 166–171.

McLaren, M., Lawson, A., Lei, Y., and Scheffer, N. (2013). Adaptive gaussian backend for robust language identification. In *Annual Conference of the International Speech Communication Association*, pages 84–88.

Navrátil, J. and Zuhlke, W. (1997). Double bigram-decoding in phonotactic language identification. In *Proceedings of the IEEE International Conference on Acoustics Speech and Signal Processing*, volume 2, pages 1115–1118. IEEE.

Nour-Eddine, L. (2015). Gmm-based maghreb dialect identificationsystem. *JIPS*, 11(1):22–38.

Penagarikano, M., Varona, A., Diez, M., Rodriguez-Fuentes, L. J., and Bordel, G. (2012). Study of different backends in a state-of-the-art language recognition system. In *Annual Conference of the International Speech Communication Association*.

Przybocki, M. and Martin, A. (2004). Nist speaker recognition evaluation chronicles. In *Odyssey: The Speaker and Language, Recognition Workshop*, pages 12–22.

Przybocki, M. A., Martin, A. F., and Le, A. N. (2006). Nist speaker recognition evaluation chronicles-part 2. In *Odyssey: The Speaker and Language, Recognition Workshop*, pages 1–6.

Ranjan, S., Yu, C., Zhang, C., Kelly, F., and Hansen, J. H. (2016). Language recognition using deep neural networks with very limited training data. In *Proceedings of the IEEE International Conference on Acoustics Speech and Signal Processing*, pages 5830–5834. IEEE.

Reynolds, D. A., Quatieri, T. F., and Dunn, R. B. (2000). Speaker verification using adapted gaussian mixture models. *Digital Signal Processing*, 10(1–3):19–41.

Reynolds, D. A. and Rose, R. C. (1995). Robust text-independent speaker identification using gaussian mixture speaker models. *IEEE Transactions on Speech and Audio Processing*, 3(1):72–83.

Richardson, F., Reynolds, D., and Dehak, N. (2015). Deep neural network approaches to speaker and language recognition. *IEEE Signal Processing Letters*, 22(10): 1671–1675.

Shon, S., Mun, S., Hansen, J. H., and Ko, H. (2016). Ku-ispl language recognition system for nist 2015 i-vector machine learning challenge. *arXiv preprint arXiv:1609.06404*.

Snyder, D., Garcia-Romero, D., Sell, G., Povey, D., and Khudanpur, S. (2018). X-vectors: Robust dnn embeddings for speaker recognition. In *Proceedings of the IEEE International Conference on Acoustics Speech and Signal Processing*, pages 5329–5333. IEEE.

Song, Y., Jiang, B., Bao, Y., Wei, S., and Dai, L.-R. (2013). I-vector representation based on bottleneck features for language identification. *Electronics Letters*, 49(24):1569–1570.

Sun, H., Nguyen, T., Wang, G., Lee, K. A., Ma, B., and Li, H. (2016). I2r submission to the 2015 nist language recognition i-vector challenge. In *Odyssey: The Speaker and Language, Recognition Workshop*, pages 21–24.

Torres-Carrasquillo, P. A., Singer, E., Kohler, M. A., Greene, R. J., Reynolds, D. A., and Deller Jr, J. R. (2002). Approaches to language identification using gaussian mixture models and shifted delta cepstral features. In *International Conference on Spoken Language Processing*.

Trong, T. N., Hautamaki, V., and Lee, K. A. (2016). Deep language: a comprehensive deep learning approach to end-to-end language recognition. In *Odyssey: the Speaker and Language Recognition Workshop*.

Villalba, J., Brümmer, N., and Dehak, N. (2018). End-to-end versus embedding neural networks for language recognition in mismatched conditions. In *Odyssey: The Speaker and Language, Recognition Workshop*.

Vogt, R. and Sridharan, S. (2008). Explicit modelling of session variability for speaker verification. *Computer Speech & Language*, 22(1):17–38.

Vogt, R. J., Baker, B. J., and Sridharan, S. (2005). Modelling session variability in text independent speaker verification. In *European Conference on Speech Communication and Technology*.

You, C. H., Lee, K. A., and Li, H. (2008). An svm kernel with gmm-supervector based on the bhattacharyya distance for speaker recognition. *IEEE Signal Processing Letters*, 16(1):49–52.

You, C. H., Lee, K. A., and Li, H. (2009). Gmm-svm kernel with a bhattacharyya-based distance for speaker recognition. *IEEE Transactions on Audio, Speech, and Language Processing*, 18(6):1300–1312.

Yu, C., Zhang, C., Ranjan, S., Zhang, Q., Misra, A., Kelly, F., and Hansen, J. H. (2016). Utd-crss system for the nist 2015 language recognition i-vector machine learning challenge. In *Proceedings of the IEEE International Conference on Acoustics Speech and Signal Processing*, pages 5835–5839. IEEE.

Zhai, L.-F., Siu, M.-h., Yang, X., and Gish, H. (2006). Discriminatively trained language models using support vector machines for language identification. In *IEEE Odyssey: The Speaker and Language Recognition Workshop*, pages 1–6. IEEE.

Zissman, M. A. (1996). Comparison of four approaches to automatic language identification of telephone speech. *IEEE Transactions on Speech and Audio Processing*, 4(1):31.

Zissman, M. A., Gleason, T. P., Rekart, D., and Losiewicz, B. L. (1996). Automatic dialect identification of extemporaneous conversational, latin american spanish speech. In *Proceedings of the IEEE International Conference on Acoustics Speech and Signal Processing*, volume 2, pages 777–780. IEEE.

Zissman, M. A. and Singer, E. (1994). Automatic language identification of telephone speech messages using phoneme recognition and n-gram modeling. In *Proceedings of the IEEE International Conference on Acoustics Speech and Signal Processing*, volume 1, pages I–305. IEEE.

13 Arabic Dialect Processing

Nizar Habash

13.1 Introduction

The Arabic language is a collection of variants among which one particular variant has the special status of being the formal written standard of the media, culture, and education across the Arab World, a region of 22 countries and over 400 million inhabitants. This variant is often referred to as Modern Standard Arabic (MSA). The other variants are mostly informal spoken dialects, henceforth Dialectal Arabic(s) (DA), that are the media of communication for daily life. Classical Arabic (CA), the primary language form of religious texts in Islam, as well as literature from pre-Islamic and early Islamic periods, is another variant. While dialect variation is not unique to Arabic, and neither is politicizing the topics of dialect, language and identity, two aspects of Arabic's linguistic situation sets it apart: (a) the high degree of difference between MSA and DA; and (b) the fact that MSA is not any Arab's native language. This leads to DA coexisting in diglossic relationships with MSA (Ferguson, 1959).

In this chapter, we discuss the ways Arabic variants (MSA and DA) differ in terms of phonology, morphology, syntax and lexicon. We also present some of the challenges Arabic poses to natural language processing (NLP), including morphological richness and complexity, and orthographic ambiguity and inconsistency. We then survey the history and state-of-the-art of dialect resources and tools. In the last 25 years, there has been a steady rise in the number of publications on Arabic and Arabic Dialect NLP (Habash, 2010; Shoufan and Al-Ameri, 2015; Guellil et al., 2019); what we present are highlights and key efforts to help NLP researchers who are starting to work in this area.

13.2 Arabic and Its Variants

13.2.1 History, Geography, and Context

All language variants exist in a continuum, both historically and geographically. The terms *language* or *dialect* are simply expressions of power and dominance of one ideology over another. In the Arab World, the politics of Arab nationalism and Islam are the primary forces that define the views on what is *the* Arabic language and what are its dialects. MSA is the official language of the Arab World, and the primary written language of media and education. MSA is syntactically, morphologically and phonologically based on CA, the language of the Qur'an. Lexically, however, MSA is more modern. DA in contrast, are the native language forms of the Arab World. They are loosely related to CA; but resulted from the interaction between different CA dialects and other languages that existed in, neighbored and/or colonized the Arab World. For example, Moroccan Arabic has a lot of Amazigh and French influences. Typically, DA are grouped along geographical lines into Gulf Arabic (GLF), Levantine Arabic (LEV), Egyptian Arabic (EGY), and North African (Maghrebi) Arabic (MAG). Recent NLP efforts have addressed some of the pitfalls of these coarse-grained classifications and started considering city dialects (Bouamor et al., 2018). DA are primarily spoken, and are not taught in schools or even standardized, although there is a rich DA culture of folktales, songs, movies, and TV shows. With the rise of electronic media, DA are becoming more written than ever before. MSA and DA coexist in a *diglossic* relationship (Ferguson, 1959) with clear domains of prevalence: formal written (MSA) versus informal spoken (DA), but there is a large gray area in between often filled with a mix of the two (Badawi, 1973; Bassiouney, 2009).

13.2.2 Linguistic Similarities and Differences

DA substantially differ from MSA and each other in terms of phonology, morphology, lexicon and syntax. We discuss these dimensions using a small parallel corpus of ten sentences from the MADAR Corpus (Bouamor et al., 2018) – see Figure 13.1. The figure pairs each Arabic script sentence with two

Variant	**Phonetic Transcription**	**Transliteration**	**Arabic Script**
MSA	kayfa ʔaṣṭaṭi:ʕu musa:ʕadataka	*kyf ÂstTyς msAςdtk?*	كيف أستطيع مساعدتك؟
Cairo	izza:y aʔdar asaʕdạk	*AzAy Aqdr AsAςdk?*	ازاي اقدر اساعدك؟
Baghdad	ʃlo:n agdar asa:ʕdak	*šlwn Aqdr AsAςdk?*	شلون اقدر اساعدك؟
Riyadh	ke:f agdar asa:ʕdek	*kyf Aqdr AsAςdk?*	كيف اقدر اساعدك؟
Jerusalem	ki:f baʔdar asa:ʕdak	*kyf bqdr AsAςdk?*	كيف بقدر اساعدك؟
Beirut	ki:f fi:ni: sa:ʕdak	*kyf fyny sAςdk?*	كيف فيني ساعدك؟
Khartoum	ke:f mumkin asa:ʕdak	*kyf mmkn AsAςdk?*	كيف ممكن اساعدك؟
Tripoli	ki:f nigder nsa:ʕdak	*kyf nqdr nsAςdk?*	كيف نقدر نساعدك؟
Rabat	kife:ʃ niqder nʕa:wnek	*kyfAš nqdr nςAwnk?*	كيفاش نقدر نعاونك؟
Tunis	kife:ʃ nnajjem nʕa:wnek	*kyfAš nnjm nςAwnk?*	كيفاش ننجم نعاونك؟

Figure 13.1 A list of ten parallel sentences from MSA and DA corresponding to the English "How can I help you?".

romanizations: an IPA phonetic transcription, and an orthographic transliteration in the Habash-Soudi-Buckwalter scheme, a one-to-one map of the Arabic script to a romanization that helps clarify the information used in Arabic orthography (Habash et al., 2007).

Phonology There are many phonological differences between MSA and DA and across different DA. Most common are vowel differences, in terms of quality and length. For example, the LEV word for "tomato" بندورة *bndwrħ* (from Italian "pomodoro"), realizes phonologically as /banadoːra/, /banaduːra/, /bandoːra/, and /banduːra/, depending on the Levantine city it is uttered in. Consonantal pronunciation differences are also common and considered strong distinctive markers of dialectal affiliations. One example is the consonant corresponding to the MSA Qaf (ق *q* /q/), which realizes in a number of ways: /q/ in Tunis and Rabat, /ʔ/ (glottal stop) in Cairo and Beirut, and /g/ in Doha and Riyadh (Holes, 2004; Habash et al., 2018). In Figure 13.1, consider the different pronunciations for the verb "I can" اقدر *Aqdr* in Cairo, Baghdad, and Riyadh. Jerusalem and Rabat use the same verb with different morphology بقدر *bqdr* and نقدر *nqdr*.

Orthography While MSA has a standard orthography, DA do not. The spelling of DA words often reflects a mix of their phonology or etymology. DA are sometimes written in the so-called Arabizi Romanization script (Al-Badrashiny et al., 2014; Darwish, 2014). Arabic orthography, similar to the orthography of some other Semitic languages (Fabri et al., 2014), does not require the spelling of short vowels and consonant duplications. In Figure 13.1, the transliteration highlights how Arabic script hides many DA pronunciation differences.

Morphology Morphological differences within Arabic variants are quite common. DA morphology tends to be simpler than MSA's in certain respects (no case, reduced paradigms), but is more complex in other respects (many more clitics). Furthermore, different DA may express the same morpheme meaning in different forms or associate different meanings with the same form. One example is the future particle which appears as +س *s+* or سوف *swf* in MSA, +ح*H+* or رح *rH* in LEV dialects, +ه *h+* in EGY, باش *bAš* in Tunisian (TUN), and +ب *b+* in GLF. This last example (+ب *b+*) also appears in LEV but as the progressive particle. In Figure 13.1, the verb قدر *qdr* conjugates in the first person "I-can" using different prefixes: اقدر+ا *A+qdr* in Cairo, Baghdad and Riyadh, and نقدر+ن *n+qdr* in Tripoli and Rabat. The additional dialectal clitics result in utterances much longer than MSA, e.g., the EGY word مابنقولهالوش

mA+b+nqwl+hA+l+w+š /ma+bi+nʔul+ha+l+u:+ʃ/ "we do not say it to him" is a three-word sentence in MSA: لا نقولها له *lA nqwlhA lh.*

Syntax Syntactic differences among DA are relatively minor compared to morphological differences (Brustad, 2000). For example, negation may be realized differently using a combination of prefixes and suffixes (ما *mA*, مش *mish*, مو *muw*, لا *lA*, لم *lam*, etc.) but its syntactic distribution is generally uniform across varieties (Benmamoun, 2012). In Figure 13.1, the examples from Cairo, Baghdad, Riyadh, Tripoli, Rabat and Tunis, all agree on a basic sentence structure employing a subordinate clause introduced without a conjunction: "how I-can I-help-you ?". This particular construction is not possible in MSA. The MSA example uses a different construction where the "help" is expressed as a nominal direct object.

Lexicon The number of lexical differences among DA, and between MSA and different DA is significant (Omar, 1976). In addition to the Levantine example of "tomato" presented above, we encounter other variants, such as قوطة *qwtħ* /ʔuːṭa/ (Cairo), مطيشة *mTyšħ* /maṭiːʃa/ (Rabat), طماطيس *TmATys* /ṭamaːṭiːs/ (Sana'a), and طماطم *TmATm* /ṭamaːṭim/ (MSA, Jeddah, Benghazi, Khartoum), among others. In the examples in Figure 13.1, there are a number of forms used for every concept: "how" is expressed as كيف *kyf* (/kayfa/, /kiːf/, /keːf/), ازاي *AzAy* (/ʔizzaːy/), شلون *šlwn* (/ʃloːn/), and كيفاش *kyfAš* (/kiːfeːʃ/); and similarly, "I-help-you" is expressed as اساعدك *AsAɡdk* (/asaːʕdak/), نساعدك *nsAɡdk* (/nsaːʕdak/), and نعاونك *nɡAwnk* (/nʕaːwnek/).

13.3   Challenges of Arabic Dialect Processing

There are a number of challenges facing work on Arabic dialect processing. We present the main issues here under five categories: morphological richness, ambiguity, orthographic inconsistency, dialectal differences, and resource poverty. None of these issues are unique to Arabic, but their combination makes DA processing particularly challenging.

Morphological Richness Arabic, in all of its variants, is morphologically rich. For each core concept, or lemma, there are numerous inflected forms varying in terms of morphological features such as gender, number, person, aspect, mood, case, state and voice, in addition to the cliticization of a number of pronouns and particles (conjunctions, prepositions, the definite article, etc.). As mentioned earlier, MSA has less clitics and more morphological features than

DA. Arabic morphology is also complex, employing a combination of templatic and affixational morphological techniques, with numerous rewrite conditions and irregular forms (Habash, 2010). This richness leads to a higher type (unique form) to token ratio compared to other less morphologically rich languages, which consequently correlates with more sparsity in machine learning models.

Ambiguity Arabic orthography employs optional diacritics to represent short vowels and consonantal gemination. Although common in children's books, these diacritics are used less than 1.5 percent of the time in news articles intended for adult readers. In MSA, the average ambiguity is 12 analyses per word corresponding to 2.7 lemmas (dictionary lexical entries) per word (Habash, 2010). While most literate Arabic readers have little or no difficulty reading, computational models can be affected by the high degree of ambiguity resulting from absent diacritics. An example of the severity of ambiguity is the word بقدر *bqdr* /baʔdar/ "I can," which appears in the Jerusalem example in Figure 13.1. The undiacritized form of the word, out of context, has the following additional readings in the Jerusalem dialect: /bʔadar/ "in the destiny," /bʔadər/ "in the level," /bʔidər/ "in the cooking pot," and /baʔaddir/ "I estimate." MSA has similar ambiguity in this case except that the verbal readings cannot happen because the progressive clitic +ب *b+* does not exist in MSA. Ambiguity can also result from different interpretation of clitic letters: e.g., MSA ورد *wrd* can be analyzed as وَرد *ward* "roses" or وَرَّد *wa+rad~a* "and he answered." Context must be employed to determine the intended meaning of the word.

It should be pointed out that since orthographic ambiguity *normalizes* some differences, it can be seen as advantageous in the context of tasks generating Arabic text for Arabic readers – speech recognition or machine translation (MT) into Arabic; as well as in the context of sharing resources from different dialects.

Orthographic Inconsistency Both MSA and DA show a lot of orthographic inconsistency. For MSA, this is not so in the context of edited text, where standards can be followed. But MSA written online is plagued with inconsistencies. Zaghouani et al. (2014) report that 32 percent of words in MSA comments online have spelling errors. In the case of DA, we cannot talk about *spelling errors* since no official standards exist. Sources of inconsistency in DA spelling are due to the differences in phonology and morphology between DA and MSA. A particular word can be written in a way that reflects how it is pronounced or how it relates to an MSA cognate. Vowels changes in DA, particularly those related to length can be specified or elided orthographically. And the additional DA clitics can also be written attached or separate. Habash et al. (2018) presented 27 ways to write the Egyptian Arabic word /mabiʔulha:ʃ/ "he does not say it" encountered with Google Search including مبيقولهاش *mbyqwl-hAš* (ق *q* is used for /ʔ/ to reflect etymology), ما بيقولهاش *mA byqwlhAš*, مبيقلهاش *mbyqlhAš*, and مبؤلهاش *mbŵlhAš*. Ali et al. (2017) report that different transcribers of EGY audio recordings had disagreement rates between 8 percent and 23 percent when asked to write in DA with minimal guidelines.

In the last few years, in the context of work on Arabic NLP, a set of conventional orthography guidelines (CODA) has been proposed for a number of dialects: EGY (Habash et al., 2012a), Palestinian (PAL) (Jarrar et al., 2014), TUN (Zribi et al., 2014), Algerian (ALG) (Saadane and Habash, 2015), and GLF (Khalifa et al., 2016a). These efforts have been recently unified under the CODA* (CODA *Star*) common guidelines (Habash et al., 2018). Eskander et al. (2013b) reported that close to 24 percent of EGY words have non-CODA-compliant spellings. In addition to the variety in Arabic script spellings, DA text in particular is also known to appear on social media in a non-standard romanization, often called Arabizi (Al-Badrashiny et al., 2014; Darwish, 2014). Obviously, the high degree of inconsistency is problematic for NLP applications because of the added sparsity and increased out-of-vocabulary rates.

Resource Poverty In terms of raw monolingual text, DA is not particularly poor. There is a large and growing body of text being produced in DA on social media (Shoufan and Al-Ameri, 2015; Khalifa et al., 2016a; Abdul-Mageed et al., 2018; Zaghouani and Charfi, 2018; Bouamor et al., 2019). This large data is naturally produced (i.e., not commissioned for NLP research and development) and suffers from a lot of noise. Identifying the specific dialects is also a challenge for working with such data (Elfardy et al., 2013, 2014; Salameh et al., 2018). However in the context of manually annotated data, DA is much poorer than MSA. The amount of parallel text for MSA and other language is orders of magnitude larger than DA parallel text, which is mostly commissioned for NLP research. Since MSA is the official language of the various countries of the Arab World, all translations of news are primarily done in it (Jinxi, 2002). Most of the parallel data for dialect-English (Zbib et al., 2012) and dialect-MSA (Bouamor et al., 2014, 2018; Meftouh et al., 2015) are commissioned and limited. Morpho-syntactic annotations of Arabic have also focused on MSA more than DA, although there is a growing body of DA morphosyntactic annotations (Maamouri et al., 2014; Alshargi et al., 2016; Jarrar et al., 2016; Khalifa et al., 2018; Alshargi et al., 2019).

Dialectal Differences Inter-DA differences and DA-MSA differences pose serious challenges for Arabic NLP since they lower the ability of using existing resources for MSA or some dialect to help develop systems for other dialects. Khalifa et al. (2016a) report that using a state-of-the-art tool for MSA morphological disambiguation on GLF returns part-of-speech (POS) tag and lemma accuracies at about 72 percent and 64 percent respectively, compared to the performance on MSA, which is 96 percent for both (Pasha et al., 2014). Moreover, since DA and MSA coexist in a diglossic situation, developing NLP systems to handle multiple forms of Arabic is an unavoidable challenge (Elfardy and Diab, 2013; Salloum and Habash, 2013; Erdmann et al., 2017; Bouamor et al., 2018; Salameh et al., 2018).

It is important to point out that all of these challenges are intertwined with each other. A morphologically rich word can be ambiguous in many ways for any number of its inconsistent spellings, all leading to a higher likelihood of the word being out-of-vocabulary in the existing limited DA or MSA resources.

13.4   Arabic Dialect Resources

MSA has, for the longest time, received most of the attention of NLP resource creation efforts. There are many parallel and monolingual data collections, richly annotated treebanks, spelling corrected and diacritized data sets, and sophisticated tools for morphological analysis and disambiguation, syntactic parsing, etc. (Habash, 2010; Zaghouani, 2014). That said, most recently there has been a noticeable shift toward work on DA. This is motivated by interest in the domains where DA is prevalent – social media, and not because MSA NLP has been in any way "solved." In fact there are many MSA domains, particularly literature, that are poorly represented still.

This section discusses patterns of research directions and interest over time exemplified with pointers to specific DA resource creation efforts. For surveys of DA NLP resources, see (Habash, 2010; Zaghouani, 2014; Shoufan and Al-Ameri, 2015). For more information on the general challenges of data collection and representation for dialects, see Chapter 6.

13.4.1   A History of Dialects of Interest

The earlier efforts on DA NLP focused on EGY (Gadalla et al., 1997). This was a natural choice given that EGY was and remains the largest single (although not majority) Arabic dialect. Iraqi Arabic (IRQ) and to a lesser extent LEV also received considerable attention particularly in the USA for obvious political reasons (Appen, 2006, 2007). The Arab World lagged on the question of building resources and tools for DA. In fact, there was considerable resistance in the 1990s and early 2000s, although there were foundational efforts in linguistics resulting in important DA dictionaries, particularly, for EGY (Badawi and Hinds, 1986) and for GLF (Qafisheh, 1997).

As large USA government funded projects such as TRANSTAC and BOLT ended, and more research groups started to grow in the Arab World (such as the Qatar Computing Research Institute, and the Computational Approaches to Modeling Language Lab in New York University Abu Dhabi), there has been more work on dialects initiated by Arab researchers and with Arab funding. Another important factor is the growing interest in research on social media text, which is dominated by DA. With this shift, came a period of interest in smaller dialects such as PAL (Jarrar et al., 2016), TUN (McNeil and Faiza, 2011; Hamdi et al., 2014; Masmoudi et al., 2014), ALG (Smaïli et al., 2014), Yemeni (YEM) and Moroccan (MOR) (Alshargi et al., 2016), and GLF (Khalifa et al., 2016a, 2018; Al-Twairesh et al., 2018).

The next direction we are seeing more and more of is to go toward multi-DA resources, and integrative resources of MSA and DA. This pattern started in projects such as COLABA in the Columbia Arabic Dialect Group in the USA (Diab et al., 2010), and in work on dialect identification (naturally) (Zaidan and Callison-Burch, 2011b). Recent efforts include (Bouamor et al., 2014, 2018, 2019; Meftouh et al., 2015; Abdul-Mageed et al., 2018).

In addition to the pattern of focusing on multiple dialects instead of one, there is a growing pattern of going from coarse-grained classifications such as MSA-DA, or five DA dialect regions (MAG, EGY, LEV, IRQ, GLF) (Zaidan and Callison-Burch, 2011b) toward finer distinctions: first toward countries such as Syrian, Palestinian, and Algerian (Bouamor et al., 2014, 2019; Meftouh et al., 2015), and most recently toward city level dialects (Abdul-Mageed et al., 2018; Bouamor et al., 2018, 2019).

Computational lexicons also saw a similar pattern with earlier efforts being dialect specific, e.g., EGY (Kilany et al., 2002) and IRQ (Graff and Maamouri, 2009), and later efforts being multi-dialectal and multi-lingual, e.g., the Tharwa four-way English-MSA-EGY-LEV lexicon (Diab et al., 2014), the University of Manchester *The Dialects of Arabic* project covering 15 countries (Matras, 2017), and the MADAR lexicon covering dialects of 25 cities plus MSA (Bouamor et al., 2018).

13.4.2   A History of Domains and Genres

Since earlier efforts on DA NLP tended toward the speech recognition task, the earlier data sets were audio-and-transcription oriented, e.g., (Gadalla et al., 1997; Appen, 2006, 2007). This eventually shifted toward MT (from Arabic to English) (Sawaf, 2010; Zbib et al., 2012; Salloum and Habash, 2013; Bouamor et al., 2018) and dialect identification (Zaidan and Callison-Burch, 2013; Elfardy et al., 2014; Salameh et al., 2018). The cost of collecting and annotating audio is naturally higher than creating translations and that is also more expensive than dialect annotation. Zbib et al. (2012), and Zaidan and Callison-Burch (2013) demonstrated how to successfully use crowdsourcing for collecting translations and dialect ids, respectively. Others worked with specific trained annotators and translators (Bouamor et al., 2014, 2018, 2019; Meftouh et al., 2015).

The rise of social media in general facilitated the collection of data. As such, we see today that the largest DA data sets originate in social media: Twitter (Cotterell and Callison-Burch, 2014; Mubarak and Darwish, 2014; Alsarsour et al., 2018; Bouamor et al., 2019), Facebook (Huang, 2015), online commentaries (Zaidan and Callison-Burch, 2011b; Almeman and Lee, 2013; Salama et al., 2014) and blogs and forums (Al-Sabbagh and Girju, 2012; Khalifa et al., 2016a). Other datasets for multi-DA include the MADAR collection which commissioned the creation of a multi-parallel data set for 25 Arab cities based on the Basic Traveling Expressions Corpus (Takezawa et al., 2002) and paired with not just English, but also French, MSA and Japanese. This set is designed for use in MT (Erdmann et al., 2017) and dialect identification (Salameh et al., 2018; Bouamor et al., 2019).

13.4.3   A History of Annotation Targets and Richness

We use the term *annotation* to cover many kinds of information enrichment tasks: dialect identification labels, audio transcriptions, text translations, tokenization, POS tagging, lemmatization, and syntactic analysis. All of these tasks require guidelines and training. Some are simple enough to be done via crowdsourcing; but others require extensive training and possibly specially trained linguists.

Orthography As mentioned above, the earlier pre-social-media days saw more focus on audio transcription, an important yet shallow annotation that requires less training than POS tagging and syntactic parsing. The main challenge for it was transcription guidelines (Gadalla et al., 1997; Maamouri et al., 2004a) given that DA do not have spelling standards. A similar challenge was present in the creation of parallel Arabizi-Arabic script data sets to support translation from Arabizi to English (Bies et al., 2014). The Conventional Orthography for DA (CODA) was an important step in the development of common standards. It built on earlier LDC efforts, and was expanded from EGY first (Habash et al., 2012a) to a number of individual dialect (Zribi et al., 2014; Habash et al., 2015; Saadane and Habash, 2015; Khalifa et al., 2016a) and eventually to the common CODA* (CODA *star*) for over two dozen dialects (Habash et al., 2018). CODA is currently used in a number of projects to represent DA words consistently in lexicons and lemmatization tasks (Diab et al., 2014; Bouamor et al., 2018).

Morphology and Syntax The Penn Arabic Treebank (PATB) was a very important point in the development of MSA NLP tools (Maamouri et al.,

2004b). It set the standard for guidelines, and training and evaluation sets for Arabic tokenization, POS tagging and syntactic parsing (Pasha et al., 2014; Shahrour et al., 2016). Many resources built on top of it (Hajič et al., 2004; Palmer et al., 2008; Habash and Roth, 2009; Taji et al., 2017). The "equivalent" resource in DA is the EGY treebank (Maamouri et al., 2014) (ARZTB) and to a lesser extent an early resource on LEV (Chiang et al., 2006; Maamouri et al., 2006). These resources are much smaller in size compared to the PATB and not as used still. Since ARZTB, a number of projects came about to annotate DA morphologically, most notably for PAL (Jarrar et al., 2016), MOR and YEM (Alshargi et al., 2016), and GLF (Khalifa et al., 2018). Most recently, Alshargi et al. (2019) presented a corpus of seven Arabic dialects in a shared annotation scheme. There are some tools with focus on Arabic that have been used for multiple DA annotation efforts, such as DIWAN (Alshargi and Rambow, 2015) and MADARI (Obeid et al., 2018). Morphological and syntactic annotation, in general, are still lagging behind as most dialects still do not have treebanks or even extensive training data sets for morphological disambiguation.

Translation Creating parallel DA-English corpora has been shown to be doable via crowdsourcing (Zbib et al., 2012). Manual translation into DA from English, MSA or other DA is a less *natural* task, and it is not uncommon for translation agencies to refuse this work as the author knows from first hand experience. Bouamor et al. (2014) was the first to attempt creating a parallel non-toy sized multi-dialectal corpus. One challenge they faced was that starting with a form of Arabic (MSA or EGY) tended to prime the translators and resulted in biased translations. Bouamor et al. (2018) minimized this effect by starting translations from English or French.

Dialect, Sentiment, and Profile Identification Dialect identification, or specifying the dialect of the speaker or writer of a particular segment of text, is, by number of words, the most common form of DA annotation. The task is typically done by crowdsourcing (Zaidan and Callison-Burch, 2011b; Abdul-Mageed et al., 2018) at the sentence (or tweet level) of collected text for coarse categories. However, there are many other variants of the task: intentional commission in translation (Bouamor et al., 2014, 2018; Meftouh et al., 2015); annotation at the document level (Khalifa et al., 2016a); DA-MSA code-switching within textual segments (Elfardy et al., 2013), and annotation for finer categories (Bouamor et al., 2014; Abdul-Mageed et al., 2018). Most recently Zaghouani and Charfi (2018) started annotations of additional profile information beyond dialectness. Bouamor et al. (2019) annotated a collection of Arabic Twitter users at the profile level for their country of origin. There have been a few efforts in sentiment annotation in Arabic dialects (Abdul-Mageed and Diab, 2014; Badaro et al., 2014; Duwairi, 2015; Medhaffar et al., 2017).

13.5   Arabic Dialect Processing Tools and Applications

In this section we discuss a number of DA processing tools, from enabling technologies intended to support application development (e.g., stemmers and POS taggers) to user-interfacing applications (e.g., MT and speech recognition). Research and development in DA tools have followed the trends and advances seen in the rest of the field of NLP over the last three decades: from rule-based to statistical corpus-based, and now to neural deep learning approaches. That said, resource poverty and noise have continued to be important factors in work on DA tools. Fortunately, such challenges are not unique to Arabic, and insights in this work have a great potential in influencing research on other low-resource languages and variants.

For more information on similar issues for other languages and in general, see Chapter 7 (for tagging), Chapter 8 (for parsing), Chapter 9 (for dialect identification), Chapter 11 (for MT), and Chapter 12 (for speech processing).

Orthographic Normalization While MSA has received considerable attention in terms of developing resources for spelling correction (Mohit et al., 2014; Zaghouani et al., 2014; Watson et al., 2018), DA struggles with even what constitutes an acceptable spelling, since there are no application-independent standards to target. In the context of applications that do not generate DA lexical forms, e.g., dialect identification or MT into English, automatic techniques such as Morfessor (Creutz and Lagus, 2005), or other aggressive normalizations employing character replacements can be used. In such contexts, the form of the DA words is just an input feature into a system. However, when targeting DA output as in the output of MT or speech recognition, some care is needed to ensure consistency for the sake of the user. This is also true when piping applications where the DA forms are part of the pipe interface. Eskander et al. (2013b) developed a system to map into CODA for EGY. Some research have been done to map from Arabizi to Arabic script (Darwish, 2014) including targeting CODA as the output representation (Al-Badrashiny et al., 2014). Other approaches addressed DA noisy spelling indirectly by learning better embeddings for low frequency types (Erdmann et al., 2018; Zalmout et al., 2018); and Dasigi and Diab (2011) and Abidi and Smaïli (2018) attempted to map DA spelling variants to each other.

Morphological Analysis Morphological analysis is the process of identifying the various possible analyses associated with an ambiguous word out of context. There is a great number of publications on MSA morphological analysis (Habash, 2010). Much of the work on MSA started in the period of rule-based approaches to NLP and has produced important resources such as the SAMA analyzer (Graff et al., 2009). The early efforts on DA morphological analysis were also rule-based. Habash and Rambow (2006) developed a common manually constructed framework for DA and MSA. Habash et al. (2012b) built a morphological analyzer for EGY (CALIMA-EGY) based on the Egyptian Colloquial Arabic Lexicon (ECAL) (Kilany et al., 2002) with semi-automatic extensions. Salloum and Habash (2014) developed a system for extending SAMA and CALIMA-EGY using hand-crafted rules for defining new DA affixes based on existing ones. Abuata and Al-Omari (2015) developed a rule-based system to segment affixes and clitics in GLF text; and Khalifa et al. (2017) built a GLF verb analyzer by creating morphological paradigms and extending them. Eskander et al. (2013a) developed a technique to generate a morphological analyzer based on an annotated corpus, by hypothesizing inflectional paradigms and completing them. Alshargi et al. (2016) applied this technique to MOR and YEM.

Morphological Disambiguation and POS Tagging Morphological disambiguation refers to the process of determining the specific in-context analysis of an ambiguous word. Morphological disambiguation is a more general form of POS tagging where all inflectional features are determined together with full diacritization and lemmatization. Stemming and tokenization refer to the processing of a word in a specific way relating to its morphological composition. Just like lemmatization and POS tagging, stemming and tokenization make decisions that in principle are contextual; although some models ignore context for the sake of efficiency (Abdelali et al., 2016; Khalifa et al., 2016b). Some approaches focus on singular aspects of the disambiguation task, such as diacritization (Abdelali et al., 2018) or segmentation (Erdmann et al., 2019), while others take a joint solution to addressing multiple aspects (Habash et al., 2013) and even multiple variants (Zalmout and Habash, 2019).

Early Arabic NLP efforts on POS tagging and morphological disambiguation focused on MSA (Diab et al., 2004; Habash and Rambow, 2005) and relied heavily on the PATB (Maamouri et al., 2004b). Habash and Rambow (2005), in their MADA system, relied on a combination of rule-based morphological analyzers and machine learning based models for disambiguation. Habash et al. (2013) extended MADA to EGY using the ARZTB (Maamouri et al., 2014) and the EGY morphological analyzer CALIMA-EGY (Habash et al., 2012b). These efforts were included in the MADAMIRA system which supports both MSA and EGY (Pasha et al., 2014). Eskander et al. (2016) presented a single pipeline to produce a morphological analyzer and tagger from a single annotation for EGY and LEV – for LEV, they used the Curras dataset (Jarrar et al., 2014). Zalmout et al. (2018) presented a noise-robust neural model for EGY morphological disambiguation. Darwish et al. (2018) presented a multi-dialectal POS tagger for Arabic tweets in four dialects. Samih et al. (2017) used DA character embeddings for word segmentation. Most recently, AlGhamdi and Diab (2019) demonstrated the use of word embeddings in POS tagging of code-switching data; and Zalmout and Habash (2019) pushed the state-of-the-art with the use adversarial multitask learning for joint multi-feature and multi-dialect morphological modeling.

Syntactic Analysis Work on Arabic syntactic analysis and base-phrase chunking has been limited in comparison to other efforts, and the majority of it focused on MSA (Diab et al., 2004; Habash, 2010; Pasha et al., 2014; Shahrour et al., 2016). One exceptional early effort is the work of Chiang et al. (2006), who compared different methods to build DA (specifically Jordanian) parsers using only a MSA treebank and a MSA-DA dictionary.

Dialect Identification Dialect identification is the task of automatically labeling a segment of speech or text with the dialect it comes from. The task can vary in a number of ways including: (a) the type of input: speech or text; (b) the unit of annotation: document, sentence, or word; and (c) the granularity of the label: region, country, or city. A number of efforts attempted to define guidelines for how to identify the dialect of text (Habash et al., 2008; Elfardy and Diab, 2012a). Zaidan and Callison-Burch (2011a), as mentioned earlier, annotated a large collection of commentaries for regional dialects; and Bouamor et al. (2018) commissioned the creation of a data set in a number of city dialects. Bouamor et al. (2019) extended the effort to include Twitter data as part of a shared task on Arabic fine-grained dialect identification that attracted over 20 teams. Some researchers focused on text dialect identification, most notably Zaidan and Callison-Burch (2013), but also Elfardy and Diab in a series of publications around their AIDA (*Automatic Identification of Dialectal Arabic*) system (Elfardy and Diab, 2012b, 2013; Elfardy et al., 2014). Salloum et al. (2014) demonstrated the value of dialect identification in MT system selection. While corpus based models seem to be popular, a number of researchers exploited linguistic phenomena or observations about the dialects in their dialect identification systems (Darwish et al., 2014; El-Haj et al., 2018). Most recently, Salameh et al. (2018) demonstrated and evaluated a method for automatic identification of city-level dialects. Their work led to the creation of an online demo tool called ADIDA (Automatic Dialect Identification for Arabic) (Obeid et al., 2019). In contrast, and quite independently, there has been work on dialect identification using acoustic features (Biadsy et al., 2009b; Biadsy and Hirschberg, 2009; Bougrine et al., 2017). In the VarDial 2017 and 2018 evaluation campaigns, a track on Arabic dialect identification targeted the recognition of the dialect of speech transcripts along with acoustic features (Zampieri et al., 2017, 2018).

Machine Translation MT is the task of automatically mapping a text in one language into another language. In the last thirty years, MT experienced two major shifts, first from rule-based approaches to statistical corpus-based approaches; and then from those to neural deep learning approaches. The shift to corpus-based approaches happened more readily for MSA where there are lots of parallel corpora. However, since DA do not have a lot of parallel data, the earlier MT efforts for DA focused on exploiting linguistic similarities between MSA and DA to translate from DA to MSA as target (Shaalan et al., 2007), or as a pivot to translate to another language, e.g., English (Sawaf, 2010; Salloum and Habash, 2011, 2012, 2013; Salloum, 2018). MT from DA to MSA was also used in non-MT contexts, such as domain adaptation for parsing (Chiang et al., 2006). These earlier efforts to exploit existing resources (namely MSA and other languages) and linguistic relatedness gave way to corpus-based statistical solutions that were based on commissioned data sets (Zbib et al., 2012). Since these results, more and more resources have been created (Bouamor et al., 2014, 2018; Meftouh et al., 2015; Erdmann et al., 2017); however, these resources are still not large enough, particularly, for neural approaches. Both Salloum (2018) and Erdmann et al. (2019) explored methods to learn segmentation models for DA and evaluated on MT as a task. Most recently, Shapiro and Duh (2019) compared the use of pipelined or integrated approaches for DA neural machine translation. For a survey on MT for Arabic dialects, see Harrat et al. (2019).

Speech Recognition Automatic Speech Recognition (ASR), one of the essential applications for the human-computer interface, has made great leaps in quality over the last few decades. ASR requires sizable amounts of training data in terms of audio and transcriptions, and in terms of monolingual data for language model training. As mentioned above, some of the earliest efforts in data creation and collection for DA were in speech corpora to support ASR. Kirchhoff et al. (2003) is one of the earliest efforts on ASR for DA, specifically EGY. The majority of work on Arabic ASR has focused on MSA (Soltau et al., 2007; Biadsy et al., 2009a). However there has been a resurgence in interest in DA ASR recently with more attention paid to the challenges of DA orthography and mining social-media sources of monolingual text (Ali et al., 2014; Wray and Ali, 2015; Zampieri et al., 2017; Ali, 2018). In the MGB-3 challenge (*speech recognition challenge in the wild*), the leading teams benefited from transfer learning and audio adaption by building background acoustic models using lots of MSA data and augmenting it with small dialectal in-domain data (Ali et al., 2017). Most recently, Ali et al. (2019) showed that the use of use of DA morphological abstractions and spelling normalization produce ASR evaluation metrics with higher correlation with human judgment.

Sentiment Analysis Sentiment analysis is, generally speaking, the task of automatically identifying the affective state communicated in text. This area has received and continue to receive a lot of attention, including for Arabic (Korayem et al., 2012; Mulki et al., 2018). Because of the relevance and popularity of sentiment analysis in the context of social media, there are numerous efforts on DA sentiment analysis (Abdul-Mageed and Diab, 2014; Badaro et al., 2014, 2015; Duwairi, 2015; Baly et al., 2017; Medhaffar et al., 2017; Alsayat and Elmitwally, 2019; Rahab et al., 2019). For a recent survey, see Badaro et al. (2019).

Dialogue Despite DA being the natural language form for dialogue in Arabic, there is a surprising absence of chatbots and conversational agents in DA. The only exception to our knowledge is Botta, an Egyptian Arabic social chatbot (Abu Ali and Habash, 2016).

13.6   Conclusion and Outlook

In this chapter, we presented a summary of the linguistic facts and computational challenges surrounding the work on Arabic dialect processing. We also presented a number of resources and tools that have been developed to address these challenges. We hope this will serve as a good starting reference for researchers in the field of NLP in general and Arabic NLP in particular.

Research on Arabic dialect NLP has been growing steadily in a number of dimensions: there are more publications on more applications, more techniques, and more dialects. While 25 years ago, work was limited to Egyptian Arabic or Levantine Arabic from relatively clean telephone transcriptions, today, researchers are working with dozens of dialects in noisy social media settings. The challenges posed when processing dialects are particularly exciting in the context of the major shift in the field of NLP toward neural networks and vector space models where the lack of dialectal data and the high degree of noise offer more interesting opportunities to push the state-of-the-art not just for Arabic dialect processing, but also for dialect and variant processing in general.

References

Abdelali, Ahmed, Darwish, Kareem, Durrani, Nadir, and Mubarak, Hamdy. 2016. Farasa: A Fast and Furious Segmenter for Arabic. Pages 11–16 of: *Proceedings of the Conference of the North American Chapter of the Association for Computational Linguistics (NAACL)*.

Abdelali, Ahmed, Attia, Mohammed, Samihy, Younes, Darwish, Kareem, and Mubarak, Hamdy. 2018. Diacritization of Maghrebi Arabic Sub-Dialects. *arXiv preprint arXiv:1810.06619*.

Abdul-Mageed, Muhammad, and Diab, Mona. 2014. SANA: A Large Scale Multi-Genre, Multi-Dialect Lexicon for Arabic Subjectivity and Sentiment Analysis. Pages 1162–1169 of: *Proceedings of the Language Resources and Evaluation Conference (LREC)*.

Abdul-Mageed, Muhammad, Alhuzali, Hassan, and Elaraby, Mohamed. 2018. You Tweet What You Speak: A City-Level Dataset of Arabic Dialects. In: *Proceedings of the Language Resources and Evaluation Conference (LREC)*.

Abidi, Karima, and Smaïli, Kamel. 2018. An Automatic Learning of an Algerian Dialect Lexicon by Using Multilingual Word Embeddings. In: *Proceedings of the Language Resources and Evaluation Conference (LREC)*.

Abu Ali, Dana, and Habash, Nizar. 2016. Botta: An Arabic Dialect Chatbot. Pages 208–212 of: *Proceedings of the International Conference on Computational Linguistics (COLING)*.

Abuata, Belal, and Al-Omari, Asma. 2015. A Rule-Based Stemmer for Arabic Gulf Dialect. *Journal of King Saud University – Computer and Information Sciences*, **27**(2), 104–112.

Al-Badrashiny, Mohamed, Eskander, Ramy, Habash, Nizar, and Rambow, Owen. 2014. Automatic Transliteration of Romanized Dialectal Arabic. Pages 30–38 of: *Proceedings of the Conference on Computational Natural Language Learning (CoNLL)*.

Al-Sabbagh, Rania, and Girju, Roxana. 2012. A Supervised POS Tagger for Written Arabic Social Networking Corpora. Pages 39–52 of: *Proceedings of the Conference on Natural Language Processing (KONVENS)*. ÖGAI.

Al-Twairesh, Nora, Al-Matham, Rawan, et al. 2018. SUAR: Towards Building a Corpus for the Saudi Dialect. In: *Proceedings of the International Conference on Arabic Computational Linguistics (ACLing)*.

AlGhamdi, Fahad, and Diab, Mona. 2019. Leveraging Pretrained Word Embeddings for Part-of-Speech Tagging of Code Switching Data. In: *Proceedings of the Sixth Workshop on NLP for Similar Languages, Varieties and Dialects*.

Ali, Ahmed, Mubarak, Hamdy, and Vogel, Stephan. 2014. Advances in Dialectal Arabic Speech Recognition: A Study Using Twitter to Improve Egyptian ASR. In: *Proceedings of the International Workshop on Spoken Language Translation (IWSLT)*.

Ali, Ahmed, Vogel, Stephan, and Renals, Steve. 2017. Speech Recognition Challenge in the Wild: Arabic MGB-3. Pages 316–322 of: *Proceedings of the Automatic Speech Recognition and Understanding Workshop (ASRU)*.

Ali, Ahmed, Khalifa, Salam, and Habash, Nizar. 2019. Towards Variability Resistant Dialectal Speech Evaluation. In: *Proceedings of Interspeech*.

Ali, Ahmed Mohamed Abdel Maksoud. 2018. *Multi-dialect Arabic broadcast speech recognition*. Ph.D. thesis, The University of Edinburgh.

Almeman, Khalid, and Lee, Mark. 2013. Automatic Building of Arabic Multi Dialect Text Corpora by Bootstrapping Dialect Words. Pages 1–6 of: *Proceedings of the International Conference on Communications, Signal Processing, and their Applications (ICCSPA)*.

Alsarsour, Israa, Mohamed, Esraa, Suwaileh, Reem, and Elsayed, Tamer. 2018. DART: A Large Dataset of Dialectal Arabic Tweets. In: *Proceedings of the Language Resources and Evaluation Conference (LREC)*.

Alsayat, Ahmed, and Elmitwally, Nouh. 2019. A Comprehensive Study for Arabic Sentiment Analysis (Challenges and Applications). *Egyptian Informatics Journal*, **21**(1), 7–12.

Alshargi, Faisal, and Rambow, Owen. 2015. DIWAN: A Dialectal Word Annotation Tool for Arabic. Pages 49–58 of: *Proceedings of the Workshop for Arabic Natural Language Processing (WANLP)*.

Alshargi, Faisal, Kaplan, Aidan, Eskander, Ramy, Habash, Nizar, and Rambow, Owen. 2016. Morphologically Annotated Corpus and a Morphological Analyzer for Moroccan and San'ani Yemeni Arabic. In: *Proceedings of the Language Resources and Evaluation Conference (LREC)*.

Alshargi, Faisal, Dibas, Shahd, Alkhereyf, Sakhar, et al. 2019. Morphologically Annotated Corpora for Seven Arabic Dialects: Taizi, Sanaani, Najdi, Jordanian, Syrian, Iraqi and Moroccan. In: *Proceedings of the Fourth Arabic Natural Language Processing Workshop (WANLP)*.

Appen, Pty Ltd, Sydney, and Australia. 2006. *Iraqi Arabic Conversational Telephone Speech, Transcripts LDC2006T16*. Web Download. Philadelphia: Linguistic Data Consortium.

Appen, Pty Ltd, Sydney, and Australia. 2007. *Levantine Arabic Conversational Telephone Speech, Transcripts LDC2007T0*. Web Download. Philadelphia: Linguistic Data Consortium.

Badaro, Gilbert, Baly, Ramy, Hajj, Hazem, Habash, Nizar, El-hajj, Wassim, and Shaban, Khaled. 2014. An Efficient Model for Sentiment Classification of Arabic Tweets on Mobiles. In: *Qatar Foundation Annual Research Conference*.

Badaro, Gilbert, Baly, Ramy, Akel, Rana, et al. 2015. A Light Lexicon-Based Mobile Application for Sentiment Mining of Arabic Tweets. Page 18 of: *Proceedings of the Workshop for Arabic Natural Language Processing (WANLP)*.

Badaro, Gilbert, Baly, Ramy, Hajj, Hazem, et al. 2019. A Survey of Opinion Mining in Arabic: A Comprehensive System Perspective Covering Challenges and Advances in Tools, Resources, Models, Applications, and Visualizations. *ACM Transactions on Asian and Low-Resource Language Information Processing (TALLIP)*, **18**(3), 27.

Badawi, El-Said, and Hinds, Martin. 1986. *A Dictionary of Egyptian Arabic*. Librairie du Liban.

Badawi, El-Said M. 1973. *Mustawayat al-'Arabiyya al-mu'asira fi Misr (The Levels of Modern Arabic in Egypt)*. Cairo: Dar al-Ma'arif.

Baly, Ramy, El-Khoury, Georges, Moukalled, Rawan, Aoun, Rita, Hajj, Hazem, Shaban, Khaled Bashir, and El-Hajj, Wassim. 2017. Comparative Evaluation of Sentiment Analysis Methods across Arabic Dialects. *Procedia Computer Science*, **117**, 266–273.

Bassiouney, Reem. 2009. *Arabic Sociolinguistics: Topics in Diglossia, Gender, Identity, and Politics*. Washington, DC: Georgetown University Press.

Benmamoun, Elabbas. 2012. Agreement and Cliticization in Arabic Varieties from Diachronic and Synchronic Perspectives. Pages 137–150 of: *Al'Arabiyya: Journal of American Association of Teachers of Arabic*, vol. 44–45. Washington, DC: Georgetown University Press.

Biadsy, Fadi, and Hirschberg, Julia. 2009. Using Prosody and Phonotactics in Arabic Dialect Identification. In: *Proceedings of the Conference of the International Speech Communication Association (Interspeech)*.

Biadsy, Fadi, Habash, Nizar, and Hirschberg, Julia. 2009a. Improving the Arabic Pronunciation Dictionary for Phone and Word Recognition with Linguistically-Based Pronunciation Rules. Pages 397–405 of: *Proceedings of the Conference of the North American Chapter of the Association for Computational Linguistics (NAACL)*.

Biadsy, Fadi, Hirschberg, Julia, and Habash, Nizar. 2009b. Spoken Arabic Dialect Identification Using Phonotactic Modeling. Pages 53–61 of: *Proceedings of the Workshop on Computational Approaches to Semitic Languages (CASL)*.

Bies, Ann, Song, Zhiyi, Maamouri, Mohamed, et al. 2014. Transliteration of Arabizi into Arabic Orthography: Developing a Parallel Annotated Arabizi-Arabic Script SMS/Chat Corpus. In: *Proceedings of the Workshop for Arabic Natural Language Processing (WANLP)*.

Bouamor, Houda, Habash, Nizar, and Oflazer, Kemal. 2014. A Multidialectal Parallel Corpus of Arabic. In: *Proceedings of the Language Resources and Evaluation Conference (LREC)*.

Bouamor, Houda, Habash, Nizar, Salameh, Mohammad, et al. 2018. The MADAR Arabic Dialect Corpus and Lexicon. In: *Proceedings of the Language Resources and Evaluation Conference (LREC)*.

Bouamor, Houda, Hassan, Sabit, and Habash, Nizar. 2019. The MADAR Shared Task on Arabic Fine-Grained Dialect Identification. In: *Proceedings of the Fourth Arabic Natural Language Processing Workshop (WANLP)*.

Bougrine, Soumia, Cherroun, Hadda, and Ziadi, Djelloul. 2017. Hierarchical Classification for Spoken Arabic Dialect Identification using Prosody: Case of Algerian Dialects. *CoRR*, **abs/1703.10065**.

Brustad, Kristen. 2000. *The Syntax of Spoken Arabic: A Comparative Study of Moroccan, Egyptian, Syrian, and Kuwaiti Dialects*. Georgetown University Press.

Chiang, David, Diab, Mona, Habash, Nizar, Rambow, Owen, and Shareef, Safiullah. 2006. Parsing Arabic Dialects. In: *Proceedings of the Conference of the European Chapter of the Association for Computational Linguistics (EACL)*.

Cotterell, Ryan, and Callison-Burch, Chris. 2014. A Multi-Dialect, Multi-Genre Corpus of Informal Written Arabic. Pages 241–245 of: *Proceedings of the Language Resources and Evaluation Conference (LREC)*.

Creutz, Mathias, and Lagus, Krista. 2005. *Unsupervised morpheme segmentation and morphology induction from text corpora using Morfessor 1.0*. Helsinki University of Technology.

Darwish, Kareem. 2014. Arabizi Detection and Conversion to Arabic. Pages 217–224 of: *Proceedings of the Workshop for Arabic Natural Language Processing (WANLP)*.

Darwish, Kareem, Sajjad, Hassan, and Mubarak, Hamdy. 2014. Verifiably Effective Arabic Dialect Identification. In: *Proceedings of the Conference on Empirical Methods in Natural Language Processing (EMNLP)*.

Darwish, Kareem, Mubarak, Hamdy, Abdelali, Ahmed, et al. 2018. Multi-dialect Arabic POS Tagging: A CRF Approach. In: *Proceedings of the Language Resources and Evaluation Conference (LREC)*.

Dasigi, Pradeep, and Diab, Mona. 2011. CODACT: Towards Identifying Orthographic Variants in Dialectal Arabic. In: *Proceedings of the International Joint Conference on Natural Language Processing (IJCNLP)*.

Diab, Mona, Hacioglu, Kadri, and Jurafsky, Daniel. 2004. Automatic Tagging of Arabic Text: From Raw Text to Base Phrase Chunks. Pages 149–152 of: *Proceedings of the Conference of the North American Chapter of the Association for Computational Linguistics (NAACL)*.

Diab, Mona, Habash, Nizar, Rambow, Owen, AlTantawy, Mohamed, and Benajiba, Yassine. 2010. COLABA: Arabic Dialect Annotation and Processing. In: *Proceedings of the Workshop on Language Resources and Human Language Technology for Semitic Languages.*

Diab, Mona T., Al-Badrashiny, Mohamed, Aminian, Maryam, et al. 2014. Tharwa: A Large Scale Dialectal Arabic-Standard Arabic-English Lexicon. Pages 3782–3789 of: *Proceedings of the Language Resources and Evaluation Conference (LREC).*

Duwairi, Rehab M. 2015. Sentiment Analysis for Dialectical Arabic. Pages 166–170 of: *Proceedings of the International Conference on Information and Communication Systems (ICICS).*

El-Haj, Mahmoud, Rayson, Paul, and Aboelezz, Mariam. 2018. Arabic Dialect Identification in the Context of Bivalency and Code-Switching. In: *Proceedings of the Language Resources and Evaluation Conference (LREC).*

Elfardy, Heba, and Diab, Mona. 2012a. Simplified Guidelines for the Creation of Large Scale Dialectal Arabic Annotations. In: *Proceedings of the Language Resources and Evaluation Conference (LREC).*

Elfardy, Heba, and Diab, Mona. 2012b. Token Level Identification of Linguistic Code Switching. In: *Proceedings of the International Conference on Computational Linguistics (COLING).*

Elfardy, Heba, and Diab, Mona. 2013. Sentence Level Dialect Identification in Arabic. Pages 456–461 of: *Proceedings of the Conference of the Association for Computational Linguistics (ACL).*

Elfardy, Heba, Al-Badrashiny, Mohamed, and Diab, Mona. 2013. Code Switch Point Detection in Arabic. In: *Proceedings of the Conference on Application of Natural Language to Information Systems (NLDB).*

Elfardy, Heba, Al-Badrashiny, Mohamed, and Diab, Mona. 2014. AIDA: Identifying Code Switching in Informal Arabic Text. Pages 94–101 of: *Proceedings of the Conference on Empirical Methods in Natural Language Processing (EMNLP).*

Erdmann, Alexander, Habash, Nizar, Taji, Dima, and Bouamor, Houda. 2017. Low Resourced Machine Translation via Morpho-syntactic Modeling: The Case of Dialectal Arabic. In: *Proceedings of the Machine Translation Summit (MT Summit).*

Erdmann, Alexander, Zalmout, Nasser, and Habash, Nizar. 2018. Addressing Noise in Multidialectal Word Embeddings. In: *Proceedings of the Conference of the Association for Computational Linguistics (ACL).*

Erdmann, Alexander, Khalifa, Salam, Oudah, Mai, Habash, Nizar, and Bouamor, Houda. 2019. A Little Linguistics Goes a Long Way: Unsupervised Segmentation with Limited Language Specific Guidance. In: *Proceedings of the Workshop of the Special Interest Group on Computational Morphology and Phonology (SIGMORPHON).*

Eskander, Ramy, Habash, Nizar, and Rambow, Owen. 2013a. Automatic Extraction of Morphological Lexicons from Morphologically Annotated Corpora. Pages 1032–1043 of: *Proceedings of the Conference on Empirical Methods in Natural Language Processing (EMNLP).*

Eskander, Ramy, Habash, Nizar, Rambow, Owen, and Tomeh, Nadi. 2013b. Processing Spontaneous Orthography. Pages 585–595 of: *Proceedings of the Conference of the North American Chapter of the Association for Computational Linguistics (NAACL).*

Eskander, Ramy, Habash, Nizar, Rambow, Owen, and Pasha, Arfath. 2016. Creating Resources for Dialectal Arabic from a Single Annotation: A Case Study on

Egyptian and Levantine. Pages 3455–3465 of: *Proceedings of the International Conference on Computational Linguistics (COLING).*

Fabri, Ray, Gasser, Michael, Habash, Nizar, Kiraz, George, and Wintner, Shuly. 2014. Linguistic Introduction: The Orthography, Morphology and Syntax of Semitic languages. Pages 3–41 of: *Natural Language Processing of Semitic Languages.* Springer.

Ferguson, Charles F. 1959. Diglossia. *Word*, **15**(2), 325–340.

Gadalla, Hassan, Kilany, Hanaa, Arram, Howaida, et al. 1997. *CALLHOME Egyptian Arabic Transcripts LDC97T19.* Web Download. Philadelphia: Linguistic Data Consortium.

Graff, David, and Maamouri, Mohamed. 2009. *Iraqi Arabic Morphological Lexicon (IAML) Version 6.5.* Linguistic Data Consortium.

Graff, David, Maamouri, Mohamed, Bouziri, Basma, Krouna, Sondos, Kulick, Seth, and Buckwalter, Tim. 2009. *Standard Arabic Morphological Analyzer (SAMA) Version 3.1.* Linguistic Data Consortium LDC2009E73.

Guellil, Imane, Saâdane, Houda, Azouaou, Faical, Gueni, Billel, and Nouvel, Damien. 2019. Arabic Natural Language Processing: An Overview. *Journal of King Saud University-Computer and Information Sciences.*

Habash, Nizar, and Rambow, Owen. 2005. Arabic Tokenization, Part-of-Speech Tagging and Morphological Disambiguation in One Fell Swoop. Pages 573–580 of: *Proceedings of the Conference of the Association for Computational Linguistics (ACL).*

Habash, Nizar, and Rambow, Owen. 2006. MAGEAD: A Morphological Analyzer and Generator for the Arabic Dialects. Pages 681–688 of: *Proceedings of the International Conference on Computational Linguistics and the Conference of the Association for Computational Linguistics (COLING-ACL).*

Habash, Nizar, and Roth, Ryan. 2009. CATiB: The Columbia Arabic Treebank. Pages 221–224 of: *Proceedings of the Joint Conference of the Association for Computational Linguistics and the International Joint Conference on Natural Language Processing (ACL-IJCNLP).*

Habash, Nizar, Soudi, Abdelhadi, and Buckwalter, Tim. 2007. On Arabic Transliteration. Pages 15–22 of: van den Bosch, A., and Soudi, A. (eds), *Arabic Computational Morphology: Knowledge-Based and Empirical Methods.* Springer, Netherlands.

Habash, Nizar, Rambow, Owen, Diab, Mona, and Kanjawi-Faraj, Reem. 2008. Guidelines for Annotation of Arabic Dialectness. In: *Proceedings of the Workshop on HLT & NLP within the Arabic World.*

Habash, Nizar, Diab, Mona, and Rambow, Owen. 2012a. Conventional Orthography for Dialectal Arabic. Pages 711–718 of: *Proceedings of the Language Resources and Evaluation Conference (LREC).*

Habash, Nizar, Eskander, Ramy, and Hawwari, Abdelati. 2012b. A Morphological Analyzer for Egyptian Arabic. Pages 1–9 of: *Proceedings of the Workshop of the Special Interest Group on Computational Morphology and Phonology (SIGMORPHON).*

Habash, Nizar, Roth, Ryan, Rambow, Owen, Eskander, Ramy, and Tomeh, Nadi. 2013. Morphological Analysis and Disambiguation for Dialectal Arabic. In: *Proceedings of the Conference of the North American Chapter of the Association for Computational Linguistics (NAACL).*

Habash, Nizar, Jarrar, Mustafa, Alrimawi, Faeq, Akra, Diyam, Zalmout, Nasser, Bartolotti, Eric, and Arar, Mahdi. 2015. *Palestinian Arabic Conventional Orthography Guidelines*. Tech. rept. Birzeit University and New York Univesity Abu Dhabi.

Habash, Nizar, Eryani, Fadhl, Khalifa, Salam, et al. 2018. Unified Guidelines and Resources for Arabic Dialect Orthography. In: *Proceedings of the Language Resources and Evaluation Conference (LREC)*.

Habash, Nizar Y. 2010. *Introduction to Arabic Natural Language Processing*. San Rafael, California: Morgan & Claypool Publishers.

Hajič, Jan, Smrž, Otakar, Zemánek, Petr, Šnaidauf, Jan, and Beška, Emanuel. 2004. Prague Arabic Dependency Treebank: Development in Data and Tools. Pages 110–117 of: *Proceedings of the International Conference on Arabic Language Resources and Tools*. Cairo, Egypt: ELDA.

Hamdi, Ahmed, Gala, Nuria, and Nasr, Alexis. 2014. Automatically building a Tunisian Lexicon for Deverbal Nouns. Pages 95–102 of: *Proceedings of the Workshop on Applying NLP Tools to Similar Languages, Varieties and Dialects*. Dublin, Ireland: Association for Computational Linguistics and Dublin City University.

Harrat, Salima, Meftouh, Karima, and Smaïli, Kamel. 2019. Machine Translation for Arabic Dialects (Survey). *Information Processing & Management*, **56**(2), 262–273.

Holes, Clive. 2004. *Modern Arabic: Structures, Functions, and Varieties*. Georgetown Classics in Arabic Language and Linguistics. Georgetown University Press.

Huang, Fei. 2015. Improved Arabic Dialect Classification with Social Media Data. Pages 2118–2126 of: *Proceedings of the Conference on Empirical Methods in Natural Language Processing (EMNLP)*.

Jarrar, Mustafa, Habash, Nizar, Akra, Diyam, and Zalmout, Nasser. 2014. Building a Corpus for Palestinian Arabic: A Preliminary Study. Pages 18–27 of: *Proceedings of the Workshop for Arabic Natural Language Processing (WANLP)*.

Jarrar, Mustafa, Habash, Nizar, Alrimawi, Faeq, Akra, Diyam, and Zalmout, Nasser. 2016. Curras: An Annotated Corpus for the Palestinian Arabic Dialect. *Language Resources and Evaluation*, 1–31.

Jinxi, Xu. 2002. *UN Parallel Text (Arabic-English), LDC Catalog No.: LDC2002E15*. Linguistic Data Consortium, University of Pennsylvania.

Khalifa, Salam, Habash, Nizar, Abdulrahim, Dana, and Hassan, Sara. 2016a. A Large Scale Corpus of Gulf Arabic. In: *Proceedings of the Language Resources and Evaluation Conference (LREC)*.

Khalifa, Salam, Zalmout, Nasser, and Habash, Nizar. 2016b. YAMAMA: Yet Another Multi-Dialect Arabic Morphological Analyzer. Pages 223–227 of: *Proceedings of the International Conference on Computational Linguistics (COLING)*.

Khalifa, Salam, Hassan, Sara, and Habash, Nizar. 2017. A Morphological Analyzer for Gulf Arabic Verbs. In: *Proceedings of the Workshop for Arabic Natural Language Processing (WANLP)*.

Khalifa, Salam, Habash, Nizar, Eryani, Fadhl, Obeid, Ossama, Abdulrahim, Dana, and Kaabi, Meera Al. 2018. A Morphologically Annotated Corpus of Emirati Arabic. In: *Proceedings of the Language Resources and Evaluation Conference (LREC)*.

Kilany, H., Gadalla, H., Arram, H., Yacoub, A., El-Habashi, A., and McLemore, C. 2002. *Egyptian Colloquial Arabic Lexicon*. LDC catalog number LDC99L22.

Kirchhoff, Katrin, Bilmes, Jeff, Das, Sourin, et al. 2003. Novel Approaches to Arabic Speech Recognition: Report from the 2002 Johns-Hopkins Summer Workshop.

In: *Proceedings of the International Conference on Acoustics, Speech and Signal Processing (ICASSP)*.

Korayem, Mohammed, Crandall, David, and Abdul-Mageed, Muhammad. 2012. Subjectivity and Sentiment Analysis of Arabic: A Survey. In: *Proceedings of the International Conference on Advanced Machine Learning Technologies and Applications*.

Maamouri, Mohamed, Buckwalter, Tim, and Cieri, Christopher. 2004a. Dialectal Arabic Telephone Speech Corpus: Principles, Tool Design, and Transcription Conventions. In: *Proceedings of the International Conference on Arabic Language Resources and Tools*.

Maamouri, Mohamed, Bies, Ann, Buckwalter, Tim, and Mekki, Wigdan. 2004b. The Penn Arabic Treebank: Building a Large-Scale Annotated Arabic Corpus. Pages 102–109 of: *Proceedings of the International Conference on Arabic Language Resources and Tools*.

Maamouri, Mohamed, Bies, Ann, Buckwalter, Tim, et al. 2006. Developing and Using a Pilot Dialectal Arabic Treebank. In: *Proceedings of the Language Resources and Evaluation Conference (LREC)*.

Maamouri, Mohamed, Bies, Ann, Kulick, Seth, Ciul, Michael, Habash, Nizar, and Eskander, Ramy. 2014. Developing an Egyptian Arabic Treebank: Impact of Dialectal Morphology on Annotation and Tool Development. In: *Proceedings of the Language Resources and Evaluation Conference (LREC)*.

Masmoudi, Abir, Ellouze Khmekhem, Mariem, Esteve, Yannick, Hadrich Belguith, Lamia, and Habash, Nizar. 2014. A Corpus and Phonetic Dictionary for Tunisian Arabic Speech Recognition. In: *Proceedings of the Language Resources and Evaluation Conference (LREC)*.

Matras, Y. 2017. *Database of Arabic Dialects. The University of Manchester*.

McNeil, Karen, and Faiza, Miled. 2011. Tunisian Arabic Corpus : Creating a Written Corpus of an "Unwritten" Language. In: *Proceedings of the Workshop on Arabic Corpus Linguistics (WACL)*.

Medhaffar, Salima, Bougares, Fethi, Estève, Yannick, and Hadrich-Belguith, Lamia. 2017. Sentiment Analysis of Tunisian Dialects: Linguistic Ressources and Experiments. In: *Proceedings of the Workshop for Arabic Natural Language Processing (WANLP)*.

Meftouh, Karima, Harrat, Salima, Jamoussi, Salma, Abbas, Mourad, and Smaïli, Kamel. 2015. Machine Translation Experiments on PADIC: A Parallel Arabic Dialect Corpus. In: *Proceedings of the Pacific Asia Conference on Language, Information and Computation*.

Mohit, Behrang, Rozovskaya, Alla, Habash, Nizar, Zaghouani, Wajdi, and Obeid, Ossama. 2014. The First QALB Shared Task on Automatic Text Correction for Arabic. Pages 39–47 of: *Proceedings of the Workshop for Arabic Natural Language Processing (WANLP)*.

Mubarak, Hamdy, and Darwish, Kareem. 2014. Using Twitter to Collect a Multi-dialectal Corpus of Arabic. In: *Proceedings of the Workshop for Arabic Natural Language Processing (WANLP)*.

Mulki, Hala, Haddad, Hatem, and Babaoglu, Ismail. 2018. Modern Trends in Arabic Sentiment Analysis: A Survey. *Traitement Automatique des Langues*.

Obeid, Ossama, Khalifa, Salam, Habash, Nizar, Bouamor, Houda, Zaghouani, Wajdi, and Oflazer, Kemal. 2018. MADARi: A Web Interface for Joint Arabic Morphological Annotation and Spelling Correction. In: *Proceedings of the Language Resources and Evaluation Conference (LREC)*.

Obeid, Ossama, Salameh, Mohammad, Bouamor, Houda, and Habash, Nizar. 2019. ADIDA: Automatic Dialect Identification for Arabic. In: *Proceedings of the 2019 Conference of the North American Chapter of the Association for Computational Linguistics (Demonstrations)*.

Omar, Margaret Kleffner. 1976. *Levantine and Egyptian Arabic: Comparative Study*. Department of State.

Palmer, Martha, Babko-Malaya, Olga, Bies, Ann, Diab, Mona, Maamouri, Mohamed, Mansouri, Aous, and Zaghouani, Wajdi. 2008. A Pilot Arabic Propbank. In: *Proceedings of the Language Resources and Evaluation Conference (LREC)*.

Pasha, Arfath, Al-Badrashiny, Mohamed, Diab, Mona, et al. 2014. MADAMIRA: A Fast, Comprehensive Tool for Morphological Analysis and Disambiguation of Arabic. Pages 1094–1101 of: *Proceedings of the Language Resources and Evaluation Conference (LREC)*.

Qafisheh, H.A. 1997. *NTC's Gulf Arabic-English dictionary*. NTC Pub. Group.

Rahab, Hichem, Zitouni, Abdelhafid, and Djoudi, Mahieddine. 2019. SANA: Sentiment Analysis on Newspapers Comments in Algeria. *Journal of King Saud University – Computer and Information Sciences*, **1**, 1–9.

Saadane, Houda, and Habash, Nizar. 2015. A Conventional Orthography for Algerian Arabic. Page 69 of: *Proceedings of the Workshop for Arabic Natural Language Processing (WANLP)*.

Salama, Ahmed, Bouamor, Houda, Mohit, Behrang, and Oflazer, Kemal. 2014. YouDACC: The Youtube Dialectal Arabic Comment Corpus. Pages 1246–1251 of: *Proceedings of the Language Resources and Evaluation Conference (LREC)*.

Salameh, Mohammad, Bouamor, Houda, and Habash, Nizar. 2018. Fine-Grained Arabic Dialect Identification. Pages 1332–1344 of: *Proceedings of the International Conference on Computational Linguistics (COLING)*.

Salloum, Wael, and Habash, Nizar. 2011. Dialectal to Standard Arabic Paraphrasing to Improve Arabic-English Statistical Machine Translation. Pages 10–21 of: *Proceedings of the First Workshop on Algorithms and Resources for Modelling of Dialects and Language Varieties*.

Salloum, Wael, and Habash, Nizar. 2012. Elissa: A Dialectal to Standard Arabic Machine Translation System. Pages 385–392 of: *Proceedings of the International Conference on Computational Linguistics (COLING)*.

Salloum, Wael, and Habash, Nizar. 2013. Dialectal Arabic to English Machine Translation: Pivoting through Modern Standard Arabic. In: *Proceedings of the Conference of the North American Chapter of the Association for Computational Linguistics (NAACL)*.

Salloum, Wael, and Habash, Nizar. 2014. ADAM: Analyzer for Dialectal Arabic Morphology. *Journal of King Saud University – Computer and Information Sciences*, **26**(4), 372–378.

Salloum, Wael, Elfardy, Heba, Alamir-Salloum, Linda, Habash, Nizar, and Diab, Mona. 2014. Sentence Level Dialect Identification for Machine Translation System

Selection. In: *Proceedings of the Conference of the Association for Computational Linguistics (ACL).*

Salloum, Wael Sameer. 2018. *Machine Translation of Arabic Dialects.* Ph.D. thesis, Columbia University.

Samih, Younes, Attia, Mohammed, Eldesouki, Mohamed, et al. 2017. A Neural Architecture for Dialectal Arabic Segmentation. In: *Proceedings of the Workshop for Arabic Natural Language Processing (WANLP).*

Sawaf, Hassan. 2010. Arabic Dialect Handling in Hybrid Machine Translation. In: *Proceedings of the Conference of the Association for Machine Translation in the Americas (AMTA).*

Shaalan, Khaled, Abo Bakr, Hitham, and Ziedan, Ibrahim. 2007. Transferring Egyptian Colloquial Dialect into Modern Standard Arabic. Pages 525–529 of: *Proceedings of the Conference on Recent Advances in Natural Language Processing (RANLP).*

Shahrour, Anas, Khalifa, Salam, Taji, Dima, and Habash, Nizar. 2016. Camel–Parser: A System for Arabic Syntactic Analysis and Morphological Disambiguation. Pages 228–232 of: *Proceedings of the International Conference on Computational Linguistics (COLING).*

Shapiro, Pamela, and Duh, Kevin. 2019. Comparing Pipelined and Integrated Approaches to Dialectal Arabic Neural Machine Translation. In: *Proceedings of the Sixth Workshop on NLP for Similar Languages, Varieties and Dialects.*

Shoufan, Abdulhadi, and Al-Ameri, Sumaya. 2015. Natural Language Processing for Dialectical Arabic: A Survey. Page 36 of: *Proceedings of the Workshop for Arabic Natural Language Processing (WANLP).*

Smaïli, Kamel, Abbas, Mourad, Meftouh, Karima, and Harrat, Salima. 2014. Building Resources for Algerian Arabic Dialects. In: *Proceedings of the Conference of the International Speech Communication Association (Interspeech).*

Soltau, Hagen, Saon, George, Kingsbury, Brian, Kuo, Jeff, Mangu, Lidia, Povey, Daniel, and Zweig, Geoffrey. 2007. The IBM 2006 GALE Arabic ASR system. In: *Proceedings of the Acoustics, International Conference on Speech and Signal Processing (ICASSP).*

Taji, Dima, Habash, Nizar, and Zeman, Daniel. 2017. Universal Dependencies for Arabic. In: *Proceedings of the Workshop for Arabic Natural Language Processing (WANLP).*

Takezawa, Toshiyuki, Sumita, Eiichiro, Sugaya, Fumiaki, Yamamoto, Hirofumi, and Yamamoto, Seiichi. 2002. Toward a Broad-coverage Bilingual Corpus for Speech Translation of Travel Conversations in the Real World. Pages 147–152 of: *Proceedings of the Language Resources and Evaluation Conference (LREC).*

Watson, Daniel, Zalmout, Nasser, and Habash, Nizar. 2018. Utilizing Character and Word Embeddings for Text Normalization with Sequence-to-Sequence Models. In: *Proceedings of the 2018 Conference on Empirical Methods in Natural Language Processing.*

Wray, Samantha, and Ali, Ahmed. 2015. Crowdsource a Little to Label a Lot: Labeling a Speech Corpus of Dialectal Arabic. In: *Proceedings of the Conference of the International Speech Communication Association.*

Zaghouani, Wajdi. 2014. Critical Survey of the Freely Available Arabic Corpora. Pages 1–8 of: *Proceedings of the Workshop on Open-Source Arabic Corpora and Processing Tools (OSACT).*

Zaghouani, Wajdi, and Charfi, Anis. 2018. ArapTweet: A Large Multi-dialect Twitter Corpus for Gender, Age and Language Variety Identification. In: *Proceedings of the Language Resources and Evaluation Conference (LREC)*.

Zaghouani, Wajdi, Mohit, Behrang, Habash, Nizar, et al. 2014. Large Scale Arabic Error Annotation: Guidelines and Framework. In: *Proceedings of the Language Resources and Evaluation Conference (LREC)*.

Zaidan, Omar, and Callison-Burch, Chris. 2013. Arabic Dialect Identification. *Computational Linguistics*, **40**(1), 171–202.

Zaidan, Omar F., and Callison-Burch, Chris. 2011a. Crowdsourcing Translation: Professional Quality from Non-Professionals. In: *Proceedings of the Conference of the Association for Computational Linguistics (ACL)*.

Zaidan, Omar F, and Callison-Burch, Chris. 2011b. The Arabic Online Commentary Dataset: An Annotated Dataset of Informal Arabic with High Dialectal Content. Pages 37–41 of: *Proceedings of the Conference of the Association for Computational Linguistics (ACL)*.

Zalmout, Nasser, and Habash, Nizar. 2019. Adversarial Multitask Learning for Joint Multi-feature and Multi-dialect Morphological Modeling. In: *Proceedings of the Conference of the Association for Computational Linguistics (ACL)*.

Zalmout, Nasser, Erdmann, Alexander, and Habash, Nizar. 2018. Noise-Robust Morphological Disambiguation for Dialectal Arabic. In: *Proceedings of the Conference of the North American Chapter of the Association for Computational Linguistics (NAACL)*.

Zampieri, Marcos, Malmasi, Shervin, Ljubešić, Nikola, et al. 2017. Findings of the VarDial Evaluation Campaign 2017. Pages 1–15 of: *Proceedings of the Workshop on NLP for Similar Languages, Varieties and Dialects (VarDial)*.

Zampieri, Marcos, Malmasi, Shervin, Nakov, Preslav, et al. 2018. Language Identification and Morphosyntactic Tagging: The Second VarDial Evaluation Campaign. In: *Proceedings of the Fifth Workshop on NLP for Similar Languages, Varieties and Dialects (VarDial)*.

Zbib, Rabih, Malchiodi, Erika, Devlin, Jacob, et al. 2012. Machine Translation of Arabic Dialects. Pages 49–59 of: *Proceedings of the Conference of the North American Chapter of the Association for Computational Linguistics (NAACL)*.

Zribi, Ines, Boujelbane, Rahma, Masmoudi, Abir, Ellouze, Mariem, Belguith, Lamia, and Habash, Nizar. 2014. A Conventional Orthography for Tunisian Arabic. In: *Proceedings of the Language Resources and Evaluation Conference (LREC)*.

14 Computational Processing of Varieties of Chinese: Comparable Corpus-Driven Approaches to Light Verb Variation

Menghan Jiang, Hongzhi Xu, Jingxia Lin, Dingxu Shi, and Chu-Ren Huang

Abstract

This chapter offers an overview of both the linguistic background and the state of the art of NLP research on varieties of Chinese as similar languages. In addition to briefly summarizing grammatical features of Mandarin Chinese, we also underline important contrasts between Chinese dialects and varieties of Mandarin Chinese. As Chinese dialects are mutually unintelligible although with a shared writing system, we focus our discussion on varieties of Mandarin Chinese. We introduce two comparable corpora containing varieties of Mandarin Chinese: the Chinese Gigaword Corpus and LIVAC as the most important resources. We also give a survey of related studies and methodology, ranging from the top bag-of-word approach in Huang and Lee (2008) to the various deep learning algorithms adopted in the 2019 VarDial shared task.

14.1 Introduction

The identification and classification of similar languages in natural language processing deal with the same set of phenomena as linguistic studies of language variations and changes. Broadly speaking, studies of language variations assume a synchronic perspective and focus on differences in terms of geographical and demographic contrasts. Studies of language changes, on the other hand, assume a chronological perspective based on the differences of the same language through time. Language variations can lead to language changes over time, and varieties of languages (or dialects) can in fact be the result of more localized language changes. Recent NLP studies on similar languages hence focus on identification and classification tasks without conscientious differentiation of variations and changes. Identification of Mandarin Chinese, being the language with the most native speakers as well as a fast growing global language, poses several interesting issues and challenges. First, the varieties of Chinese share a semantics-driven character-based system; thus, phonetic and phonological variations are not reflected and do not play significant roles in identification of similar languages. Second, the writing system has two variants, namely simplified and traditional characters, that are encoded differently. However, encoding based identification of the variants is highly unreliable, as any text can be automatically converted between each other. Given these two characteristics, identification and classification of variants of Mandarin Chinese have not been systematically attempted until recently, and previous linguistic studies focused mostly on lexical alternations. In this chapter, we will provide a general overview of the Chinese language and its grammar, as well as the background of variations of Mandarin Chinese. It is followed by an introduction to previous linguistic studies of variations in Chinese. It will conclude with survey on recent NLP research on the identification of Chinese varieties as well as the main approaches adopted and future developments.

In what follows, we will first provide a comprehensive background of the complex issues of Chinese dialects and varieties of Chinese. After that is an overview of the grammar of Mandarin Chinese, which is then followed by a summary of past linguistic studies of variations in Mandarin Chinese. Finally, the focal part of this chapter introduces various computational approaches to varieties of Chinese, which is followed by conclusion.

14.1.1   Chinese Language or Languages: From Similar Languages, Dialects, to Varieties

Mandarin Chinese, or simply either Mandarin or Chinese, is one of the most commonly learned first or second languages in the world currently. In fact, Mandarin Chinese, with over 900 million native speakers, is one of the ten main dialect groups of Chinese, along with Yue, Min, Wu, and others (often also referred to as Sinitic languages). Commonly accepted dichotomy of language and dialect is not easily applicable in the context of Chinese language(s). Cantonese, Min, Hakka, and Wu are traditionally referred to as dialects (方言 fāngyán) of Chinese but are mutually unintelligible. Different Chinese dialects/Sinitic languages are in fact "similar languages" and are fairly easy to differentiate with significant differences at all linguistic levels, from lexicon to phonology and morpho-syntax. Each dialect/Sinitic language may obtain distinguishable lexical or syntactic features, e.g., Southern Min dialect (Huang, 1988b; Chen, 2011), Yue dialect (Yue-Hashimoto, 1991; Lin and Kwok, 2010), or other Chinese dialects (Dwyer, 1992; Wang et al., 2012). However, these "Chinese dialects" share a common writing system and literary textual tradition is shared among them, which allows speakers to have a shared linguistic identity. In fact, in some of these "dialects," such as Cantonese, Hakka, and Southern-Min, there are two co-existing linguistic systems at morpho-phonology level. The "colloquial" system is the indigenous system, while the "literary" system is a close mapping to the common language–Mandarin. It is easier to envision that these are in fact "dialects" when the "literary" system is considered. Yet, the "colloquial" systems are also clearly very different from each other. To overcome the mutual unintelligibility problem, a variant of Northern Mandarin Chinese, is designated as the common language about a hundred years. Mandarin (i.e., the language of the mandarins (the officers)) has been the official language of the government by convention for over a thousand years but has also become the common language both in spoken language and written text by constitution in the modern era, first by the Nationalists (ROC) after 1911, and then by the Communists PRC in 1949. In this chapter, we continue to use the term "dialects" in its traditional meaning of referring to the group of languages in the Sinitic family, e.g., Cantonese, Hakka, (Northern) Min, Southern Min, etc. In our discussion of varieties and variations, on the other hand, we refer to varieties of Mandarin Chinese.

In daily nontechnical usage, both Chinese and Mandarin refer to the standard Mandarin that is generally accepted in a wide range of public discourse, such as government, education, broadcasting, and publishing (Huang et al., 2014). This standard language is referred to as 普通话 *pǔtōnghuà* common language' in Mainland China (hence force, Putonghua), and Macau, and as 国语 *guóyǔ* "national language" in Taiwan (hence force, Guoyu), while both terms are used in Hong Kong (Huang and Shi, 2016). Mandarin itself is not all uniform and standardized. The most obvious variations are from standard Mandarin used in different regions. Despite the same linguistic heritage, Mandarin Chinese in different regions has evolved in different ways as a result of political, economic, cultural, and social reasons (Huang et al., 2013). For example, although Putonghua in Mainland China and Guoyu in Taiwan share the same lexical and syntactic system, variations arose since 1949 for several reasons between Mainland and Taiwan (Lin et al., 2018). First, and most of all, the two varieties developed in relative isolation from each other and under different political systems for about 40 years during the Cold War era. Although the thawing that eventually leads to frequent exchanges, direct travel links, and close commercial ties between Taiwan and Mainland China today, 40 years of total isolation from each other did allow the language use to develop into different varieties (Huang et al., 2014). Second, each has its own regulating bodies as well as different contextual influences. Third, Guoyu has more southern influences than Putonghua, even though both are based on Beijing Mandarin. Note that Putonghua in China is written with simplified Chinese characters with Pinyin romanization for pedagogy; while Guoyu in Taiwan is written in traditional characters and uses the Zhuyin system (sometimes called bopomofo) for pedagogy. With recent more frequent exchanges at different levels of Mainland China and Taiwan, some of the differences have begun to get absorbed.

It is important to note that compared to the differences among Chinese dialects, the differences among different varieties of Mandarin used in different regions are subtle. Furthermore, the differences among varieties of Mandarin tend to be differences in frequency or preference (more conventionalized versus less used) instead of un/grammatical differences (Huang et al., 2013). For instance, Jiang and Huang (2017b) have shown that Taiwan VO compounds present a tendency of taking event-denoting objects while Mainland has more preference of taking common NP as the object. Therefore, to differentiate the varieties of the standard language (Mandarin/Putonghua/Guoyu) used in different regions poses a challenge in Natural Language Processing, especially when only texts are available.

14.1.2   Grammatical Features of Chinese

A brief syntactic overview of Chinese grammar, especially morphology and syntax, is given in this section before a short discussion on the implication on the processing of varieties of and similar languages.

We mentioned earlier that one of the most salient differences between the two main varieties of Mandarin (Mainland and Taiwan) is the simplified and traditional writing systems. To understand that, it is important to understand the Chinese writing systems.

A character is the smallest unit of the writing system in Chinese. A character typically, but not always, stands for a morpheme (as the smallest meaningful unit) which can often be used a word (as the smallest unit with independent syntactic functions). Phonologically, each Chinese character represents a syllable. And semantically, a Chinese character usually encodes a lexicalized concept. Each Chinese character as a glyph can be further decomposed as components (部件 bùjiàn). The majority of Chinese characters are formed by semantic-phonetic composition (形声 xíngshēng), with one semantic radical and one phonetic part. Hence the radical+phonetic structure has been treated as the default structure of Chinese characters and can often be leveraged in processing (Chen et al., 2019). The most typical order of compositional is either left–right or top–down.

Most native Chinese morphemes are monosyllabic, as in 花 huā 'flower' and 好 hǎo "good." Native disyllabic morphemes are few in number and a large portion of them have either a consonant alliteration, such as 蜘蛛 zhīzhū "spider," or a vowel rhyme, such as 迷离 mílí 'bewildered' (Huang and Shi, 2016). Inflection does not play a crucial role in Chinese grammar. The few inflectional morphemes which do play a role include the plural marker 们 *men* that is a suffix to personal pronouns and certain human nous such as 学生们 *xuéshēngmén* "students," aspectual marker 着 *zhe*, -了 *le*, and -过 *guò* that are suffixes to verbs such as 看着 *kànzhe* "looking at," and, to a certain extent, infixes like 得- *de* '-able' or its negative form 不 *bù* 'NEG' that appear inside a V(erb)-R(esultative) complex word (Huang and Shi, 2016), such as 看得见 *kàndejiàn* 'be able to see'. Generally speaking, word token frequencies are dominated by monosyllabic words and word type frequencies are dominated by disyllabic words, although longer words are not unusual. This leads to typical word length average to between 1.3 and 1.4, roughly equivalent when measured in terms of character, morpheme, or syllable.

Most Chinese morphemes, no matter whether free or bound, or whether content or functional, are active in word formation. Word formation rules include derivation, such as reduplication (e.g., 看看 *kànkan* 'take a look'), and compounding. Compounding is by far the most prevalent device for word formation in Chinese and can be classified in terms of relation between the two stems, such as Verb+Object compound (e.g., 读书 *dúshū* "attend school"), Subject+Predicate compounds (e.g., 心疼 *xīnténg* "heart-ache," etc.), as well as Verb+Resultative, Noun+Noun, Adjetive+Noun, etc.

Words in Chinese can be assigned parts-of-speech just like other languages. However, there are three exception categories that behave differently from more familiar languages such as English. First, classifiers are an essential component of NP and provide the units of enumeration. Second, sentential particles conveying eventive information are a separate category that typically occurs at the end of a sentence, such as the interrogative particles 吗 *ma* and 呢 *ne*. These particles are typically in neutral tones. Third, conceptual equivalents of adjectives are typically state verbs that can occur alone as sentential predicates. There are only a handful of true adjectives that requires a head verb (e.g., 非常 *fēicháng* 'exceptional, unusual').

Sentences and phrases in Chinese are quite similar to English and share the SVO word order. The main components of a sentence are a subject and a predicate. Yet topicalization is also common in Chinese. Since a topic typically takes the sentence-initial position, it is not usual to have a general topic, i.e., a topic that does not have other grammatical functions, or a pre-posed object as a topic. Given the SVO word order and the prominence of topics, one long standing linguistic issue in Chinese is the differentiation of topic and subject. At phrasal level, Chinese noun phrases are typically head final, while verb phrases are typically head initial.

The predominant way to negate a proposition in Mandarin is to insert a negative morpheme into the clause bearing the proposition. The most commonly used negative morphemes are 不 *bù* "not," which negates predicates with an imperfect aspect, and 没有 *méiyǒu* "not" or its shortened form 没 *méi* "not," which negates predicates with a perfect aspect.

There is no grammatical tense in Chinese, although it has a complex aspectual system instead. Aspectual markers are attached to predicates, usually on the head, indicating the status of the event or action, as well as the relation between the time of action and the time of reference. Commonly used aspectual marker in Mandarin mainly include 了 *le*, 过 *guò*, 着 *zhe*, and 在 *zài*.

Another important feature of Chinese that does not fall clearly into the category of either syntax or morphology is cliticization or phrasal affixation. Many important grammatical constructions involve cliticization, such as the sentential particles as sentential clitics (Huang, 1989a); the relative clause marker 的 *de* and nominalizer 者 *zhě* as NP clitics (Huang, 1988a, 1989b) etc. This creates great challenge in traditional pipeline models of NLP as word formation cannot be completed without phrasal formation and vice versa (Huang, 2015).

Among the grammatical characteristics, three stands out from the perspective of identification and classification of varieties or similar languages. The first is the poverty of morphology and the dominance of compounding. As Chinese has only a few inflectional and/or derivational affixes, very little morphological cues can be used for processing of variants. The second is the dominance of a stable orthography for over 2000 years as well as the use of Chinese characters (instead of phonological alphabets like the writing systems of the majority of languages in the world). This means that very little variations can be detected by orthography and almost none at the morphemic-character level. The third is the richness and varieties of the tonal system. This fact means that the detection and classification of varieties of spoken Chinese are much easier to conceptualize and implement than written texts. Hence past literature contains a significant number of studies on detection of varieties of speech but only a handful dealt with written texts.

14.1.3   Grammatical Studies on Chinese Language Variations

Although the differences between Mainland China and Taiwan variants of Mandarin Chinese attracted considerable interests in linguistics, no comprehensive and systematic studies on the grammatical variations between them have emerged yet. Most past linguistic studies focused on individual lexical differences. With the availability of corpora of both varieties, more recent studies make use of naturally-occurring data and go beyond individual lexical items, e.g., Fang (2013, 2014, 2015). And only a few studies, e.g., Huang et al. (2014) and Lin et al. (2014), adopt computational and statistical tools to process the data. A good number of existing grammatical studies were conducted by listing or briefly discussing the individual grammatical constructions.

A selected sample of studies based on individual lexical or constructional variations are introduced below to outline the range of grammatical variations between these two variants. Wei (1984) and Kubler (1985) focus on the development of Mandarin in Taiwan and point out several distinctive grammatical constructions in Taiwan Mandarin, including 有 *yǒu* "have"+VP, 会/不会 *huì/búhuì* "can/cannot," 来/去 *lái/qù* "come/go" and 来去 *láiqù* "come and go," 给 *gěi* "give," 用 *yòng* "use" with nominalized verbs, 在 *zài* "at" as an auxiliary verbs, and so on. Huang (1988b) also investigates the variation of several grammatical constructions based on Taiwan novels: reduplication (Liao, 1999), use of classifiers, comparative sentences, 到 *dào* "reach" constructions, etc. Diao (2000, 2012a,b,c,d,e) has also conducted a number of studies on the variation differences in different grammatical constructions between Mainland and Taiwan Mandarin, including 获 *huò* "receive" constructions (Diao, 2012a), 遭 *zāo* "suffer" and 被 *bèi* "BEI" constructions (Diao, 2012c, 2013), 将 *jiāng* "will" constructions (Diao, 2012f), the uses of 而已 *éryǐ* "nothing than" (Diao, 2012d) and so on. Zhu and Zhou (1990) mainly focus on the differences in the transitivity of VO compounds, uses of clitics, reduplications of adjectives and modal verb usages between Mainland and Taiwan Mandarin. Qiu and Fan (1994) describe the grammatical differences mainly based on V+neg+V question, and word order of double object construction. Zhao and Shi (2014) talk about the different usages of 有信心 *yǒuxìnxīn* "have confidence" constructions in Hong Kong, Taiwan, and Mainland Mandarin.

In addition to the observations on individual grammatical constructions, Diao (1998) also discusses the variation differences between Mainland and Taiwan Mandarin from the perspective of language characteristics/properties. He points out that there are several characteristics of Taiwan Mandarin: the remnants of classical Chinese and Japanese, the mixing of different grammatical forms, and the influence of Southern Min. Other studies also mention the influence of Southern Min and English for Taiwan Mandarin (Dai and Zhao, 2009; Mao, 2007; Huang, 1988b; Kubler, 1985, among others).

14.2   Computational Approaches to Language Variations in Chinese and Other Languages

Having laid out the overall issues involving Chinese, Mandarin Chinese and their varieties, we focus on corpus based computational approaches to language variations.

14.2.1   An Overview of NLP Methods for Language Variation

With the development of social media, large amounts of linguistic data have become available online. Concomitantly, NLP, more specifically machine learning technologies, has developed at an unprecedented rate due to the need for the analysis of this new big data. Using NLP methods to answer questions in linguistics research has become a rather common methodology in quantitative linguistics. NLP technologies can be used in two different ways: the traditional methodology starts with a hypothesis which is then tested, with a result that either supports or rejects the hypothesis; secondly, NLP approaches have the advantage of capturing potential correlations between variables over traditional statistical methods. Given a set of linguistic features representing the data entries, the technology can automatically identify salient patterns in the data, e.g., by measuring the similarities between data entries. NLP technologies have been used in various language variation studies, including phonetics, lexical semantics, syntax, and pragmatics. Studies have shown that the NLP approach could find consistent results with the conclusions drawn from previous linguistic studies, as well as discovering patterns that are not found previously (Abramov and Mehler, 2011; Bloem et al., 2014; Hamilton et al., 2016).

The identification of languages is an important task in NLP, especially in an environment where code-switching is common (Solorio et al., 2014). In linguistics, classifying languages into proper families is also an important topic; this research area traditionally relies on studying a large set of linguistic typological features. With NLP technologies, especially clustering algorithms, these languages can be automatically grouped together based on various automatically extracted features. Batagelj et al. (1992), for example, use hierarchical clustering to gradually merge similar languages into groups with different similarity measures, including Levenshtein distance, cosine, etc., based on the senses of sixteen commonly-used words in sixty-five languages. Blanchard et al. (2011) use a similar method and test it with fifty Indo-European languages and fifty Austronesian languages by automatically constructing the language taxonomy. Due to the gradual maturation of syntactic parsing systems, there are also studies that use features that have been extracted based on syntactic structures, rather than simple collocations, for automatic parsing, e.g., Abramov and Mehler (2011); Bloem et al. (2014).

A less prevalent trend is to focus on the variations of a particular linguistic construction. By doing so, these studies shed light both on how languages vary as well as on the linguistic account of the particular constructions. Interestingly, light verbs are among the most targeted construction based on this approach (e.g., Samardžić and Merlo, 2010; Huang et al., 2014).

Statistics has been used in the study of dialectology as early as Séguy (1971) and computational/NLP technologies were applied to dialectology (geographic variation) studies to measure the linguistic distance between dialects by Nerbonne et al. (1999), and Nerbonne and Heeringa (2001). Most of the recent works studying geographic language variation are done with social media data such as Twitter and Facebook, e.g., (Doyle, 2014; Eisenstein et al., 2014; Huang et al., 2016; Donoso and Sánchez, 2017) in English and other languages.

The VarDial workshop series inspired a new stream of research in identifying similar languages and language variations. The shared tasks in VarDial 2017

(Zampieri et al., 2017) and VarDial 2018 (Zampieri et al., 2018) highlighted the challenge and potential of applying NLP technologies to similar languages and language variations. The tasks cover an eclectic yet impressive list of similar languages: Arabic Dialects; German Dialects; Dutch and Flemish in Subtitles; Indo-Aryan Languages; among Bosnian, Croatian, and Serbian; Malay and Indonesian; Persian and Dari; Canadian and Hexagonal French; Brazilian and European Portuguese; and Argentine, Peninsular, and Peruvian Spanish. The third campaign in 2019 has the following tracks, and the relevant track on Chinese will be discussed later: German Dialect Identification (GDI), Cross-lingual Morphological Analysis (CMA), Discriminating between Mainland and Taiwan variation of Mandarin Chinese (DMT), Moldavian vs. Romanian Cross-dialect Topic identification (MRC), Cuneiform Language Identification (CLI).

In most of the submitted systems in the VarDial workshop series, the most frequently used features are still based on n-grams, or skip n-grams, either in character level or in word level. Such features, however, have largely compromised in capturing semantics, and will be affected by the distribution of the data across different domains. This limit certainly applies to the study of light verbs, where traditional n-gram based features are likely to reflect the domain difference rather than the difference in their true usages.

The recent development of distributional semantics allows representations of word meanings using a vector of continuous values (word embeddings), e.g., Word2Vec (Mikolov et al., 2013), and this allows for the analysis of semantic variation in both geographical and chronological dimensions. Hamilton et al. (2016), for example, use SVD, Neural Network, and Word2Vec models to trace the lexical meaning changes and found the results consistent with what have been found by linguists. Peirsman et al. (2010) also adopt the word embeddings approach to uncover geographic lexical variations between Belgian Dutch and Netherlandic Dutch.

Although word embeddings appear to be the dominant trend for lexical semantic analysis, a key issue of the current technologies of generating word embeddings is that it assumes a single sense for a single word form. This causes problems for the linguistic studies where differentiating senses is necessary. Huang et al. (2014), Lin et al. (2014), and Xu et al. (2020), hence adopted a different assumption for the identification of Mandarin light verb variations. They assume that each instance of a light verb in the text represents a single usage of it. In other words, instead of summarizing all occurrences of a single word form into a single vector, they represent each occurrence of a light verb as a separate data point. This assumption avoids the data sparseness problem by extracting features in a higher level (more abstract) that together represent the usage of a light verb in a particular context.

14.2.2 Automatic Detection of Chinese Dialects Based on Spoken Language

Due to the significant differences in morpho-syntax among Chinese dialects as well as the fact that they share a single writing system and a single standardized written language, past studies on detection and classification of dialects are mainly based on speech.

Dialect identification based on speech is an important task. It is particularly important for speech recognition. Dialects of one language can have big differences in terms of almost all linguistic levels including lexical choice, morphology, syntax, semantics, and pragmatics. Thus, identifying language dialects allows a system to build different models for the next-step speech recognition. This is the case for various languages such as Arabic languages (Biadsy, 2011, cf. chapter 13; Ali et al., 2015), Kurdish (Hassani and Medjedovic, 2016), Malayalam (Sunija et al., 2016), Hindi (Rao and Koolagudi, 2011), Java and Sunda dialects (Rahmawati and Lestari, 2017), and Chinese (Chang and Tsai, 2000; Lim et al., 2005; Hou et al., 2010; Chen et al., 2011; Zhang et al., 2013; Qiu et al., 2017).

Features for dialect identification include low-level acoustic features, typically modeled with Gaussian mixture model (GMM), and phonetic features, e.g., phonemes in various representations and suprasegmental information such as prosody, tone and stress, etc., as well as their combinations. The phonetic features are processed categories, which are highly dependent on the representation framework and theory. In addition, the recognition of such categories will introduce errors and noise, which will be accumulated in the succeeding dialect identification. Thus, for simply dialect identification, acoustic features yield better performance, while phonetic features are more linguistically informed and will provide more insights about the differences between the dialects. However, studies show that careful selection of the n-gram features can help improve accuracy (Zhang et al., 2013). Identifying Chinese dialects is slightly different from identifying the other languages in that Chinese is a toned language. This makes the suprasegmental features more important compared to other languages.

Dialect identification does not necessarily require any domain-specific features due to its nature that what mostly matters is the phonetic space of the dialect. Global statistics of phonetic features can help improve the performance as well (Lim et al., 2005). Qiu et al. (2017), for example, propose a system that adopts prosodic features to differentiate five Chinese dialects including Min, Yue, Wu, Jianghuai, Zhongyuan and standard Mandarin using Deep Neural Network and achieved a good result.

Chinese people typically have two or more spoken languages, namely Mandarin and her/his local language. This applies to those whose native language is

Mandarin as there are many dialects of Mandarin that are significantly different from the standard language (Putonghua/Guoyu). Native speakers can clearly identify the difference between Mandarin and their own language. So, the mandarin of different speakers in China will show different accents. This is similar as, e.g., American English versus Indian English. Sproat et al. (2004) propose a speaker adapted speech recognition system for Mandarin Chinese and find a big performance improvement. Hou et al. (2010) propose a system that combines different levels of features to identify Chinese accents and found a significant improvement compared to a system that only uses single level features.

14.2.3 *Automatic Detection of Lexical Variations in Mandarin Chinese*

Understandably, the study on varieties of Mandarin Chinese started with studies on lexical variations and produced rich literature. In these years, a variety of studies have been conducted for lexical variations among different Mandarin speaking communities, such as region-specific neologism, meaning variations of the same word, and the use of different words to express the same meaning (Huang et al., 2013).

Although a variety of researches have been conducted to help resolve any misunderstanding problems and to facilitate the communication among different Chinese speaking communities, research on lexical variation has been dominated by qualitative and/or judgement based studies. There have been very few quantitative and/or (semi-)automatic studies. A few exceptions include Hong and Huang (2008), in which a corpus-based and collocation-driven approach is utilized to study the lexical contrasts between Taiwan and Mainland Mandarin. Šimon et al. (2008) has introduced a novel approach for automatic extraction of divergent transliterations of foreign named entities between Taiwan and Mainland China, by bootstrapping co-occurrence statistics from tagged Chinese corpora. Xu and Li (2019) have made a metrological comparison of different features of language used in sports news in terms of coverage between Mainland and Taiwan Mandarin. The results show that language used in sports news between cross-straits can be effectively differentiated by various linguistic features, including lexical density, word frequency, word length, sentence types, etc.

In addition, a series of linguistic studies have been conducted by the Hong Kong Polytechnic University team, based on automatically extracted data from the Annotated Chinese Gigaword Corpus, and by adopting statistical analysis. Jiang et al. (2016) and Jiang and Huang (2017b) adopt a comparable corpus-based approach, with the assistance of statistical modeling to investigate the light verb/VO compound variations in Mandarin and Taiwan Chinese, and have shown that the verbs of Taiwan Mandarin have a higher degree of transitivity than the Mainland counterparts. Other studies (e.g., Jiang and Huang, 2017a,

2018) have also shown that the language use in different Mandarin speaking communities can be distinguished by syntactic features, and statistical modeling is very effective in detecting differences among varieties of standard Mandarin.

The LIVAC synchronic Chinese corpus (Linguistic Variations in Chinese Speech Communities) also generated exciting and comprehensive studies on lexical variations among different Chinese communities. For example, based on LIVAC, corpus-based studies and comparisons have been carried out on topics such as thesaurus (Kwong and Tsou, 2006a,b, 2008; Tsou and Kwong, 2006), Chinese news headlines (Chin, 2007), celebrity coverage in the Chinese press (Tsou et al., 2005), judgment terms (Kwong and Tsou, 2005), normalized verbs (Kwong and Tsou, 2003), the usage of Quadrasyllabic Idiomatic Expressions (QIEs) in the pan-Chinese context (Tsou and Kwong, 2015), and loan words in Mandarin Chinese through other Chinese dialects (Tsou, 2017).

14.2.4   Chinese Comparable Corpora

It is important to note that, with only one exception, all the above studies are inspired by the availability of two comparable corpora of varieties of Chinese: the Chinese Gigaword Corpus, and the LIVAC synchronic Chinese corpus. Both will be described in this section.

14.2.4.1 Tagged Chinese Gigaword Corpus 2.0: A Fully Tagged Comparable Corpus for Varieties of Mandarin Chinese   The Tagged Chinese Gigaword Corpus 2.0 (Huang, 2009) was produced by Linguistic Data Consortium (LDC).[1] This is a comprehensive archive of newswire text data that has been acquired from Chinese news sources by the LDC over several years. It contains over 2.8 million documents, roughly 1.1 billion characters which are segmented to nearly 832 million Chinese words, each tagged with a part-of-speech. The sources include more than 500 words from Taiwan Central News Agency (CNA), more than 300 million words from Mainland China's Xinhua News Agency (XNA), and over 18 million words from Singapore's Lianhe Zaobao newspaper. All documents are categorized into four distinct 'types':

story	this type of DOC represents a coherent report on a particular topic or event, consisting of paragraphs and full sentences
multi	this type of DOC contains a series of unrelated "blurbs," each of which briefly describes a particular topic or event: "summaries of today's news," "news briefs in ..." (some general area like finance or sports), and so on
advis	these are DOCs which the news service addresses to news editors, they are not intended for publication to the 'end users'
other	these DOCs clearly do not fall into any of the above types; these are things like lists of sports scores, stock prices, temperatures around the world, and so on

---

[1] Catalog number LDC2009T14 and ISBN1-58563-516-2.

The full corpus is segmented and POS tagged with the reduced tagset from Sinica Corpus (Chen et al., 1996; Huang et al., 2017). Segmentation and tagging are performed after all texts are converted to the same character set hence users can choose to access the full corpus as either simplified or traditional characters. Supervised automatic tagging is performed first. Then, both systematic and spot-checked errors (based on a one million sample) are corrected. The estimated segmentation precision is about 0.96, while POS tagging precision is about 0.985 (Ma and Huang, 2006).

14.2.4.2 The LIVAC Corpus   The LIVAC corpus (Linguistic Varia-tions in Chinese Speech Communities) is a synchronous corpus which con-tains representative media texts from the communities in the Pan-Chinese region including Hong Kong, Macau, Taipei, Singapore, Shanghai, Beijing, Guangzhou, and Shenzhen (Tsou et al., 1997).

By 2016, more than 600 million characters of news media texts (mainly including textual samples drawn from editorials, local and international news, cross-Formosan Straits news, as well as news on finance, sports and entertain-ment) have been processed and analyzed and have yielded an expanding Pan-Chinese dictionary of 2 million words from printed media. Through conducting rigorous analysis based on computational/information methodology, LIVAC has accumulated a large amount of meaningful statistical data on the Chinese language and their speech communities in the Pan-Chinese region (Kwong and Tsou, 2006b).

14.3   Classification of Varieties of Mandarin Chinese

In this section, we introduce published computational classification studies on classification of varieties of Mandarin Chinese:

14.3.1   Bag-of-Words and Feature Similarity Based Approaches

The first attempt at classification of varieties of Chinese is most likely Huang and Lee (2008), which, unsurprisingly, is based on the Chinese Gigaword Corpus. They try to classify three varieties if Mandarin Chinese, namely Mainland China, Taiwan, Singapore, according to the similarity of the top frequency words. Five months of data (from 2000 or 2003) is selected from each variety, hence 15 text groups. Half of the data is set aside as test data and half as training data. Top 5000 words are extracted for each variety and three classifiers are constructed based on three top BoWs (as the three BoWs have different members and will produce different similarity scores). The similarity between any two BoWs are between 60 and 69 percent. Since three classifiers are used, majority voting is adopted for classification if the classifiers do not agree. All 15 text groups are correctly classified based on this approach and 9 of the 15 groups were classified correctly by all three classifiers. Other than providing a base-line approach for future studies, this study also shows that a robust approach can successfully differentiate different similar languages even when sizes of data are different. In this particular experiment, text sizes vary greatly. For instance, for the 2000 data, Taiwan text is roughly twice the size of Mainland data and six times the size of Singapore data.

Xu et al. (2016) provide a multi-feature based SVM classification system for sentence level similar language classification from six areas of greater China, including Mainland China, Taiwan, Singapore, Hong Kong, Macao and Malaysia. They use Huang and Lee (2008)'s BoW based system as baseline. Interestingly, their system performs well when simplified/traditional character encoding difference is kept (and hence character form features obtain high accuracy). However, when they follow Huang and Lee (2008) and convert the texts to uniform encoding, their system in fact does not outperform the BoW approach. This suggests that variations among Mandarin Chinese varieties are rather subtle. It interesting to note that Wu et al. (2019) also adopt a similar (multi-feature based SVM) approach in the VarDial/DMT sharetask and also achieved good results.

14.3.2 Linguistic Knowledge Informed Approaches

The first attempt to leverage linguistic knowledge for automatic classification of varieties of Mandarin Chinese (or World Chineses) is reported by Lin et al. (2014) and Huang et al. (2014), following the earlier manual analysis of Huang et al. (2013). Their study focus on sentences containing light verbs from Taiwan and Mainland China that are extracted from the Chinese Gigaword Corpus. These sentences are then annotated with a full set of grammatical features that are claimed in the literature to show variations between Mainland and Taiwan Mandarin. Lin et al. (2014) differentiate the usage of five Chinese light verbs and Huang et al. (2014) classify the sentences containing these light verbs to Mainland China or Taiwan Mandarin texts based on the features of these two varieties by these light verbs extracted earlier. They show that identifying features from various linguistic levels including syntactic collocation, grammatical aspect, lexical aspect of the event verbs, part-of-speech tags, inner-lexical features, speech register, etc., can contribute to the varieties of a language. Both Uni- and Multi-variate analysis are applied with, as expected, multivariate analysis showing advantage. The results are then adopted for machine learning classification of the two varieties of Chinese and of the five light verbs. What these studies focus on are how NLP tools can help us to analyze, classify, and understand the patterns and motivations of language variations and changes.

14.3.3   *VariDial/DMT 2019 Campaign*

The first shared task for classification of Mandarin Chinese was held in the sixth VarDial workshop (Zampieri et al., 2019). The task named "Discriminating between Mainland and Taiwan variation of Mandarin Chinese (DMT)" is to predict whether a sentence is from the Mainland China corpus or Taiwan Mandarin corpus. The training corpus contains 10,000 sentences belong to news articles that are either from Mainland China or Taiwan.

Traditional machine learning methods such as Nave Bayesian (NB), SVM have shown promising results. For example, Jauhiainen et al. (2019) use NB with simply character N-Grams and achieves the best result in the campaign. Yang and Xiang (2019) use NB with pre-trained word embeddings and also got promising results. Bert (Devlin et al., 2018) has been noticed recently due to its performance in training effective language models. Different from the traditional language models that are based on original corpora, the BERT model begins by masking some low token frequency items in the corpora, and then uses deep neural network to train word embeddings. The benefit comes from the fact that by masking the low frequency items, the model actually groups together rare items that are mostly nouns (common or proper) whose domain is not related to the specific task but mostly provide a syntactic category that matters for their neighbor words.

The results from different teams that adopt n-gram features in both character and word levels, and pre-trained word vectors show surprisingly good performance. The best team achieves an F1 score above 90 percent. This shows that there are potentially important features hiding in the n-grams and word embeddings that can well discriminate the two variants. For example, it can be the salient n-grams existing preferably only in one variant that show the specific lexical items, or the collocations that are either phrasal or syntactic in nature. However, it is still unclear which of them play the main role. In addition, the n-gram features are still compromised from the linguistic perspective as it fails to capture long distance dependencies and falsely captures some random noise as well.

Deep Neural Networks including CNN, RNN, bi-LSTM, etc., can discover more complicated patterns from the data. However, the training of such models requires big data. That is probably the reason why such systems did not perform well in this task due to the closed nature of this task (they are not allowed to use other resources outside this task). In addition, the mysterious nature of Deep Neural Network also makes it more appropriate to be used in the engineering domain rather than studying the nature of the language. The studies on light verbs in Huang et al. (2014) and Lin et al. (2014), on the other hand, are based on linguistically concerned features that the linguists discovered. Some of the features are highly semantically or pragmatically enriched, which are very difficult to be captured in n-gram features. Thus, the study will have merits in linking the NLP domain by suggesting more linguistically informed features and also evaluating and testing the theories that are proposed in linguistic studies by putting them in machine learning frameworks.

14.3.4   Classification of Regional and Genre Varieties of Chinese

One issue that has not been explored in NLP approaches to similar languages is if there are any significant differences between with variety variations and within variety variations, that is, are the variations among different similar languages similar to or different from within-language variations such as genre and register, and can the same text classification methods be applied to both, and if so, how to differentiate similar language from different genres in the same language. Hou and Huang (to appear) propose a robust text classification and correspondence analysis based approach to the identification of similar languages based on the hypothesis that each variety of similar languages is a self-adaptive complex system. Under this hypothesis, the power relation between linguistic units and their constituents is one of the most readily accessible characteristics of language variations and changes. In particular, they propose to use universally available clause and word length data to model similar languages. To test the self-adaptive complex system hypothesis as well as the robustness of the proposed methodology, they included both regional and genre varieties of Mandarin Chinese as targets of classification. The results show that (1) the complex adaptive system driven approach as they propose is effective for both regional and genre variations, yet (2) genre varieties do have compounding effect on classification of similar languages, hence the hypothesis that language variations at different levels arise because of the self-adaptive nature of languages as complex systems are corroborated, and that (3) robust real world application of classification of similar and related languages must also take into considerations other variables such as genre. The two corpora chosen are the Sinica Corpus (Chen et al., 1996) and the Lancaster Corpus of Mandarin Chinese (McEnery and Xiao, 2004), from Taiwan and Mainland China, respectively. The texts were represented by the clause length distributions and their fitted parameters, word length distribution and their fitted parameters, respectively.

14.4   Conclusion

This chapter gave an overall survey of the study on computational and corpus-based approaches to identification of varieties of Chinese. We started with a brief introduction to Chinese as well as dialects and varieties of Chinese, which is followed by a very brief overview of the grammatical features of

Mandarin Chinese. The main part of the chapter introduces NLP approaches to similar language, with comprehensive discussion of NLP studies on varieties of Chinese. It is interesting to see that Huang and Lee (2008)'s BoW approach is still relevant today. Unsurprisingly, current studies mostly use feature selection systems, and apply them to either supervised or unsupervised learning tools. Two approaches that are note-worthy are the one adopted by Lin et al. (2014) and Huang et al. (2014), as well as the one by Hou and Huang (to appear). The former takes an approach involving rich linguistic knowledge and aims at both understanding the linguistic motivations and cues of language variations and changes, as well as providing solution to long-standing issues. The latter is developed based on previous studies on textual classification and genre/register clustering. They show that both can be treated as complex self-adaptive systems and that such systems can be classified with model fitting. With the establishment of the VarDial shared task and the wider context of new topics and approaches, studies on changes and variations in Chinese will surely boom and bring us new knowledge and better technology.

References

Abramov, Olga, and Mehler, Alexander. 2011. Automatic language classification by means of syntactic dependency networks. *Journal of Quantitative Linguistics*, **18**(4), 291–336.

Ali, Ahmed, Dehak, Najim, Cardinal, Patrick, et al. 2015. Automatic dialect detection in arabic broadcast speech. *arXiv preprint arXiv:1509.06928*.

Batagelj, Vladimir, Pisanski, Tomaž, and Keržič, Damijana. 1992. Automatic clustering of languages. *Computational Linguistics*, **18**(3), 339–352.

Biadsy, Fadi. 2011. *Automatic dialect and accent recognition and its application to speech recognition*. Ph.D. thesis, Columbia University.

Blanchard, Ph, Petroni, Filippo, Serva, Maurizio, and Volchenkov, Dimitri. 2011. Geometric representations of language taxonomies. *Computer Speech & Language*, **25**(3), 679–699.

Bloem, Jelke, Versloot, Arjen, and Weerman, Fred. 2014. Applying automatically parsed corpora to the study of language variation. Pages 1974–1984 of: *Proceedings of COLING 2014, the 25th International Conference on Computational Linguistics: Technical Papers*.

Chang, Wen-Whei, and Tsai, Wuei-He. 2000. Chinese dialect identification using segmental and prosodic features. *The Journal of the Acoustical Society of America*, **108**(4), 1906–1913.

Chen, I. Hsuan, Zhao, Qingqing, Long, Yunfei, Lu, Qin, and Huang, Chu-Ren. 2019. Mandarin Chinese modality exclusivity norms. *Plos one*, **14**(2), e0211336.

Chen, Keh-Jiann, Huang, Chu-Ren, Chang, Li-Ping, and Hsu, Hui-Li. 1996. Sinica corpus: Design methodology for balanced corpora. Pages 167–176 of: *Proceedings of the 11th Pacific Asia Conference on Language, Information and Computation*.

Chen, Nancy F, Shen, Wade, Campbell, Joseph P, and Torres-Carrasquillo, Pedro A. 2011. Informative dialect recognition using context-dependent pronunciation modeling. Pages 4396–4399 of: *2011 IEEE International Conference on Acoustics, Speech and Signal Processing (ICASSP)*. IEEE.

Chen, Weirong. 2011. The Southern Min dialect of Hui'an: morphosyntax and grammaticalization. *HKU Theses Online (HKUTO)*.

Chin, A. 2007. A sociocultural comparison of Chinese news headline verbs between Hong Kong and Taiwan. Pages 444–450 of: *Proceedings of the First International Workshop on Intercultural Collaboration -IWIC 2007*.

Dai, Zhaoming, and Zhao, Yifan. 2009. "港台式"语法及其对内地汉语的影响 (Grammar of Hong Kong/Taiwan Mandarin and the influence on Mainland Mandarin). 191–205.

Devlin, Jacob, Chang, Ming-Wei, Lee, Kenton, and Toutanova, Kristina. 2018. Bert: Pre-training of deep bidirectional transformers for language understanding. *arXiv preprint arXiv:1810.04805*.

Diao, Yanbin. 1998. 台湾话的特点及其与内地的差异 (The characteristic of Taiwan Mandarin and its differences between Mainland Mandarin). *Zhongguo Yuwen*, **5**, 387–390.

Diao, Yanbin. 2000. 差异与融合: 海峡两岸语言应用对比 *(Divergence and Convergence: A Cross-Strait Language Comparison)*. Nangchang: Jiangxi Education Press.

Diao, Yanbin. 2012a. 两岸四地"获"字句对比考察 (The comparative study of the sentence with huo in the four places across the Taiwan Strait). *TCSOL*, **2**, 67–76.

Diao, Yanbin. 2012b. 两岸四地现代汉语常用词 "进行" 使用情况对比考察与分析 (Comparison and analysis of the usage of jinxing in the four places across the Taiwan Strait). *Journal of Wuling*, **3**, 116–124.

Diao, Yanbin. 2012c. 两岸四地的 "遭" 字句及其与 "被" 字句的差异 (The Contrast Study about zao and bei Sentences in the Four Places across the Taiwan Strait). *Language Teaching and Linguistic Studies*, **5**, 70–77.

Diao, Yanbin. 2012d. 试论海峡两岸语言的微观对比研究———以 "而已" 一词的考察分析为例 (A microscopic comparison of cross-strait varieties: The case of eryi). *Journal of Beijing Normal University*, **4**, 44–51.

Diao, Yanbin. 2012e. 台港澳地区 "搞" 的使用情况及其与内地的差异 (On the usage of Gao in the regions of Taiwan, Hong Kong and Macao and the differences with the Mainland). *Journal of Weinan Normal University*, **9**, 80–83.

Diao, Yanbin. 2012f. 两岸四地"将"字句及其使用情况考察 (Research on Jiang construction in modern Chinese in the four places across the Taiwan Strait and its usages). *Journal of Nanyang Normal University*, **5**, 37–43.

Diao, Yanbin. 2013. 两岸四地 "被" 字句对比考察 (The comparative study of the sentence with BEI in the four places across the Taiwan Strait). *Linguistic Researches*, **2**, 17–23.

Donoso, Gonzalo, and Sánchez, David. 2017. Dialectometric analysis of language variation in Twitter. *arXiv preprint arXiv:1702.06777*.

Doyle, Gabriel. 2014. Mapping dialectal variation by querying social media. Pages 98–106 of: *Proceedings of the 14th Conference of the European Chapter of the Association for Computational Linguistics*.

Dwyer, Arienne M. 1992. Altaic elements in the Línxìa dialect: Contact-induced change on the Yellow River Plateau. *Journal of Chinese Linguistics*, **20**(1), 160–179.

Eisenstein, Jacob, O'Connor, Brendan, Smith, Noah A, and Xing, Eric P. 2014. Diffusion of lexical change in social media. *PLoS ONE*, **9**(11), e113114.

Fang, Qingming. 2013. 基于口语库统计的两岸华语语气标记比较研究 (A contrast study of the mood markers between Taiwanese Mandarin and Mandarin Chinese: Based on the Spoken Chinese Corpus). 华文教学与研究 *(TCSOL)*, **3**, 58–65.

Fang, Qingming. 2014. 基于口语库统计的两岸华语指示标记比较研究 (A contrast study of the demonstrative markers between Taiwanese Mandarin and Mandarin Chinese: Based on the Spoken Chinese Corpus). *Linguistic Sciences*, **13**(2), 131–139.

Fang, Qingming. 2015. 基于口语库统计的两岸华语程度副词比较研究 (A contrast study of the degree adverbs between Taiwanese Mandarin and Mandarin Chinese: Based on the Spoken Chinese Corpus). *Shijie Huawen Jiaoxue*, **01**, 88–98.

Hamilton, William L, Leskovec, Jure, and Jurafsky, Dan. 2016. Diachronic word embeddings reveal statistical laws of semantic change. *arXiv preprint arXiv:1605.09096*.

Hassani, Hossein, and Medjedovic, Dzejla. 2016. Automatic Kurdish dialects identification. *Computer Science & Information Technology*, **6**(2), 61–78.

Hong, Jia-Fei, and Huang, Chu-Ren. 2008. 语料库为本的两岸对应词汇发掘 (A corpus-based approach to the discovery of cross-strait lexical contrasts). *Language and Linguistics*, **9**(2), 221–238.

Hou, Jue, Liu, Yi, Zheng, Thomas Fang, Olsen, Jesper, and Tian, Jilei. 2010. Multi-layered features with SVM for Chinese accent identification. Pages 25–30 of: *2010 International Conference on Audio, Language and Image Processing*. IEEE.

Hou, Renkui, and Huang, Chu-Ren. (2019). Classification of Regional and Genre Varieties of Chinese: A correspondence analysis approach based on comparable balanced corpora. Natural Language Engineering, 1–28.

Huang, Chu-Ren. 1988a. Towards a morphosyntactic account of Taiwanese question particle kam. *Bulletin of the Institute of History and Philology*, **59**(2), 425–447.

Huang, Chu-Ren. 1989a. Chinese sentential clitics and theories of clicization. Pages 247–287 of: *LSA Annual Meeting at Seattle*.

Huang, Chu-Ren. 1989b. *Cliticization and type-lifting: A unified account of Mandarin NP de*. Indiana University Linguistics Club.

Huang, Chu-Ren. 2009. Tagged Chinese Gigaword Version 2.0, LDC2009T14. *Linguistic Data Consortium*.

Huang, Chu-Ren. 2015. What you need to know about Chinese for Chinese language processing. Pages 23–24 of: *Proceedings of the Tutorials of the 53rd Annual Meeting of the ACL and the 7th IJCNLP*.

Huang, Chu-Ren, and Lee, Lung-Hao. 2008. Contrastive approach towards text source classification based on top-bag-of-word similarity. Pages 404–410 of: *Proceedings of the 22nd Pacific Asia Conference on Language, Information and Computation*.

Huang, Chu-Ren, and Shi, Dingxu. 2016. *A reference grammar of Chinese*. Cambridge University Press.

Huang, Chu-Ren, Lin, Jingxia, and Zhang, Huarui. 2013. World Chinese's based on comparable corpus: The case of grammatical variations of jinxing. *Open image in new window*, 397–414.

Huang, Chu-Ren, Lin, Jingxia, Jiang, Menghan, and Xu, Hongzhi. 2014. Corpus-based study and identification of Mandarin Chinese light verb variations. Pages 1–10 of:

Proceedings of the First Workshop on Applying NLP Tools to Similar Languages, Varieties and Dialects.

Huang, Chu-Ren, Hsieh, Shu-Kai, and Chen, Keh-Jiann. 2017. *Mandarin Chinese words and parts of speech: A corpus-based study.* Routledge.

Huang, Guoying. 1988b. 台湾当代小说的词汇语法特点 (The lexical and grammatical property of Taiwan Contemporary Fiction). *Zhongguo Yuwen*, **3**, 194–201.

Huang, Yuan, Guo, Diansheng, Kasakoff, Alice, and Grieve, Jack. 2016. Understanding US regional linguistic variation with Twitter data analysis. *Computers, Environment and Urban Systems*, **59**, 244–255.

Jauhiainen, Tommi, Lindén, Krister, and Jauhiainen, Heidi. 2019. Discriminating between Mandarin Chinese and Swiss-German varieties using adaptive language models. Pages 178–187 of: *Proceedings of the Sixth Workshop on NLP for Similar Languages, Varieties and Dialects.*

Jiang, Menghan, and Huang, Chu-Ren. 2017a. Lexicalization, separation and transitivity: A comparative study of Mandarin VO compound variations. Pages 354–362 of: *Proceedings of the 31st Pacific Asia Conference on Language, Information and Computation.*

Jiang, Menghan, and Huang, Chu-ren. 2017b. Transitivity variations in Mandarin VO compounds – A comparable corpus-based approach. Pages 564–575 of: *Workshop on Chinese Lexical Semantics.* Springer.

Jiang, Menghan, and Huang, Chu-Ren. 2018. A comparable corpus-based study of three DO verbs in varieties of Mandarin: gao. Pages 147–154 of: *Workshop on Chinese Lexical Semantics.* Springer.

Jiang, Menghan, Shi, Dingxu, and Huang, Chu-Ren. 2016. Transitivity in light verb variations in Mandarin Chinese – A comparable corpus-based statistical approach. Pages 459–468 of: *Proceedings of the 30th Pacific Asia Conference on Language, Information and Computation: Posters.*

Kubler, Cornelius C. 1985. *The development of Mandarin in Taiwan: A case study of language contact*, vol. 9. Taiwan Student Book Press.

Kwong, Oi Yee, and Tsou, Benjamin K. 2003. A synchronous corpus-based study of verb-noun fluidity in Chinese. Pages 194–203 of: *Proceedings of the 17th Pacific Asia Conference on Language, Information and Computation.*

Kwong, Oi Yee, and Tsou, Benjamin K. 2005. A synchronous corpus-based study on the usage and perception of judgement terms in the Pan-Chinese context. Pages 519–532 of: *International Journal of Computational Linguistics & Chinese Language Processing, Volume 10, Number 4, December 2005: Special Issue on Selected Papers from CLSW-5.*

Kwong, Oi Yee, and Tsou, Benjamin K. 2006a. Feasibility of enriching a chinese synonym dictionary with a synchronous chinese corpus. Pages 322–332 of: *International Conference on Natural Language Processing (in Finland).* Springer.

Kwong, Oi Yee, and Tsou, Benjamin K. 2006b. Regional variation of domain-specific lexical items: Toward a pan-Chinese lexical resource. Pages 9–16 of: *Proceedings of the Fifth SIGHAN Workshop on Chinese Language Processing.*

Kwong, Oi Yee, and Tsou, Benjamin K. 2008. Extending a thesaurus with words from Pan-Chinese sources. Pages 457–464 of: *Proceedings of the 22nd International*

Conference on Computational Linguistics-Volume 1. Association for Computational Linguistics.

Liao, Liping. 1999. 台湾小说单音形容词的重叠形式-海峡两岸词的重叠形式的对比研究 (The reduplication form of monosyllabic adjectives in Taiwan Novels – A contrastive study of the reduplication forms of cross-strait words). *Journal of Xuzhou Normal University*, **3**, 66–68.

Lim, Boon Pang, Li, Haizhou, and Ma, Bin. 2005. Using local & global phonotactic features in Chinese dialect identification. Pages I–577 of: *Proceedings.(ICASSP'05). IEEE International Conference on Acoustics, Speech, and Signal Processing, 2005*, vol. 1. IEEE.

Lin, Huayong, and Kwok, Bit-Chee. 2010. The grammaticalization of the directional verbs qu (去, go) and lai (来, come) and the convergence of their functions in the Lianjiang Yue dialect [J]. *Studies of the Chinese Language*, **6**, 516–525, 575–576.

Lin, Jingxia, Xu, Hongzhi, Jiang, Menghan, and Huang, Chu-Ren. 2014. Annotation and classification of light verbs and light verb variations in Mandarin Chinese. Pages 75–82 of: *Proceedings of Workshop on Lexical and Grammatical Resources for Language Processing*.

Lin, Jingxia, Shi, Dingxu, Jiang, Menghan, and Huang, Chu-Ren. 2018. Variations in world Chineses. In *The Routledge Handbook of Applied Chinese Linguistics*, ed. by Chu-Ren Huang, Zhuo Jing-Schmidt and Barbara Meisterernst. London: Routledge.

Ma, Wei-Yun, and Huang, Chu-Ren. 2006. Uniform and effective tagging of a heterogeneous giga-word corpus. Pages 2182–2185 of: *LREC*.

Mao, Zhongmei. 2007. 台湾书面语中的闽南方言特点初探-以台湾报刊语言为例 *(The Code-Mixing of Taiwanese in Taiwan Mandarin Newspapers)*. Master's thesis, Shanghai: East China Normal University.

McEnery, Anthony, and Xiao, Zhonghua. 2004. The Lancaster Corpus of Mandarin Chinese: A corpus for monolingual and contrastive language study. *Religion*, **17**, 3–4.

Mikolov, Tomas, Sutskever, Ilya, Chen, Kai, Corrado, Greg S, and Dean, Jeff. 2013. Distributed representations of words and phrases and their compositionality. Pages 3111–3119 of: *Advances in Neural Information Processing Systems*.

Nerbonne, John, and Heeringa, Wilbert. 2001. Computational comparison and classification of dialects. *Dialectologia et Geolinguistica*, **9**(2001), 69–83.

Nerbonne, John, Heeringa, Wilbert, and Kleiweg, Peter. 1999. Edit distance and dialect proximity. *Time Warps, String Edits and Macromolecules: The theory and practice of sequence comparison*, **15**, 5–15.

Peirsman, Yves, Geeraerts, Dirk, and Speelman, Dirk. 2010. The automatic identification of lexical variation between language varieties. *Natural Language Engineering*, **16**(4), 469–491.

Qiu, Yuanhang, Ma, Yong, Jin, Yun, Li, Shidang, and Gu, Mingliang. 2017. Chinese dialects identification using attention-based deep neural networks. Pages 2051–2058 of: *International Conference in Communications, Signal Processing, and Systems*. Springer.

Qiu, Zhiqun, and Fan, Dengbao. 1994. 台湾语言现状的初步研究 (A preliminary study on the current situation of Taiwan language). *Zhongguo Yuwen*, **4**, 254–261.

Rahmawati, Rita, and Lestari, Dessi P. 2017. Java and Sunda dialect recognition from Indonesian speech using GMM and I-Vector. Pages 1–5 of: *2017 11th International Conference on Telecommunication Systems Services and Applications (TSSA)*. IEEE.

Rao, K Sreenivasa, and Koolagudi, Shashidhar G. 2011. Identification of Hindi dialects and emotions using spectral and prosodic features of speech. *IJSCI: International Journal of Systemics, Cybernetics and Informatics*, 9(4), 24–33.

Samardžić, Tanja, and Merlo, Paola. 2010. Cross-lingual variation of light verb constructions: Using parallel corpora and automatic alignment for linguistic research. Pages 52–60 of: *Proceedings of the 2010 Workshop on NLP and Linguistics: Finding the Common Ground*. Association for Computational Linguistics.

Séguy, Jean. 1971. *La relation entre la distance spatiale et la distance lexicale*. G. Straka, Palais de l'université.

Šimon, Petr, Huang, Chu-Ren, Hsieh, Shu-Kai, and Hong, Jia-Fei. 2008. Transliterated named entity recognition based on Chinese word sketch. *International Journal of Computer Processing of Languages*, 21(01), 19–30.

Solorio, Thamar, Blair, Elizabeth, Maharjan, Suraj, et al. 2014. Overview for the first shared task on language identification in code-switched data. Pages 62–72 of: *Proceedings of the First Workshop on Computational Approaches to Code Switching*.

Sproat, Richard, Liang Gu, IBM, Li, Jing, et al. 2004. Dialectal Chinese speech recognition. In: *CLSP Summer Workshop*.

Sunija, AP, Rajisha, TM, and Riyas, KS. 2016. Comparative study of different classifiers for Malayalam dialect recognition system. *Procedia Technology*, 24, 1080–1088.

Tsou, Benjamin K. 2017. Loanwords in Mandarin through other Chinese dialects. Pages 641–647 of: Sybesma, R, Behr, W, Gu, Y, Handel, Z, Huang, C-T, and Myers, J. (eds.), *The Encyclopaedia of Chinese Language and Linguistics*, vol. 2. Leiden; Boston: BRILL.

Tsou, Benjamin K, and Kwong, Oi Yee. 2006. Toward a Pan-Chinese Thesaurus. Pages 2391–2394 of: *LREC*.

Tsou, Benjamin K, and Kwong, Oi Yee. 2015. LIVAC as a monitoring corpus for tracking trends beyond linguistics/LIVAC 追料探索泛地言以外的演. *Journal of Chinese Linguistics Monograph Series*, 25, 447–472.

Tsou, Benjamin K, Lin, Hing-Lung, Liu, Godfrey, et al. 1997. A synchronous Chinese language corpus from different speech communities: Construction and applications. Pages 91–104 of: *International Journal of Computational Linguistics & Chinese Language Processing, Volume 2, Number 1, February 1997: Special Issue on Computational Resources for Research in Chinese Linguistics*, vol. 2.

Tsou, Benjamin KY, Yuen, Raymond WM, Kwong, Oi Yee, Lai, Tom BY, and Wong, Wei Lung. 2005. Polarity classification of celebrity coverage in the Chinese press. Pages 531–537 of: *Proceedings of International Conference on Intelligence Analysis*.

Wang, Yue, Chen, Jun, and Zhang, Ji-Jia. 2012. Using Mandarin and dialect together: Dialect psychological research and its development. *Advances in Psychological Science*, 20(8), 1243–1250.

Wei, Hsiu-ming. 1984. 国语演变之研究 (*Changes in the Mandarin Language in Taiwan*). Taipei: National Taiwan University Press.

Wu, Nianheng, DeMattos, Eric, So, Kwok Him, Chen, Pin-zhen, and Çöltekin, Çağrı. 2019. Language discrimination and transfer learning for similar languages: Experiments with feature combinations and adaptation. Pages 54–63 of: *Proceedings of the Sixth Workshop on NLP for Similar Languages, Varieties and Dialects.*

Xu, Fan, Wang, Mingwen, and Li, Maoxi. 2016. Sentence-level dialects identification in the Greater China region. *International Journal on Natural Language Computing (IJNLC),* **5**(6), 9–20.

Xu, Hongzhi, Menghan Jiang, Jingxia Lin, and Chu-Ren Huang. "Light verb variations and varieties of Mandarin Chinese: Comparable corpus driven approaches to grammatical variations." Corpus Linguistics and Linguistic Theory 1, no. ahead-of-print (2020).

Xu, Lei, and Li, Quan. 2019. 海峡两岸体育新闻语言多特征计量对比研究 (A multi-feature metrological comparative study of language used in sports news on the two sides of the Taiwan Straits). 江汉学术*(Jianghan Academic),* **38**(3), 111–118.

Yang, Li, and Xiang, Yang. 2019. Naive Bayes and BiLSTM ensemble for discriminating between Mainland and Taiwan variation of Mandarin Chinese. Pages 120–127 of: *Proceedings of the Sixth Workshop on NLP for Similar Languages, Varieties and Dialects.*

Yue-Hashimoto, Anne. 1991. The Yue dialect. *Journal of Chinese Linguistics Monograph Series,* No. 3, Language and Dialects of China, 292–322.

Zampieri, Marcos, Malmasi, Shervin, Ljubešić, Nikola, et al. 2017. Findings of the VarDial evaluation campaign 2017.

Zampieri, Marcos, Malmasi, Shervin, Nakov, Preslav, et al. 2018. Language identification and morphosyntactic tagging: The second VarDial evaluation campaign. Pages 1–17 of: *Proceedings of the Fifth Workshop on NLP for Similar Languages, Varieties and Dialects (VarDial 2018).*

Zampieri, Marcos, Malmasi, Shervin, Scherrer, Yves, et al. 2019. A report on the third VarDial evaluation campaign. In: *Proceedings of the Sixth Workshop on NLP for Similar Languages, Varieties and Dialects (VarDial 2019).* Association for Computational Linguistics.

Zhang, Qian, Bořil, Hynek, and Hansen, John HL. 2013. Supervector pre-processing for PRSVM-based Chinese and Arabic dialect identification. Pages 7363–7367 of: *2013 IEEE International Conference on Acoustics, Speech and Signal Processing.* IEEE.

Zhao, Chunli, and Shi, Dingxu. 2014. 两岸四地汉语 " 有信心 " 句式的异同 (Syntactic difference of youxinxin between Mainland Chinese and Hong Kong, Macau and Taiwan Chinese). *Chinese Language Learning,* **2**, 27–36.

Zhu, Jingsong, and Zhou, Weiwang. 1990. 台湾 " 国语 " 词汇与普通话的主要差异 (The lexical differences between Taiwan Mandarin and Mainland Mandarin). *Journal of Anhui University,* **1**, 91–100.